Engendering MEN

WITHDRAWN FROM
MACALESTER COLLEGE
LIBRARY

Charles Nielson with J. Ogle (behind glass) (1937), by George Platt Lynes. Reproduced with permission of the Lynes Estate.

Engendering MEN

THE
QUESTION
OF MALE
FEMINIST
CRITICISM

EDITED BY

JOSEPH A. BOONE & MICHAEL CADDEN

ROUTLEDGE · NEW YORK AND LONDON

Published in 1990 by

Routledge
An imprint of Routledge, Chapman and Hall, Inc.
29 West 35 Street
New York, NY 10001

Published in Great Britain by

Routledge
11 New Fetter Lane
London EC4P 4EE

Copyright © 1990 by Routledge, Chapman and Hall, Inc.

Printed in the United States of America

All rights reserved. No part of this book may be reprinted or reproduced or utilized in any form or by any electronic, mechanical or other means, now known or hereafter invented, including photocopying and recording, or in any information storage or retrieval system, without permission in writing from the publishers.

Library of Congress Cataloging-in-Publication Data

Engendering men / Joseph Boone and Michael Cadden [editors].
    p. cm.
  Includes bibliographical references.
  ISBN 0-415-90254-1; ISBN 0-415-90255-X (pbk.)
  1. Feminist literary criticism. 2. American literature—History and criticism. 3. English literature—History and criticism.
4. Sex role in literature. 5. Criticism—United States. I. Boone, Joseph Allen. II. Cadden, Michael.
PS152.E49 1990
810.9'9287—dc20
                            89-78222

British Library Cataloguing in publication data also available

Contents

Editors' Introduction

Imagine an untenured male professor of English arriving at a neighboring university to address its Feminist and Gender Theory Group about "men and feminism" and meeting there a man—of comparable age and faculty status—who is to introduce his talk. In the course of said talk, the speaker humorously refers to a voluminous footnote in his script that cites twenty names of other men in the profession doing similar work on issues of gender and sexuality—two of whom are in his audience. The obligatory reception follows, during which these two men put their heads together and—*voilà!*—realize that nothing would be easier than using that epic list as a starting point for editing a collection of essays on the question of male feminist criticism—a collection rather similar to the one now in your hands.

A pretty story, but a fantasy. While a heroic male birth narrative might require the declaration that the two of us were solely responsible for initiating this project (and that whatever readers may find exciting or original about its aims and achievements primarily owes to our founding inspirations), the genesis of this anthology is significantly more convoluted than that; its originating circumstances form, in fact, an allegory of the very phenomenon this collection attempts to describe. For the truth is that neither of us even thought of editing such a project at the time. It took a female member of that Feminist and Gender Theory Group to bring up the idea over wine and cheese: "You two really *should* do this; it's your issue and a political statement that needs to be made."

It strikes us as important to relate this anecdote here, at the beginning of this collection, because it so vividly sums up the relation of our entire project to feminism. Without this friendly push from Elaine Showalter, an established feminist critic who had the savvy to recognize a good opportunity for her less experienced younger colleagues, *Engendering Men* might never have gotten off the ground. Likewise, without the *fact* of feminist theory, now part of our general intellectual inheritance, the men writing for this anthology would not have had available the basic terms for articulating the developing perspectives on gender and sexuality featured here. Feminism has engendered us, even as we strive to engender a practice that might not always be *the same* as feminist practice, but that remains in contiguity with its politics.

Initially we worried that our title might be overly cute or inappropriately punny. In the small world of contemporary literary criticism, the mere mention of the word *gender* (especially in the same breath as the words *race* and *class*) all too often serves as only a profession of this year's fashion—the less threatening, postmodern way of declaring vaguely feminist sympathies without alienating students or, in a competitive job market, more conservative colleagues and potential employers. But we grew into our title as the essays we solicited began to arrive. If we were not entirely aware of the fact from the genesis of this collection, it soon became clear that there now exists an entire generation of male critics, many of whom, having been educated by "first generation" feminist scholars, have in turn been "engendered" by feminism. As offshoots of the feminist movement, both in its academic and non-academic manifestations, such men have not only taken to heart but begun to embody the feminist injunction to return gender to the universal term *Man*, in their work as well as their lives.

Essential to this process, of course, has been the way in which feminism has foregrounded sexuality as a crucial component in any thoroughgoing analysis of textuality, both authorizing a revolution in the way we read and underlining the necessity of taking responsibility for our gendered subject positions, male and female alike, as reader-critics. In particular, while feminism has obliged the male critic to see the "men" in the supposedly transhistorical and genderless species called "Man," it has simultaneously freed each of us to begin to articulate the "me" in "men" itself. Needless to say, if it is with an awareness of the many me's in me(n) that we write, it must be understood that the "we" we now invoke in this introduction is an editorial "we" that does not and cannot always encompass the variety of voices and opinions gathered here under the aegis of "engendering men."

As for our subtitle, we feel that the designation "male feminist criticism" remains, and ought to remain, a question, rather than a definitive classification of the following work—work that by its very nature is yet in search of its own (im)proper "name." The "question of male feminist criticism," that is, must necessarily remain such so long as men live in a society in which most of our sex (white, straight, middle-class men) have been, and continue to be, the beneficiaries of an asymmetrical sexual system that oppresses women; however much we as male critics may want to retheorize our position within patriarchal culture, our efforts at engendered self-clarification cannot help but be complicated by our access to male privilege. Men have traditionally had recourse to both universality *and* particularity—an access guaranteed, at least in English, by the generic term *man*. Indeed, the male "I" has enjoyed something of a psychic and cultural monopoly on subjectivity that needs to be dissolved. It is our hope that in opening up for critique the essentializing homogeneity of patriarchal discourse, this collection's alternative project of "engendering men" by giving their individual voices a forum will contribute to the deconstruction of such privilege.

A collection of essays professing a politics grounded in feminism yet featuring an all-male cast may strike some critics as a professionally self-serving and sexist appropriation of feminist discourse. Indeed, the example of some previous attempts to write on men and feminism is not promising, partially because those essays and collections—no doubt wary of valorizing male ventures into a previously all-female preserve—have been somewhat defensively structured to represent (and in the process create) a contestatory relation between female and male critics with feminist interests. While these previous narratives suggest a territorial battle between female "natives" and male "colonists," we prefer to avoid geopolitical metaphors that necessarily disenfranchise those who come later and who come differently. For us, feminism is a matter of vision and revision, a mode of critical perception that has introduced us to new ways of interacting with our worlds and our lives, our literatures and our cultures. No one has more eloquently expressed the difference such revision can make than Adrienne Rich:

> Re-vision—the act of looking back, of seeing with fresh eyes, of entering an old text from a new critical direction—is for us more than a chapter in cultural history; it is an act of survival . . . We need to know the writing of the past, and know it differently than we have ever known it; not to pass on a tradition but to break its hold over us.[1]

To "[see] with fresh eyes," we would argue, is a revolutionary task in which both men and women can—indeed must—participate if we are to create a nonsexist future. And for the man who abjures the "male gaze" and thereby learns to "re-see" in the name of a materially engendered rather than transcendent "I/eye," revision is a transformative act: he who acknowledges the absolute necessity of, in Rich's words, "know[ing] differently" inevitably participates in an effort common to feminism but with an agenda that is *also* specific to his own gender: "not to pass on [the] tradition [of male privilege] but to break its hold over us."

A corollary of this process, of course, is that while the investigations of gender to be found in this volume could not exist without the (continually evolving) feminist models we have inherited, neither are they necessarily parallel to those produced by our female colleagues. These essays draw upon a wide variety of existing method-ologies (Marxist criticism, deconstruction, New Historicism, psychoanalysis) and experiment with an equally wide range of voices (confessional, lyrical, scientific, journalistic) in the shared effort to create a field of study that, as yet, remains amorphous and—as we've already noted of our subtitle—a question.

At one end of the spectrum, for instance, some of our contributors explore the gynocentric concerns of classical feminism (domesticity, chastity, sisterhood), offer new perspectives on well-established women writers (Anne Bradstreet, Emily Dick-inson), and champion both the centrality of neglected women writers (Sylvia Town-send Warner) and the significance of contemporary female authors (Wendy Was-serstein). Other essayists respond to Myra Jehlen's call for, and Sandra Gilbert and Susan Gubar's practice of, a simultaneous reading of male and female traditions and canons: thus Warner's achievements are seen in relation to those of George

Gissing, Mark Rutherford, and Arnold Bennett; Gwendolyn Brooks' lyrics in relation to those of Paul Laurence Dunbar and Claude McKay. The central interest of the majority of our contributors, however, remains the task of retheorizing the male position in past and present Anglo-American culture. Not surprisingly, many of the essayists find a model for their practice in the newly emergent and rapidly growing field of gay studies; their work ranges from theoretical attempts to define "gay reading," "gay criticism," and "gay subjectivity" to practical extensions of Eve Kosofsky Sedgwick's analysis of male homosocial desire into new sexual and cultural arenas. This interrogation of male sexuality, gay or otherwise, often spills over into the more general critiques of masculine subject positions that preoccupy still other of our writers. Thus we have some essays that focus primarily on textual and cultural images of "manliness" (the soldier, the cowboy, the explorer), other essays that focus on the anxieties of gender occasioned in specifically male (and, interestingly, most often American) writers, from Edward Taylor and Michael Wigglesworth to Henry James and Wallace Stevens, and still other essays that focus on the status of the male reader or critic (be he F. O. Matthiessen, Frank Lentricchia, or the contributor himself). In sum, what we have gathered under the aegis of "male feminist criticism" is clearly not just one thing, nor does it speak in a single voice, as the various styles and tonalities incorporated in these essays, moving from the personal to the postmodern, attest.

As editors, we have found ourselves faced with the vexing question of how to order the contents of the rich but differently textured voices that make up this collection. Recognizing that any taxonomy will to some extent be gratuitous, we have nonetheless found it useful to suggest, via the division of these essays into four thematic categories, some of the more important filiations that exist among our contributors. Although several essays could legitimately have been placed under more than one of these divisions, we are hopeful that these sections best represent the principal concerns that *Engendering Men* seeks to address.

Part I, "Men, Feminism, and Critical Institutions," offers an engendered perspective on the profession of literary criticism, especially as practiced at American universities in this century. Joseph Boone provides an overview of the whole phenomenon of "male feminist criticism" as it has evolved at conventions and in anthologies over the last few years and indicates several avenues from which a practical criticism by men professing a feminist politics might emerge. Michael Cadden, Lee Edelman, and Jacques Lezra focus on three very different male critics working in three different periods in order to call attention to the complicated relations that exist between critical discourse and the gender of the critic. Cadden takes up the strange case of F. O. Matthiessen, using his letters to his gay lover of twenty-five years as a way of discussing how gender issues get elided both in Matthiessen's critical work and in fictional and academic treatments of his career. Edelman's essay takes a recent interview with Frank Lentricchia as its point of departure in order to analyze one way in which feminism has been attacked so as to appropriate for straight men a universal copyright on cultural subversiveness;

Edelman counters this strategy with one of his own—a reading of Wallace Stevens that critiques Lentricchia's male sexual positioning (and posturing) from an explicitly gay perspective. In focusing on how the examples in a Renaissance rhetorical handbook (George Puttenham's *Arte of English Poesie*) formalize a position of, and a specific gender construction for, the reader, Jacques Lezra argues that current critical efforts to move "beyond formalism" toward a materialist concept of language depend to some extent on the same strategy. Finally, Michael Cooper extends this section's focus to the practice of pedagogy within the profession of literary criticism; taking his cue from the master-disciple relationships depicted in James' tales of literary life, Cooper sees both the study and the classroom as stages where teachers and students enact scenes of subjection replete with ambiguous sexual implications.

The essays grouped in Part II, "Power, Panic, and Pathos in Male Culture," illuminate the anxieties that attend the process of acculturation undergone by all men growing up in a patriarchal society. Just how a crisis in the ideology of familialism impacts on representations of manhood in contemporary popular culture is the focus of Andrew Ross' essay, a wide-ranging survey that traces the transformation of the masculine codes of the classic Western—popularized in television's *Bonanza*—into Spielbergian fantasies of Empire and Lucasian showdowns in outer space. In fascinating contrast to this cinematic projection of mass cultural anxiety about gender redefinitions onto an uncertain future, Walter Hughes' essay locates a parallel anxiety about the meaning of manhood in America's very origins: its Puritan forefathers. Specifically, Hughes interrogates the homoerotic strain—and attendant homosexual panic—that arises when the male Puritan poet, in contrast to his female counterpart, addresses his male God as a lover. This tension between (religious) vocation and male panic is repeated in mid-nineteenth-century America, Robert K. Martin argues, in the case of Nathaniel Hawthorne, whose anxieties about the feminizing effects of his vocation as artist surface in his ambivalent representation of female artist figures. In a continuation of the subject of the making of the American man, Mark Seltzer's essay takes us up to the turn of the century, focusing on the sado-masochistic paradoxes embedded in American naturalist writing and the renegotiations of the male "natural" body in machine culture—renegotiations mediated by Boy Scout manuals, the disciplines of systematic management, and the coming-of-age stories of Stephen Crane and Jack London.

Although all four essays of Part III, "Cleaning Out the Closet(s)," attempt to theorize gender issues as experienced specifically by gay men, many also interrogate the meaning and purpose of establishing a potentially essentializing category of gender ("gay") as a separate analytical tool, whether in the field of literature, film, television, psychology, or literary criticism. Nowhere is the latter impulse more apparent than in the opening essay, Ed Cohen's thought-provoking meditation on his own position as a man who "professes" a field and an identity that are only now beginning to take on some shape. A fitting prologomenon to the inquiries that follow, Cohen's piece, like Boone's in Part I, investigates the inevitably problematic relation of the gay "male feminist" to the professional and academic worlds that seek to "institutionalize" him and provides a startling contrast to Cadden's inventory of Matthiessen's closet. In his study of Oscar Wilde's prison writings, *De Profundis* and "The Ballad of Reading Gaol," Wayne Koestenbaum offers a different perspective on institutionalization by speculating on how these works, produced while Wilde was condemned to "hard labor," might have given rise to "the birth of gay reading." (Koestenbaum's theory of "gay reading" bears comparison to Edelman's formulation of "a gay reading practice.") Michael Warner reads two other "seminal" figures, Sigmund Freud and Jacques Lacan, against Simone de Beauvoir, in order to argue that the equation of narcissism and homosexuality in the psychoanalytic tradition is in fact the basis of modern *hetero*sexuality—a misprision tied to the Western cultural assumption that gender provides us with our only access to otherness. Arguing that Eve Sedgwick's model of homosocial desire depends upon the repression of the homosexual into the homosocial, Christopher Castiglia begins "Rebel Without a Closet" with a gay appropriation of Nicholas Ray's classic *Rebel Without a Cause* before moving on to an investigation of the policing of sexuality in films such as *Consenting Adult* and *Nightmare on Elm Street 2: Freddy's Revenge*.

In Part IV, "Revolutionary Alliances: Call and Response Across Gender," the collection treats the subject of mutual engendering as our essayists specifically address the work of women writers and critics. Marcellus Blount provides us with the motif of this section in his treatment of how female and male Afro-American poets (Henrietta Cordelia Ray, Paul Laurence Dunbar, Claude McKay, Gwendolyn Brooks) have used the sonnet, one of the staples of a Western patriarchal literary discourse from which they are supposedly disenfranchised, in order to offer one another revisionary models of black masculinity and femininity. Tom Foster, in dialogue with feminist Americanist critics and historians, also works in the revisionary mode, depicting the ways in which Emily Dickinson represents the home as the site of contradiction between her desire for a female haven and her resistance to mid-nineteenth-century ideologies of domesticity—the same ideologies Robert Martin identifies as the source of Hawthorne's fears of feminization. In contrast to these Americanist schools, Robert Caserio's critical conversation is transatlantic, as he reclaims Luce Irigaray from recent Marxist-feminist attacks in order to illuminate the representational politics of the novelist Sylvia Townsend Warner, one of the lost voices of the female and lesbian literary traditions. Caserio shows how Warner's coupling of themes of celibate sisterhood and the topos of revolution responds both to an earlier British male tradition and to her own remarkable blend of feminist, modernist, Marxist, and even mystical thought. Robert Vorlicky returns us to the present—a present in which men and women live together, work together, and all too often grieve together, as he analyzes Wendy Wasserstein's Pulitzer Prize-winning play, *The Heidi Chronicles*, in relation to a female friend's response to the so-called wilding rape in Central Park in the summer of 1989. More than any other contributor, Vorlicky laments the invisibility of heterosexual, bisexual, and gay male feminists both in contemporary literature and, despite their demonstrable feminist activity, in the culture at large.

And, of course, it is this invisibility that *Engendering Men*, in its literal embodiment as an essay collection, attempts to redress. Bringing together a community of male critics whose insights into issues of sexuality and gender have been enabled and empowered by feminist insights, we hope to make more visible the efforts of all those individual men throughout the academy who have already begun the task, perhaps too often in isolation, of reconceptualizing themselves as men and hence as critics of the literary and cultural texts that we have inherited and are in the process of recreating. In engendering ourselves, in making visible our textual/ sexual bodies, we thus acknowledge our part in a movement whose time, we hope, has come.

In writing this introduction, we have benefited from the helpful advice and criticism of a number of individuals, including Laura Doyle, Diana Fuss, Deborah Nord, Patsy Yaeger, and, not least, our not always easy to please but always interested contributors. We also owe a debt of gratitude to A. Drake Baer and Dale M. Wall for proofreading the manuscript when our eyes failed. Finally, we are grateful for the generous monetary support allotted this project by the Harvard University Hyder Edward Rollins fund and the Princeton University Committee on Research in the Humanities and Social Sciences fund.

I

Men, Feminism, and Critical Institutions

1

Of Me(n) and Feminism:
Who(se) Is the Sex That Writes?

Joseph A. Boone

[Since the essay that follows was originally written in 1987 for inclusion in another essay collection, *Gender and Theory: Dialogues on Feminist Criticism* (1989), its reprinting here may benefit from a few words of explanation. First, despite the fact that it may initially read like a review-essay of Alice Jardine and Paul Smith's 1986 anthology, *Men in Feminism*, it was conceived in response to a much broader series of impressions I had been gathering for some time prior to the publication of the Jardine and Smith volume. *Men in Feminism* is best seen, then, as the *triggering* event, rather than sole offender or culprit, motivating me to articulate my uneasiness about the way in which men's relation to feminist criticism was at the time being politicized in academic circles. Since it seemed to me that a critical discourse had formed around the subject that almost necessarily precluded its potential, I decided to use the occasion of my essay to examine some of the stages whereby "men and feminism" had become the "issue," the "topic," of the moment.

Even though the debate over men's relation to feminism has far from abated, I am relieved to discover that some of my most immediate worries seem less relevant in light of the two years that have intervened between the writing of this essay and its reappearance here. For in these two years an increasing number of male critics dedicated to the exploration of their gendered subject positions have begun *to do the work*, not just theorize about, what I was then calling "male feminist criticism," and in the process they have begun to assemble an impressive array of methodologies for critiquing patriarchy, masculine subjectivity, and issues of sexuality in general. In face of this productivity, the issue of naming—whether to take on the label, for instance, of "male feminism"—now strikes me as perhaps less urgent than measuring the degree of commitment to a feminist politics demonstrated in these men's newly engendered methods of analysis.]

The lead essay in the collection *Men in Feminism* opens with an eye-catching assertion, one that is as provocative as it is literally and figuratively *arresting*. "Men's relation to feminism," Stephen Heath writes, "is an impossible one. This is not said sadly nor angrily . . . but politically."[1] Heath's claim to dispassionate objectivity and political correctness notwithstanding, the contents of this volume fairly bristle with the antagonistic emotions conjured forth by the subject matter announced in the controversial title of the volume—an antagonism fueled by the very wording of that title, in which the loaded preposition *in* is made to bear the weight of a rather questionable relation between men and feminism. But that relation, according to Heath, is also supposedly "an impossible one," and it is telling to note how Heath's formulation has set the tone for, as well as defined the limits of and boundaries to, nearly all the discussion that follows: one critic after the other in *Men in Feminism,* whatever his or her personal reading of the issue, nonetheless accedes to the *theoretical impossibility* of men ever being "in" feminism *except* as an act of penetration, violence, coercion, or appropriation.

I'd like to suggest, however, that "being *in*" isn't the only relation possible between men/feminism and redirect our attention to the *possibilities* (rather than impossibilities) inherent in the potential conjunction of men *and* feminism. For if we can find our way out of Heath's incapacitating metaphor of arrest, we may also find a way out of an equally incapacitating anger over the issue of inclusion/ exclusion. This is not to ignore the very real political ramifications of questions of being "in" or "out," nor is it, I hope, to overlook the dangers of speaking for such "possibility" in a phallocentric world where power is still overwhelmingly male-identified; rather it is an attempt to chart a path whereby these points of contention, these potential limits, do not automatically bar our *thinking through* the issue of men and feminism. At the same time, I'd also like to suggest that theorizing the topic, as Heath and company often eloquently do, while it is obviously essential, also risks becoming essentializing; the issues suffusing the topic of men and feminism should not come to be perceived merely as set of grammatical relations ("in" or "for" or "against"), at the expense of the simultaneously lived and practiced dimensions of that relation.

Thus, I'd like to risk personalizing the issue in the pages that follow, rather than leaving it an exclusively theoretical one. And one way of doing this, as the first half of my title suggests, will be to coax forth a bit of the "me," the personal pronoun hidden in the word *men,* the biologically determined category to which that pronoun also belongs—that individual "me" in this case being the voice of a male literary critic who for years now has found in feminism a theory, praxis, and way of life that have become synonymous with his, my, sense of identity. In exposing the latent multiplicity and difference in the word *me(n),* we can perhaps open up a space within the discourse of feminism where a male voice professing a feminist politics *can* have something to say beyond impossibilities and apologies and unre-solved ire. Indeed, if the male critic can discover a position *from which* to speak that neither elides the importance of feminism to his work nor ignores the specificity of his gender, he may also find that his voice no longer exists as an abstraction, but that it in fact inhabits a body: its own sexual/textual body. In this regard, the really crucial question for feminists —male and female alike—is how to formulate terms for presenting the issue of "men and feminism" so as not to limit its possibili-ties, overdetermine its body, from the outset.

And my analysis will begin with precisely this danger. For in the field of literary criticism in particular, it strikes me that to date the most important *public* discussions of the topic have been cast, however unconsciously, in terms of a two-dimensional oppositionality that has negatively structured our very perception of the issue, both as a theory and as a reality. In focusing on the disjunctions and alliances between men and the feminist movement in a specifically institutional sphere—that of academic criticism—I do not mean to give short shrift to those many other "nonacademic" contexts where feminism counters male opposition as well as encounters male support: instead I wish to suggest that those "intellectual" debates that the public often conceives as (in both senses of the word) purely "academic" are not without a certain charge for even the so-called real world: the rhetorical formations that underwrite rarified "academic" theory may also illuminate the politics, and communicative impasses, that have accompanied the ongoing feminist struggle in its movement into the streets, the home, and the workplace.

In order to examine the debate surrounding men and feminism in my own "workplace," along with the premises underlying the articulation of that debate, I have chosen to focus on five seemingly random moments: (1) Elaine Showalter's publication of "Critical Cross-Dressing" in 1983, the first prominent survey of the "male feminist" phenomenon in literary criticism; (2) the panel "Men in Feminism I & II" presented at the 1984 Modern Language Association Convention, the annual meeting to which tens of thousands of literature professors, willingly or not, flock; (3) another MLA panel on "male feminist voices" in which I participated in 1986; (4) Alice Jardine and Paul Smith's editing of the *Men in Feminism* essay collection (stemming from the panel of the same name); and, finally, (5) Linda Kauffman's invitation that I participate in the essay collection, *Gender and Theory*, for which this essay was conceived. There is nothing absolute or binding about these stages, I hasten to emphasize, for they consist of events to which I have had very personal and indeed subjective relations—be it as friend, outsider, spectator, or contributor. But that is part of my point, for it has been in the very intimacies and awkwardnesses of my position in relation to each of these events that I have recurrently experienced the aforesaid gap between the "me" and "men" in "me(n)." And, as the following section will now detail, it has been my experience of this discontinuity that has in turn inspired me to question the discursive formations in the literary critical institution whereby the concept of men and feminism, transformed into a territorial battlefield, has attained an "impossible" status.

Impossible Narratives

Although feminism has always remained acutely aware of its relation to men, the reverse situation hasn't necessarily been true. One of the insights of Elaine Showalter's witty "Critical Cross-Dressing: Male Feminists and the Woman of the Year" was to pinpoint the formation of one such moment of reversal. For, by tapping into two seemingly unrelated cultural events to show the same masculine anxiety operating in both, Showalter proposed a link between an unexpected, and unexpectedly popular, phenomenon in several early 1980s films—the rise of the female impersonator or male heroine—and an equally unexpected phenomenon in academic circles—the avowal, by several prominent male literary critics, of their "conversion" to feminist literary theory.[2] In particular, the pseudofeminism embodied in the film *Tootsie* (where Dorothy Michaels' *female* "power," after all is said and done, is only a *man's* masquerade) provided Showalter with a fascinating analogue for analyzing as instances of "critical cross-dressing" the recently donned garb of feminist theory apparent in Jonathan Culler's *On Deconstruction* (1982) and Terry Eagleton's *The Rape of Clarissa* (1982). The irony of Culler's attempt to bring feminism positively to bear on deconstruction, Showalter points out, lies in his reluctance to foreground the relation of his own gender to such an endeavor; much as he advocates deconstruction's incorporation of feminist methods as a positive gain, he himself remains the untainted deconstructor, the removed and authorizing interpreter or "analyst of feminist critical work" (126) who has (safely) positioned himself *outside* the feminist readings that he is, in actuality, often producing.[3] Showalter also points out how Eagleton's claim to find an ally for Marxist theory in feminism disguises a desire to compete with, dominate over, and ultimately recuperate feminism for his own agenda. Rather than a "revolutionary" coupling of the two -isms, Eagleton's reading of *Clarissa* might be said to recapitulate a traditionally figured marriage, with the Marxist "groom" ultimately silencing his feminist "bride" by speaking over-loudly for and on behalf of her.

Through such perceptive readings, Showalter's review gives expression to the very understandable fear of the appropriation or "raid" (129) of feminist criticism by male critics eager to cash in on its early successes. But Showalter's focus, from its very beginning, also unconsciously problematizes the issue she is investigating, by making what she calls the "first wave of male feminist criticism" (131) appear synonymous with what is in fact a highly select group of critics—well-known and very powerful men in the academy already identified with specific schools of criticism other than feminist criticism and with strong preexisting allegiances that have perhaps almost inevitably modified their professions of feminist sympathy. By not raising the possibility that the most empathetic, least appropriative feminist critical practice might be happening *elsewhere*—away from public view, by precisely those men who lack the academic power, rank, or numerous publications of Showalter's named "cross-dressers"—"Critical Cross-Dressing" therefore creates the illusion of a discursive field in which "male feminism" can be perceived only in terms of a struggle for power among superpowers (Showalter versus Eagleton, say) and hence as potentially antagonistic, intrusive, or threatening to those who have fought for years to legitimize feminism within the academy. There is a catch here, of course, for the problem is *not* Showalter's ignorance of an "other side" to male feminism, as many of her male colleagues and male students can attest. The catch is in the simple fact that "Critical Cross-Dressing" was designated, from its beginnings, as a review article of a handful of books published in 1982–83; and the trends that Showalter finds in that published work, augmented by her perception of the suspect "feminism" of films like *Tootsie,* are indeed congruent with her conclusions. The irony is that the terms that her overview evolved out of its highly specific context—that of the book review—quickly became for many other feminists the basis for viewing the whole phenomenon of men and feminism solely as one of appropriation: that is, of "men *in* feminism."

In speaking of the contexts that shape a text's reception, however, I owe an explanation of the personal as well as institutional contexts shaping my own reception of this article. In this case, the "institutional" context was provided by Harvard's Center for Literary Studies, which in the autumn of 1984 created its Feminist Literary Theory Seminar—a "first" in the university's tradition-bound history. And the topic of discussion for the inaugural meeting, as one of my colleagues, Marjorie Garber, informed me, was to be Showalter's article. My initial excitement was brought to a halt, however, when Marge apologetically added that, against her own recommendation, men were specifically not invited; some of the founding members felt that the topic was too sensitive, that the women in the seminar needed to reach a group consensus before opening its doors to men. "But I'll pirate you my copy of the essay," Marge said with a complicitous wink, "Under the circumstances, I'd love to hear your reactions!" On the one hand, I can't say that I didn't find it somewhat ironic that women from as far away as Dartmouth and Wesleyan could come to my institution to discuss "male feminism," while I—one of the only nominally practicing "male feminists" I knew on campus at the time—couldn't. But, on the other hand, I'd been in the field too long to dismiss lightly the claims of separatism at specific historical junctures, and so I tried to convince myself not to make too much out of this one incident. *Nonetheless,* as might be well imagined, the immediate result was that I read the Showalter article with special care, determined to discover my difference from the negatively represented "male feminists" of the article's title. It's little wonder that "Critical Cross-Dressing" came to mark a significant plateau in my perception of "male feminism" as a more problematic issue than I'd previously experienced it to be.

These reflections are intimately connected to the second event that I have chosen to examine as a significant moment in the politicization of the concept of male feminism: the volatile double panel, organized under the title "Men in Feminism: Men and Feminist Theory," that took place at the 1984 MLA Convention in Washington, D.C. For, once again, it was a personal exchange —again involving my tenuous relation to Harvard and Harvard's tenuous relation to women's studies— that first brought this particular event to my attention. The setting for this exchange was a dinner held for one of the English Department's candidates for a women's studies position—exactly one week, incidentally, after the second meeting of the Feminist Literary Theory Seminar, to which men *had* been invited. Seated at a long table at a Cambridge restaurant named Autre Chose, Alice Jardine and I literally found ourselves *les autres,* shunted to the far end of the table so that the senior faculty members in attendance could grill the candidate from its center, as it were. It turned out to be a fortuitous exclusion from the dominant discourse, however, since it brought Alice and me into dialogue for the first time since we'd arrived on campus as beginning junior faculty. As we got to know each other, Alice mentioned the problems she was having coming up with a satisfactory response paper for an MLA panel she was on, a panel on men and feminism: she didn't find the two papers (Heath's and Smith's) she'd received very helpful, didn't want to come off sounding dictatorial or better-than-thou about what they, or other men interested in feminism, should be saying, but didn't want to let these guys entirely off the hook for being so persistently abstract either. Even now I can remember wondering why *these* men were the ones speaking to the subject if their views were so problematic, but at the time I decided to wait till the convention and judge for myself.

For, despite Alice's ambivalence (with which I could empathize, given her position as respondent), the intention of the panel from my position (as one of its subjects) seemed entirely credible and potentially admirable—namely, to give voice to the growing perception among men and women alike that the increased participation of men in feminist discourse added a new if problematic dimension to the history of feminist criticism. But the very constitution of the panel, as I was to discover two weeks later, posed the enunciation of the problem in an equally problematic way. Male panelists—not Showalter's now (in)famous "cross-dressers" but, as Jardine stressed, "those men who are *really trying* . . . our allies" (56)— were invited by the panel's organizer, Paul Smith, to *theorize* about their relation to feminism for the first session, whereupon, in the second meeting, the female respondents took the men to task for theorizing rather than practicing what they preached. The collective response that emerged included a tone of general weariness at having, once again, to be the ones to say, in Alice's paraphrase, " 'That's not quite it . . . you're not there yet' " (54) and a shared suspicion that to the extent that men were "there" in feminism at all, it was, again in Alice's words, "to speak about 'something else,' some 'larger issue' " (55).[4]

But while much of the criticism of male appropriations of feminist theory for "larger" ends, as in Showalter's essay, was clearly on target, the *very format* of the two panels disturbingly seemed to reproduce the two-sided oppositionality against which the feminist concept of difference ideally sets itself: men as a unified body visually and temporally set against women as a unified body; men speculating about "entering" the ranks of feminist women; and the latter reprimanding the former for their bad behavior, "rather tired" (88) imitations of feminist theory, and "all too familiar" (72) arguments "which do not take us very far" (71). In effect, potential dialogue had become confrontation between two "sides" aligned by gender, sides whose interaction was thereby doomed to reinforce stereotypes of both sexes (men blunder in, women scold). In the process the question of differences within and between the men's perspectives, much less the women's, were set aside.

Sitting in the audience, eager to see an issue so close to home being treated seriously yet frustrated by its very airing, I experienced a series of contradictory reactions. First of all, throughout the men's talks, I kept thinking how they were *not* speaking for me, for the "me" in "men," or, for that matter, for my male friends; in particular, Heath's and Smith's attempts to intellectualize their relation to feminism seemed a detour for setting that relation into practice—for all their words and wordplays, for all their confessional techniques, their texts seemed void of any body, any immediate presence. During the question period that followed and intermittently throughout the second panel, moreover, I found myself siding with the women's anger against those hypothesized male entrepreneurs jumping on the "feminist theory bandwagon" (57) now that most of the groundwork had been done; the intrusiveness of such critics happened at my expense too, I found myself thinking; I had "been there" years before the arrival of these belated converts, with their too-easy criticism and how-to mandates. And yet a third impression simultaneously set in, for, as the female critiques accelerated, I began to feel a belated sympathy for the actual men (rather than the hypothesized appropriators) who had participated in the morning's session. They, after all, by virtue of their age and lack of professional status alone, were far from being the "born-again" Bandwagoners or "Divide and Conquerors" (56) under censure, and yet the format they had either helped organize or agreed to participate in was setting them up, it struck me, in a no-win situation.[5] As I left the panel, I kept trying to imagine where my voice fit in the spectrum I had just witnessed, and, more pointedly, which of the two panels I would have chosen to participate in, had I had the choice: in either case, in my case, in the case of feminist scholarship at large, *whose* is the sex, finally, that speaks?

I had my chance to appear on the other side of the podium two years later, when I was asked by Laura Claridge and Elizabeth Langland to moderate an MLA panel they were arranging on "Male Feminist Voices Within a Patriarchal Language"— the focus this time around being on the "sympathetic" male writer, rather than the male critic, attempting to write in a nonphallic mode. At the time I couldn't imagine a more ideal situation. Laura and Elizabeth were seeking a moderator in name so that they could at once organize the panel and present papers on it, and thus I would get a free trip to the MLA with a minimal amount of work—merely introducing the session and the speakers. Moreover, the panel's prospectus struck me as very much a step in the right direction. It suggested that we locate the male voice as a third or odd term in a gendered discourse that consists of (at least) man, woman, and the dominant culural ideology that we call patriarchy: that is, maleness needn't be assumed to be coeval with patriarchy, with woman symmetrically positioned on the other side of the proposition. But the very *construction* of the panel—as I found when I read the selected papers—tended to blur this important move and reinstate, once again, a male-female opposition. Part of the problem was, simply, the plain old element of chance that enters into the arrangement of any panel. For it so happened, first, that all the chosen panelists were women (although both men and women applied), and second, that all their papers, while excellent, nonetheless focused on *men writing about women*. Whether the subject was Shelley on feminine ideality, Emerson on Margaret Fuller, Forster on the Schlegel sisters, or Hardy on

Tess, "male sympathy" was shown to transform itself into a form of linguistic appropriation as the authorial voice inevitably became entangled with the patriarchal rhetoric against which it was ostensibly rebelling.[6]

Such critiques, however applicable to these authors, couldn't begin to address a number of other questions that such a panel *might* have opened up. What difference, for instance, might the perspective of a man on the panel have made? Had any panelists—male *or* female—examined a male author's exploration of his own sexuality, might a more "authentic" male—as opposed to phallocentric and appropriative—desire been located? What of the male writer writing from a gay or otherwise marginalized perspective of race or class? (Forster, the one homosexual author under consideration, was examined, tellingly, only in regard to his views on women, not on how his difference from a heterosexual male norm might have influenced that relation.) And even when the male writer focuses on the "feminine," might there be alternatives beyond "appropriation"—instances, however rare, when he has let femaleness transform, redefine, his textual erotics, allowed himself *to be read through* femininity and femaleness, rather than seeking to become the authorizer speaking on behalf of it?

Having unconsciously precluded an exploration of these differences—the modalities of position that would have indeed rendered man as a third or odd term for analysis in the investigation of gendered discourses—the panel's very constitution had in fact reconstituted "man" as a homogeneous entity, the "fall-guy" for a one-sided rather than really radical deconstruction. Moreover, as the one man on stage, I found the question of positionality all the more immediate. There I was, by virtue of having been listed in the program as the panel's moderator and having introduced its speakers, in the perceived position of having selected this panel, endorsed its version of "male feminism," and authorized four women to speak to the subject (a double-bind: not only for potentially offending some women by seeming to assume a "male" right to authorize their voices, but equally for offending some men by seeming to cede their story, their voices, to women). And yet there I was, just the same, the one male among four women on stage and the one person whose participation was peripheral to the main event in a discussion, ironically enough, of male feminist voices.

Beyond panels often lie essay collections-in-the-making, which has proved to be the case for both the panels I've mentioned: we now have Jardine and Smith's *Men in Feminism*, and Claridge and Langland's *Out of Bounds: Male Writing and Gender(ed) Criticism* is forthcoming. The fourth stage I would like to examine in the emerging academic discourse on men and feminism centers on the way in which a widely read anthology like *Men in Feminism* can unconsciously limit what might be said about men's participation in feminist criticism. For I would suggest that as a totality *Men in Feminism* almost unwittingly seems to recapitulate the problems inherent in the panel from which it originated. Telling in this regard is the semi-apologetic tone of the brief introduction written by the coeditors, Jardine and Smith. For while they seem to agree in feeling the "question of 'men in feminism' [to be] a relatively unpromising one" (vii), they do not *restate* the issue to make it less "unpromising" or less problematic, either for themselves or for their potential readership. Another warning sign emerges a few lines later, when they announce that "it became clear almost immediately. . .that most (though, finally, not all) of our contributors would be straight, white academics," which they admit to be one of the book's limitations (viii). Just why or how the latter fact "became clear almost immediately" gave me pause when I first read it: *who*, I wondered, had they sought out as potential contributors? For what seems "unpromising" or limited here is not so much the topic itself as any *framing* of the question (symbolized in the deliberate retention of the controversial title, "men *in* feminism") that would make it "clear almost immediately" that most of its male contributors would more likely than not be men "in(to)" feminism in the most troublesome sense of the word.[7]

As if in confirmation of this suspicion, the collection includes as "experts" on the subject Jacques Derrida, Robert Scholes, Denis Donoghue (in small print), and Terry Eagleton (in reply to Showalter)—prominent critics whose relation to feminism has never gone unquestioned. In opting for name-recognition by including such men among the seven added male contributors, the editors merely reproduced the problem that I've already noted in relation to Showalter's essay: for the price of spotlighting "famous" names as THE representatives of a movement that inevitably forms elsewhere than in the dominant discourse is to risk precluding what can be said differently, other than in the language of the "straight, white academic." Given this set-up, there's a certain uncanny poetic justice to the fact that, by the last essay in the collection, Jardine's "bandwagon" has been transformed by Rosi Braidotti into a veritable "bulldozer": "Blinded by what *they* have learned to recognize as 'theory,' *they* bulldoze their way through feminism . . . *They* are walking all over us . . . *'They'* are the best male friends we [women]'ve got, and *'they'* are not really what we had hoped for" (234–35; emphasis added). Braidotti's very rhetoric of repetition has transformed "men" into an army of indistinguishable, unnamed "they's"; in the process any idea of "me(n)" has vanished altogether.

The problem of choosing one's contributors—an editorial problem not unrelated, of course, to the exigencies of the marketplace—takes on a different slant when one turns to the *female* critics not originally on the panel but included in *Men in Feminism* and to the way that, as a group, their essays construct—or avoid— the subject of "male feminism" itself.[8] For example, Naomi Schor's "Dreaming Dissymmetry: Barthes, Foucault, and Sexual Difference" strikes me as superb criticism, one of the best essays in the entire collection; nonetheless, by virtue of its rather exclusive focus on Barthes and Foucault, it has the effect of shifting the discussion from "male feminism" to yet more examples of—if we stretch our imagination—men "into" feminism. Instead of Showalter's Anglo-American cross-dressers, we get, this time round, an elite class of male French poststructuralists whose fascination with castrati and hermaphrodites becomes the basis for theories of sexual discourse that ultimately enforce dreams of sexual "in-difference" (in Schor's apt phase), of a lost paradise of blissful indeterminacy that transcends sexual specificity. But in so attempting to move *beyond* difference, Barthes and Foucault in effect also *refuse* feminism's claim of female difference, leading Schor to generalize that "no feminist theoretician *who is not also a woman* has ever fully espoused the claims to a feminine specificity . . . Even the most enlightened among the male feminists condone claims to female specificity *only* as a temporary tactical necessity" (109; emphases added). While Schor's reading of Barthes's and Foucault's displacement of sexual difference is right on target, this larger generalization, however, depends on what is in fact a highly selective focus of two. Indeed, the trajectory of Schor's argument unconsciously repeats the *clinamen*, or "shift away from" (103), of which she accuses Barthes and Foucault—a swerve in argument whereby two men with only an implicit relation to feminism are transformed into universal exemplars of "even the most enlightened. . .male feminists," *all* of whom, it would appear, have gotten it wrong.

Another of the collection's highlights is Nancy Miller's unpacking of the male anger hidden behind platitudes of universal judgment in Denis Donoghue's attack on Gilbert and Gubar's *Norton Anthology of Literature by Women* in the *New Republic*.[9] But, like Schor's essay, Miller's "Man on Feminism" in the long run gives us only what her title announces: *a* man, *one* man unfortunately speaking for too many men, holding forth *on* feminism, certainly *not* speaking on behalf of the male feminist. By definition, then, Miller's essay addresses not the subject or practice of male feminism, but rather its antithesis. Nonetheless, I would suggest, the specific terms of the case she makes against Donoghue *do* turn out to be highly relevant to the hidden imperatives shaping this collection's presentation of that subject. For in revealing the way in which Donoghue's gripe with feminism actually disguises his battle with poststructuralist theory "over ownership of (literary) discourse" (141)—that is, a struggle between the Big Daddies of Humanism and Deconstruction, in which feminist criticism serves as the pretext, the agency of mediation—Miller's argument made me realize the degree to which many of the contributors to *Men in Feminism* use the subject "male feminism" in much the same way, as *their* pretext to wage other critical wars. In the process, ironically, "male feminism" comes to occupy in structural terms the traditional position of women in patriarchy—the ultimately expendable item of exchange that merely gets the conversation going. No wonder my vague discomfort, then, with several of these selections. For it is not that any of them is "bad," but that they often have other, hidden, or not-so-hidden, agendas. Thus, for example, when Jane Gallop uses the occasion of her essay to unmask the sexism of Jean Baudrillard's theories of seduction, it turns out that her real interest is in addressing the relation of French theory to feminism (the idea of men and feminism, or even antifeminism, has entirely dropped out of the picture by the last paragraph). Likewise, Robert Scholes' "Reading Like a Man" actually serves more as an occasion to attack Culler's deconstructive practice (in reading "as a woman") than as any kind of exploration of the subject announced in his title (broached only in his concluding sentence). In the end, it is no surprise that *Men in Feminism* becomes a territorial battlefield, reproducing the discursive thrusts of its title, when the very issues at stake have been so clouded, disguised, or otherwise silenced.

My criticisms notwithstanding, it is also important to note the collection's many merits, not the least being the very fact of its having raised the issue in the first place—and "first" statements are always more difficult to make. Not only does it include Schor and Miller's excellent work and Alice Jardine's sorely needed outline of what a male feminist praxis might really include, but it features the thoughtful commentary of three added male critics—Richard Ohmann, Cary Nelson, and Craig Owens. Indeed, with more contributions like these, the volume would have avoided the pitfalls that I have sketched above.[10] The Claridge and Langland volume also promises to move beyond its panel format in exciting directions; several male contributors, none easily assimilable to the other, are being included, and at least some will be talking about men's experiences.

But the danger is always there of reinstating those potentially blinding symmetries that a feminist understanding of difference should instead encourage us all as feminists to unravel, to move beyond. Thus, as a kind of coda to this part of my essay, I'd like to present a vignette that has to do with the form—and formulation— of Linda Kauffman's 1989 *Gender and Theory: Dialogues on Feminist Criticism*, the collection for which this essay was conceived. One of Linda's agendas, as I understood it, was to give voice to less well-known critics; another was to redress the imbalances of the *Men in Feminism* collection, and the format of essay-plus-response was self-consciously conceived as a means of making an ongoing *dialogue* part of that redressing process. Yet, curiously, what did I find when I looked back at the wording of the letter I received inviting me to become a contributor? Inevitably: "the collection is arranged so that *male essayists* are responded to by *feminist theorists*, and vice versa, and presently includes the following" (emphases added). "Male essayists" versus "feminist theorists"; once again, two sides of a divide, leaving me unclear where *I*, claiming to be both "male" and "feminist," belong. For note, the wording does *not* stipulate "*female* feminist theorists," although that is the obvious, albeit perhaps unintentional, implication, since all of "the following" in Linda's letter turn out to be male-female pairs. So I have chosen, for my peace of mind, to take advantage of this slight opening in phraseology and, rather than considering myself one of the "male essayists," to include myself among the "feminist theorists"—not that I prefer being considered more of a "theorist" than an "essayist," but in hopes of creating a bit of healthy confusion, a field of imaginative play that might contribute to the liberation of our current discourses on and around the subject of "men and feminism." For, when it comes to feminist criticism, I repeat, only half facetiously, whose *is* the sex that writes?

Possible Narratives

I'd now like to pick up on various hints strewn throughout the prior commentary that, if stitched together, might help shift the direction that the issue of men and feminism has hitherto followed and, in the process, redirect our attention to various areas from which a critical practice by men invested in a feminist politics might logically *emerge* rather than sink in (Heathian) impossibility. The following, of course, is only a partial list.

1. One such directive is for concerned literary feminists to stop looking to prominent figures like Derrida for the final word on men's potential to theorize their relation to feminist theory and practice. This is not to say that Derrida's wish to "write as a Woman" or Culler's prescriptions for "reading as a woman reading as a woman" might not be of interest; but it is to suggest that more relevant scholarly work—work more aptly described as feminist and worthy of feminists' attention—is being carried on elsewhere.

2. Second, we need to account for an important generational factor if we are to begin to measure with more discrimination the multiplicities of men's relations to feminism. For, as Andrew Ross has rightly pointed out, there are now "men [in academics] young enough for feminism to have been a primary component of their intellectual formation."[11] The emergence of a whole generation of young men educated in feminism does not in itself allay the problem of recuperation or appropriation, but it does, I would argue, create a scenario qualitatively *different* from the "Bandwagoning" or "Divide and Conquer" theories of male feminism offered by Jardine and others. Such theories generally are more applicable to male critics with, as Ross puts it, a significant "pre-feminist" past, who thus tend to respond to feminism as either an alluring "other" or an overwhelming threat, or both at once. Moreover, if the presence of feminist-educated men makes a difference, so too, potentially, does its correlative: that there are now young women in the academy whose education in feminism has at least partially been shaped by men with feminist interests, both in their lives and their scholarship. Again, this is not to say that this new situation does not pose its own dangers, but simply to recognize a reality, one that has already begun to shift the way in which our current students— tomorrow's scholars—will think of men's participation in feminist studies.

3. A third, related point that has emerged from what I've had to say thus far concerns the danger of lumping all "men" together as a uniform category. What I hope we've begun to learn in this regard is that all feminists, male and female alike, need to be particularly attentive to those marginalized male voices whose interests may intersect with, or move along paths that are congruent to, but not the same as, those already marked out by feminist interests to date. If men are to take to heart Jardine's warning against the "suppression of the diversity and disagreement within the [feminist] movement itself" (57), women and men alike need to keep the same principle in mind when judging the possibilities of a male feminist critical activity, its own potential for diversities, divergence, and disagreement. This recognition is exactly what Stephen Heath elides when he resigns himself to the belief that men's attempts at a "male writing" can only reproduce itself, turn out more of the "same." Tellingly, he leaves unexplored a parenthetical qualification that he inserts at this

very moment: "(unless perhaps [such writing emerges] in and from areas of gay men's experience . . .)" (25).

For, at this historical juncture, many of the men in the academy who are feminism's most supportive "allies" *are* gay. Somehow this fact and its implications have often been forgotten in many of the discussions surrounding the "male feminist" controversy, especially those represented in the *Men in Feminism* volume. From Heath's to Braidotti's essays, too many of the generalizations made about men's desire to become a part of feminism *take for granted* the "heterosexual" basis of that desire—the predominant imagery of penetration is but one clue to the preponderance of these assumptions. In contrast, a recognition of the presence and influence of gay men working in and around feminism has the potential of rewriting feminist fears about "men *in* feminism" as a strictly heterosexual gesture of appropriation. The annual conference of the three-year-old Center for Lesbian and Gay Studies at Yale, while not without its own discursive struggles, has gone far to dispel such fears. Indeed, what impressed me most about the center's inaugural conference, held in 1987, was the extent to which "gay studies" as an intellectual event was able to *begin* at a highly sophisticated, theoretical level precisely *because of* the informing influence of feminism; what I saw demonstrated throughout was a convergence of feminist method and gay studies—epitomized in the conference's presiding intellectual "presence," Eve Sedgwick—in the service of creating a discipline and an agenda that claim to be neither superior to nor the same as feminism, but rather in an ever-present relation of contiguity with the originating politics of feminism.

Hence, in acknowledging the possible plurality of male feminist voices, gay or otherwise defined, along with the many possible directions that such work might take, we would do well to recall Nancy Miller's caution to those who would reduce the feminist enterprise to a pat formula, bearing in mind the potential applicability of her words to male feminist criticism as well: "feminist criticism is not about more of the same. It is about the imagination of difference that does not break down into two agendas, but (that) opens onto a complicated map of contiguities" (141–42).

As with any political theory, there is always, of course, the very real danger of feminism being used irresponsibly by men, particularly when it leaves its established domains. Thus, I'd like to close this essay with a few observations, garnered from my own subjective experiences, that other male academics interested in feminist criticism might consider.

1. My first impulse is simply to encourage men to *identify with* feminism, taking on without fuss or ado the label of "feminist" *if* that's indeed your interest and appropriate to the work you're producing. Too many people, men and women, shy away from the appellation as if the word had the power to diminish their scholarship. A feminist politics, to the contrary, is about taking risks, about assuming the responsibility of a name or label, if only as a temporary political strategy.[12]

2. Second, men participating in feminism should make their own oppressive

structures (ideological, social, psychological) *present* for critique, rather than hiding them under a veil of abstract musing. Part of this process, for example, is simply to remember the multiple ways in which the "me" in "me(n)"—whose cause I've been advocating all along—is nonetheless gendered male, *does* belong, after all, to the biological and social group "men." This is an identification for which, at some point, all of us feminist men must take responsibility. What, for example, happens when we academic "me(n)" must take part in specifically male spheres of action or power? To what degree do we choose to disguise, or not, our commitments to feminism? How do we sometimes take advantage of our born status as "men" to negotiate the treacherous process of establishing a professional identity and continuing to exist within the limitations of our specific institutional circumstances? Whenever such circumstances tempt us to "pass" as "men" rather than "me(n)," what do we do with, where do we leave, our female allies?

3. Third, men with a commitment to a feminist politics need to be willing to forge self-definitions of themselves *as men* that make room for the acknowledgment of a difference and a sexuality that is truly heterogeneous. Which means, really, to quote Jardine quoting Hélène Cixous, *that men still have everything to say about their sexuality*. This is one of the logical, crucial, and, I hope, inevitable directions in which an enlightened discourse of masculinity will develop. For instance, what do the texts we men read and produce and teach say—or avoid saying—about the relation of son to father, man to his gendered subjectivity, to his physical body, to his homoeroticism, to desire and its multiple effects on his and others' pleasures? In this regard, I find Jardine's entire list of "appropriate" areas of exploration for the would-be male feminist in her essay in *Men in Feminism* right to the point. My only caveat is that many of these have already been put into practice by the male critics I know, men who, in Jardine's phrase, are learning "to speak as . . . body-coded male(s)" (60) precisely in order to reimagine man. Which is inevitably to change the shape of patriarchy and its discourses as well.

4. Such acts, hence, are not only theoretical but also political, which ties in with a final observation I'd like, tentatively, to make. Women in the feminist movement have for two decades successfully shared their ideas collectively, seeking each other out in communal networks of relationship. How eventful it would be if more men professing a politics grounded in feminism did likewise. This is not to suggest we should begin forming exclusive men's clubs (that would indeed be only to produce more of the same), but to remind ourselves that we can learn from each other, as well as from our female friends. I would like to think that such a phenomenon—*men really trusting men*—would signal a cataclysmic change in the structures of our contemporary society, dealing the traditional notion of the Old Boys' Network a blow from which it might, I hope, never recover.

But, my friend Patsy Yaeger, reading this essay, said musingly: here is the one point in your paper where I begin to feel uncomfortable and need to be convinced by something more; how can you trust groups of men not to repeat the old order, or not to erase women altogether in forming their cozy communities? I hesitate, too:

I want to assure Patsy that the "me(n)" for whom I've been speaking are different, not in-different to such dangers. Then I think back to my hypothesis, following my reading of Nancy Miller's essay, of the way in which our current discourses on "male feminism" have already constituted such men as the odd element, the expendable item of exchange, in current critical debates; and, to the degree that truly feminist-minded men also occupy the position of outsider in the homosocial transactions that make up patriarchy, perhaps, just perhaps, the linking together of their, our, individualities is to establish a counter network of exchange necessarily subversive of traditional masculine networks of power. A community *with* phalluses, rather than the community *as* Phallus, need exist only as a threat to the existing patriarchal order, not to women individually or to feminism as a movement.

So I tell myself, telling Patsy, but I don't know: this may be *my* dream of utopia (as opposed to Barthes' or Foucault's), marking in fact an "impossible" limit beyond which male feminism cannot go—and yet, even so, that limit of possibility is one that I'd like, for now, for me, for men, to keep in view.

2

Engendering F. O. M.: The Private Life of *American Renaissance*

Michael Cadden

To work out:—The sexual bias in literary criticism . . . What sort of
person would the critic prefer to sleep with, in fact."[1]

—E. M. Forster

" '*Dosce, doce, dilige*.' 'Learn, teach, love.' For me I know no better."[2]

—F. O. Matthiessen

When I was an undergraduate at Yale, I was very aware of the ethnic and religious backgrounds of the men and (few) women who taught me literature. Complaining about the gods of the English Department who had shot down our most recent arguments, my friends and I spoke of Father Wimsatt and Father Brooks, Rabbi Bloom and Rabbi Hartman. We did so, as I recall, out of a profound sense of respect for what we saw as the connections these men had made between their various traditions and their work as critics. If we didn't agree with, say, Wimsatt in *The Verbal Icon*, "that the greater poetry will be morally right"[3] and that, consequently, *Antony and Cleopatra* is demonstrably inferior to *King Lear*, we at least knew where he was coming from. Some of us saw him at Mass on Sundays. It never occurred to us to think of criticism as a neutral enterprise in which personality is effaced; we had too many great examples to the contrary at hand.

Given our undergraduate interest in connecting at least some aspects of the critic with his or her work, it may seem surprising in retrospect that we rarely thought of our teachers as having any sexuality. We might have taken Wimsatt's comment on Shakespeare as saying as much about his heterosexual monogamy as about his Catholicism, but we simply hadn't been taught to think in those terms. The only time a professor's sexuality became an issue was when you heard a rumor or caught a pass. The mere mention of sexuality could mean only homosexuality at the all-male Yale (as it was for my first two years); the speakable variety went largely unspoken. And certainly no one ever thought about how a professor's rumored "queerness" might affect his work. Literary criticism was a thing of the mind and the soul; for the body such men had recourse, it was whispered, to vacations in Morocco with Arab boys or in Venice with the gondoliers.

There was one professor whom I might have had at Yale and who might have taught me something about embodied criticism; that is, had he lived, and had his alma mater made him the offer he longed for, and had he been an altogether different sort of man. In 1925 a young Rhodes Scholar, with a little visionary help from Walt Whitman, wrote to his physically reluctant male lover of his desire to join mind, body and, soul both in his life and in his work:

> You say our love is not based on the physical, but on our mutual understanding and sympathy and tenderness. And of course that is right. But we both have bodies: 'if the body is not the soul, what then is the soul?' . . . Blend together the mind, body and soul so that they are joined in a mighty symphony. The mind and the soul give an idealisation and exhaltation to the body; and the body in its turn gives an intuitive, impalpable channel of expression to the soul and mind. (*Rat* 86, 88)

These words from Francis Otto Matthiessen—F. O. Matthiessen on his book jackets, F. O. M. in his introductions, "Matty" to his friends, and "the Devil" to his lover.

Best known as the author of *American Renaissance: Art and Expression in the Age of Emerson and Whitman*, F. O. Matthiessen was one of the most celebrated critics of his time. A graduate of Yale, class of 1923, he studied at Oxford on a Rhodes Scholarship before returning to the United States to do graduate work at Harvard. He taught for two years at Yale, from 1927 to 1929, before taking up a job back at Harvard. By the age of thirty-two Matthiessen had published three books—on Sarah Orne Jewett, Elizabethan translation, and the poetry of T. S. Eliot. His *American Renaissance*, published in 1941, helped to create and legitimize the field of American Studies; college teachers throughout the country still use his title for their courses in nineteenth-century American literature. Active as a Christian Socialist, the vice-president of the Harvard Teachers' Union, and a member of the Progressive Party and innumerable leftist defense committees, Matthiessen continued to be productive until his suicide in 1950, shortly before he was to testify before the House Un-American Activities Committee about his political sympathies.

As Jonathan Arac reminds us in his book *Critical Genealogies*, there are now two F. O. Matthiessens in print—the author of the above-mentioned critical volumes *and* the author of a series of letters written over a period of twenty years to his lover, the American painter Russell Cheney. Matthiessen met Cheney in 1924 on a voyage to England prior to his second year at Oxford, and the two remained lovers until Cheney's death in 1945, corresponding daily whenever they were apart. In 1978, Matthiessen's friend and Yale classmate Louis Hyde, acting on hints in Matthiessen's will and in the letters themselves, published *Rat and the Devil: The Journal Letters of F. O. Matthiessen and Russell Cheney*. In his chapter on Matthiessen, Arac calls attention to the extraordinary differences between Matthiessen's critical and personal voices and the ways in which such differences highlight both the "struggle of the will to define, formulate, mobilize and authorize an American Renaissance"[4] and the cost of that institutional struggle. In the process, Arac cites the difference between Matthiessen's homosexually explicit treatment of Whitman in the letters and the rather more pansexual version in his *magnum opus*; as Arac writes, to "create the centrally authoritative critical identity of *American*

Renaissance, much had to be displaced or scattered or disavowed."[5] But in concentrating on Matthiessen's *political* displacements, scatterings, and disavowals, Arac succeeds in doing to Matthiessen what Matthiessen did to Whitman in *American Renaissance*: in both cases, politics displaces sexuality as the proper issue for scholarly investigation.

We can see this displacement at work in Arac's treatment of Matthiessen's visit to Wells Cathedral, where he had what he describes as a Whitmanesque encounter with a

> workman—husky, broad-shouldered, forty . . . the perfect Chaucerian yeoman.
> We stood there talking for a quarter of a minute, and as he went on I deliberately
> let my elbow rub against his belly. That was all: there couldn't have been anything
> more. I didn't want anything more. I was simply attracted by him as a simple open-
> hearted feller, and wanted to feel the touch of his body as a passing gesture. (*Rat*
> 124)

In Arac's analysis, the elbow rub becomes a figure for all that was lost in the "harmonizing, centralizing, normalizing and identifying"[6] process of writing *American Renaissance;* as Arac puts it, "Loose elbows had to be tucked in."[7] But Arac tellingly paraphrases one particular line of Matthiessen's, and this paraphrase, I would contend, works as a metaphor for the desexualization of Matthiessen that Arac's essay, like all post–*Rat and the Devil* treatments of F. O. M., eventually effects. Arac tells us that, during his encounter with the workman, Matthiessen was "sexually excited."[8] Matthiessen's own description is more colloquial: "I had a hard on." (*Rat* 124). For me, the lovely, blunt statement of the fact of the matter embodies Matthiessen—gives him a body: the body of an upper-class, gay man— in a way that his criticism rarely does. Throughout the letters to Cheney, the gay critic barely perceivable beneath his canonical drag emerges from the closet of professional and patriarchal mastery hard on in hand, thereby exposing and demystifying the "Phallus" that "disseminated" an entire Renaissance.

A Matthiessen even more decorously sober-sided than Arac's is on display in May Sarton's 1955 novel, *Faithful Are the Wounds*.[9] Like Arac, Sarton chooses to concentrate on the Matthiessen of the public witchhunt rather than the private hurt. Sarton's story focuses on the last days of Edward Cavan, an English professor at Harvard University (with a resumé closely approximating Matthiessen's) who commits suicide largely out of his sense that former political allies have abandoned him. Although Cavan's principal political involvement is with a safely liberal "Civil Liberties Union," Sarton's fictionalization reflects the usual leftist position on Matthiessen's suicide in the 1950s—that he was America's Jan Masaryck, a just man suicided by an unjust society. But as Harry Levin has observed, the publication of the Matthiessen-Cheney letters brings out "the disingenuousness of [Sarton's] effort to center a novel upon his person while ignoring the basic psychological facts,"[10] most especially Matthiessen's inability to continue his interest in life after the death of his lover.

Within the world of the novel, Sarton seems to justify her silence on the subject of Matthiessen's closet by allowing two of her characters to admit to their ignorance about Cavan's private life and then, oddly enough, to deny its relevance to his suicide:

> "But who were Edward's lovers, if he had a lover?"
> "I don't know."
> "Of course you don't. And neither do I. Don't you see? There are whole areas of Edward's life that we never touched, never could touch."
> "People like Edward Cavan don't commit suicide for love—a man of fifty—really, Orlando, what a romantic you are!" (*FW* 162)

Yet like Arac and, to a certain extent, Matthiessen himself, Sarton teases her readers with suggestions of a possible (homo)sexually oriented interpretation of literary life/artifact. Of course, publishing in 1955, Sarton probably felt she could not be explicit in her references to Matthiessen's/Cavan's sexuality; no doubt even Matthiessen's friends would have considered such a breach of confidentiality an attempt to besmirch the reputation of an honorable man. Hence, although Cavan has never married and is possessed of a "personal dignity" that "almost . . . precluded intimacy" (*FW* 127), his status as an "outsider" (one of the novel's key terms) is established only in relation to his *public, overtly political* self.

But Sarton provides the occasional encoded bit of information for those who might want to speculate about why her hero remains such a *personal* cipher. When Cavan is about to depart from a friend's house, one character muses about his next destination in ways that betray a knowledge different from that possessed by the novel itself: "He would go to one of those bars in Scollay Square, she supposed, carrying his word *solidarity* like a banner which no one could see, drink with the sailors who called him Professor and treated him like a harmless drunk, walk the streets half the night, and then not sleep" (*FW* 132). It would be ten years before Sarton, herself a lesbian, published a novel dealing explicitly with gay and lesbian issues—*Mrs. Stevens Hears the Mermaids Singing*—but in passages such as this one, we can hear the content in the closet rattling around, almost begging to be let out. When a character explains that Cavan "couldn't communicate the very essence of his belief and that was his tragedy" (*FW* 209), Sarton perhaps unconsciously signals the novel's tragic inability to name at least one important part of its hero's essence. What's missing is the Whitmanesque hard on.

It was his encounter with Cheney that made Matthiessen read Whitman in a new way, "not solely because it gives me an intellectual kick . . . but because I'm living it" (*Rat* 26). The combination of his physical experience with Cheney and his intellectual experience with *The Intermediate Sex*, by Whitman's British disciple, Edward Carpenter, provided Matthiessen with a new vision of the sexual condition he had earlier assumed would be condemned to inexpressibility, the "idea that what we have is one of the divine gifts; that such as you and I are the advance guard of any hope for a spirit of brotherhood" (*Rat* 47). He saw Cheney and himself as pioneers in a new sexual landscape:

> Of course this life of ours is entirely new—neither of us know [*sic*] a parallel case. We stand in the middle of an uncharted, uninhabited country. That there have been other unions like ours is obvious, but we are unable to draw on their experience. We must create everything for ourselves. And creation is never easy. (*Rat* 71).

As a student of American literature and culture, Matthiessen was aware that the gender territory he inhabited was not entirely unpeopled. His request to write his dissertation on Whitman, a request turned down by his Harvard mentors, suggests that he might have entertained hopes from early on in his career to profile some fellow pioneers. Indeed, at moments in *American Renaissance* itself, Matthiessen appears to want to make good on the observations and claims of the letters; he seems to provide a coded roster of undercover soldiers for a nascent gay political avant-garde, a map of the previously uncharted landscape of same-sex affection, and a genealogy of gay relationships.

Matthiessen's chapter on Whitman has been attacked for politically incorrect statements about Whitman's sexual identity, especially when compared to the invocations of the great gay poet in the letters where, as William E. Cain remarks, "Matthiessen tapped his passionate reading of Whitman to voice his love for Cheney."[11] Yet many of Matthiessen's comments about Whitman seem to beg for a recognition of the gay specificity of his critical analysis. Of course, it is certainly the case, as most contemporary commentators feel obliged to point out, that Matthiessen displays signs of internalized homophobia in his observation about Whitman that "in the passivity of the poet's body there is a quality vaguely pathological and homosexual."[12] But many other passages invite a more celebratory reading of the "Calamus" Whitman. He praises the earthiness of Whitman's language and its roots in "the power of sex" (*AR* 523), and he provocatively suggests the existence of a coterie clientele for the poet's most homoerotically suggestive work:

> Actually Whitman's language approximates only intermittently any customary colloquial phrasing, though the success of some of his best shorter poems, 'As I lay with my head in your lap camerado,' or, probably the most skillfully sustained of all, 'When I heard at the close of day,' is owing to their suggestion of intimate conversation. This fact raises the ambiguous problem of just who his audience was. (*AR* 556)

In quoting from one audience member's review of Whitman's letters to Pete Doyle (the notorious 16.4 of the poet's alphabetically encoded journals), Matthiessen implies that Henry James himself was one intimate of the Whitman reading circle. In a footnote to the James observation, Matthiessen attempts to answer "the much disputed question of what [Whitman] meant by comradeship" (*AR* 582) by quoting at length from a steamy Whitman letter to yet another "loving comrade," the soldier Benton Wilson. He thus wittily if elusively effects a textual four-way among James, Whitman, Doyle, and Wilson.

Two other guest appearances in the Whitman chapter indicate that Matthiessen may have been dropping hints as to the existence of a literary homintern, if not a self-conscious gay literary tradition. After documenting the fears Gerard Manley Hopkins had of appearing too Whitmanesque, the critic comments, "He must have been referring to Whitman's homosexuality and his own avoidance of this latent strain in himself" (*AR* 585). Matthiessen sees Hopkins' own homosexuality at its most obvious in the sonnet "Harry Ploughman," where "this feeling rises closest to the surface in his pleasure in the liquid movement of the workman's body" (*AR* 585). A reader of the Matthiessen-Cheney letters, and particularly of the Wells Cathedral episode, cannot help observing here the creation of something like a gay literary tradition, a band of scribbling brothers united by their class-determined common attraction to common workmen.

It was probably the painter Cheney who introduced Matthiessen to another kindred spirit found in the Whitman chapter of *American Renaissance*—Thomas Eakins. Taking for his example *The Swimming Hole* (a reproduction of which appears in the book for consultation and delectation), Matthiessen seems almost coy in his fantasy about the poet's imagined response to one of the painter's most homoerotic canvases: "What would have appealed most to Whitman was the free flexible movement within the composition, and the rich physical pleasure in the outdoor scene and in the sunlight on the firmly modelled flesh" (*AR* 610).

Like Eakins' *The Swimming Hole* and like Skull and Bones, the secret society at Yale that provided Matthiessen with his longest friendships, the critic's collection of kindred literary spirits is exclusively male. When he writes, "The one common denominator of my five writers, uniting even Hawthorne and Whitman, was their devotion to the possibilities of democracy" (*AR* ix), he ignores another, more obvious connection: as a number of feminist critics have pointed out, Matthiessen, like many other male theorists of American literature, excluded all women authors from the national canon he created in *American Renaissance*.[13] The man who worried that he had the "blurred and soft" voice of a "fairy" (*Rat* 197) did everything he could to insure a manly tradition purged of the effeminate. While his discussion of Whitman's poems of psychic transvestism[14] (Section 5 of *Song of Myself*, "The Sleepers") tends to betray a certain embarrassment at the poet's "fluidity of sexual sympathy" (*AR* 535), it is clearly Matthiessen's own fluidity of (homo)sexual sympathy that in part determines the womanless world of canonical greatness.

Nonetheless Matthiessen had no intention of becoming the Edward Carpenter of literary criticism. Neither in his work nor in his life was Matthiessen a sexual politician or rabble-rouser. Throughout his career, he remained an insider's outsider

and an outsider's insider, cultivating a schizophrenic division between his relationship with Cheney and his professional mien even as he glorified the rhetoric of
wholeness; dedicated as he was to consensus of all kinds, Matthiessen felt obligated
to elide those personal (and political and literary) facts that challenged (and continue
to challenge) the dream of a single, organic, democratic community. According to
Joseph Summers' and U. T. Miller Summers' entry in the *Dictionary of American
Biography*, Matthiessen's homosexuality was strictly an affair of the heart; it had
few consequences in the great worlds of the university or the profession: "For most
of his students and younger colleagues Matthiessen's homosexuality was suggested,
if at all, only by the fact that his circle was more predominantly heterosexual than
was usual in Harvard literary groups at the time and that he was unusually hostile
to homosexual colleagues who mixed their academic and sexual relations."[15] (*Plus
ça change*.) This graphic example of Matthiessen's refusal to connect his professional and sexual lives and hence to develop any kind of sexual politics in his life
or his work suggests that this refusal may have ultimately lead to his destruction
every bit as much as the overt political reasons that are usually attributed to his
suicide. He could begin *American Renaissance* by quoting the architect Louis
Sullivan to the effect that the test of "true scholarship" is that it be "for the good
and enlightenment of all the people, not for the pampering of a class" (*AR* xv), but
tragically he could not see himself as part of a collective sexual identity smaller
than "all of the people."

At times Matthiessen's closeted position seems to have been a source of extreme
pain. He wrote to Cheney in January of 1930:

> My sex bothers me, feller, sometimes when it makes me aware of the falseness of
> my position in the world. And consciousness of the falseness seems to sap my
> confidence of power. Have I any right to live in a community that would so utterly
> disapprove of me if it knew the facts? . . . I hate to have to hide when what I
> thrive on is absolute directness. (*Rat* 200)

But directness about his sexual identity would have placed Matthiessen on the
margins of the very culture he sought to center. The price of engendering an
American Renaissance was directness about gender itself.

Given Matthiessen's total investment of his sexual identity in the person of
Russell Cheney, it should come as no surprise that, when he suffered a breakdown
in 1938–1939, he and his doctors connected it to his fears of Cheney's death.
Cheney was twenty years older than Matthiessen and an alcoholic. At fifty-six,
Cheney had good reason to believe that his health would not hold up; in a moment
of desperation, after a particularly bad spree, he told Matthiessen that he wanted
to die. Soon after, Matthiessen's own suicidal feelings began.

Arac and others have testified to the many political, literary critical, and sexual repressions that might have precipitated both this breakdown and his later suicide. In his own journal account of the genesis of his condition, Mattiessen seems to downplay the political and professional problems he was facing, but his language suggests a critical schizophrenia with roots in his position as a gendered subject:

> Why? That is what is so baffling, so unfathomed. Because my talent is less than I thought? Because, on the first outset, I couldn't write the book I wanted? . . . Even though it should turn out that I am an enthusiast trying to be a critic, a Platonic rhapsode trying to be an Aristotelian, that means a fairly hard period of readjustment, but scarcely grounds for death for a man of thirty-six. (*Rat* 246)

It was important for Matthiessen that he tame "the enthusiast," "the Platonic rhapsode" in himself—the persona given full reign in the letters to Cheney—in order to create his "Aristotelian" masterpiece. Neither "Matty" nor "the Devil" could perform the work of authorizing an *American Renaissance*. Yet Matthiessen also acknowledges, in relation to his reaction to Cheney's death wish, that without the man who gave birth to the rhapsode in him, his own life would become meaningless:

> Having built my life so simply and wholly with Russell's, having had my eyes opened by him to so much beauty, my heart filled by such richness, my pulse beating steadily in time with his intimate daily companionship, I am shocked at the thought of life without him. How would it be possible? How go on from day to day? (*Rat* 247)

Without Russell, there would be no work for the body; the body of work might go on, but not in the vital way that it had. Without the Whitman in his life, there would be only the Whitman of *American Renaissance*, an unsexed Aristotelian version of the Platonic original and of his unsexed Aristotelian critic.

Later in this same journal entry, Matthiessen records a conversation with his doctor in language that recalls an earlier letter about his depression at being separated from Cheney ("There seems to be a film between me and everything. Nothing seems really vital: books are just a procession of words and I can't find significance in my work" [*Rat* 173]). Significantly, here Cheney is not the explicit subject; subliminally, however, he is figured as Matthiessen's connection to everything that is most important in his life and work:

> At one point in our talk I broke into tears, and said that I loved life, that I had felt myself in contact with so many sides of American society and believed there was so much work to be done, absorbing it, helping to direct it intelligently. And now I felt a film of unreality between me and everything that had seemed most real, that I had to find some way to break through it. (*Rat* 248)

Surely one of the major sides of American society that Matthiessen was most in contact with was the homosocial and homoerotic literary and social traditions. He knew it from books—through his work on Jewett, Melville, Whitman, James, and others. And he "lived it" with Cheney and the men he cruised on the streets of Boston, London, and Paris. But the connection between the tradition and the life existed only in his person, not in his book; without Cheney, the "film of unreality" would reappear, and he would be left not with a utopian sexual and political project, but with its pallid representation in *American Renaissance*.

Cheney died in 1945, six years after Matthiessen's breakdown. They had been together for over twenty years. Although Matthiessen continued to be professionally and politically active (he seconded the nomination of Henry Wallace at the Progressive Party convention in 1948), he could not sustain himself for long. In 1950, at the age of forty-seven, he fulfilled his 1938 fantasy of "jumping out of a window" (*Rat* 247) by leaping from the twelfth floor of a Boston hotel. His suicide note read: "I am exhausted . . . I can no longer believe that I can continue to be of use to my profession and my friends" (*Rat* 367).

Twenty-five years before, Matthiessen had written Cheney from Oxford:

> I don't want to be well-informed. I want to be truly myself and by that comfortably vague statement I mean that I want to follow what I feel to be my bent to the full. I want to study the essence of the human spirit and I want to live to the full. You remember me telling you Langland's motto: '*Dosce, doce, dilige*.' 'Learn, teach, love.' For me I know no better. (*Rat* 101)

It was a harder motto to live up to than he knew. F. O. Matthiessen became the scholar and teacher; Matty the Devil lived in love. While it is true, as Eric Cheyfitz has suggested, that "Matthiessen lacked or resisted a critical vocabulary that could translate his democratic politics into the writing of literary history,"[16] it is also the case that Matthiessen lacked a sexual politics (and a resultant critical vocabulary) that could allow him to connect his many kinds of work and the life he lead with Russell Cheney.

Let me end on a fantastic and utopian note, borrowed from the imagination of Virginia Woolf.[17] Let the feminism I came of professional age with do for me what Matthiessen could not do alone—engender and legitimize the Platonic rhapsody. Let me imagine, then, since facts are so easy to come by, what would have happened had Matthiessen had a wonderfully gifted brother, called Michael, let us say. Like Francis, Michael went to Yale. Like him, he studied in England on a generous fellowship. But there their paths diverged. While in England, Michael met E. M. Forster, and one fateful day, Forster touched Michael's backside in the same way that Edward Carpenter had once touched Forster's. As if by magic, the effect was the same. In Forster's words, which Michael cherished, "It seemed to go straight through the small of my back into my ideas, without involving my thoughts."[18]

Michael found another sentence in Forster, a much shorter one, that also meant a lot to him, resonated for him in ways different from the way it did for his friends: "Only connect . . . "[19] It seemed an invitation. To what he could not yet say. Let us now suppose that Michael returned to Yale, worked very hard, got a job at the very school that brother Francis most wanted to teach at, and fell in love with the most wonderful man in the world. Michael was nearly as productive as his now famous brother and, because he wrote the right sort of books, eventually received tenure. But he was not content with his work.

After the death of his brother, Michael reflected on their parallel lives and began to ask some very startling questions: "Could I be thinking about my work in the wrong fashion? Doesn't who and what I love affect the way I write and teach? Shouldn't who and what I love make its way into my work and into my classroom? Doesn't it do so whether I like it to or not? Isn't there a history of people who have loved as I do? Is this country as uncharted and uninhabited as Francis thought? Haven't many of our kind been writers and teachers and critics? Wouldn't it be good to tell their stories? There will be problems, of course. Who counts and who doesn't? Based on what information? And where is it in the text? But wouldn't it be worthwhile nonetheless? To at least begin the map? Yes, and with others who cannot find themselves represented there for company."

By the time I arrived at Yale in 1967, Michael Matthiessen was a legend—the great gay critic, we called him, because he seemed to like that queer word. Some felt awkward around him. I did myself at first. I'd certainly never met anyone as honest and open—in his work, in his classroom, and in his life—about something everyone else found so unspeakable. His learning, teaching, and loving were all of a piece, all connected. And, like most Yalies of the period, I had to admit that the best course I ever took was the one he cotaught with a feminist colleague based on the book they cowrote—*The Other American Renaissance*.

3

Redeeming the Phallus:
Wallace Stevens, Frank Lentricchia, and the
Politics of (Hetero)Sexuality

Lee Edelman

The critical literature written about Wallace Stevens for over half a century now offers little that could be understood as providing a "gay reading" of the poet or his work—this despite the fact that it is remarkably easy to view Stevens in a purple light, easy, that is, at the very least, to see him in terms of a fin-de-siècle aestheticism evocative of a culturally identified "decadence" inseparable from associations with sexual irregularity. As early as 1924, after all, Stevens' poetry could be described in the highly charged language of self-conscious perversity and artifice that characterizes the following passage from a review of *Harmonium:*

> Just as in the 'nineties, golden quill in hand, Aubrey Beardsley, seated under a crucifix, traced with degenerate wax-white finger pictures that revealed a new world, a world exact, precise, and convincing, squeezed out, so to speak, between the attenuated crevices of a hypersensitive imagination, so in his poetry Wallace Stevens chips apertures in the commonplace and deftly constructs on the other side of the ramparts of the world, tier upon tier, pinnacle upon pinnacle, his own supersophisticated township to the mind.[1]

Eight years later another reviewer, foregoing such gorgeously elaborated syntax, proposed a similar reading of Stevens by describing him more concisely as "a very Proust of poets"[2]; in 1935 Ronald Lane Latimer suggested a relationship between Stevens' poetry and the work of Ronald Firbank, leading Stevens to acknowledge that he had read Firbank's novels, although he insisted that he had "long since sent the lot of them to the attic"[3]; and as late as 1953, only two years before the poet's death, William Empson raised once more the question of Steven's literary and intellectual brotherhood when he proposed that "Mr. Wallace Stevens, very well-to-do it appears, and growing up in the hey-day of Oscar Wilde, was perhaps more influenced by him than by Whitman."[4]

I cite these comments, on the one hand, to evoke the way in which Stevens, virtually from the outset of his public poetic career, was defined in relation to a literary culture already associated—more or less explicitly—with homosexuality; but I cite them, on the other hand, to indicate by synecdoche the sort of analysis that this essay will not endeavor to produce. Instead of engaging the question of a "gay style" or a "gay aesthetic," I want to consider in the following pages some ways in which a gay reading practice that attends to the social inscriptions of ideology can make visible certain definitive stresses inhabiting our culture's texts— stresses that might seem to have little relation to what our critical institutions continue to define as the narrowly specialized (i.e., insignificant) concerns of gay men and lesbians. I plan to proceed with that consideration by examining some strategies by which literary criticism in particular attempts to evade, contain, or dismiss what it tendentiously—and defensively—construes as "the homosexual"; I will refer to Stevens' poetry, therefore, not primarily as a body of texts through which to trace the workings of a deeply embedded (hetero)sexual ideology, but more obliquely as an instrument of analytic leverage that can help to articulate a critique of those gestures whereby criticism refuses or denies its own positioning within a framework that a gay theory might enable us to read.

I

Let me start by quoting from an interview with Frank Lentricchia that was conducted by Imre Salusinszky. Near the beginning of the conversation, Lentricchia assails American literary feminists for their alleged inability to distinguish between a "woman of privilege" and a "working woman," between, as Lentricchia puts it, "Nancy Reagan and [his] mother." He explains that he cannot be wholly sympathetic with the American feminist project until, as he phrases it later in the interview, feminists attend to "the contextualization of sexuality within economic realities." His withholding of total sympathy produces the following exchange:

[Salusinszky]:   One finds the same tensions between the radical left and, for example, the Gay Rights Movement, which is, even more than feminism, primarily a bourgeois oppositional group.

[Lentricchia]:   I've said to very close gay friends of mine that they're very radical on one issue, and they're with Reagan on most of the other issues. They don't much disagree.

[Salusinszky]:   But the "one issue" of feminism is an all-embracing one, in a way that the gay rights issue is not.

[Lentricchia]:   Well, the one issue of feminism *may* be an all-embracing one, if it doesn't conceive of female sexual identity and the socialization of females as some sort of isolatable territory for Elaine Showalter and Sandra Gilbert to examine.[5]

It may be worth mentioning in passing that the possibility of a gay theory of reading, a gay literary practice that might serve as a more appropriate analogue to American literary feminism, is not conceivable within the context of this interview recorded in March of 1986; but what I want to focus on more carefully here is the implicitly validated—because unrefuted—assertion that the "gay rights issue is not" an "all-embracing one." Within this dialogue the token of the limited scope of gay rights as an issue is its isolated status in the political agenda of Lentricchia's "very close gay friends." In the midst of an argument with American feminism grounded in his resistance to what he sees as its tendency to universalize women's experiences and naturalize gender difference by ignoring the significance of such social determinants as ethnicity, class, and race, Lentricchia nonetheless adopts easily and unself-consciously a familiar and insidiously totalizing perspective that allows his "very close gay friends" to stand in rhetorically for gay people as a whole. The effect of this substitution—independent of any question of motivation or intentionality on Lentricchia's part—is to reinforce an always potent strand of American homophobic ideology whereby the Left in particular envisions its antithesis in the image of the narcissistically self-absorbed gay man: politically reactionary, indeed, Reaganesque, except in defense of the right to pursue the gratification of his own desires. Implicit in the mobilization of this broadly accessible post-Wildean construction of male homosexuality is the assimilation of gay men to a repudiated realm variously defined as that of aristocratic privilege or of self-aggrandizing bourgeois ambition to embody an elitist high cultural ideal.[6] Although the invocation of this particular construction of male homosexuality could lead us back to the images cited earlier of Wallace Stevens as dandy or rarefied aesthete, I want to take a route back to Stevens that is simultaneously more circuitous and more direct: more direct because Lentricchia follows up on his remarks by using Stevens to exemplify the interdependence of "sexual and economic self-consciousness," more circuitous because I want to approach Lentricchia's ideas by looking at two of his essays in which the reading of Stevens briefly sketched in the interview finds fuller articulation.

Both of the essays I have in mind appeared initially in *Critical Inquiry*. The first, "Patriarchy Against Itself—The Young Manhood of Wallace Stevens," was published in the summer of 1987 and reprinted as part of the final chapter of Lentricchia's recently published book, *Ariel and the Police;* the second, "Andiamo!," appeared in the winter of 1988, and it constitutes Lentricchia's response to two published responses to his earlier piece: one written by Donald Pease, the other jointly authored by Sandra Gilbert and Susan Gubar. The argument propounded in "Patriarchy Against Itself" repudiates what Lentricchia describes as the essentializing tendency of American literary feminists; the essay asserts that by failing to recognize the self-contradictory structure of patriarchal ideology—an ideology in which gender difference is naturalized as the determining ground of identity at the expense not only of women but also of men or "patriarchs" themselves[7]—these feminists, represented in Lentricchia's essay by Showalter and Gilbert and Gubar, unwittingly wind up espousing the system of values "that patriarchy invents" (777). To escape yet another repetition of that "manichean sexual allegory" (775), Lentricchia explores the construction of the modernist literary tradition in terms of its anxious positioning between an economic sphere construed by the bourgeoisie as the definitive arena of masculine self-fashioning and a cultural sphere construed as the province of a genteel, ineffectual, and marginalized femininity.

By examining Stevens in such a context, Lentricchia, as Donald Pease appreciatively writes, "makes audible a previously unheard cultural voice, a voice calling from the feminist unconscious of the male patriarchate."[8] Summarizing Lentricchia's argument (in a way that Lentricchia largely endorses in his response), Pease explains how such a voice arises:

> Before the patriarch can dominate others he is divided from within into two figures, the dominant or "masculinized" and the submissive or "feminized" male. In the patriarchal unconscious, the figure who demands conformity to certain imposed standards of masculinity is in a necessary relation to another figure who must conform to those standards. Whether this figure conforms or not does not matter. As the figure who should do the conforming, he is what Lentricchia describes as the feminized male cohabiting the identity of the masculine patriarch. In submitting (or more pointedly in failing to submit) to the patriarchal demand to be masculine, this male experiences "becoming masculine" as cultural feminization.[9]

Lentricchia phrases this notion succinctly; in his view "the basic ideological point has to do with social engenderment, and it means, among other things, if you're male, that you must police yourself for traces of femininity" (743). This necessity arises because "the ancient social process called 'patriarchy' consists also in the oppression of patriarchs; the 'interest' of patriarchy lies also in the confusion of men, in teaching men who will not conform how to alienate and despise themselves, and even men who do conform" (774–75).

One might, at this point, be struck by the sense of having heard this all before— of having heard it in a variety of different contexts and in the service of differing political agendas; indeed, it may be hard *not* to hear it most resonantly as a repetition of the "manichean sexual allegory" that Lentricchia himself has dismissed. That allegory, however, now returns with a difference: internalized within the space of the male psyche (seen here as doubly victimized insofar as it suffers both its "masculinized" and its "feminized" aspects as oppressions) this revisionary manichean scheme assures that the historical experiences of women within modern patriarchal social structures can now be read as ancillary to a larger and male-centered project of ideological deconstruction by which "patriarchy against itself dismantles itself from within" (775). Without disputing that patriarchy operates coercively on men as well as on women (though from the benches of governments to the bleachers of ballparks, the world is filled with vast numbers of men who "conform" to the " 'interest' of patriarchy"—and thus gain access to social power— without, unfortunately, seeming to "despise" themselves in the least), one can nonetheless become suspicious when Lentricchia goes on to declare: "Patriarchy does not and cannot understand the self-subverting consequences of what it conceives . . . as its 'interest.' If we can speak of a social process as having intention, then we have to follow through and say that it also has an unconscious"(775). What troubles here is not the notion that patriarchy "has an unconscious," but that its unconscious is one more *thing* that patriarchy can *have*. The "deconstruction" of patriarchy that Lentricchia would perceive when "patriarchy against itself dismantles itself from within" serves not to dismantle but to reinforce the coherence of patriarchal identity by insisting that patriarchy and its unconscious share the same name, the same patronymic: that the unconscious is not something fundamentally other but the other as appropriated or domesticated by the same.

Feminism, in other words, can become an "all-embracing issue" only when it ceases to be an "isolatable territory for Elaine Showalter and Sandra Gilbert to examine" and becomes instead a province susceptible to colonization by oppressed patriarchs claiming access to the unconscious of patriarchy itself—an unconscious that may be viewed as "feminized" but must not be construed as female. The absolutes of gender binarism have not been dismantled here but merely displaced; read not as fixed biological determinants but as culturally specific psychic positions, the masculine and the feminine—even when their operations are situated "within" the male psyche—still derive their efficacy from the ways in which they function as social and historical tropes. They necessarily participate, that is to say, in the process whereby biological differences come to ground ideologies of gender. Lentricchia's internalization of those binary positions, therefore, does not evade, but merely relocates, the manichean schematization that informs the social consequences of gender as it is ideologically construed.

To some extent the manichean conflict that is thus repositioned in Lentricchia's essay must always get reproduced so long as the argument is framed in terms of gender alone. Indeed, what is striking about Lentricchia's reading of authority in the literary culture of modernism is his failure to consider the numerous ways in which the awareness of homosexual possibilities and the insistence of homophobia as a mode of social control both complicate and reorient "social engenderment" in Western cultures—and in particular, the ways it effects the "social engenderment" of what he chooses to identify simply as the "feminized male."[10] In fact, one reason for the familiar sound of Lentricchia's evocation of the patriarchal insistence that men "police (themselves) for traces of femininity" is that it echoes, but in a less satisfying way, observations made earlier and more cannily by Eve Sedgwick concerning the emergence of those terroristic regulatory mechanisms that have reshaped the interpretive contours of all relationships between men: "Not only must homosexual men be unable to ascertain whether they are to be the objects of 'random' homophobic violence, but no man must be able to ascertain that he is not (that his bonds are not) homosexual. In this way, a relatively small exertion of physical or legal compulsion potentially rules great reaches of behavior and filiation."[11] My purpose in citing this passage is not merely to place Lentricchia's categories beside Sedgwick's so as to find the former wanting; instead, I would view Lentricchia's argument as a representative cultural instance of the way in which some of the most sophisticated, politically engaged, and ideologically self-conscious literary criticism of our moment founders in its efforts to interpret the social and literary inscriptions of gender by refusing to recognize that for modernist culture lesbian and gay issues may also be "all-embracing" and require a theoretical articulation that would illuminate not only our literary texts but also the various maneuvers that make possible the gestures whereby literary criticism refuses and resists that recognition. And that refusal is all the more noteworthy in this case because Lentricchia himself addresses the question of homosexuality in his essay on Stevens.

Lentricchia argues that Stevens, in his anxious response to a society that "masculinized the economic while it feminized the literary" (766), felt the need to "recover poetic self-respect, whose name was necessarily phallic" (757). He sees the enactment of this imperative in the seventh section of "Sunday Morning," where the poet imagines "a ring of men," "supple and turbulent," who "chant in orgy on a summer morn." The production of this vision, in Lentricchia's reading, serves to distance Stevens from the effeminacy that Keats and such poets as Stedman, Stoddard, and Taylor seemed to represent. If Keats became "a word signifying sexual otherness to the econo-machismo of Stevens' culture" (761), Stevens, according to this logic, had to produce a poetry that would repudiate Keats—and thus the feminization that Keats came to signify—in the name of a phallic masculinity that, as Lentricchia argues, finds its most compelling American literary precedent in Whitman.

What seems particularly interesting, and particularly suspicious, about this account of the patriarchal insistence upon an oppressively phallic masculinity is that Lentricchia identifies this vision of phallic insistence with homosexuality. When he first evokes Stevens' vision in section 7 of "Sunday Morning," a vision he will later characterize as the "absurd no woman's land" (775) of patriarchal fantasy, Lentricchia describes it as the imagination of a community that is "homogeneously male and in some sense homosexual" (757). The casual imprecision with which he deploys the category of the "homosexual" here allows him to inflect its significance shortly afterwards by referring to an American tradition of "homoerotic pleasure"— a tradition that acquires both its distinctive tone and its political resonance in Lentricchia's essay from the way in which it echoes, of all things, the earlier work of Leslie Fiedler.[12] Thus Lentricchia sees Stevens as joining himself with mainline American visions of male utopias, including:

> certain raft passages in *Huckleberry Finn*, the "Squeeze of the Hand" chapter in *Moby-Dick*, Rip Van Winkle's fantasy in the Catskills of men at play, many, many things in Whitman and, more recently, the Brooks Range conclusion of Norman Mailer's *Why Are We in Vietnam?* What Stevens imagines for the social future is a place without women; men who work, but whose work cannot be distinguished from the homoerotic pleasure of sexual indulgence . . . The contradictions of Stevens' early life and poetry—work, poetry, and nature itself, the conventional realm of female authority—all are reclaimed for a masculine totality, fused in an image of masculine power: Father Nature. (759)

As this passage suggests, what is designated in Lentricchia's reading as "in some sense homosexual" not only becomes complicitous with, but provides the very pattern for the patriarchal imperative to stigmatize and discredit all that is feminine, including, significantly, the feminized male himself. In the totalitarian resonance of the "power" informing this "masculine totality" Lentricchia evokes the dark obverse of what he describes as its "language of fraternity . . . and equality" (759). For this "homosexual" community embodies the social energies that perform the exclusionary operations of patriarchy; and though "seductive" even to Lentricchia, the representation of communal "orgy" in this "astounding" poetic vision merely recuperates the privilege of the phallus and thereby, given the logic of his reading, implicitly defines as "homosexual" the libidinal energy that underlies the oppressive mechanisms of "social engenderment."

This reading of the relationship between homosexuality and the socio-economic structures of patriarchy may recall, ironically, a similar analysis offered by Luce Irigaray. Echoing Lentricchia's vision of "homosexual" masculine totality, Irigaray asserts, in "Women on the Market":

> The work force is thus always assumed to be masculine, and "products" are objects to be used, objects of transaction among men alone.
> Which means that the possibility of our social life, of our culture, depends upon a hom(m)o-sexual monopoly? The law that orders our society is the exclusive valorization of men's needs/desires, of exchanges among men.[13]

Irigaray proceeds to unpack the logic of this position as she declares: "Reigning everywhere, although prohibited in practice, hom(m)o-sexuality is played out through the bodies of women, matter, or sign, and heterosexuality has been up to now just an alibi for the smooth working of man's relation with himself, of relations among men."[14] In his reading of "Sunday Morning," Lentricchia, like Irigaray, unmasks the "power" of patriarchy—and of patriarchy's oppressively exclusionary fantasies—as a force working toward the production of utopian communities whose relationships nakedly emerge at last as "in some sense homosexual." One could productively apply to Lentricchia, therefore, the analysis that Henry Louis Gates, Jr., so persuasively offers of Irigaray: "Plainly, this 'revelation' is intended to confirm the corruption of the patriarchal order. Plainly, too, Irigaray's redemonization of an already demonized category is not just an unhappy coincidence."[15] For Lentricchia this implicit "redemonization" of homosexuality participates in an effort to redeem the heterosexual male from complicity with the mechanisms of patriarchal oppression; he is seen, therefore, not as the agent of patriarchal power but as its victim, and, in prospect, as its vanquisher. The covert invocation of Fiedler in Lentricchia's interpretation of "Sunday Morning" figures in this exculpatory strategy by appealing to Fiedler's ideological construction of male homosexuality as an anxiously misogynistic evasion of mature heterosexual relationships; Lentricchia draws upon this prejudicial analysis of "American visions of male utopias" in order to label as "homosexual" the libidinal economy subtending the operations of patriarchal authority. Where homosexuality was regressive psychologically for Fiedler, it is regressive politically for Lentricchia; like the latter's "very close gay friends," homosexuality itself in this analysis is allied with Reagan on every issue except for the right to experience the "homoerotic pleasure of sexual indulgence."

II

To frame within the context of a gay reading Lentricchia's own framing of homosexuality, I must make rather quickly a number of preliminary observations. To begin, Lentricchia studies Stevens' resistance to the bourgeois feminization of literary culture in the context of his own attack on American literary feminism— an attack focused largely on feminism's failure to engage the specificity of economic determinants in the construction of social history. But Lentricchia's repudiation of literary feminism for tending towards an "aristocratic social model" (782) and for privileging a "formalism of gender" (775) to justify a critical practice that "leap(s) to the literary" (781) at the expense of the economic, reenacts the same "capitalist" (761) logic of "econo-machismo" that he analyzes in Stevens: a logic that led Stevens to "phallicize" his poetry as a defense against the socially disengaged— or "feminized"—formalism practiced by the aesthetic aristocracy of his day.[16] It is all the more interesting, therefore, that Lentricchia, himself a male at work in a culturally "feminized" profession,[17] should claim the ability to articulate the "self-subverting consequences" (775) of patriarchal organization while arguing that feminism, like that which he defines as "in some sense homosexual," actually serves the patriarchal interest by "insist[ing] on the values of the phallus" (777).

Lentricchia returns to this last assertion in "Andiamo!" where he replies to Gilbert and Gubar's response to "Patriarchy Against Itself" by referring to their essay's epigraph from Stevens—an epigraph in which, with Lentricchia in mind, they cite the following lines from "The Bird with the Coppery, Keen Claws": "He munches a dry shell while he exerts / His will, yet never ceases, perfect cock, / To flare, in the sun-pallor of his rock." Lentricchia counters that Gilbert and Gubar misread not only his own representations of gender, but Stevens' as well, and they do so, he says, because they "take the 'perfect cock' even more seriously than some of us boys do. Certainly more seriously than Stevens does in the poem from which they quote the phrase."[18] The logic of his earlier essay implies that it is inevitable that feminists and homosexuals would take the "perfect cock" too seriously since they are the ones who complicitously enact the "values of the phallus." But "some . . . boys" (should we read, some *heterosexual* boys?), who gain cognitive authority by their positioning outside the fetishistic realm of phallic fixation, are capable of articulating the self-subversion implicit in the patriarchal ideology of the phallus. Lentricchia thus seeks to absolve his enterprise from the taint of patriarchal coopta-tion even while that enterprise attempts to appropriate the power of radical subversiveness for the implicity heterosexual and implicitly male (or male-identified) critic who has been able to master the hurly-burly world of economic realities.

But the phallus will out, and the discursive contexts in which Lentricchia gestures toward the exposure of his own may tell us something about what is at stake in his attempt to reconfigure the politics of gender. Had I space I would consider a telling moment from Salusinszky's interview with Lentricchia in which he reveals the extent of the phallic investment at issue in his work by responding as follows to critics who challenged his view of de Manian deconstruction: "If I'm wrong about de Man: well, show me. I've shown you mine, now you show me yours" (205). But a similar, and more significant, moment is inscribed at the outset of "Andiamo!" Before addressing Gilbert and Gubar, Lentricchia comments briefly on the analysis of his essay offered by Donald Pease. In the process Lentricchia alludes to a quotation from Kenneth Burke cited by Gilbert and Gubar as another epigraph to their response: "The picture of Frank Lentricchia on the jacket of his *Criticism and Social Change*," Burke comments, "is enough to make an author feel relieved on learning that Lentricchia is largely on his side."[19] Taking issue with a particular aspect of Pease's reading, Lentricchia writes: "Those of you who know Don will appreciate why the mere thought of disagreeing with him makes me go limp. Consequently, it comes as a great relief to me (and to my wife) to learn that he is largely on my side."[20]

Surely Lentricchia would say of this what he said of "the infamous photograph"[21] referred to by Burke: that it should be understood in "a tradition of self-mocking send-ups of macho stances" and that it offers "not a defense of stereotypical masculinity but its comic subversion."[22] With such assertions Lentricchia claims access to subversive energies that in some as yet unspecified way dismantle patriarchy from within; but he fails to see that "sending up" may be synonymous with erection. Indeed, Lentricchia's "relief" on discovering that Pease is "largely on [his] side" and able therefore to reinforce his potency rather than making him "go limp" must be read in relation to the parenthetical, because logically obtrusive, insistence on the heterosexual uses toward which Lentricchia's potency is put: the relief, he assures us, is experienced not only by himself but by his wife as well. We can only imagine what sort of relief is provided by such a gratuitously objectifying invocation of his wife as the guarantor of his virility.

Through all of this, of course, Lentricchia is not taking the " 'perfect cock' too seriously"; he's having fun displaying the phallus and "subverting" it at once. What could be more delightful or further from the dour and patriarchal seriousness that marks the feminist or "homosexual" investment in the phallic? But might it not be useful, even at the risk of seeming to take Lentricchia's self-representations too seriously, to inquire just what, if anything, is getting subverted here or to ask how the miming of heterosexual male privilege by a heterosexual male differs from the persistently oppressive enactment of that privilege in the culture at large? After all, isn't one of the hallmarks of that privilege the right to claim that it's all in fun— since, as Lentricchia himself might suggest, "some of us boys" will, in fact, *be* boys? Let me be clear about what I am suggesting: Lentricchia has not only stated but demonstrated his sensitivity to gay rights as a matter of social policy. Indeed, at the end of "Andiamo!" he insists that he "can think of one sexual difference in Reagan's America, which threatens to override all differences: gay men, regardless of class and race, may face criminalization and indefinite detention on the sole basis of their "sexual orientation."[23] Yet he fails, nonetheless, to recognize that the scope of this "sexual difference" extends beyond questions of social policy alone. For like the question of feminism, to which it may never be entirely assimilable but from which it is never wholly separable either, homosexuality is indeed an "all embracing issue" whose decisive effects in the shaping of modern ideologies of gender and sexuality can be traced in the strategic blindness at work in his own cultural critique.

III

Rather than examine in detail how that blindness inscribes itself in Lentricchia's reading of Stevens, I want to suggest how Lentricchia reproduces the sexual ideology that his essay anatomizes by glancing at a provocative, though rarely examined, work from the middle of Stevens' career, a work that Stevens decided to exclude when he compiled his *Collected Poems*. The poem is "Life on a Battleship," and the battleship to which the title refers is quite pointedly identified as *The Masculine*.[24] The poem presents a series of meditations on the "rules of the world" (30) as drafted by the captain of the ship, who speculates, as does the poem itself, about the possible relations between the parts and the whole in the organization of society. Describing the captain as an "apprentice of / Descartes" (31–32), "Life on a Battleship" explores the ideological implications of efforts to codify the "grand simplifications" (32) of life as dogma, as the *"Regulae Mundi"* (31) by which to determine the governance of human interactions, and it does so in a context that reinforces the relation between questions of social power and questions of masculinity.

Like the photographic representations of Lentricchia and their relation to the iconography of phallic empowerment, however, "Life on a Battleship" has occasioned disputes about its meaning that center on questions of tone. Harold Bloom, for instance, declares that the poem is "almost a mockery"[25] while Joseph Riddel emphasizes its "belligerantly [*sic*] rhetorical posture" and defines both the poem and its hero as "self-mocking and yet serious."[26] Thus the instability in the relationship of send-ups to seriousness and subversion is already inscribed in the various critical interpretations of this particular text, and that instability, significantly, emanates from a work that self-consciously reads gender, sexuality, and class in terms of a social organization centered on phallic authority.

"Life on a Battleship" repudiates a Marxist-inspired ideal of collective society in favor of an Emersonian celebration of individual autonomy, and it does so by analyzing this ideological conflict as itself an enactment of differing ways of constructing masculinity. Thus the collectivist vision (as the poem represents it) fetishizes a phallocentric notion of unity and imagines transforming *The Masculine*, as battleship, into "the largest / Possible machine, a divinity of steel" (12–13) that would become "the center of the world" (15). As "both law and evidence in one" (37), *The Masculine*, in this ideological framework, appears to be simultaneously self-evident and self-authorizing: "a divinity / Like any other, rex by right of the crown, / The jewels in his beard, the mystic wand" (41–43).

Such rhetoric makes clear that the collectivist ideal, at least from the poet's perspective, reproduces the hierarchy of aristocratic privilege against which it defines itself; as the captain of *The Masculine* observes: "The war of the classes is / A preliminary, provincial phase, / Of the war between individuals" (3–5). Class struggle must give way to the conflict of individuals and the collectivist ideal of a workers' paradise must produce instead a "paradise of assassins" (7)—a world of collective antipathy in which the desire for individual distinction and privilege necessarily reasserts its appeal.[27] For Stevens as for Lentricchia this return of the aristocratic is inscribed within a realm that takes its ideological tint from its contiguity with that which can be viewed as being "in some sense homosexual"— its contiguity, that is, with the erotics of power in a domain that is, definitionally here, portrayed entirely as *The Masculine*. For the privilege of authority aboard this embodiment of *The Masculine* finds expression in the captain's ability to make the men on the battleship bend to his word—a word whose authority is reinforced by the might of "ten thousand guns" (22). As Stevens notes in a passage that pinpoints the phallic imperative whose logic governs this reductively unitary world: "On *The Masculine* one asserts and fires the guns" (75). Imagining a future in which he has seized this phallic authority so completely that he "would only have to ring and ft! / It would be done" (19–20), the Captain delights to envision a world in which all men "did / As [he] wished" (25–26): "fell backward when [his] breath / Blew against them or bowed from the hips, when [he] turned / [His] head" (26–28). In this fantasy the bodies of the other men respond to his every desire; they must obey the most whimsical or sadistic command that he voices "to please [him]self" (20).

The sort of intimacy implied by the physiological specificity of this language locates this exercise of power in the realm of sexual authority; and the rapacious interchangeability in the poem of sexual and political authority is precisely what is at issue in the text's revitalization of the socioeconomic metaphor that governs its opening lines: "The rape of the bourgeoisie accomplished, the men / Returned on board *The Masculine*" (1–2). Class conflict or the conflict of economic ideologies achieves its representational force here through the image of sexual violation. The bourgeoisie, already feminine in the French from which the term is borrowed, is envisioned as having been violently overpowered by the champions of the working class who dwell aboard *The Masculine*. But since Stevens, as Stevens himself knew well, was nothing if not, in his public life, the embodiment of a bourgeois ideal, it is possible to see this "rape" as the expression of his anxious positioning in relation not only to questions of "social engenderment," as Lentricchia would have it, but also to the unarticulated questions of sexuality that intersect with, inflect, and complicate the historically specific interpretations of gender.

Interestingly, while both Stevens and Lentricchia conduct arguments against particular ways of construing the economic—Stevens attacking the phallic insistence of a socialism that masks an older dream of aristocratic privilege and luxury while Lentricchia attacks the phallic insistence of a bourgeois ideology he defines as "econo-machismo"—the discredited positions are located in each instance in relation to sexual interactions between men: interactions that are culturally articulable in terms of "homosexuality." Such a maneuver, for Stevens as for Lentricchia, allows these interactions to embody an ideology that each can "expose," though in different ways, as fundamentally conservative in its enshrinement of authority and privilege. And this appears to be structurally necessary so that each can reappropriate, in the name of an ideology allegedly more open to difference, the very phallic authority that he claims to subvert by sending-up.

Thus in Stevens' poem the quasi-Emersonianism with which the poet refutes the collectivist vision does not disavow the dominance of the masculine, but seeks to redefine masculinity as always already containing within itself the subversion of phallic bravado:

if

It is the absolute why must it be
This immemorial grandiose, why not
A cockle-shell, a trivial emblem great
With its final force, a thing invincible
In more than phrase? There's the true masculine,
The spirit's ring and seal, the naked heart. (46–52)

This "true masculine," with its capacity to see through the "grandiose" posturings of anxious phallicism (and to acknowledge its own vulnerability by defining itself as the "naked heart"), finds its parallel in Lentricchia's effort to define a position from which the male might escape the symptomatic "phallic gestures" enforced upon him by "patriarchy in its capitalist situation" (413). But even when dressed as a "cockle-shell" in modest self-effacement, the "perfect cock" of "the true masculine" neither conceals nor subverts itself: rather, it seeks to become still more perfect, "invincible / In more than phrase," by appropriating even the power of subversion as its own.

My purpose, however, is not to argue for some more "authentically" subversive position, but to show through what agencies and at whose expense the alleged subversion effected by this ideological framing of the issue is produced. And toward that end it is important to note that the phallus—which, as "mystic wand" (43), presided over the tendentious fantasy of authority that colored the captain's reduction of law to a unity not wholly distinguishable from *The Masculine* itself—returns at the end of "Life on a Battleship" to empower the poet's own belated Emersonian assertions. "The good, the strength, the scepter moves / From constable to god" (88–89), he writes, tracing, as he does in "Sunday Morning," the process by which the law, like other mechanisms of human authority, finds justification through a projective displacement that misreads it as a transcendent structure of meaning, a divine and thus absolute mandate that enforces a univocal truth. The disciplinary entitlement of the "constable," the ability to act as the representative of the law, springs from a relation to the "scepter" whose "circle" (90) or sphere of influence grows larger as it moves toward the hand of the deity imagined to underwrite its authority. But here, as in "Sunday Morning," Stevens suggests the imaginative poverty inherent in this fictive projection of divinity; the authority assumed to originate from the divine hand holding the "scepter" travels in the opposite direction instead, "from constable to god, from earth to air" (89). And as a weak mythological misrecognition of the imagination's own strength, as a phantom constructed by men unwilling to assume the burden of their creative potency and centrality, the divine hand inevitably "fails to seize" (92) the phallic "wand" that would represent, in such a worldview, the source of all authority. With that failure Stevens rejects any trajectory of power that depends upon the originating fiat of a divine father whose presence can seem to anchor not only the poetic imagination but also the ontotheological system within which that imagination operates. Repudiating so central— and so centrally masculine and imperial—a source of authority, the poem concludes with the poet foreseeing a future in which the phallic scepter "returns to earth" (80) to underwrite a version of Emersonian self-reliance. Liberated from subjection to a transcendental masculinity embodied in a master seen as the "immemorial grandiose," every man is now empowered—but also, and more problematically, *required*—to become the king in his own castle. Such a notion, as Eve Sedgwick lucidly explains while discussing a passage by Juliet Mitchell, carries with it a powerful charge as a representative instance of bourgeois ideology at work:

> The phrase "A man's home is his castle" offers a nicely condensed example of ideological construction in this sense. It reaches *back* to an emptied-out image of mastery and integration under feudalism in order to propel the male wage-worker *forward* to further feats of alienated labor, in the service of a now atomized and embattled, but all the more intensively idealized home. The man who has this home is a different person from the lord who has a castle; and the forms of property implied in the two possessives (his [mortaged] home / his [inherited] castle) are not only different but, as Mitchell points out, mutually contradictory. The contradiction is assuaged and filled in by transferring the lord's political and economic control over the *environs* of his castle to an image of the father's personal control over the *inmates* of his house.[28]

The return of the scepter, therefore, cannot be read outside the historical context of middle-class male self-definition. Indeed, its critical significance for Stevens derives from its relation to a discourse of autonomy that intersects with and makes possible a discourse of visionary self-articulation. For when the scepter returns to earth after the banishment of the gods,

> It will be all we have. Our fate is our own:
> Our good, from this the rhapsodic strophes flow,
> Through prophets and succeeding prophets, whose prophecies
> Grow large and larger. Our fate is our own. The hand,
> It must be the hand of one, it must be the hand
> Of a man, that seizes our strength, will seize it to be
> Merely the center of a circle, spread
> To the final full, an end without rhetoric. (102–109)

As an American prophet who would have his "strophes" succeed the rhapsodies of Emerson, Stevens here draws a larger circle—a circle "spread to the final full"— around that earlier traced by the Emerson of "Circles."

The language with which this circle is "spread," however, demands attention; for the spreading of the circle—and thus the act of empowerment through which the poet becomes autonomous, becomes, himself, a man—requires in the first place, as Stevens puts it, that "our strength" be "seize[d]" by the "hand of a man," requires, in other words, the intervention of a power that is explicitly gendered and implicitly made sexual. "Seize," the verb that articulates the violent force of that intervention, is the same verb that named the activity by which the Captain envisioned his appropriation of *The Masculine:* "Suppose I seize / The ship, make it my own and, bit by bit, / Seize yards and docks, machinery and men" (7–9). Such acts of seizure cannot evade coloration by the initial reference to "rape" and it might not be far-fetched to suggest that the language with which "Life on a Battleship" concludes leaves itself open to the sort of analysis that would read a textual reinscription of that rape in the activity whereby "the hand / of a man . . . seizes our strength . . . to be / Merely the center of a circle, spread / To the final full." Such a reading would define the final image as "an end without rhetoric" indeed.

Pace Lentricchia, this does not make the scene of phallic empowerment "in some sense homosexual"—nor will it do to resolve the issue by calling it "homosocial" instead.[29] For what distinguishes this enabling seizure or rape of one male by another is its determining *hetero*sexuality—its participation, that is, in a psychic economy that defines itself *against* that which is culturally identified as "homosexual." The poem represents this scene, in which, as it were, a man is made, as one of necessary and productive violence; the issue is not one of same-sex desire but rather of submission to phallic Law so as to earn the privilege of inhabiting the "center of a circle, spread / To the final full." Thus desire in this scene attaches only to the affirmation of the poet's centrality and "strength"; and the act of seizure signifies only to the extent that it makes possible a socially sanctioned introjection of masculine authority. What may at first glance appear to figure a scene of "homosexual" rape, then, should be viewed instead as a sort of apotropaic fantasy that phobically reflects the anxiety of the heterosexual male about the meaning of his desire for the phallus *as signifier* of autonomy and social entitlement—an anxiety made all the more urgent by the necessity that his own phallic power only represent or reenact a social authority identified with the phallic pre-eminence of the father(s). Thus the focus at the conclusion of "Life on a Battleship" falls on the poet's achievement of a position from which to declare the self-dependence, the autonomy, that distinguishes those who wield the "scepter": "Our fate is our own," he twice proclaims, marking the "strength" of his own imagination in contrast to the impotence of those who receive their intellectual insemination from others.

The intersection of the literary and the economic in this credo becomes more apparent when the phrase is juxtaposed against a passage cited by Lentricchia from Stevens' journal of 1900, a passage in which Stevens discusses Phillip Henry Savage, a poet who had died the previous year: "Savage was like every other able-bodied man—he wanted to stand alone. Self-dependence is the greatest thing in the world for a young man & Savage knew it."[30] This fiscal Emersonianism surely participates, as Lentricchia argues, in a broad nexus of class and gender issues; but as the last lines of "Life on a Battleship" imply, it is also informed by an ideology of sexuality intricately bound up with those very questions of gender and class. It bespeaks, that is, a deeply rooted concern on the part of bourgeois heterosexual males about the possible meanings of dependence (emotional or economic) on other males—a dependence whose danger lies not in the threat of a "feminization" that would destabilize or question *gender*, but in the threat of a "feminization" that would challenge one's (hetero)sexual identity. In this way the bourgeois ideology of male economic "self-dependence" effects its self-definition, at least in part, against a "homosexuality" construed in terms of the indolence and wealth of an economically unproductive aristocracy.

Neither homosexual nor homoerotic, the conclusion of "Life on a Battleship" disavows all dependence on other men even as it unfolds a narrative of submission to the power of the phallus as the necessary *precondition* to the achievement of phallic autonomy. This narrative defines the scene of submission not as the fulfillment of a "homosexual" desire at the core of patriarchal phallicism, but as the product of an embattled male heterosexuality that expresses therein its disquieting—and dangerous—confusion about how to respond to its culturally mandated investment in the phallus.[31] The trajectory of the poetic narrative, in consequence, is toward the rehabilitation of the phallus, its affectionate re-erection in a place of privilege and respect, through the repression of its violent power as the "immemorial grandiose"—as the signifier, in other words, of the law and as the violent agent of "rape"—and through the representation of it instead as "a trivial emblem great / With its final force, a thing invincible / in more than phrase"—in short, as "the true masculine, / The spirit's ring and seal, the naked heart." Lentricchia similarly manifests a desire to effect such an act of redemption when he observes with unmistakable sympathy and perhaps no small amount of wistfulness: "In the literary culture that Stevens would create, the 'phallic' would not have been the curse word of some recent feminist criticism but the name of a limited, because male, respect for literature" (767).

In this way, for Lentricchia, as for Stevens, the larger project is one that undertakes the redemption of the phallus, that seeks to transform its image, to make it, as it were, more likable. No longer the emblem of repression and rigidity that humorless feminists and homosexuals fetishize, the new phallus has gotten in touch with its emotions and dares to let it all hang out. Having begun by looking at an interview with Lentricchia, so I will conclude by referring to another interview in which he figures prominently. I have in mind a fictive interview that Lentricchia includes in "Andiamo!.," an interview in which he literalizes the scene of patriarchal indoctrination by imagining a moment of sexual instruction by his father. Having been accused by Gilbert and Gubar of suffering from male hysteria, or "testeria," Lentricchia asks:

> FL: Dad, what's testeria?
> Dad: *Figlio!* What happened to your Italian? It's TestaREEa! *Capisce?*
> FL: Yes.
> Dad: Tell me.
> FL: A store where they sell that stuff.
> Dad: In big jars!
> FL: Let's go there![32]

This fantasy of male empowerment takes shape as a revisionary anecdote of the jars, an anecdote sufficiently significant to Lentricchia that he titles his essay by rendering its punchline, "Let's go there," in his father's Italian, "Andiamo!" That return to the language of the patriarch seems very much to the point, for here, as throughout Lentricchia's argument, the phallus returns to the father. Thus what Lentricchia writes with regard to Stevens' "Anecdote of the Jar" seems applicable here as well: "Jars . . . seem to have designs upon power."[33] Indeed, the ambiguous "stuff" of desire dispensed from the jars of this "TestaREEa" constitutes the very essence of phallogocentric power insofar as it conflates associations of heads (the Italian *testa*) and texts (the Italian *testo*) with sperm (the "stuff" of testicles) and testosterone (the "stuff" of maleness).

This fantasy, of course, expresses itself rhetorically as a joke; but here as elsewhere Lentricchia's humor reinforces an ideological investment that he otherwise denies: it reinforces, that is, the alleged ability of heterosexual men to occupy positions more authoritative (because derived from the sexual authority of their fathers) than those identified with the feminists or the lesbians or the gay men who find themselves excluded both from Lentricchia's humor and from the invitation that his title "Andiamo!" would extend. After all, it is as a response to the challenge embodied by feminists, lesbians, and gay men that the fantasmatic "TestaREEa" is conjured in the first place—conjured as a zone of traditional security, familiarity, and empowerment: as a haven in which heterosexual men accused of suffering from "testeria" can find shelter from attack and safely indulge in their celebration of male (hetero)sexual potency while continuing to deny that they take too seriously the prerogatives of the phallus.[34] Lentricchia's scene of paternal instruction may offer us phallicism with a baby face, but it celebrates the same old phallus of Western patriarchal power.

The "subversive" effect of Lentricchia's intervention in the politics of gender, then, is undermined by his inability to recognize its relation to the sexual ideologies of modernism, ideologies that require interpretation not only in terms of gender binarism, but also in terms of the cultural analysis that a gay reading can provide. In the absence of such an analysis, the redemption of "the phallic" from its status as the "curse word of some recent feminist criticism" will signal only the patriarchal redemonization of feminism and homosexuality; and Lentricchia, like the critical institutions for which he serves here as a representative, will continue to misrecognize his investment in the enterprise of the "TestaREEa": an investment that makes him not merely a consumer, but a profit-making shareholder in the ideology it purveys.

4

"The Lady Was a Litle Peruerse": The "Gender" of Persuasion in Puttenham's *Arte of English Poesie*

Jacques Lezra

Notorious for its self-serving definitions of decorum, George Puttenham's *Arte of English Poesie* (1589) seems to join an explicitly pedagogical motive with consistent definitions and uses of gender and rhetoric. Not only does the *Arte* envision itself as a manual for the formation of courtiers, but it also implicitly fashions a definition of the appropriate position for women under a female monarch, even (or particularly) for anyone "a litle peruerse, and not disposed to reforme her selfe by hearing reason."[1] The happy combination of the language of rhetoric with a formal reliance on the persuasions of pedagogy has eased the appropriation of the handbook by both formalist and historicist approaches to the English Renaissance. To these, Puttenham provides either a contemporary terminology for describing textual mechanisms or an example of the ideologico-political consequences or motives of rhetorical practices common in Elizabeth's court, and in either case he understandably appeals to a criticism that seeks in part the reformation of its readers, or at any rate their education to the inscription of power in the contemporary language of gender. For this critical reformation occurs in part, as in the *Arte of English Poesie*, not only by hearing texts' reasons, but by learning how to read them, as it were, perversely, where reading seems least called for and where such "learning" most resists formulation. However imperfect in itself, the *Arte* (and, more broadly, the genre of which it is an example) seems to indicate the possibility that reading itself will provide a common institutional and discursive ground between such forms of criticism—a way of moving, in Patricia Parker's recent phrase, "beyond formalism, differently."[2]

The project that this movement announces is compelling, and to some degree it is underway—if, however, in directions that can seem contradictory. Efforts in this country to align the strategies of rhetorical reading with the concerns of feminism have begun to problematize and extend dated or conceptually limiting analyses of the linguistic and ideological construction of sexuality.[3] At the same time, historicizing criticism that seeks to describe the "power of forms," whether in the English Renaissance or elsewhere, has tended to substitute for reflection theories of history the more dynamic mediation of discursive power in the formation of a dominant ideology persuasively coordinating the formal and the empirical. The institutional effects of this distinction have at time been suggestively bitter, perhaps because the tacit agreement between deconstructive, cultural materialist, and certain feminist criticism about what lies *beyond* formalism is threatened by incompatible under-standings of the term "beyond." Not only is *matter*, the term that organizes this effective critical accord, the site of, rather than the solution to, the temporal and epistemological impasses encountered by the desire to move through reading "beyond formalism," but the concept of material mediation, conceived in dialectical terms that should not be applied uncritically (and in particular not to the representa-tions of sexuality with which Renaissance rhetoricians sought to educate and persuade their readers), is the subject of some confusion.[4] For to the extent that textual production, understood as either reading or writing, provides access to matter, however equivocal the status of that access, it become dispensable or contingent. Unless the terms are correlative, proceeding beyond formalism then becomes a way of going beyond reading, a project whose ease and desirability depend more on deliberate misreadings of the term "reading" than on consistent critiques of its "politics." Such correlation, however, cannot without simplification be expressed in terms that relate notions of *praxis* to the practice of reading or writing.[5] That this dilemma is in turn taken to suggest that we can in no sense go "beyond" reading seems to bring into question the passage from this notion of materiality to the more familiar, if equally opaque concept of matter associated with empirical events and with political and ideological resistance and change.[6]

Retaining for the moment only the outlines of this problem, I want in this essay to address the possibility that the distinctions between formalist and historicist criticism that Puttenham's manual allows us to pose, if not to resolve, themselves arise as a way of displacing other difficulties. These concern the more general question of whether gender and gender difference—as they come to be represented and used in a theory of persuasion—can be aligned with either the historicity of forms or that of empirical events. The question is on the face of it contradictory, even if the analogy at work is not trivial. Persuasion, after all, involves a use of language that seems strictly intersubjective, one which it is entirely appropriate to define as one would the exchange between a forming and a reformed self, and by extension between the recognizable figures of the teacher and pupil or, as in Puttenham, between an argument and its representation in examples, or between man and woman.[7] It is no news that the definition of this exchange has suffered a considerable theoretical elaboration, both in aesthetic and in explicitly historical terms, and most notably as the concept of mediation is introduced and what Luce Irigaray has called its "old dream of symmetry" is opened to question.[8] The subordination of the second terms—the reformed self or persuaded subject, the pupil, the example, the woman—in the analytical sciences of logic, education, and the law not only follows analogous discursive patterns, but often has the same content. And it also remains an open question whether the "alignment" of gender difference with formal or empirical categories does not itself repeat this gesture of subordination. It is only in the most deliberate cases that *reading* escapes from the problematic of what has been called the "reontologization" of the *chora*, the "essentially mobile and extremely provisional articulation constituted by movements and their ephemeral stases" that we find in Kristeva and Irigaray and whose very resistance to the geometry of position—being between or mediating—becomes symbolic law.[9]

It is no coincidence, then, that when Puttenham's *Arte* reflects upon its primary formal categories—persuasion, denomination—it does so in examples not only constructed to persuade or educate, but understood to be externalizations by which the form of language reflects upon itself. To suggest that the language in which this reflection and questioning are to occur necessarily repeats the asymmetries it discloses, and that for this reason it must take into account and in part be *about* this repetition, is to say that in its most perversely rigorous form this language is necessarily that of rhetoric. And to suggest that the necessity of this argument comes from the desire to displace its asymmetry is to say that the epistemology of rhetoric is inseparable from a reflection on the difference of gender. Rhetoric, and in particular the rhetoric of examples, will always have been the "demoiselle aux miroirs" in which this reflection finds its term. Jean Paulhan's celebrated phrase reflects the logic binding the analytics of externalization to both rhetoric and the figure of the woman, but it is subtle in suggesting that the status of this figure is itself far from clear.[10] The allusion to the "caballero de los espejos" episode in *Don Quixote* shows to what extent relations between "demoiselles" and "caballeros," rather than serving to wed linguistic concerns to the empirical figure of gender, tend instead to express these as the abyssal intertextuality of literary history. Whatever its practical consequences, this tendency should remind us that what we call "desire"—the desire, for instance, to move "beyond formalism"—is not only, or not primarily, a subjective or libidinal function. Desire names the disjunction between the discourse of subjectivity that structures our understanding of reading and the rhetorical form of language's epistemology. And because in this sense it is strictly a nominal mechanism for *producing* text, the desire to move differently beyond formalism becomes in every instance the matter of reading.

This is perhaps why in Puttenham's examples it becomes increasingly difficult to understand the discourse of rhetoric by analogy to the very representations of gender that serve to instance it *empirically*. At the same time, however, it becomes impossible to refer to *formal* distinctions to begin to understand what difference, if any, this displacement of the empirical might make for a description of the rhetoricity of gender in Elizabethan texts. The insistence with which Puttenham returns to the issue of sexual difference—principally in stories of rape, seduction, or instruction, but also of generation and/or infanticide—constitutes already a perverse reformation of rhetorical problems whose resistance to being read as symbolic externalizations is neither empirical nor formal. In addressing the question of the positional power of reading—what it can serve to "align" with what—we will in fact be asking what this resistance is and seeking to define its odd materiality. To conclude his chapter on "How our writing and speaches publike ought to be figuratiue, and if they be not doe greatly disgrace the cause and purpose of the speaker and writer," Puttenham, a most exemplary Elizabethan, has recourse to the following fable:

> And because I am so farre waded into this discourse of eloquence and figuratiue speaches, I will tell you what hapned on a time my selfe being present when certaine Doctours of the ciuil law were heard in litigious cause betwixt a man and his wife: before a great Magistrat who (as they can tell that knew him) was a man very well learned and graue, but somewhat sowre, and of no plausible utterance: the gentlemans chaunce, was to say: my Lord the simple woman is not so much to blame as her lewde abbettours, who by violent perswasions haue lead her into this wilfulnesse. Quote the iudge, what neede such eloquent termes in this place, the gentleman replied, doth your Lordship mislike the terme [*violent*], and me thinkes I speak it to great purpose: for I am sure she would neuer haue done it, but by force of perswasion: and if perswasions were not very violent, to the minde of man it could not haue wrought so strange an effect as we read that it did once in Aegypt, and would haue told the whole tale at large, if the Magistrate had not passed it ouer very pleasantly. (153)

Two related judgments are at issue when "eloquent termes" come before the law. In the first place, the objection, on the basis, presumably, of the code of decorum that the term *plausible* suggests, to characterizing persuasion as "violent." In the second place, an objection to the telling of the tale that would have justified or explained this use—this time, also presumably, on the more practical grounds that the "litigious cause" risks becoming a Shandean morass if metalinguistic anecdotes of this sort are allowed. Both considerations have a less pleasant corollary, however, that is no longer presumptive but a matter of structure. Once it is admitted, even anecdotally, that persuasion can violently sway the will (of the judge, for example), the aspect of law that depends for judgment and expression not on "plausible utterance" but on the realm of empirical knowledge invoked by the narrator ("on a time my selfe being present . . . *as they can tell that knew him*") can, like the unfortunate litigant's wife, be led astray. The resulting appearance of judicial "wilfulnesse" (or unwillfulness) would be at odds with the concepts of legal consistency, repeatability, and tradition that the Magistrate's learning and gravity seem to figure.[11] The Magistrate's interruption reflects a necessary unwillingness to have wrought upon him and the law the type of persuasions that may have led to the litigious cause in the first place.

For Puttenham's narrator, however, the example's risks are of a different nature, and the fable's content has a certain persuasiveness that leads him to continue the gentleman's anecdote. "Now to tell you the whole matter as the gentleman intended," he continues, "thus it was":

> There came into Aegypt a notable Oratour, whose name was *Hegesias* who inveyed so much against the incommodities of this transitory life, and so highly commended

death the dispatcher of all euils; as a great number of his hearers destroyed themselues, some with weapon, some with poyson, others by drowning and hanging themselues to be rid out of this vale of misery, in so much as it was feared least many moe of the people would haue miscaried by occasion of his perswasions, if king *Ptolome* had not made a publicke proclamation, that the Oratour should auoyde the countrey, and no more be allowed to speake in any matter. Whether now perswasions, may not be said violent and forcible to simple myndes in special, I referre it to all mens iudgements that heare the story. (153–54)

For the narrator, then, the value of this example is to show precisely that the type of laws that separate such stories from what they exemplify cannot be "passed over" except as it were below the surface (to return to the fluid metaphors he invokes: "because I am so farre waded into this discourse of eloquence"), becoming part of what they are intended to distinguish. [12] What then happens below the surface, within the very matter of the discourse of eloquence, assumes a regulative function that the law itself obeys. The banishment of the Orator thus echoes the interruption and passing over of the Magistrate, adding one more to the list of ways in which the barrister's (and Puttenham's) tale tends to resemble aspects of its interrupted frame narratives. [13] "Resemblance" pertains formally first to the similarity between what the example represents and the argument it bolsters—in this case, between the outcome of the Orator's too persuasive powers and the argument for a judicious use of such powers with which Puttenham closes his defense of figurative language. [14] The category of "similitude," involving necessarily some form of historical or mythological precedence ("as we read that it did once"), is thus in Puttenham the defining feature of example, which is to be taken, in "matters of counsell and perswasion," in the strong sense of a paradigm or moral exemplar. At the same time, however, "similitude" becomes the foundation for the representation of the law, the category regulating the wisdom and gravity of a judge whose task it becomes to see in particular litigations (between a man and his wife, say) examples of previously adjudicated cases which form the body of precedent. This regulation depends, indeed, on the law's power to make its subjects similar before it, of downplaying the class and economic differences figured, in this courtroom, as sexual difference.

Three types of similitude, then, seem to be articulated in the example that concerns us. With the strict decorum of a court, the forms of resemblance that pertain to reading, to the law, and to representation function together with an exemplary harmony. The contrast with the matter the Magistrate is trying is deliberate and pedagogical: formal matrimonies (even *ménages à trois*) based on such close resemblance do not, it would seem, fall into litigious causes, for they incorporate regulative and adjudicative principles as a constitutive part of their relation. One should understand this harmony, however, as reflecting a wish or a vow rather than the state of events. Puttenham's text, like many promising marriages, is in fact divided by the very similarities it seeks to join. Indeed, the criterion of resemblance is peculiarly in need of "learned and graue" control when it comes into contact with examples, and precisely because of its capacity to cross formal bounds. In the gentleman's anecdote resemblance comes to seem threateningly independent of the aims of the argument—it would, for example, be a poor story for Puttenham's purposes if it incited "all mens iudgements that heare the story" to banish eloquence as Ptolomey does, and a poorer one still if it further incited them to "miscarry by occasion of [its] perswasions" as Hegesias' words do. The fluid metaphor that the narrator invokes ("I am so farre waded") and that at first represented for us the submerged regulative force of the rhetorical structure of similitude itself becomes rather too fluid for such formal determinations. Rather than "resembling" it, the metaphor seems to become an example of the overdetermination of the category of resemblance. This leaves one not only with the persistent sense that the rule Puttenham is gravely establishing in this court is a pragmatic one, based on and mandating a discriminating use of eloquence that keeps its violent consequences from simple minds, yet able to manipulate its plausible utterances at will, but also with the sense that a theory of legal precedent that rests upon it may be more violent than one would like. This persistent sense can become a kind of precedent. To the same extent that it threatens, by reason of an unregulated invocation of resemblance, to fail as an example, the fable becomes paradigmatic of the necessity of regulating a reading understood to be based on resemblance ("as when we read," the gentleman begins his digression). To the extent, in other words, that the fable's content can be said to reflect, resemble, or pass over into its frame, it succeeds in exemplifying also, and most importantly, the pragmatic necessity of distinguishing among the forms, frames, or levels that it tends to elide.

The importance of this dialectical precedent does not seem to flow much beyond the limits of Puttenham's fable, or—at most—those of a particular marital litigation. It is worth noting, nonetheless, that Puttenham's previous example tells the story of a "noble woman of the Court" who, refusing to listen to a speaker both eloquent and wise, is asked "why . . . had your Ladyship rather heare a man talke like a foole or like a wise man? This was," the narrator continues,

> because the lady was a little peruerse, and not disposed to reforme her selfe by hearing reason, which none other can so well beate into the ignorant head, as the well spoken and eloquent man. (153)

The narrator's introduction to Hegesias' cautionary fable, "my selfe being present when certaine Doctours of the ciuil law were heard," resonates somewhat differently in this context, since the "reformation" of the reader into a well-spoken and eloquent man is precisely the task he advocates—and since, for this reason, Hegesias' story can become an example of the "beating" the previous example alludes to. The regulation of reading is figured as an instruction or (re)formation of the self in the act that first the narrator (who finds himself interjecting an anecdotal *I* into his argument), then the Magistrate, and finally the King perform: the discrimination of the sociolegal power and decorum of "eloquence and figuratiue speaches."[15] The self being instructed, the argument follows, *resembles* (in the strong sense Puttenham associates with "matters of counsell") that of the reader who gazes into the text as into a mirror or a pool ("and because I am so farre waded into this discourse") that regulates the forms it reflects. Reading becomes an example, the privileged example, of and for the formation of the self. The historical persuasiveness of this logic is clear. It accounts in part for the *Arte*'s becoming a crucial example of social and rhetorical self-fashioning in the image of the state and the law that has been seen to motivate eloquence and certain aspects of figurative language under Elizabeth and (somewhat differently) under James.[16]

Two difficulties remain, however, in the story's telling. In the first place, it becomes necessary to take into account the specific function that the genders have in the two examples—in other words, to account for their (representational) context as well as their formal logic. The reason for this is not only one of completeness: the twin oppositions of content-form and matter-form are the subject of the gender alignment, which takes the form of a chiasmus. Reason, aligned with the "wise man," is set into opposition to "a little perverseness," aligned with the noble woman who is in want of reformation. The perlocutionary force of the example is to "reforme her selfe by hearinge reason"—a goal that then allows the category of *form* itself to be aligned with both reason and the male figure. The pedagogical formalism of the *Arte of English Poesie* is specifically figured, in this sense, as a constitutively male attribute of the text; and its examples would then tend to become the pedagogical instrument with which reason is beaten into the ignorant (female) head. The implicit alignment of the figure of the/a woman with the nonformal, which is the polemical burden of much contemporary feminist criticism that follows Luce Irigaray, can in this way be shown to obey the very laws (of eloquence and speech) it most seeks to undermine.[17] The very precision that the formal analysis of resemblance in the example seems to require—the distinction of thematic and other levels disrupted in Hegesias' example, for instance, or the positing of a figure of reading to be educated by the text—is erected against a perverseness, a mis-turning or mis-troping that seems to have wandered from the form of reason. Puttenham's prefixes are significant: the issue is not forming, but re-forming; it is not troping or turning itself that is to be corrected, but an error in turning, a perversion. Within the example—again, within the fluid material of eloquence—there should by contrast be found an originary turning (upwards) that retains the form of reason, a figure that is both rational and pedagogical, to which one returns in and through the instruction of the *Arte*. It is this figure that the example of Hegesias, the example of the function of persuasion, is intended to instance and elucidate.

But it is, in the second place, no less important to reflect on what this example of persuasion comes to mean by example than it is to explain the value of the various violences in the two examples. In the courtroom, this understanding takes the form of an apparent paradox. It is necessary to interrupt the barrister's story in order to establish the formal parallel between the Magistrate and Ptolomey, although it would have been equally plausible formally to have the Magistrate refrain from interrupting the barrister, since the story that was to be told would have legitimated the act of juridical interruption, of "passing over very pleasantly," which thematically represents the point of analogy between Ptolomey and the Magistrate. Moreover, it is not entirely clear that the example is persuasive as a representation of the necessity of such interruptions, for it draws a firm line between persuasion and example, or, more precisely, between persuasion and a self-reflexive representation, in the very figure of the orator that we are conflating with the barrister. Persuasive though Hegesias is, his discourse on no account takes the form of an act—his own suicide, for example—that could itself be taken as an example. On the contrary, his example—that is, himself as an example—is that of a peripatetic, very much living, cynic. He persuades although he cannot be taken as an example—that is, as the subject—of what he advocates. The subject, it is being suggested, cannot be the exemplary instrument of a pedagogy. One cannot teach reason—or beat it into a woman's head—by appealing either to oneself (as a man already "eloquent," "wise," and "grave"—Puttenham's narrator, for example) or to the instrument that comes to hand—one's example, for example.

The persuasion proper to this rhetoric can no longer easily be said to resemble or to rely upon either a representational or a dialectical use of language. Neither, however, can one rely upon a specular formalism that makes Puttenham's language the subject of his example—as if, wading into the discourse of eloquence, one found this "wading" itself already a figure and the "wader" no different from the pool or stream. For if we now seek to reapply the model of a continuous, self-reflexive flow between the nested narratives and the exemplary story, we find ourselves in a genuine impasse—hardly a comfortable place if one is fording a stream or crossing a pond. Puttenham, who floats deep in the discourse of eloquence and figuration, gives us for example the story of a trial in which a persuasive example is gracefully interrupted. This interruption itself, it will transpire, comes to instance the pragmatic law to be drawn from the example, the necessity of incorporating the exclusion of eloquence within the very legal system in which it is used. So far, we are within the fluid intricacies of a theory of representation based on resemblance, but as soon as this representation eddies one last time to reflect the contents of the example itself, something else surfaces. The figure of the Orator, who was supposed to become an example of persuasion, an example of the persuasiveness of example, becomes instead the very example of the noncoincidence between (self-)example and persuasion. A further example of such noncoincidence arises when the representation of such reflection itself comes into the picture,[18] both in the linguistic pool in which the narrator finds himself and even more explicitly in the series of self-reflexive acts characterized as different techniques of suicide, or, rather, as the same act using different instruments ("some with weapon, some with poyson, others by drowning and hanging themselues"). This series can in no empirical sense be said to add up to a story with a single or plural narrator (as in the impossible "I (or we) slew myself with a weapon, and then I (or we) poisoned myself, and then I/we drowned myself, and then I/we hanged myself"), to be predicated of a single subject (whether first person singular or plural), or strictly speaking to be within the purchase of the law, much less the civil law being heard in this court. Suicide is an empirically unrepeatable act that can be the occasion for the administration of the law and that can be legally proscribed in advance, but that can never have any legal consequence for the self. What is proscribed in the example is not suicide but Hegesias' (and the lawyer's) speech, which can be said to cause suicide but not by example.[19] The example then "represents" the violent separation between acts (like suicide) and eloquence in its insistence on the pragmatic criteria on which one can act to distinguish between ontologically similar uses of eloquence, an insistence that is itself a figure (of the law), but in this case a violent, improper figure, neither rational nor pedagogical, that appears to draw together things that cannot otherwise be joined, particularly not on the basis of resemblance.

One should not be misled by the pathos of such descriptions. The example is structured around a logic of exclusion that dictates that Puttenham is not—or not only—narrating the story of his narrator's self-drowning, of how, once "waded into this discourse of eloquence and figurative speaches," he is willingly or not swept in deeper and deeper, to drown finally in a linguistic violence that lies outside the law. The self is nowhere present in this courtroom. Rather, the fable narrates from the first a scene whose principal actors are figures of thought and speech and that is, in fact, an exemplary recapitulation of the tropes given in the *Arte*. The law at issue in the example concerns this "representation" and can be said to function as both a regulative and a generative principle for the differential relation among tropes. One can carry out the demonstration at a number of levels, from noting the extent to which the similarities between tales operate metonymically to substitute container for contents, to enumerating the figures each "character" employs, to speculating on the allegorical function of the scene itself. This law momentarily places the reader who follows Puttenham in the magisterial position of the judge who administers and embodies the law (and who may authoritatively question the place of figurative speech before the law).

On the other hand, a reader who at this point interrupts, feeling (like the "peruerse" woman of the previous example) perhaps a bit abused by such textual willfulness, fares no differently. Objecting "What need is there here for the language of figures? does it not somehow do violence to what is clearly no more than an exemplary anecdote?" ("what neede such eloquent termes," interjects the Magistrate), such a reader finds herself or himself also aligned with Puttenham's judge, eliciting like him a narrative explanation that is then summarily passed over— where "passing over," of course, is itself the paradigmatic name of a trope, the figure of transport or trope of trope, metaphor.[20] Without in fact abandoning a specular structure, we seem to have replaced one system that tells the tale of the education of the self with an entirely homologous one that tells the tale of the legislation of rhetoric. The substitution also defuses the relatively menacing possibilities opened by the example's formal transports, reforming them so that they do not stray from the bounds of a model of rhetoric, however much it may resemble a pedagogy. But this symmetry itself can pose certain problems. For the empirical reader, being transported formally into a specific relation to the text, even into the magisterial figure of the judge, is likely to be experienced in the less comforting sense of a legally mandated banishment (to the colonies, for example), or as a cudgeling reformation of the sort aligned in the previous example with women's irrationality, or, finally, in the sense already common under Elizabeth, as a figure for death or execution. Unlike the Magistrate's objections to the gentleman's eloquence, however, these violent reformations have nothing to do with and in no way resemble the decorum of reading: they are the formal preconditions of a theory of example based on resemblance.

The juxtaposition of the two scenes, one of instruction and one of legislation, suggests that the allegory of tropes remains an example of the allegory of the positing of the subject—a conclusion that, if it is not quickly qualified, can lead to the more threatening inference that the positing of the subject also becomes an example of the allegory of tropes, that the subject can always be—indeed, has already been—transported as easily and with as little say in the matter from reading (the *Arte of English Poesie*) to being read (its rights at a trial in which it does not know whether it is the defendant, the prosecutor, or the judge). The solution to the example's two logics—the privative, formal logic that pertains to the act of legislation and the fluid, figural logic that pertains to what is legislated—seems to lie in replacing its self-reflexive subject, represented in the chain of suicides, with a subject whose predicate serves to bridge the formal differences the examples represent—the generalized subject of the barrister's "as when *we* read." This, then, is a *we* that can neither be interrupted nor passed over, general enough to function at any level of the example—to pass over or pass under any formal distinction—and for that reason exempt from the specific difficulties (of gender-construction, of instrumentalization, and so on) that haunt the reformed self in Puttenham. We read Puttenham's example—an irreducible event whose certainty depends neither on what we take it to mean, nor on what it comes to teach us, nor on who we are. A theory of the self based on resemblance is shown to "hide" a theory of tropes; and this "hiding" itself hides another name for an allegory that functions to unbalance the threatening symmetry between the production of the empirical self and the legislation of tropes, an allegory of the production of a subject so highly formalized that no phenomenal quality can be predicted of it. Separated from its empirical attributes, the event of our reading becomes the very form of ontological predication.

This, however, means that what we read when we read the narrator's "and if perswasion were not very violent, to the minde of man it could not haue wrought so strange an effect as we read that it did once in Aegypt" turns on an unintelligible, entirely *un*readable proposition. Not only can "as when we read" no longer be accounted for within the system of formal displacements that it serves to found; "read," which grounds the *Arte*'s turn to education or pedagogy and serves as the ontological predicate of the allegorical "we," can only be read as bearing an absolutely contingent relation to the empirical project of reading Puttenham's *Arte* *of English Poesie*. The word *as*, which seems to work as a grammatical hinge wedding the analogy's two readings, is in fact the very mark of linguistic contingency—indeed, the notions of resemblance we bring to bear at this moment are the result of reading "As when we read" as when we—empirical subjects—read (the text of Puttenham's *Arte*, for example) as if it (that is, "we") were here, like us, both subject to the same law, in the same courtroom. In order to read "we read" as when we read (for instance) the law, we (in order to remain distinct from Puttenham's "we") first cast onto it the face, voice, and gender of a subject who can answer back, as in a court of law. Like the statement "we read," the mechanism described by the conjunction *as* and by the verb *to cast* is neither figurative nor literal: it neither links one term to another, nor substitutes for another term, nor names a literal moment or event that empirically takes place in any relation to the text. In the same instant and to the very extent that "we read" defines the originary event of the subject's predication, that definition is cast and becomes readable to us—to "we"—only as when we are read as an example of the empirical categories apparently excluded from "our" ontological predication. This is comforting if "we" are cast in the position of the Magistrate, but less so if "we" end up as the plaintiffs in a case in which, as it turns out, "our" wife has so far forsaken the form of law to be "by violent perswasions" led into willfulness; and perhaps it is most troubling if "we," brought before the law by "our" husband, can offer only violence against "ourselves"—whether literal or figurative—as a defense. The *Arte of English Poesie* is most coercive precisely where it offers its reader a choice—between, for example, rejecting or being persuaded by its lessons, or being cast as Magistrate or defendant in the court it defines—for at such moments the handbook rigorously thematizes the impasse it finds when seeking to define the event of its reading. Neither a formal nor an empirical condition, the indecision that marks this splitting of the subject of reading, the extravagant internal resistance that separates these two predicates, pertains to what can only, and very improperly, be called the *material* event of their coincidence. Like the lawyer's unintelligible "as," this definition names the violent articulation between reading and rhetoric, between the claims to a formal reduction and its empirical constraints. We can lament, like Puttenham's Magistrate, the apparent hyperbole of this formulation—but we should remember that the objectionable *violence* of its tone also names a figure of speech, the particularly deceptive one that Puttenham calls "Catachresis, or the Figure of abuse":

> But if for lacke of naturall and proper terme or worde we take another, neither naturall nor proper and do untruly applie it to the thing which we would seeme to expresse, and without any iust inconuenience, it is not then spoken by this figure Metaphore or inuersion as before, but by plaine abuse. (190–191)

It is not coincidental that this impossible position should itself be named in a context that cannot be disengaged from the representation of violence, literal or figurative, exercised against a woman. The reformation of the subject to which any theory of rhetoric as persuasion lays claim necessarily consists in forming or "taking another," in Puttenham's words, "for lacke of naturall and proper terme or worde." However careful its formulation, de-forming reading so as to avoid "any iust inconueniencie" repeats this very violence by reading its examples as allegories of the "lacke of naturall or proper terme" to which they refer. Even though *matter* is the term erected, however improperly, in its place, we seem in fact only to have repeated, at a slightly different level and with different terminology, an ontologization inseparable from the example's formal logic. Catachresis, the necessary deformation of the possibility of moving beyond formalism, operates then as a familiar dynamic of lack and supplementation that would seem to express (only) the just or unjust severing and application of Puttenham's terms to his thing—his argument, examples, and *Arte*.

Whatever the rewards, however, it is all too convenient to read Puttenham as when we read in Lacan of the subsistence of ideality in the signification of the phallus. For when the *Arte of English Poesie* seeks to move beyond or towards formalism from within its impasses, it has recourse not to the language of castration, but to an epistemological troubling of the notion of position that resists being formulated according to the couples of absence and presence, literal and figurative, lack and supplement.[21] This is Puttenham's definition of *aporia*, called "the *doubt-ful*, because oftentimes we will seeme to cast perils, and make doubt of things when by a plaine manner of speech wee might affirm or deny him, as thus of a cruell mother who murdred her owne child":

> Whether the cruell mother were more to blame,
> Or the shrewd childe come of so curst a dame:
> Or whether some smatch of the father's blood,
> Whose kinne were neuer kinde, nor euer good,
> Mooued her thereto, &c. (234)

If Puttenham's text seeks to teach us by example to read which, of the languages of the de-formation and re-formation of the subject (of gender), is the mother and which the child, it cannot do so without casting also "some smatch of the father's blood" into the choice that moves us to it. In this case an exchange of qualities occurs at a level that has to do with "what mooues" the woman, what makes her change her "natural" position in the genealogy and exchange it for that of the murderess. The way these perils are cast is summarized in the grammatical *or*, which constructs the doubt; but the example's positions are troubled in a different way. The child is "shrewd," in the sense of naughty, but also in having been literally set upon by the "curst dame," in having been be-shrewed. Understood this way, the child's fate reflects also the agentive sense of "shrewing," and its murder can then be taken as a displaced castration, its loss the loss of what distinguished the "shrewd" child from its shrewd mother. To read the castration story in the problem of genealogy, however, ignores complications to which Puttenham's example and "we" who might choose its strategy are also moved, and in precisely the same way. The mother, who may have acquired "some smatch of the father's blood" that "mooued her thereto," becomes, as it were, herself the father. Her "shrewing" of the child not only first casts on it the father's sex, but in thus casting "her" sex also removes the "smatch" of blood that marks her kinship to the father. All of the figures in Puttenham's example, then, are matched by the circulation of the father's blood among their positions. That this matching crosses from paronomasia to a grammatical amphibology to a question of logical implicature confirms that the impasses the example represents are at worst momentary. The blood's circulation, a literalization of the analogy between families and natural organisms, is also a figure for the dispersal of the logic of cause ("Whether the cruell mother . . . Or the shrewd child") in the field of language.

But this in no way coincides with what the example explicitly serves to illustrate. *Aporia* as it were freezes the blood, makes impassable the way—the movement— from the act to its cause, makes doubt of things as well as arguments. It retains and exacerbates both the need for the affirmation or denial of cause and the resistance persuasion can oppose to its logic. It is, in other words, absolutely incompatible with the example's tropological matching of positions. At this level, then, Puttenham's text comes closest to the "plaine manner of speech" it forbids itself: there is and can be no movement or match between the trope and its illustration, other than as a permanent interruption. They cannot be read to refer to each other, and this second-order impasse must itself be read *in place of* the story the example tells. Literally in the same place, although with a difference: thus although the term *shrew* can be applied equally to both male and female, the child can be thought at the same time as both sexes only when "mooued . . . thereto" by a desire for the "plaine speech" that the child's plain- ness makes unavailable. The child's sex remains utterly in doubt, and this doubt, like the aporia to which it corresponds, resists being described either in the language of castration and circulation that it generates or as the pre-Oedipal undifferentiation it suggests. And this resistance makes the positions acquired and vacated by the father and mother in Puttenham's family romance unintelligible according to a genealogical law.

The perils of such a law, in which reading for examples (of how by "plaine manner of speech" one can avoid or move beyond formalism, for example) beguiles itself, fatally contemplating what it takes to be another's face matched in its own blood, are those of Narcissus and of Hermaphroditus. But the rigorously *material* reading that feminism and its deconstructions can exemplify does not move differ- ently beyond form by remaining where affirming or denying the other takes the form of repetition or of mourning. Rhetorical reading in feminism becomes a political program only when the material resistance opposed by the particular to the law of example is itself taken as exemplary. To learn to "read" the difference of this second exemplarity, to understand that it in no way resembles, echoes, or seeks its reflection in the first, is neither to remain within formalism nor to legislate its unintelligibility to itself: it is already to learn the perpetual need to break its law. What remains necessarily in doubt is the genealogy of this lesson.

5

Discipl(in)ing the Master, Mastering the Discipl(in)e: Erotonomies of Discipleship in James' Tales of Literary Life

Michael A. Cooper

While writing my dissertation on what I call "apostolary" narratives—those fictions whose narrators, like Nick Carraway and Marlow, represent themselves as relatively subsidiary characters in stories with more exemplary, or at least more narratable, protagonists—I became interested in discipleship. Many of these narratives, I realized, can be said to enact discipleship; the narrators register themselves as having become disciples through the act of narrating the story of the person who obsesses them, together with their own part, however minor, in the plot.[1] By releasing yet another Sherlock Holmes adventure to the public, Dr. Watson not only performs another deed of sedulous devotion to his renowned friend but also reestablishes his position as Holmes' biographer and the public's main conduit to the romantic arena of the reclusive detective. Stumped for an adequate word to denote the class of human behavior to which discipleship belongs—does one call it a relationship? a connection? an affiliation?—I have coined the word *erotonomy*, on the model of *economy*, to emphasize what I view as the constitutive elements of such behavior: a mutual desire of the participants for personal interaction with each other and a mutually accepted system for exchanging satisfactions. By describing the apostolary relationship as an erotonomy, I deliberately mean to associate it with a vast array of other human systems of intimacy, including friendships, garden-variety sexual relationships, the nuclear family, and extreme but not necessarily sexualized relationships of domination and submission.

The primary erotonomy around which most canonical apostolary narratives coalesce is, perhaps unsurprisingly, a homosocial relation between men, although theoretically such a relation between an obsessive narrator and a visionary protagonist could be motivated purely sexually, and a woman could step into either role or both. While the bald fact that the narrator tells a story not his own does not hamper him from asserting a subaltern authority to narrate, it does constrain much of his narration to the business of justifying this authority, explaining how he knows what he does about the protagonist, and speculating for the reader on the protagonist's subject position. In *Lord Jim*, for instance, Marlow, the narrator, offers up the evidence of a whole series of interviews with other characters to justify both the narratability of his story and his views on Jim, the protagonist. Like a critic, Marlow essentially *reads* Jim and interprets him. When it eventually struck me that while an apostolary narrator resembles a critic, the resemblance also flows in the contrary direction, I began to notice that my academic enterprise, *the* academic enterprise, is structured by the sorts of erotonomies that structure these fictional texts. Not only does criticism often reduce to the attempts of critics to establish themselves as the true apostles of author *x* (or of all the authors, sometimes of everybody, from period *y*), but the university itself reduces to an institutionalization and bureaucratization of erotonomies of discipleship—most especially so at the level of graduate research. By focusing on discipleship as represented in and enacted by works of literature, I aim to shed light on, or at least to raise questions about, the academic kind.

I choose here, not entirely arbitrarily, to look at the example of Henry James. His novels, woven around the theme of coming to consciousness, supply numerous familiar instances of erotonomies of patronage that evoke the relation between disciple and master, where an older and wiser character attempts in some measure to enlist and to impart knowledge and experience to a younger, more lively one.[2] But James reserves an even more complex and direct treatment of erotonomies of discipleship for his tales of the literary world. Out of more than one hundred stories, written over a span of forty years, approximately a score of them focus sharply on the literary life. If the entire body of tales stands, to quote Tzvetan Todorov, "as so many theoretical studies in which James poses the great esthetic problems of his work,"[3] these literary stories pose the problem of his working at all. All of them portray authors as largely encompassed by demanding, uncomprehending readers— or nonreaders, as the case may be; many are narrated by or limited to the viewpoint of the one sympathetic male reader, the one disciple, who believes he possesses a privileged understanding of the author.

The most plaintive of the literary stories, "The Middle Years" (1893)—written during James' own middle years, when anxiety over not having achieved great popular success most consumed him—offers an excellent example of this format, expressing as it does a powerful fantasy of adulation and care that centers on the relationship between a dying middle-aged author, Dencombe, and his handsome young doctor and most devoted fan. Uncustomarily told from the author's viewpoint, the story endows the young Dr. Hugh with every ounce of critical intelligence, physical beauty, medical knowledge, and selfless devotion that could possibly bring happiness and bodily comfort to the ailing Dencombe. Considering that James in his diary entries often describes his own raptures using images of health, relief from care, disburdening, and relaxation, one can see that Dr. Hugh, an agent of these salves, would embody a considerable emotional appeal for him. Indeed, a real Dr. Hugh was what James spent a good deal of energy throughout his life looking for. "From all appearances, James . . . never made love either to a woman or to a man," Leon Edel concludes; "He had ended up with a personal aloofness which probably shut him into auto-eroticism."[4] James' primary psychic gratification, however, obviously came from his relations with men; his correspondence reaches its greatest heights of tenderness when addressed to any of the younger men, including Hendrik Andersen, W. Morton Fullerton, Jocelyn Persse, and Hugh Walpole, whom he cultivated in earnest beginning in the mid-1890s and for the rest of his years.[5]

A passage from a letter of 8 August 1907 to Fullerton gives some idea of the intensity of feeling that James expressed in these relationships:

> My dearest Morton!
> My difficulty is that I love you too fantastically much to be able, in intercourse and relation with you, in such a matter as answering your celestial letter, to do anything *but* love you, whereby the essence of the whole thing is simply that you divinely write to me and that I divinely feel it. (*Letters* IV:453)

That James should attribute such intensely erotic sensations to the mere apprehension of text and that he should characterize them in terms of religious ecstasy are typical of his most intimate mode of human interaction. Edel relates a story of Sherwood Anderson's that imagines James recoiling in timidity from an outright sexual proposition by Hugh Walpole (*Letters* IV:ix–xx). But the exchange of written pseudoerotic asseverations of devotion with his favorites was for James matched in pleasure only by his long private walks or drives with them. Later on in his letter to Fullerton, James, speaking in the third person and again lapsing into religious language, revels in his responses at the thought of his disciple's expression of personal interest, which he figures as an examination under a magnifying glass:

> His communion with your exquisite intelligence is poor dear H. J.'s supreme luxury and source of thankfulness—and to feel you play that fine burning-glass over him from any point of vantage or seat of authority whatever is an idea to make him sit as still and as tight as possible, lest he cry out, when scorched, with the beautiful intensity of the sensation! (*Letters* IV:454)

James, as we shall see, viewed his privacy as sacrosanct, so it is no accident that he represents his offer of "communion" with Fullerton as a masochistic surrender to the domination of a sexualized gaze. Psychologically too bound up by what Eve Kosofsky Sedgwick calls "male homosexual panic" to give his physical body to his beloved disciples, James instead generously allows the initiated to roam behind the wall of his reserve.[6] But however much he describes himself as submitting to the initiated, he always retains the titular power in these erotonomies. In answer to Hugh Walpole's query, when their relationship began to deepen, about how he should address James, he replies: "Say '*Très*-cher Maître,' or 'my very dear Master' (for the present), and believe how faithfully I am yours always and ever." (*Letters* IV:520). Insofar as his tales of the literary life depict successful relations between harried authors and worshipful admirers, they sail the deepest waters of James' fantasies.

The tales of the literary life all center on the conceit of the author's having two incarnations, one physical and one textual, each separately capable of being known, interacted with, and mistreated. Where the tales focus mainly on the author's physical body, they delineate the material conditions enhancing the production of literature and the impediments blocking it. Where they focus on the author's textual body, his *corpus*, they begin with the assumption that it represents "the quality of the mind of [its] producer"[7] and from there derive rules of engagement with it that mirror ordinary bodily etiquette—for instance that one should feel as embarrassed about reading work of the author's not prepared for publication as one should feel spying on him undressed at home. The tales form an expression of boundless wonder that the author's two incarnations should ever be treated differently. The *donnée* of "The Author of Beltraffio," for example, is a marriage in which the husband and wife like each other well enough as persons, although the wife takes moral offense at her husband's writings. In "The Private Life," the author's two bodies literally take the form of two identical persons, a clever one who constantly sits alone at his desk writing and a dull one who socializes endlessly and provides material for the other aesthetically to transfigure. James most deplores the prevailing tendency to prefer the physical body to the textual one, to engage the person rather than the work, even though the fact of the work, not anything about the physical person, is the source of the author's attraction.

In most of these tales James builds his model for negotiating approaches to the author's two bodies into plots of triangular desire. Here I am thinking of the concept as René Girard develops it in *Deceit, Desire, and the Novel* rather than as Eve Kosovsky Sedgwick strongly, but fruitfully, misreads it in *Between Men*. To advance her illuminating discussion of homosocial relations between men, Sedgwick takes from Girard his observation about erotic triangles that "the bond that links the two rivals is as intense and potent as the bond that links either of the rivals to the beloved" and then proceeds to argue that men's methods of expressing and negotiating homosocial desire—exchanging or competing for women, for example—have since the late eighteenth century increasingly reflected "homosexual panic," the fear that one may be taken for, or may unconsciously be, a homosexual. Hence she focuses mostly on whether and how sexual desire is configured among the angles of the traditional erotic triangle: two "straight" men and one woman. Girard, however, concerns himself as much with metaphysical as with physical desire. For him the essential characteristic of triangular desire is simply the presence of a "mediator" between the desiring subject and his or her object of desire. In the Girardian triangle the subject acts not from a desire originating in the self but in imitation of a desire exhibited by the mediator. Thus Don Quixote, rather than inventing his own goals and his means of obtaining them, "pursues objects which are determined for him, or at least seem to be determined for him, by the model of all chivalry [Amadis]," just as the Christian pursues objects determined for him by his mediator, Christ.[8]

James does deploy the structure of triangular desire in ways that could almost stand as paradigms of Sedgwickian homosociality.[9] But James also turns Sedgwick's homosocial triangle on its side, most strikingly by often positioning the middle-aged male author, rather than a desirable young woman, at its apex. In this version, the young male disciple may be set in rivalry for the author's attention with the latter's wife or lover ("The Right Real Thing," "The Author of Beltraffio," "The Aspern Papers") or the disciple may fall in love with and marry his rival/partner-in-devotion-to-the-author ("The Death of the Lion," "The Figure in the Carpet," "John Delavoy"). James, a middle-aged author himself by the time he writes these stories, frankly feminizes the author position, making it the passive object of desire, the battleground over which the author's physical and textual admirers, and those who may not distinguish so clearly between the two camps, enact the struggle for ownership of the claims on his desire.

In these battles James generally figures women, however triumphant, in negative terms. Importunate wives, who insist that their author-husbands support them in style, encourage the production of lucrative trash. Desirable sweethearts, who claim attention and refuse to appreciate the author's art, distract his mind from his noble calling. Salon-steering socialites, who control the traffic in celebrities with which the leisure class ornaments its intricate hierarchies of prestige, feed the author and house him so long as he stays away from his work. The newspapers and fashionable contemporary journals, which ignore the author in favor of his manifest inferiors except occasionally to ask him embarrassingly pointed questions about his personal life, are, although run by men, clearly associated with women, their predominant readership. Only the young male disciple strives to protect the enfeebled and misunderstood author from the sensory barrage of contemporary life and the threat of objectification by predatory women. The homosocial bond with this disciple becomes the fertile relationship that allows the feminized male author the space in which to bear his aesthetic offspring.

Balanced against desire for the author-character, which inspires these triangular erotonomies and focuses the narrative interest of the stories, always hangs anxiety about his eventual death. These stories play upon the reader's sympathetic fears of losing the author's voice, of the narration's suspension, of the absconding of authority. Paraday's great manuscript, for example, disappears on a train. Dencombe dies before he can put to use the brilliant "late manner" he has only finally developed after a lifetime of literary experience. "The Jamesian narrative," says Todorov, "is always based on *the quest for an absolute and absent cause*."[10] These hoped-for texts, adumbrated but unwritten, paraded before us as a desideratum but at last denied us in the deaths of their authors, are such a cause and come to stand for, in a sense, the essence of literature, the motivation for reading: the nugget of wisdom always over the horizon of the unturned page. The despair of a disciple who no longer imbibes fresh inspiration from the fountain of his master's invention clouds the endings of these stories and gives them an elegiac, or occasionally a mock-elegiac, tone—elegy being the original mode of claiming a relation of discipleship towards an acknowledged master.

Where the threat of the author's death does not constitute one of the events of the plot, it is usually because he dies before they fairly commence. His having died supplies the condition that starts them congealing. Only when the corpus takes the baton from the corpse and sprints into posterity do the problems and contradictions arising from the author's two incarnations appear to vanish. The textual remains become the central focus for the author's devotees. But when the textual incarnation alone persists, even loyal disciples, who would normally distinguish between savoring the author's works and barging into his home, have trouble distinguishing legitimate from illegitimate approaches to and expressions of desire for him. "The Aspern Papers," for example, dramatizes how a critic's obsession with intimate textual knowledge about a dead author corrodes his soul. The critic, in hopes of gaining some of his idol's unpublished correspondence which he learns a pair of elderly ladies possess, fraudulently prevails on them to lodge him, after which, with hardly a qualm, he seduces one and rifles the possessions of the other. The stories of the dead authors, then, want to remind the reader that relations toward the author-as-text require as much propriety as those toward the author-as-person.

Anxiety over the way he himself would be textualized after death lies latent in many of James's writings. In his 1875 review of *The Last Journals of David Livingstone in Central Africa, from 1866 to his Death, Continued by a Narrative of His Last Moments and Sufferings, etc.*, by Horace Waller, F. R. G. S., James criticizes Waller's lack of biographical discrimination:

> The journal is largely interspersed with religious reflections *and ejaculations intended solely for Dr. Livingstone's own use.* They are interesting to students of character, for they help to explain the sources of the great explorer's indomitable resolution and patience. . . . But *it seems a rather cruel violation of privacy to shovel these sacred sentences, written in the intensest solitude, into the capacious lap of the public,* in common with all sorts of baser matter—including the rather sensational and not particularly valuable illustrations with which the volume is adorned. It is as interesting as it ever was to be admitted behind the scenes of a man's personality, but it is more important than it ever was that the privilege should not be offered to all the world, but *reserved for the few who can present a certain definite claim to initiation.* (*Essays* 1142; emphases added)

The "cruel violation" as James figures it here—Mr. Waller's shoveling into the "capacious lap of the public" "ejaculations intended solely for Dr. Livingstone's own use," composed "in the intensest solitude"—amounts to the public's witnessing, and even becoming a prurient party to, the great explorer's masturbation. As bad as this is, what makes it worse is the inclusion of "rather sensational and not particularly valuable illustrations"—in short, *National Geographic*–style images of aborigines *en petite tenue*. That purely sensational masturbatory images should accompany the unexpurgated text of the great explorer's private ejaculations is almost too much for James to bear. Why, one wonders, is it *now*—"more than it ever was"—important that the privilege of being "admitted behind the scenes of a man's personality" "should not be offered to all the world, but reserved for the few who can present a certain definite claim to initiation"? Who, one wonders, can present such a definite claim to initiation? What would such a claim look like?[11]

The story "The Real Right Thing" agonizes over these issues. Each of James' stories operates by adumbrating what form the satisfaction of narrative desire *could* take in the story and then proceeding to frustrate that satisfaction (thereby, of course, satisfying the desire for narrative frustration). "The Real Right Thing," like "The Aspern Papers," represents intimate communion with the dead author through perusal of his most private documents as the greatest satisfaction, then denies such a communion. The tale concerns George Withermore, a young disciple of the recently deceased author Ashton Doyne, who has been selected by Doyne's widow to write a "Life" of her husband. In the margins of the story hovers the suggestion that Mrs. Doyne was, if not unfaithful to her husband sexually, at least uninterested in him textually, and that the proposed "Life" would in some sense assuage her guilt and create for her a public statement of intimacy with him that never existed in his lifetime:

> a sense of what she had lost, and even of what she had lacked, had betrayed itself, on the poor woman's part, from the first days of her bereavement, sufficiently to prepare an observer at all initiated for some attitude of reparation, some espousal even exaggerated of the interests of a distinguished name. George Withermore was, as he felt, initiated; yet what he had not expected was to hear that she had mentioned him as the person in whose hands she would most promptly place the materials for a book.[12]

Also in the margins hovers the suggestion of a possible liaison between Withermore and Mrs. Doyne, if only one created by the fact of their occupying opposite angles of the Jamesian author-oriented triangle. This possibility increases as Withermore begins working in her husband's old study, reading his private notes, letters, and journals. The story can be figured in Oedipal terms: Withermore stands poised to supplant his absent father/mentor in the study and the bedroom. This figuration, however, by emphasizing only conflict, misses the erotic component of Withermore's relation to his master. Both he and Mrs. Doyne confess to sharing a sense of the author's continued spectral presence. The ghost, they imagine, seems to bestow himself on them each alternately. At last Withermore realizes that the dead author is actually attempting to *prevent* them from penetrating further into his secrets. In confirmation of this hypothesis the ghost appears to him one last time blocking the entrance to the study. After this, when Mrs. Doyne refuses to accept the young man's caution against continuing the biography, she suffers, the reader is led to imagine, a particularly horrible manifestation of spousal ectoplasm, and, again from the narrative penumbra, the sense emanates that it serves her right. "I give up," she says to Withermore, and their budding relationship dissolves with the project. The end of the story leaves the implied nonfeminist reader, though probably not the actual reader, simultaneously holding two opposed attitudes towards the identical punishments meted out to each of them: frustration at the tragic abscission of communion between Withermore and his master and satisfaction at the comic come-uppance dished out to the supposedly manipulative, pathetic wife.

At the center of the story is James' meticulous depiction of the relationship Withermore believes he is creating with Ashton Doyne's spirit through nightly visits to the author's drawers. The young man names as his motivation the possibility of communion with Doyne, not the money. The "chance of spending his winter in an intimacy so rich" has "been simply dazzling":

> It hadn't been the "terms," from the publishers . . . it had been Doyne himself, his company and contact and presence—it had been just what it was turning out, the possibility of an intercourse closer than that of life. Strange that death, of the two things, should have the fewer mysteries and secrets! The first night our young man was alone in the room it seemed to him that his master and he were really for the first time together. (475)

Believing that Doyne's specter materializes to encourage his explorations, Withermore begins to "wait . . . for the evening very much as one of a pair of lovers might wait for the hour of their appointment" (477). The simile is apt considering the ensuing descriptions of the young author's encounters with his master's ghost:

> There were times of dipping deep into some of Doyne's secrets when it was particularly pleasant to be able to hold that Doyne desired him, as it were, to know them. He was learning many things that he had not suspected, drawing many curtains, forcing many doors, reading many riddles, going, in general, as they said, behind almost everything. It was at an occasional sharp turn of some of the duskier of these wanderings "behind" that he really, of a sudden, most felt himself, in the intimate, sensible way, face to face with his friend; so that he could scarcely have told, for the instant, if their meeting occurred in the narrow passage and tight squeeze of the past, or at the hour and in the place that actually held him.

Although on the face of it the imagery pictures the two men simply passing each other by in a narrow secret corridor, a suggestion of a sexual encounter lurks for the modern reader in the accumulation of such vaguely euphemistic phrases as "the duskier of these wanderings 'behind,' " "the intimate, sensible way, face to face with his friend," and "the narrow passage and tight squeeze." Perhaps James feels free to use such explicit terms because Doyne is incorporeal. But now that the dead author can be approached only through texts, now that his presence can only be ghostly, not only can the latent sexuality of the relation between master and disciple come to the fore, but so also may the coercive nature of this relation. Withermore, "drawing many curtains, forcing many doors," like a guileless Iachimo unthinkingly abuses the literary remains of his friend, all the while fantasizing that Doyne genuinely craves his intimate attentions, that it pleases the master to show himself privately, utterly, to his disciple.

As the scene continues, the imagined intimacy loses a fraction of its purely sexual charge but acquires a corresponding aura of tenderness. Here James depicts the fantasy of mutual exchange that underlies the erotonomy: in return for ministrations at "his altar," Ashton Doyne caters to the youth's bibliophilia:

> There were moments, for instance, when, as [Withermore] bent over his papers, the light breath of his dead host was as distinctly in his hair as his own elbows were on the table before him. . . . That he couldn't at such a juncture look up was his own affair, for the situation was ruled—that was natural—by deep delicacies and fine timidities, the dread of too sudden or too rude an advance. What was intensely in the air was that if Doyne *was* there it was not nearly so much for himself as for the young priest of his altar. He hovered and lingered, he came and went, he might almost have been, among the books and the papers, a hushed, discreet librarian, doing the particular things, rendering the quiet aid, liked by men of letters.

The spirit watching fondly over Withermore, his light breath blowing in the youth's hair—what makes this image of the two poignant, especially in view of the story's subsequent repudiation of their relation, is that it recreates a fantasy James secretly maintained about his own guiding genius, whom he frequently addressed in his private diaries as "*mon bon*." In an entry in the notebooks from 4 January 1910, James comments on his newly returning imaginative potency after a long bout with illness, envisioning his guiding genius once again perched behind him like the ghost of Doyne behind Withermore:

> Thus just these first little wavings of the oh so tremulously passionate little old wan[d] (now!) make for me, I feel, a sort of promise of richness and beauty and variety; a sort of portent of the happy presence of the elements. The good days . . . come back to me with their gage of divine possibilities and I welcome these to my arms, I press them with unutterable tenderness. I seem to emerge from these recent bad days . . . and the prospect clears and flushes, and my poor blest old Genius pats me so admirably and lovingly on the back that I turn, I screw round, and bend my lips to passionately, in my gratitude, kiss its hand.[13]

Commenting on this passage, Leon Edel solemnly notes that James' turn to face his genius "derives from the pleasure principle and the search for catharsis and purge. The kiss is warm and tender, a kiss of love and gratitude. The orgasmic overtones suggest an extraordinary state of exaltation behind which lay years of immense devotion and industry."[14] One might also point out that the kiss is one of submission, that James here represents himself as both dependent upon his genius for inspiration and praised by him with a pat on the back for living up to the genius's expectations. Presumably this notebook passage, taken from Edel's edition, is precisely the sort of confidence that James complains Waller shovels into the public's lap. But where Livingstone addresses his most private ejaculations to his Creator, James addresses his to a created mentor.

James, unsurprisingly, left behind few written reports of his being sexually aroused. That so many of these appear in the context of discussing the process of creation justifies speculation that (save when corresponding with his young favorites) it was perhaps only when writing, when losing himself in the complex emotions and situations of his created characters, that he allowed guiltless ardor to wash freely over his psyche. By authoring a narrative, he could bind himself into a Girardian triangle across which his passion would then string itself; he would invent characters as mediators whose desires, instead of his own, would satisfy him. In his notes for *The Ambassadors*, for example, he states that the climactic stroke of the story, Strether's rejection, for Chad's benefit, of Mrs. Newsome and her financial advantages, allows Strether "a little super-sensual hour in the vicarious freedom of another." For James, it seems, the more vicariously he experienced this freedom, the more supersensual his experience.

The description of Withermore's hours in the vicarious freedom of Doyne, then, holds a double erotic value for James: as a sensuous portrayal of one person's obsessive involvement in the experience of another it eroticizes voyeurism; and as a replication of James's own fantasy of creative direction from his genius it eroticizes submission. The story thus makes explicit the erotonomy that underpins the relation between disciple and master. The disciple fantasizes occupying the subject position of the master, literally taking the master's place (at home, in person and social relations, as creator of an oeuvre). Far from assuming conflict between the two persons, this fantasy relies for its erotic value on the master's approval of, compliance with, and even authority over his or her displacement. Indeed, the disciple's fantasy figures the process of supplantation as mutually arousing. Withermore, luxuriating among the artifacts of his master, imagines Doyne as assisting him "not nearly so much for himself as for the young priest of his altar." Of course, this is but the disciple's fantasy. The master by contrast fantasizes a disciple who regards the master as he or she needs to be regarded, who has no interest in those aspects of the master's person or personality about which the master takes no pride. "The Real Right Thing" begins as a disciple's fantasy and ends as a master's; it replaces the pleasures of voyeurism with those of submission. That Withermore bows without question to Doyne's spectral reassertion of authority proves that the young critic, unlike Doyne's own wife, really is a loyal disciple foremost. The renunciation that the story enacts bears the semblance of libidinal repression characteristic of James' most powerful writing. Despite the fact of Withermore's evident "initiation," despite the obvious erotic pleasure the disciple takes in "the possibility of an intercourse closer than that of life," despite the author's inability to exact more punishment from beyond the grave than to make the disciple feel guilty, the young critic comes to realize that morally such a renunciation must occur: the invasion of the artist's textual privacy without invitation is, to James' mind, the worst transgression. [15]

Where "The Real Right Thing" laments the invasion of the textual privacy of the dead author, "The Death of the Lion" positively excoriates those who invade the physical privacy of the living one. In this story James shows how the mass market mistakenly commodifies storytellers, rather than the works they produce, as a consequence of the masses' craving for, to use these terms in their Benjaminian sense, information instead of wisdom. Being established as a celebrity, being lionized by the public, although apparently an amplification or transmigration to the social level of the private relation between disciple and master, reduces in James' eyes to being invested with mere exhibition value. By substituting the artist for the artwork as the prime object of contemplation, James shows, the modern popular media jeopardize the ideal relation between the storyteller and his or her true disciples—a relation wherein the storyteller transmits wisdom, not information, to the disciple, and the disciple invests the storyteller with a maximum of cult and a minimum of exhibition value. [16]

"The Death of the Lion" tells the story of an author melted by the glare of publicity like a snowman in the noonday sun. The narrator, a young journalist sent to write up author Neil Paraday in the best modern fashion—abundant details about the author's personal life and minimal literary discussion—experiences a "change of heart" and writes a sympathetic appraisal of his latest novel instead. During the narrator's visit, Paraday reads aloud to him a manuscript outline of his work in progress. Realizing that Paraday's latest novel will soon become widely enough read, or at least discussed, to put its author into the limelight, the narrator resolves to devote himself to helping Paraday ward off interviewers, autograph hunters, and lionizers so that he may finish this beautiful fragment, which the young man perceives will be his greatest work yet. Sure enough, Paraday soon becomes the toast of the town and, despite the narrator's protective efforts, is invited down to Prestidge, the country home of Mrs. Weeks Wimbush, to be displayed among her other important guests, including Guy Walsingham, a woman novelist who writes under a man's name in order to be more sexually frank; Dora Forbes, a florid, bald, red-mustached gentleman who writes under a woman's name because women novelists seem in the ascendant; and a large princess of a small European state. The only person, indeed, whom the narrator manages successfully to prevent from bothering Paraday is a young lady, Fanny Hurter, who wants to acquire the author's autograph. Having convinced her that out of love for Paraday's work she should avoid bothering the author personally at all costs, the narrator falls in love with her himself. From Mrs. Weeks Wimbush's country home, where he goes to attend Paraday, the narrator sends Fanny letters that detail most of the rest of the story: Paraday, wearied from his hostess' constant demands that he display himself as charming and clever before the other guests, suffers a relapse of an earlier illness, declines rapidly, and dies. His last request is that the narrator arrange to publish the beautiful fragment of the work in progress. Unfortunately, Mrs. Wimbush, without reading it, has lent it to someone, who, without reading it, lent it to someone else, who packed it away in a suitcase and may have left it on a train. Nobody ever finds it.

This casual summary cannot express the intensity of the satire that the story directs against the popular press and its craving for information at the expense of storytelling. James makes clear that Paraday's storytelling should stand by itself as the central commodity in question, through which the public might achieve the ultimate desideratum of his wisdom. Failing that, the young journalist's "little finicking feverish study of [the] author's talent," a narration with an aesthetic position, presumably sketching the wisdom in the author's work, ought to occupy the papers. Instead, the narrator's editor, Mr. Pinhorn, "whose definition of genius was the art of finding people at home" and whose "great principle . . . was just to create the demand we required," insists that his employee "be personal"—which consists, if the actions of the lionizing journalist Mr. Morrow offer any example, in observing the design of the author's home and inquiring about his attitudes towards literary representations of sex (asking, for instance, whether he "goes in for the larger latitude"). The newspaper not only attacks the author's privacy, it also competes with him for a share of the market. The ironic paradox that serves as the *donnée* of "The Death of the Lion" is that while articles *about* Paraday sell the journals and while because of them he becomes a literary lion, the center of every social gathering, his work itself sells "but moderately." As Paraday confides to the narrator, "No one has the faintest conception of what I'm trying for . . . and not many have read three pages that I've written; but I must dine with them first— they'll find out why when they've time."

If the story displays fear of the information impulse in newspapers on the one hand, it also displays a tremendous fear of powerful women on the other. Mrs. Weeks Wimbush, the socialite at whose door Paraday's death literally can be laid, controls the exchange of artists and minor royalty that occupies the feminized world of the leisure class in the story. As long as the organs of information reproduce sufficiently the "fact" that the author's *textual* body merits praise—or, better, that some accredited expert praises it—then the author's *physical* body acquires the Benjaminian aura, a sense of uniqueness combined with a sense of cultural significance, that puts it into circulation and justifies the reproduction of further facts about *it*. The author's (or painter's or composer's) textual body serves only to launch his or her physical body into circulation, like a motorized plane that drags a glider to its proper altitude before releasing it to fly off on its own. In "The Death of the Lion," the world of celebrity-commodification is run by middle-aged women, who, not being empowered to act in the political sphere, gain pseudopolitical power by feminizing male artists and circulating them among themselves as, presumably, they themselves were circulated as young women among empowered men.[17]

The relations among the characters in "The Death of the Lion" form a series of triangles, at the apex of most of which we find Paraday. The main triangle that structures the plot is, of course, that formed by the battle between the narrator and the feminized forces of Mrs. Wimbush. That they desire different forms of satisfaction of Paraday is not surprising, and, indeed, is precisely James' point. The young narrator spells out the nature of the differences in asserting his loyalty to Paraday:

> I should make it my business to take care of him. Let whoever would represent the interest in his presence . . . I should represent the interest in his work—or otherwise expressed in his absence. These two interests were in their essence opposed; and I doubt . . . if I shall ever again know the intensity of joy with which I felt that in so good a cause I was willing to make myself odious. (280)

The interest "in his absence" that the narrator represents is plainly James' own interest. An author, in James' view, should precisely be a present absence or absent presence. (A very conscious pun on "presence," James' frequent word for ghost, gives resonance to Ashton Doyne's haunting of George Withermore). One comes to know authors properly only in their absence, through the mediation of their texts. This is the only initiation that can properly lead to discipleship and a personal relation. Since the Wimbushites aim to accrue and exchange authors rather than become disciples of them, they have no use for initiation. Mrs. Wimbush's desire for Paraday is triangular in the Girardian sense not only by being opposed to the narrator's, but also by being mediated through the representations of the mass media informing her that Paraday merits adulation. Like Stendhal's *vaniteux*, in Girard's view, Mrs. Wimbush desires Paraday because others do.[18] Her desire expresses rather competition with her mediators—those who, like the narrator, truly value Paraday—than devotion to its pretended object. Unable to conceive an alternative system of value, she foolishly accuses the young journalist of harboring a similarly mediated desire for Paraday, of wanting to "monopolise" him in order that the author might advance his literary career, of cultivating intimacy so as to stick Paraday like a feather in his cap.

The young journalist does not monopolize Paraday to advance his own career. But he does monopolize him, at least in part, to advance his own sexual goals. Fanny Hurter—the one woman in the story who, because she refuses to commodify Paraday, does not represent a threat to him—becomes the focus of the journalist's ardor. Once persuaded that she can "perform an act of homage really sublime" towards Paraday by succeeding "in never seeing him at all," she goes out of her way to avoid the author, performing, "for consistency's sake, touching feats of submission." The narrator relishes her masochism:

> Nothing indeed would now have induced her even to look at the object of her admiration. Once, hearing his name announced at a party, she instantly left the room by another door and then straightway quitted the house. At another time . . . at the opera . . . I attempted to point Mr. Paraday out to her in the stalls. On this she asked her sister to change places with her and, while that lady devoured the

great man through a powerful glass, presented, all the rest of the evening, her inspired back to the house. To torment her tenderly I pressed the glass upon her, telling her how wonderfully near it brought our friend's handsome head. By way of answer she simply looked at me in charged silence, letting me see that tears had gathered in her eyes. (288)

Although the pronounced ritualistic form of renunciation she enacts here—the presentation of her backside to Mr. Paraday and the whole opera house—appears to signify her devotion to Paraday, the person for whom this public submission is enacted, the one who must be allowed to witness the tears, is the narrator, who compels her to accept him as her mediator in their triangular erotonomy. He "torments" her by eroticizing the object of their interest, using the phallic technology of the opera glass to bring the "friend's handsome head" closer spatially, and forcing her to dramatize the author's absence by moving away from him.

Parodying the standard (two-straight-men-eroticizing-one-woman) romantic triangle, this scenario brings out the desires that only lie latent in that one. In the ordinary triangle, to invoke Sedgwick's analysis, homosexual panic prevents the desiring male subjects from recognizing that their mutual desire for the female object brings them closer to each other than it does to her. But by making one of the two desiring subjects in this story a woman, James takes down the barrier of homosexual panic normally separating the desiring subjects and allows a consummation ordinarily impracticable. Homosexual panic here transfers instead to the relation between the narrator and his "dear master," where it is held in check by both the homosocial framework of discipleship and the demands of social occasions at which the narrator can do "nothing . . . but exchange with [Paraday] over people's heads looks of intense but futile intelligence." Because the narrator's relation with Paraday must not be sexual and must therefore be mediated, he takes pains to ensure that the relation of his rival, Miss Hurter, with Paraday, which could quite easily be sexual, be similarly mediated.

By standing between Miss Hurter and his master, the narrator prevents his dispossession as Paraday's principal disciple and enjoys the sexual attentions of Miss Hurter that would presumably be directed at Paraday, had she access to him. In effect, by seducing a woman attracted originally to Paraday, he sexually usurps Paraday's subject position. Moreover, he uses Paraday's writings to center his relationship with Fanny. "We read him together," he remarks of Miss Hurter and himself, ". . . and the generous creature's sacrifice was fed by our communion" (287). The narrator's religious language emphasizes the high cult value the two place on Paraday and the mystical quality of the rapport sparked by their mutual perusal of his textual body. They seek him "in his works," the narrator tells us, "even as God in nature." This statement suggests a final triangular erotonomy in the story: author, text, and reader. Paraday's texts, in the proper relation of reader to author, mediate his disciples' desire for him. The text, having at its heart, as James so often remarks, "the quality of the mind of the producer," the author's "personal, direct impression of life," leads the reader to the author along the approved path. One thinks one loves one's author, but really one loves only the text's mediation of him or her. One loves the author's absent presence in the text.

But *is* it the author as a physical self who stands behind the text's mediation as one reads? James' use of the words "the mind of the producer," "the personal, direct impression of life" suggests something more. I think he would ultimately have agreed with Walter Benjamin's hypothesis that the *wisdom* of the author, not the person, is the true desideratum—the author's experience, consciousness, outlook. This brings us back to the relation of discipleship, putting it into a clearer light. Sometimes one reads for narration (mystery stories, Harlequin Romances), sometimes for information (the newspaper, textbooks); but to read as a disciple reads is to pursue the author behind the text, and more. Disciples pursue authors, read their texts, invade their notebooks and letters, occupy their private studies, because the *authors themselves mediate* the disciples' desire for a yet more distant object, namely the intangible and ineffable seat of power that is the author's wisdom. In the last analysis, the author's wisdom occupies the apex of a Girardian triangle, the author and the reader angled separately below. Authors make themselves desirable by packaging their wisdom in such a way as to encourage the belief that one's reading them as a disciple will be satisfying. Ultimately what the disciple dreams of, as Girard points out, is to adopt the subject position of the mediator in order to stand in direct relation to the object. Don Quixote wants to be Amadis; Madame Bovary, the romantic heroines that inspire her; Dr. Watson, Sherlock Holmes; Plato, Socrates; and Bradley Headstone, Mortimer Lightwood.

In "The Death of the Lion," the unnamed narrator wants to become Paraday. To do so, however, involves a not always disinterested, or sexually innocent, mastery over others: over Fanny, as we have seen, who is required to submit passively to the narrator's sadistic desire that she abjure Paraday, and, finally, over the master himself. Although the narrator figures himself as striving to prevent the death of the lion, it is only by virtue of Paraday's death and the narrator's unique knowledge of its circumstances and comprehension of its ironies that he earns his place before the reader. As is the case with Doyne and Withermore, paradoxically the author's death at last allows the disciple the intimacy of consummation. But while "The Real Right Thing," in moving from the pleasures of voyeurism to those of submission, begins as a disciple's fantasy and ends as a master's, "The Death of the Lion," moving from the pleasures of care to those of domination, begins as a master's fantasy and ends as a disciple's. This difference in trajectory explains the stories' difference in narrative point of view: unlike Doyne's disciple, whose projected "Life" never bears fruit, Paraday's disciple, having assumed the master's chair, gains authoritative voice and narrates the tale. In either case the erotonomics of the relation between master and disciple become entangled—upon close examination, submission and domination frequently exchanging attire—and the purity of affiliation becomes more than suspect.

Postscript: Mastering the Academy Today

The contemporary cultural institution that has a particular interest in perpetuating the structure of discipleship as James delineates it is, of course, the academy. In the humanities, at least, discipleship takes two paths, which occasionally cross. First, we typically read as disciples the authors in whom we specialize. We read biographies of them and their letters, as well as their more consciously aesthetic creations; perhaps, when in the neighborhood, we visit their birthplaces. In all of these acts we try, like George Withermore, to recapture and appropriate for ourselves as much as we can the subject position of our Ashton Doynes. Second, as graduate students, we were, or we still are, or we could or should have been, to some extent disciples of our professors; and as professors, "masters" of our students. Our system of graduate education operates largely by professors' manufacturing disciples, for whose benefit they model their own discipleship toward their authors, and further, toward their old professors, laying bare the chain of an elaborate erotonomic descent. Behind the idea of a purely "professional" academy lies the suggestion that professors should exist simply to transmit information, that they should erase themselves as media of transmission. Perhaps they should. But this view ignores the fact, however blameworthy or laudable, that many students, especially many good students, operate on the model of Withermore—they learn how and what to learn by working to inhabit the subject position of those whose wisdom, or *Weltanschauung*, they value. This view also ignores the fact, however blameworthy or laudable, that persons become professors to transmit what Benjamin calls wisdom—i.e., their subject position—rather than simply information; to eroticize themselves (I do not mean, or mean only, make themselves sexually available) in the display of what they know; to implicate their identities inextricably in the knowledge they transmit.

Working at its best, discipleship in the humanities almost automatically, structurally, promotes some of the values classically associated with humanistic study— the capacity for empathy, for example, or the craving for knowledge, or respect for the evocative power of cultural records. The emotional bonds of discipleship often bring about, in both participants, the same salubrious psychic effects commonly attributed to monogamous romances. Great disciples of great masters become great masters in their own right. There is no better example of this effect than the genealogy of scholars of James, which in its more theoretical branch begins with Percy Lubbock and descends through Joseph Warren Beach and Wayne Booth to engender American point-of-view criticism. The tradition of American Puritanism scholars affiliated with Harvard (to choose an example with which I am familiar), starting with Perry Miller and descending through Alan Heimert and Andrew Delbanco, offers a typical instance of the system plugging along reasonably respectably. But working at its worst, discipleship in the academy promotes intellectual conservatism, sexual discrimination, and psychic harassment. Academic departments throughout the country are burdened by blocs of voting faculty made up of two, three, or even four generations of (mostly male) masters and disciples hunched over the same bailiwick, each generation more etiolated and feckless than the one before. The notorious imperviousness of these old-boy integuments to the quests for departmental legitimacy of women's studies, African-American studies, and gay studies needs no extensive rehashing here.

To mitigate this male hegemony, women (to focus here only on gender difference) have been making some, though all too few, inroads into both kinds of discipleships, textual and institutional, with perhaps some greater success in the former area than in the latter. The familiar stumbling block in the latter area is the role played by sexual desire in interpersonal relationships. In Sedgwickian terms, homosexual panic creates the elaborate structures of mediation and exchange that defuse, or at least desexualize, the relations between male professor and male disciple. Because of homosexual panic, it never occurs to many men entangled in erotonomies of discipleship that the possibility even exists to negotiate them sexually. Between women and men, however, far from there being an equivalent to institutionalized male homosexual panic, there is a positive social presumption of sexual attraction. Indeed, as James shows in such stories as "The Death of the Lion" and "The Figure in the Carpet," where the two competing desiring subjects in the triangular erotonomy are heterosexuals of opposite sexes, when the man occupies the position of relative authority and of access to the author's wisdom, then the woman has little choice but to accede to sexual domination as the price of maintaining that access.[19]

For the most part, James's stories of the literary life depict discipleship as it was almost universally constructed in the academy well into the 1960s and as it still often is—a male homosocial relation of deep intimacy into which women are expected not to thrust themselves at all. "The Death of the Lion" paints Fanny Hurter's total exclusion from intercourse of any sort with Neil Paraday as a noble, indeed sexually arousing, characteristic of *hers*, rather than as a condition the narrator imposes upon her. "The Real Right Thing" punishes Mrs. Doyne for attempting, out of remorse, to assert a kind of discipleship post mortem, while partially rewarding Withermore, for committing the identical transgression, with an intensely experienced pseudosexual fantasy. The only proper form of discipleship for women in James is one that is thoroughly mediated by texts—except when discipleship becomes mingled with sexual attraction. Similarly, in the academy female students of male professors are too often either excluded from discipleship in favor of male students or must suffer from the positive cultural presumption of heterosexual attraction (whether presumed by professor, student, or local quidnunc).

One conclusion that my argument unfortunately appears to be slouching towards is that heterosexual erotonomies of discipleship might benefit from a fundamental, culturally inscribed structuring principle akin to male homosexual panic, which would automatically and violently channel libidinal energy through an intellectual, or in any event a nonsexual, medium of exchange. If, say, at the simple thought of desiring a female student many heterosexual male professors experienced a reaction of guilt powerful enough to threaten their sexual identities, the incidence of sexual harassment would perhaps decrease. Whether any such panic may be brought by fiat into existence is doubtful, but may be worth investigating. I call my conclusion unfortunate because male homosexual panic—whatever its power to keep the minds of ostensibly straight men focused on the medium of exchange (be it women, guns, information, or eurobonds) between them rather than on each other—seems always to presuppose domination and submission, if not always the complex and ambiguous ways of exchanging them that this essay has traced in James. At any rate, male homosexual panic afflicts only certain male heterosexuals whose present majority membership in erotonomies of discipleship dwindles measurably with each passing year. What remains unclear is how erotonomies of discipleship will be negotiated, if they will at all, in a future where, owing to the long-overdue influx of women and openly gay men into the academy, male homosexual panic will be increasingly useless to structure that subjection. How will discipleship look when as many "masters" are women as men? When heterosexuality will no longer be every unknown person's assumed sexual orientation? I suspect that lesbian erotonomies of discipleship function differently from those between heterosexual males and that all of these function differently from those between gay males, but I have not seen any research to this effect, and my personal experience supports no generalizations. To understand and encourage the erotic energy that drives pedagogy, while at the same time preventing its being deployed to establish sexualized structures of domination and submission—this must become a central and abiding aim of the academy.

II

*Power, Panic, and
Pathos in Male Culture*

6

Cowboys, Cadillacs and Cosmonauts: Families, Film Genres, and Technocultures

Andrew Ross

"I feel just like a guy at the shopping center with the groceries waiting for his wife."
—Pete Conrad, waiting to store equipment on the lunar module of *Apollo XII*

In Barry Levinson's 1987 film *Tin Men*, set in Baltimore in 1962, the lunchtime banter of four aluminum siding salesmen (the tin men of the title) often revolves around the shared suspicion that "*Bonanza* is not an accurate depiction of the West." One of the characters, who claims that ordinarily he isn't "too picky" about such details, says that he "is beginning to think that the show doesn't have too much realism." Why? Because it depicts "a fifty-year-old father with three forty-seven-year-old sons." A companion who points out, with mock humility, that he is no "authority" on the TV show, casts further suspicion on the Ben Cartwright patriarch, who must, he says, possess "the kiss of death" to have had three children from "three different wives who all die at childbirth." In addition, they agree that the characters seldom show any interest in the topic of women. No one, not even Little Joe or Hoss, ever talks about getting horny or getting laid.

In recent years, we have seen a rising tide of complaints about standardized depictions, in media and advertising, of a nuclear family model that bears little resemblance to real, demographic families in the United States, where, it is pointed out, the nuclear family has long been in decline. While the ideology of familialism is everywhere, the families themselves are increasingly hard to find. The complaint of Levinson's tin men about *Bonanza*'s weird, one-parent family expresses some of this current critical anxiety, but the comments of these characters are also set within a conventional filmic context that invokes a number of historical perspectives about the apparent incoherence of the nuclear family unit.

Tin Men, as I will show later, bristles with references to the generic codes of the classic Western, especially those that demarcate the genre's obsession with masculinity and its technological extensions. But the film is also a 1980s nostalgia film, depicting the innocent, prelapsarian conditions of 1962, which are nonetheless seen to contain the seeds of the oncoming decline of the United States' postwar social stability and economic prosperity. As in the classic Western, an ideal masculine way of life on the New Frontier is shown to be threatened with extinction. While the film tries to establish the threat objectively, in economic terms, I would argue that it is more fully displayed in a reconfiguration of courtship and marital relations that interrupts the utopian temporality of male camaraderie so shrewdly and passionately described in Levinson's films generally. Consequently, the debate in the diner about *Bonanza* takes on an added significance, not only for the film's own play of narratives, but also for the historical timespan—1962–1987—that the film mediates.

The *Bonanza* family debate can be seen, then, in the context of the messages it bears about the structural conventions of the Western itself, straining, by now, under the historical burden of recalling the days of frontier settlement and the origin of American imperialist expansionism in the nineteenth century. In particular, this strain is increasingly manifest in the genre's difficulties in resolving the contradiction between, on the one hand, the opportunistic brand of male self-reliance that is often referred to as "rugged individualism" and, on the other, the communal domesticity represented by the settlement family, each threatened in different ways by the arrival from the East of technological development and government regulation. As a cultural genre, the Western does not hold the copyright on telling this story, anymore than the Old West should always be invoked as a privileged site of the nation's foundational mythologies. If the Revolutionary War would seem a more likely candidate for mythologizing masculine and national identity, it is nonetheless clear that there are ideological risks involved in dwelling upon armed resistance to colonial vassalage. More well known to us, largely as a result of the cultural work done by the Western, are the advantages of focusing upon a period of territorial aggrandisement—the exploitation of land and labor through the codes of "lawlessness," the justification of genocide through the codes of "manifest destiny," and the legitimation of wild misogyny through the codes of maverick male autonomy. What has been repressed, of course, is the debt of the Southwestern cowboy mythology to the Mexican *vaquero* culture of cattlemen, which it appropriated wholesale, along with the culturally specific macho codes of the *rancheros:* "everything that served to characterize the American cowboy as a type was taken over from the Mexican *vaquero:* utensils and language, methods and equipment."[1]

In the pages that follow, I will track the logic of the Western codes governing masculinity (and its technological extensions) and nuclear familialism (in its successive management of crises) as their legacy is rearticulated in other film genres— the oil melodrama, the automobile nostalgia film, and science fiction, both naive and postmodern.

Ponderosa Lost

Although weakened by genre burnout in print, on film, and now on TV, the Western, by the 1960s, was still a convenient vehicle for playing out the conflict between male restlessness and familial domesticity.[2] With the Cartwrights' baronial settlement, the Ponderosa, playing a starring role, *Bonanza* had become the most successful of the TV "property Westerns" in which social and kinship affinities governed solely by property relations had come to replace the codes of gunmanship as a determining structural feature of the genre's preoccupation with possessive individualism. Since Hollywood made its first horizontal penetration of the television industry in the mid-1950s with shows starring already established Western stars like Gene Autry, Roy Rogers, and William Boyd, the development of the TV Western had managed to reflect, over the course of ten years, each successive historical stage in the violent settlement of the Western states:[3] from the genteel frontiersman to the mercenary hired gun; from the bustling cattle boom of the 1880s to the shlocky performance art of Buffalo Bill Cody's Wild West Shows; from the glorification of outlawed prole desperadoes like Billy the Kid and the James Gang to the style fetishism of the rodeo dudes.

In the space of that TV decade, then, the atomistic rituals of the roving cowboy, bound to early libertarian codes of social action, had first been augmented by family or spouse substitutes in the form of celebrity horses like Trigger, Silver, and Champion, each famed for selfless loyalty and trust, and by "ethnic" sidekicks like Tonto and Pancho, equally valued for their unquestioning obedience. Subsequently, the introduction of advanced gun technology and the heyday of the independent, maverick gunfighter in *Gunsmoke*, *Wyatt Earp*, and *Colt 45* reinforced a typical male ambivalence about the values of domestic settlement, even as the rationale for the gunfighter's presence was to secure moral and territorial space for the settlement of families. In turn, the advent of the drover team or herd Westerns, like *Rawhide* and *Wagon Train*, celebrated the trail life of ideal male communities, paternalized by the wagon master, and serviced by a stereotypical cook whose sexually ambiguous associations are still perpetuated in ads like the recent homophobic Nut 'n Honey TV commercial. By the time of *Bonanza* and other property Westerns like *High Chaparral* and *The Virginian*, the domestic cook is Chinese.

The guidelines for *Bonanza* scriptwriters show how strict taboos were enforced to keep intact the show's formulaic view of family, property, and race relations:

> We often have a surfeit of Indian stories. Forget, too, any stories concerning a "wife" showing up, or someone claiming to own the Ponderosa, or the young, misunderstood rebel who regenerates because of the Cartwrights' tolerance and example.[4]

As is clear from these and other guidelines, the trajectory of the TV Western was one that safely bypassed the history of Native American genocide and the appropriation of Mexican culture and lands, just as it sweetened the history of the brutal carving out and baronial colonization of cattle kingdoms at the expense of small homesteaders.[5] With the cumulative popular appeal of the genre behind it, *Bonanza* might have soldiered on for much longer without taking account of either of these histories. It was the structural absence of a Cartwright wife, however, that finally sealed the fate of the new "suburban" phase of this genre, just as this absence had underscored the show's continuity with the atomistic characterology of the early Western. Even if the thrice-widowed Ben's paternalism mellowed visibly over the years, the crisis of filiation under which the three absurdly infantilized sons labored was too much to bear for a consistently persuasive representation of this one-parent family for a modern TV audience. One son left, another died, and the series, increasingly confused about the nonmarital status of its characters, ended amid a controversy over the representation of the murder of Alice Cartwright, Little Joe's bride.

On the other hand, the popularity of the show's nonnuclear family over the course of its thirteen-year run (1959–1973) might still attest to its success in somehow representing values that are invariably associated with the nuclear 1950s TV family as depicted in their suburban form by *Father Knows Best* and *Ozzie and Harriet* or in the regional homilies offered in the 1970s by *The Waltons:* the close-knit, property-owning family as the privileged site of caring, stability, moral authority, and emotional security. While the nuclear, two-parent family has no ultimate rights over such values, my examples intend to suggest that the ideology of familialism is so closely identified with these values that any set of alternative living arrangements that seeks to claim them is still obliged to define itself as a "family," whether extended and thus tribal/communal, or else reduced to essential, dyadic bonding. The popularity of a show like *Bonanza* showed, perhaps, how pliant that ideology was, while the reinforced familialism of the 1980s proves how efficiently it has absorbed and contained the powerful countercultural challenge to traditional family structures in the late 1960s and early 1970s, which ran the gamut from decentered hippie communities, modeled on the egalitarian Native American tribe, to the nomadic feudal patriarchalism of the thirty-five-member Manson "family."[6]

Arguably the most successful, and problematic, of the 1960s' attempts to romanticize pre-industrial kinship values were those made *in the service* of postindustrial ideology. None were more persuasive than those of Marshall McLuhan, who advocated an "Orientalization" and "retribalization" of families in advanced industrial societies through the medium of new cultural technologies like television. The chief obstacle in the path of postindustrial utopia, as McLuhan saw it, was the tendency of its new technological environments simply to reflect the content of outdated environments, a phenomenon he called "rear-view mirrorism." Writing in 1966 at the height of U.S. domination of the world's media markets, McLuhan cited *Bonanza*'s popularity as an example of this contradictory face of technologist ideology:

> *Bonanza* is not our present environment, but the old one; and in darkest suburbia we latch onto this image of the old environment. This is normal. While we live in the television environment, we cannot see it. . . . Anyone who talks about centralism in the twentieth century is looking at the old technology—*Bonanza*—not the new technology—electric technology. . . . Our thinking is all done still in the old nineteenth-century world because everyone always lives in the world just behind— the one they can see, like *Bonanza*. *Bonanza* is the world just behind, where people feel safe. Each week 350 million people see *Bonanza* in sixty-two different countries. They don't all see the same show, obviously. In America, *Bonanza* means "way-back-when." And to many of the other sixty-two countries it means a-way-forward when we get there.[7]

Here McLuhan proposed a cultural parable for advanced technological societies. As I have elsewhere pointed out, it is also "a parable about underdevelopment in many of the sixty-two countries (almost a hundred finally, in *Bonanza*'s case) in which a technologically advanced culture's own imaginary and anachronistic relation to its past development is being introduced."[8] In imagining the point of view of consumers in the foreign media markets upon which Hollywood film and network TV programming were being dumped, McLuhan saw only the witty, anachronistic side of culture shock, predicated upon assumptions about the inevitable linear shape ("when we get there") of technological progress along the Western model, assumptions that would not go uncontested in the decade ahead.

McLuhan's working concept of technological environments is nonetheless a useful one if we do not attribute to it the functional homogeneity and absolute determinist power that he does. It can be understood instead as a set of discursive rules, and in this respect it is similar to the concept of the genre, which, however imprecisely defined, impure, and variable in its permutation of rules and conventions, is still a model of efficiency, rather like the Colt revolver, the result of the first "American" production system of interchangeable parts. Genres are like technological environments inasmuch as their uneven influence, over a period of time, helps to shape our collective responses to perceived social contradictions. The cultural work that they perform serves to transform a set of material conditions into a narrative economy.

The Oil Crisis

If McLuhan had chosen to consider that the sponsor of *Bonanza* was General Motors—it was a highly visible sponsorship—then a different kind of political economy and a different understanding of technological environments might have underscored his comments about the show. It would be a story that looked backwards to the "heritage" of empire and settlement in the Old West but that drew, for its current cultural and economic sense, upon the iconography and the oil-rich resources of the New West. At the time when McLuhan was writing and *Bonanza*'s ratings were at their peak, the oil-dependent automobile industry, economic guarantor of the postwar Pax Americana, accounted for 10 percent of all manufacturing and one out of every six jobs. No single product before or since is ever likely to dominate the economic base and imagination of a world power to the same extent as the automobile did in the postwar age of consensus. The decline of the U.S. auto industry was completely synonymous with deindustrialization and the flight of U.S. capital overseas.

Just as there is an economic narrative that puts cowboys and Cadillacs together without too much in the way of contradictions, the cattle-rich base of the Cartwrights' property wealth rests uneasily, but not anachronistically, alongside the new social organization of the Western oil family dynasty. Cattle ranching is a labor-intensive business in principle—though not always on TV (the Ponderosa's 600,000 acre spread was worked by no more than four hired hands). On the oil ranch, there isn't much to do, except spend more time with the family. Hence the great Western melodramas like *Written on the Wind, Hud, Giant,* and the long-running TV equivalent *Dallas,* each of which focused on internal family tensions, on crises of filial succession and inheritance, and on the moral dissolution and decadence of a leisure class—all of the problems, in short, of that specific North American type of late capitalism, the aristocratic family with a suburban imagination. But if oil wells had become a dishonorable replacement for ranching and the dissolute dynasty represented a falling off from the close-knit cattle clan, the West and the Western were still ideological places for working out what exactly it is that a man "has to do."

This enduring legacy is quite evident in Levinson's *Tin Men,* a film that has fully absorbed the popular consciousness about the meaning of these Western narratives and oppositions. At the same time, it presents a clever reframing of the conflict between technological environments that helps to define masculine identity inside and outside the family. Punctuated with references to all of the generic phases of the Western, *Tin Men* dramatizes the end of an equally mythical period when North American men's relation to both their independent and familial identity was mediated across the lavishly styled surfaces of their new Cadillacs. The central action is provided by a prolonged conflict between two tin men: BB, a natty, maverick type, single and enterprising, and Tilley, a frustrated citizen type, married and unimaginative. This conflict involves several showdowns, involving destructive attacks on their respective cars, at, among other sites, a local race track and a bar called the Corral Club and against the backdrop of a Western shoot-out on a drive-in screen. Revenge, for the rogue male BB, takes the form of "stealing" Tilley's wife, Nora, but she ends up outlawing the cowboy in him with a series of speeches and actions that displays her protofeminism. Investigating evidence of their hustling, fraud, and misrepresentations as aluminum-siding salesmen, a government Home Improvements Commission revokes both of their licenses. Tilley, the populist "small man" victim, who is everywhere harried by the IRS, views this as a McCarthy-style outrage, while BB, the shrewd sharpie, sees it as a symptom of "the future," otherwise depicted throughout the film by BB's close attention to the humble appearances on Baltimore streets of the Volkswagen Beetle. The closing scene ends with a reconciliation that leads the spectator to assume that the enemies might romantically team up and seek their fortune together in the new business of selling Volkswagen automobiles. Nat King Cole croons over the credits: "Now I've found my joy / I'm as happy as a baby boy / With another brand new choo-choo toy / When I met sweet Lorraine, Lorraine, Lorraine."

Like the classic Western, the film registers the end of a golden age of male autonomy: the Law has moved in to cramp the male style, and suddenly, the world, like its new automobiles, is a smaller and more restricted vehicle in which to maneuver. In the home improvements business, selling, in which each man had a style all of his own, had nonetheless been a story of hucksterism, of livelihoods dependent upon hoodwinking women about how to "beautify" the exterior of their homes. In the business of male bonding and male rivalry, it had been a story that posited the economy of the automobile, with its own "beautified" and feminized exterior, against the economy of the home and the family—an opposition in which a dented car, equated with a dented virility, could arbitrarily determine the fate of the family. The causes and symptoms of decline are manifest everywhere; the interventionist state is clamping down on the old, unregulated enterprise, the appearance of "economical" import cars on North American streets heralds the end of the Golden Age of Detroit-style production and consumption, and women aren't going to stand by their men anymore. If, in the face of all of these threatening horizons, *Tin Men* is a "nostalgia" film, it is because it is typically Western—it says that white males, even if they have the right stuff, will never be able to get up to the same tricks again, while enjoying the technological legitimacy and confidence they shared along with Detroit's latest hurrah or the feudal allegiances they could once expect from their families. For these tin men, struggling to survive the coming shift in technological environments, both economic and sexual, the contours of their masculinity may have to be redesigned, for life on the Ponderosa will never be quite the same again.

Francis Ford Coppola's *Tucker* (1988) offers a more conscious narrative about U.S. economic decline through the vehicle of the automobile nostalgia genre. Here, the typical Coppola opposition between the utopian family community and the ruthlessly anonymous face of big business is economically posed as a contest over the technological definition of "the family car," that benign, iconic model of Fordist production in the immediate postwar period. A visionary techno-entrepreneur, Tucker plans and designs an authentic "family car" that will truly embody family values—a safe, caring, ethical car that looks the future confidently in the face, just as it respectfully pays tribute to the decor and furnishings of a less streamlined past. The production of this car becomes a family business in every sense, strongly identified in promotional events with Tucker's own happy family and based on a small, close-knit production team that militates against the big Fordist ethic of Detroit. In his inclusion (daring in the postwar years) of a Japanese-American engineer in the production team, Tucker unconsciously but symbolically gestures toward a future in which the struggle for technological innovation and supremacy, just recently waged against imperial Japan, will be lost.

Tucker's family enterprise falls victim to the corruptions of power generated by the Detroit manufacturers' influence in Washington, and Coppola's film embraces its small-guy Capraesque logic in full consciousness of the future decline of the auto industry. Complaining in the classical rhetoric of populist nostalgia that he has been a "generation too late," Tucker's courtroom speech appeals to what appear to be embryonic (but are, in fact, long-established) resentments about a technologically administered society: "Bureaucrats would squash Benjamin Franklin. . . . Let's not close out the small guy. One day, we'll be buying cars from our former enemies. That's what happens if the bureaucrats squash the innovators."

In contrast to the fantasmatic historical sense of Rockwellian films like *Back to the Future*, *Tucker*'s idealistic picture of the happy 1950s family is at least technologically grounded. By this I mean that it takes to the letter many of the mythical values and meanings now associated with the iconic "family car" of the 1950s and seriously attempts to ground them within a more or less credible world of representations. In the benign picture of the household economy associated with Tucker's car, Coppola offers a productionist version of the atomized family utopias of the new suburban landscapes that had been organized around consumerism in the 1950s. Like the covered wagon and the "iron horse," the automobile was linked to the creation of "pioneer" suburban communities, whose domestic technological environments were similarly organized around privatized mobility. But while *Tucker*'s tight-knit household economy emphasizes the cohering effects of the automobile on family life, it ignores the dispersing effects. The intrusion of the car on family life just as often facilitated an escape from repressive family rituals and habits, while it provided an alternative domestic space for more adventurous teenage family romances; youth films from *Rebel Without a Cause* to *American Graffiti* celebrate this other, liberating side of automobile culture.

Similarly one-sided is the film's representation of the family not as a consumerist economy whose source of authority and power lies ultimately in the home, but rather in terms of a (male) productionist unit that takes over, and subsequently masquerades as, a gendered household economy. In the former, alternative version, the mother would have had to play much more of a leading role, if only in fostering and shaping the redeeming values of the family through its members. In fact, the culture of consumerism was organized around this very premise, just as the nineteenth-century cult of domesticity and its ideological blueprint, preached in the manuals of persuasion, for a Christian "family state" centered in the home, had earlier presented the female-dominated household economy as a utopian alternative to the world of trade, manufacturing, and government.[9] As a result of its conflation of these two economies, *Tucker* manages to resolve the contradictions between market individualism and domestic collectivity that are present in a conservative ideology of the family—an ideology where the *market ideal* of the self-supporting (male) individual must somehow be reduced to the *moral ideal* of a collective family unit, supported, of course, by a single male breadwinner.[10] Given the recent contribution of women to factory wartime production, Mrs. Tucker's intimate role in the "production" of the automobile, even if she figures mostly in a promotional context, tells yet another tale about the containing, or incorporative, power of familialist ideology in the film.

Empire of the Son

One might still be surprised, however, by the extent to which Coppola commits himself so fanatically to a cohesive family ideology, even in the light of his long obsession with the family, from *The Godfather* to *Peggy Sue Got Married*. But

Coppola's stories, and his obsessions, are as much an outcropping of the Hollywood imagination as they are an ideological critique of the Hollywood system. Coppola's own Hollywood reputation as an outlawed, visionary techno-entrepreneur is itself heavily overlaid with paternalistic features. In his dual role as technological pioneer and paternal protector of his film "people," he embodies the contradictions of familialism as seamlessly as his Tucker. So too, in the mythology of the new Hollywood genre cinema devoted to techno-worship, Coppola might take his place as father, godly or not, within the holy trinity completed by Stephen Spielberg and George Lucas. Within this canonically motherless family, Spielberg is cast in the filial role of the eternal *Wunderkind*, and Lucas is the Holy Ghost in the machine, the facilitator, the brother of invention.

The naive science-fiction genres favored by Spielberg and Lucas (children's films made for adults, or, as the marketing slogan goes, "for kids of all ages") have all but replaced the Western as the dominant Hollywood genre for speaking about the foundational myths of masculine and national identity. As modern narratives of empire, science-fiction films today increasingly borrow more conventions from the Western than from the horror genres that were their primary source in the 1950s. If they no longer speak to the history of an internally colonized settlement, their concern has been with external conquests in space, the "final frontier." On the other hand, they share the xenophobia and the euphoric nostalgia of the classic Western, providing, in the figure of the "alien" (as the *unfamiliar*, and thus outside the family), one of the most fully articulated image repertoires of racist and racially marked types in North American culture.

The figure of the alien is now so current in the Hollywood imaginary that the semantic distance it has maintained with respect to the typology of the "alien" generated by the U.S. Immigration Service has collapsed upon itself. For example, the 1988 film *Alien Nation*, directed by Graham Baker, is the story of the absorption of a stray alien population, genetically altered for slavery, into the U.S. labor force as a new underclass, working with methane and other poisonous substances to which the aliens are immune.[11] ACLU lawyers defend the newcomers' rights, but discrimination is rife, alien ghetto crime proliferates, and racist jokes abound. With all the promise of a bad cop–buddy movie, the film depicts the course of bonding between a white hard-ass bigot officer and the first alien to achieve the rank of detective in the Los Angeles Police Department (indeed, it is the alien who has an "Ozzie and Harriet" family and who helps to bring together the separated family of his new buddy). Presented explicitly as an allegory of immigration racism and primitive capitalist exploitation in Southern California, the film recycles too many familiar racist moves, however, to render it critical. The *Alien National Inquirer*, a promotional newspaper distributed at theaters where the film showed, reproduces uncomfortable racist mythologies in its advertising section: lazy aliens (the La-Z-Alien Recliner), the well endowed alien (Chippenaliens), alien hair obsessions, "exotic" foods (Chief Boyar Dee's Beaveroni), and so forth.

But for all its troubled intimacy with the discourses of racism, *Alien Nation* is symptomatic of a new wave of *domestic* alien pictures that overtly address questions of race and class, a tendency brilliantly heralded by John Sayles' *Brother from Another Planet* and figured, more indirectly, in Julian Temple's *Earth Girls Are Easy*, where a racially diverse trio of aliens are freely and easily submerged into the hedonistic subcultures of valley life in Southern California. This tendency, however, is far removed from the ideology of science-fiction promoted by the Spielberg-Lucas school, whose most domesticated alien has been E.T., a charmingly deformed infant-savant, and whose most xenophobic productions have been spectacular theological sagas about final conflicts and crusades against dark, totalitarian empires. Much has been written about the close association of *Star Wars'* Cold War mysticism with the global agenda of the North American New Right. The critique has been so accurate, in fact, that the popularity of the Lucas films has sufficiently blurred the line between imperial fiction and technological reality for it to have helped to legitimize the plans for SDI (Strategic Defense Initiative), a new permanent arms economy linked to the industrialization and militarization of the space frontier.

More problematic for critics of the Spielberg-Lucas school has been the phenomenon of the infantilization of the spectator. This is an effect inscribed within the films not only in terms of the Oedipal configurations worked out around the usually centralized family milieu, but also in relation to the wondrous gee-whizzery of magically clean technology. Robin Wood has described these films' appeal in terms both of a regression to childhood and of the narrative of the restoration of the father in Hollywood cinema.[12] Vivian Sobchak extends this analysis by pointing to the born-again father-as-child as a figure for resolving the crisis of patriarchy.[13] Historically speaking, in these parables about science-fiction technology, which regularly evoke as their frames of reference a 1950s TV boyhood, the narrative of "going back to the future" is a powerful conservative recuperation of the postlapsarian present. It is a familiar way of imaginatively predating the less-than-mythical breaks that divide us historically from the 1950s: post-Oedipal maturity, the real economic decline of U.S. supremacy, the erosion of the nuclear family, the loss of the political "innocence" of the postwar "youth culture," the breakup of the liberal middle-class consensus, the ignominy of U.S. interventionism, and so on.

In fact, the postimperial nostalgia espoused by Spielberg and Lucas has taken on a visibly generational form, comprising a narrative that can be told in the space of a single generation—specifically, their own generation—which spans the postwar period of the rise and fall of "American" empire. The generational framing of this narrative is not yet explicitly moral; it has not become a conventional feature of the filmic narrative itself, as it is in, say, the most nostalgic of classic Westerns.[14] Lacking the historical distance provided by the Western, Spielberg-Lucas nostalgia has been interpreted as a much more personalized and Oedipalized investment on the part of the directors themselves, especially in the case of Spielberg, whose valorization of the infantile presexual male and the restored nuclear family, with or without a *real* father, has been an invariable feature of his films.

When Spielberg does address real historical conditions and events, it is symptomatically in the context of two films, *1941* and *Empire of the Sun*, that relate to Japanese imperial power and the U.S.–Japanese military struggle for aerial supremacy. *1941* is a forgettable slapstick farce set in a hysterical California weeks after Pearl Harbor, during the violently racist "zoot suit riots," in which U.S. servicemen attacked Mexican-Americans wearing fashions pioneered by black jazz musicians. The sexual angle of the farce is developed through a female character who is turned on by airplane technology; she "has a serious interest in strategic bombers." This identification with phallic, aerial firepower was to find its vintage Spielbergian formulation in *Empire of the Sun*.

Empire of the Sun (1987) transforms J. G. Ballard's bleak memoir of a neocolonial childhood in Shanghai into an astonishing story about a boy's education in what Walter Benjamin saw as the specifically fascist aestheticization of technology and power. Jamie Graham, the precocious and resourceful boy-hero of the film, is growing up in an idealized British bourgeois family setting in a Shanghai that is threatened by the imperial Japanese invasion. Having abandoned the God of Anglicanism and lacking any sense of patriotic affiliation, his sympathies in the coming conflict are becoming quite clear; at the age of ten, he is "thinking of joining the Japanese air force" because they have the better pilots and the superior technology that his comic books valorize. Separated from his parents in the confusion of the invasion, his male survivalist education in the hard school of wartime labor camps is governed by a series of affiliatory maneuvers and deals that he negotiates with representatives of different nationalities in the labor camp. He has little patience for the old paternalistic British code of decency, fair play, and humanistic respect for elders and finds the tough camaraderie and competitive individualism of the U.S. community more attractive and exciting; he becomes an honorary North American, with an Americanized name, Jim, a flying jacket, baseball cap, and entrepreneurial manner to accompany these acquisitions. His ultimate respect, however, is reserved for the "honorable" militaristic codes of the Japanese pilots whose airfield abuts the labor camp.

Between his schooling in unprincipled North American male pragmatism and his training in the deferential master-slave code demanded by the Japanese camp commander, his education as a protofascist youth looks to be almost complete. During a bombing raid on the airfield, in which the smell of cordite overexcites his imagination and his body, he is struck by the thought that he cannot remember what his parents look like. The rest of the film looks toward the final restoration of the family. The Americans betray him, and the Japanese are humiliated in war. But there is no real satisfaction for him in the reunion with his parents at the close of the film. Instead, gratification is provided by a rejuvenation of his faith in aerial military technology, this time as a result of his mystical, proto-orgasmic encounter with the moment of origin of a new empire of the sun, the artificial sun of the atom bomb's white light on the horizon. In Ballard's autobiography, this is a gloomy if not nihilistic scenario. In Spielberg's version it is an altar scene of awe and techno-worship; for Jim, the explosion is "like God taking a photograph."

If only because of its explicit historical setting, *Empire of the Sun* is the most politically clearcut of Spielberg's allegories of born-again boyhood. Structurally, the hero is faced with a difficult choice among a number of imperialist lifestyles: the bankrupt British code of being a "decent chap," the busy commercial Darwinism of North American "pragmatism," or the rigorously demanding ideology of Japanese "honor." His Oedipal choice à la Spielberg proves to be a disinterested, disembodied one, a mystical identification with the new atomic technology that is posed as beyond sexuality, race, class, and nationality, after which choice his parents can then reappear as the *familia ex machina*. The "West," then, with its outdated codes of masculine ethics, is no longer the natural site of the Spielbergian *Bildungsroman*. It is an "empire of the son" in aerospace that Jim chooses, an empire of promise that has yet to commit atrocities and fail expectations and that is offered its own originary code of manifest destiny by the appearance of the atomic omen in the sky.

(Not) Lost in Space

The technological miracle in the skies that so inspires Spielberg's Jim is the barbaric origin, not just of the Cold War and the United States' permanent arms economy, but also of what Dale Carter has called the Rocket State, which is imaginatively aimed at realizing a technological environment for the colonization of space.[15] The backdrop to all postwar science fiction, from the germophobic, anti-Communist films of the Cold War to the clean, wonderworld technology of *Star Wars*, was the development of an aerospace industry to meet the national challenge of world supremacy. The aerospace imaginary fostered its own folk heroes in astronauts with a national iconic function, even though they were eventually exposed as "tin men," with little opportunity, within the strict operational environment of the space program, to prove that they had the "right stuff" of frontiersmanship.

In the development of the Rocket State, partial erosion of the sexual division of labor has given rise to the need for representations of women in iconic, pioneering roles hitherto exclusively reserved for men, and it is through these roles that the near future of postmodern familialism is being introduced. Consequently, the *Challenger* disaster that involved Christa McAuliffe in 1986 was a difficult event for liberal narratives about equal opportunity to absorb and contain. The McAuliffe mission was planned in every respect as an "ultimate field trip" and also as a gender-blind history lesson in national identity for students. McAuliffe herself had underscored the continuity of colonialist history when she compared her mission to that of the pioneering women of the Old West who had traveled across the Plains in Conestoga wagons, keeping personal journals of their experiences and writing letters back East.[16] So too, the multi-ethnic family that made up the *Challenger* crew—a black, a Jew, and an Asian-American from Hawaii, in addition to two women—was a *Star Trek* melting pot community, boasting a range of cultural diversity that would be conspicuously absent from the all-white, male makeup of the next shuttle crew.[17]

Beyond its many resonances with Western and science-fiction genres, the Christa

McAuliffe story could also be told as the story of what happens when Mother leaves the family to go out and work. (Her job, in this case, was not a skilled job; much of her training "consisted of stern admonitions to 'never touch those switches.' "[18]) In this respect, the McAuliffe story was shot through with symptoms of the new national anxiety about mothers in the workforce. Forget the pioneering women in the covered wagons. Self-supporting individualism of the sort valorized by a conservative ideology of the family depends today upon easy access to day care, and this is not the stuff of which pioneering legends are easily made. No more helpful toward a successful representation of the space family was the overplanned control technology of the space program, notoriously responsible for casting its astronauts as helplessly passive, even as victims, rather than sovereign rulers of their interplanetary fates.

The tragic failure of the McAuliffe mission, then, inadvertently called attention to the difficulties involved in presenting "pioneer" women in ways that appeal to equal opportunity and to sexual difference alike. Time-honored codes that had served to resolve the contradictions, rooted in the Western genre, between male individualism and familialism could not perform the same effortless role for women in a similar position. Between femininity and familialism lay the technologies of reproduction; there was no clean technological break or separation of public and private environments. Nowhere was this difference more fully addressed than in science-fiction film, from the naive narratives about body-invading mutant offspring of science-out-of-control experiments to the more lovable aliens of recent control technology environments. If, as Vivian Sobchak has argued, the pressure of conservative patriarchalism à la Spielberg and Lucas has produced a number of successful if unstable narratives in the born-again–father mold, a similar story might be told within Hollywood film about attempts to rewrite the relation of women to the new reproductive technologies. For it is in the new technological environments of human reproduction, more germane to femininity than to masculinity, that the contest over definitions of familialism is currently being waged. Consider, then, the case of Ripley, the most famous heroine of modern science fiction, whose adventures in *Alien* and *Aliens*, respectively, tell a disturbing story about a woman who is professionally trained in the use of aerospace technology but who is consequently an amateur or "natural" when faced with a crisis involving reproductive technology.

When it appeared in 1979, *Alien* was almost immediately recognized as a film that stretched the limits of modern science-fiction and naive horror genres in order to comment explicitly on *commercial* and *patriarchal* attempts to colonize female control over reproduction. The film starts out by presenting a gender-coded dialogue between the technological environment of the Nostromo and that of the alien spaceship.[19] Because it is a dystopian film, the surfaces are not friendly and appealing: the grungy, hardware-confining spaces of the Nostromo prove to be unsafe and claustrophobic, while the fossilized, biomechanoid design of the Alien's terrain, gestating even as it wears the look of death, is replete with female reproductive imagery, which the film, in line with classical science-fiction codes, presents as threatening. In using a human male body as an incubator for part of its life cycle, the alien environment manages to reproduce itself with all of the iconographic trappings of a destructive rapist. This dystopian picture of reproductive technologies is set within a sharp critique of the capitalist logic that is sending pioneer families and mining crews out into space to colonize mineral resources and whose android agent and computer are programmed to decide that human lives are expendable in the Company's pursuit of new organic technologies for its bioweapons division.

In *Alien*, Ripley is the only character who is able to survive the Alien's rampage. She survives not because she is a true professional, responsibly in control of the technologies of control, and not because, in the confrontation scene, she evokes "feminine intuition" by wishing on a "lucky star." She survives because she alone is in a position to recognize the logic of the film's narrative about reproductive technology; she is in a position to greet the Alien as a "son of a bitch," just moments after she has named the Company's computer "Mother, you Bitch" for failing to deactivate the self-destruct program. She alone can see that the Alien's blend of autogenetic self-sufficiency and aggressive individualism—"a perfect organism, whose structural perfection is matched only by its hostility" in the admiring words of Ash, the Company's android—is perfectly complict with the patriarchal logic of the Company that allows the Alien free destructive rein over her companions' bodies. From her point of view, the Alien technoculture can be seen as the full embodiment of the dream of womanless reproduction, since its autogenesis is dependent upon the colonization of other *male* bodies—the only bodies that the film wants us to see being used in this way.

In *Aliens*, the militaristic, nationalistic sequel, Ripley's position and her lucidily critical point of view are realigned and rewritten to meet the demands of more conservative narratives of gender and race. The Aliens' colonization of other bodies is more indiscriminate than in the original film, and indeed we actually *see* female bodies being colonized. So too, *Alien*'s precise critique of the Company's capitalist logic has dissipated; exploitation is personified in the individual figure of the Company agent, Burke, the bad guy who acts independently of his employers. As a result, when Ripley criticizes the motives behind the Company's appropriation of alien technologies, she can only blame the human species as a whole; she says, "at least the aliens don't fuck each other over for a percentage."

In contrast to her role in *Alien*, Ripley's role in the sequel is not only clearly gender-coded as female, but is also marked from the very beginning of the film as maternal. The opening scenes establish Jonesy the cat as her surrogate child, and her nightmare birthing dreams indicate unresolved maternal anxieties and desires. We are also offered the spectacle of our heroine going weak at the knees at the thought of the endangered colonist families on the terraformed planet. *Alien*'s clear critique of corporate logic is bypassed by the way in which the sequel takes up the question of motherhood, surrogate or otherwise, in order to establish a mythical showdown, *High Noon*–style, between good and bad mothers. In the final analysis, personalizing the queen Alien as a "bitch," as Ripley does in the confrontation scene, is arguably less of a critical perception than a recognition (as in the original film when she reserves the term *bitch* for Mother, the name of the company computer) of the common logic of aggressive colonization shared by the Company and the Alien offspring. In effect, the "natural" vengeance of the grieving Alien mother comes to displace the logic of genocide, colonization, and the dream of womanless reproduction as motives for aggression. If Ripley ends up with a strange kind of one-parent family to look after—the adopted, feral child, Newt, and two castrated men, Bishop, the decapitated android, and Hicks, the wounded lieutenant—it is nonetheless the best that the film can offer in the way of solutions to the crisis of the family.

As part of the final, Western showdown between the good and bad mother, *destructive* "human" technology in the shape of Ripley's appropriation of the marines' arsenal of firepower is seen as justified in the fight against *reproductive* "alien" technology. The film's move to make Ripley into a female Rambo, bristling with state-of-the-art weaponry while recklessly but heroically protecting her adopted child, can and has been read as one way of taking technology into one's own hands, an unavoidable move if we are to have strong female heroines looking after their own. But what may prove, I think, to be more important about the film's dominant image of Ripley—guns, flamethrowers and cannons blazing—is not that she is a woman or a (step)mother, but rather that she is a *North American*, and a white North American at that. Nor does it really matter what she is firing at, anymore than it matters whom Stallone, Schwarzenegger, Bronson, or Eastwood are firing at. What she does when she strikes this pose is to take on a recognizably national identity, marked by the gesture of *shooting from the hip*, the properly casual North American style of blowing away an adversary.

For whom, finally, is Ripley pulling the trigger of her Peacemaker? Not for some universal good mother, not for the protection of her otherwise defenseless adopted family, but for a particular audience, constructed within the national imaginary as defined by the history of Hollywood genre film, especially the Western, and as responsive as ever to a trigger-happy technological environment. The iconography of this pose is quite culture-specific; it belongs to a rhetoric of violence spoken, in film theaters around the world, in a North American accent and acted out with the deathless swagger of empire. The story of the assimilation of Ripley into this Western-masculinist posture is thus a remarkable example of the conservative power of generic narratives to tailor the representation of technological environments to fit a body that is as much untroubled by sexual difference as it is secure in its assumption of a national identity founded on the genocide of aliens. In fact, Ripley's story shows some of the moves by which women can be, and increasingly will be, presented as accomplices, unwilling or not, in the particular national tradition of "engendering men" that I have been describing here.

7

"Meat Out of the Eater": Panic and Desire in American Puritan Poetry

Walter Hughes

I find my desires . . . to the study of
points of divinity another while ready to
grow to a lust.
—The Diary of Michael Wigglesworth

Readers of seventeenth-century religious poetry have often sensed an erotic strain in the devotional meditations of English poets: Herbert details his seduction by "Love" in *The Temple*, and Donne in the *Holy Sonnets* pleads with God to "ravish" him. What many readers do not know is that this theme fascinated poets on the other side of the Atlantic as well. Not only did the three major American Puritan poets—Anne Bradstreet, Michael Wigglesworth, and Edward Taylor—all make use of eroticism in their religious poetry; they brought it to a level of intensity that would surprise anyone who believes that Puritans were "puritanical" about sex. In fact, the imagery in which they embodied their relation to God would probably strike their self-styled descendents as downright pornographic. Latter-day "puritans" might be particularly shocked by the efforts of Wigglesworth and Taylor, whose work shows the stress of a different kind of erotic strain: the tension these male poets felt when addressing a male God as a lover, a tension that both tormented and inspired them.

Historians have long reiterated that the Puritans were not prudish about the subject of sex; their letters and diaries show them capable of erotic candor and appreciation. Although, like all Christians of their time, they were hostile toward extramarital and "deviant" sex, Puritans eagerly celebrated the pleasures of "wedded love."[1] Furthermore, their theology and hermeneutics actually encouraged them to figure their relation to God as a sexual one. Many Puritans understood the Calvinist doctrine of election, for example, as a sign of his love for his chosen saints, a love that had to be accepted and returned on pain of damnation. The changes in Christian piety wrought by the English Reformation bestowed a new importance on the salvation of the individual: Protestants, particularly those with Puritan tendencies, came to see their personal relation to God as the most important, as well as the most intimate, aspect of life. God began to appear more like a lover than a father.

Puritan typological readings of the Old Testament confirmed this tendency by focusing their attention on the Song of Songs, which they read as an adumbration of Christ's love for his church. This interpretation of the love poetry of Canticles served as a way of infusing spiritual life with erotic imagery and energy, not as a prudish desexualization of the text. Because Puritans emphasized the personal nature of salvation, they increasingly heard Christ's seductive overtures as directed not only to the church, but to the individual churchgoer as well. Edmund Morgan and Philip Greven have described how Puritans of both sexes, following the Song of Songs, frequently wrote of themselves as "brides of Christ," spiritually committed to a divine "husband" and eagerly awaiting a consummation of their union with their divine "beloved."[2] This figure became a commonplace in Puritan writing; in his diary, the minister and poet Michael Wigglesworth could address God with such plaintive blandishments as "will the Lord now again return and embrace me in the arms of his dearest love? will he fall upon my neck and kiss me?"[3] In this context, grace, the center of the Puritan religious experience, took on particularly erotic connotations. To many Puritans, this sudden, exhilarating, even violent infusion of the divine into the human inevitably suggested sexual intercourse. As the poet Edward Taylor rather bluntly put it, "The Soule's the Wombe. Christ is the Spermodote / And Saving Grace the seed cast thereinto."[4]

None of these doctrines or images was unique to American Puritanism, but the isolation and increasingly enforced consensus of New England created a kind of cultural hothouse in which many Puritan ideas underwent exotic growth and even bore forbidden fruit. Scholars who generalize about American Puritanism acknowledge that at the heart of the movement was a *desire* for God, not a filial sense of obligation; Perry Miller called it "Augustinian" piety.[5] More recently, Andrew Delbanco has isolated this longing for intimacy with God as a "feminine" strain within Puritanism that had a special appeal for women.[6] But how did Puritan men respond to a form of piety that placed them in the anomalous position of receiving the attentions of an insistent, masculine suitor? How could they respond to an omnipotent male deity that made their salvation contingent upon an outpouring of homoerotic passion? Can we assume that for most of them this imperative of desire necessarily aroused contrary feelings of fear, repulsion, even panic? The implications of the figurative homosexuality within the religious lives of Puritan males has gone largely unexplored.[7]

Poetry seems the most fruitful literary form in which to scrutinize the use of an erotic metaphor for the individual's relation to God. The sixteenth-century English sonnet tradition had cemented the connection between the lyric and the erotic; seventeenth-century meditative poetry added the religious element (as did the Song of Songs). However, American Puritans found other, more subtle links among religion, sexuality, and poetry. In New England, sexuality and religion had both a private and a public face: essentially personal concerns, they nevertheless had major social consequences and therefore fell under the jurisdiction of government and church. Poetry likewise moved between public and private spheres. Anne Bradstreet wrote poetry about the private realm to which her society restricted her, poetry that friends made public without her consent. Michael Wigglesworth addressed his society in didactic verse that translated private experiences, recorded only in a secret diary, into a public idiom. Edward Taylor wrote poems, unpublished for centuries, that privately prepared him for participation in a public religious ceremony. Because poetry, like religion and sexuality, formed part of the crucial nexus between public and private, it should best record the consequences of the irresistible yet perilous blending of the spiritual and the erotic.

Anne Bradstreet: The Continuity of Desire

Bradstreet's writings (c. 1635–1670) confirm the assertion that Puritan religious experience was predicated upon desire. In her prose meditations, she defines the human soul as a principle of insatiability within each person:

> The eyes and ears are the inlets or doors of the soul, through which innumerable objects enter; yet is not that spacious room filled, neither doth it ever say it is enough, but like the daughters of the horseleach, cries "Give, give"; and which is most strange, the more it receives, the more empty it finds itself, and sees an impossibility ever to be filled but by Him in whom all fullness dwells.[8]

For Bradstreet, the first step toward faith is the realization that nothing our senses present to us will satisfy the appetite that is the soul. This desire can be defined as *erotic* in that it orients itself toward a succession of "objects," in both the sense of perceptible things and that of focuses or goals. However, all material objects fail as ultimate objects of desire, because the desiring soul is so ravenous that it can consume them all without ever being filled. In short, we must search beyond sensual experience for the fulfillment of sensual desire. The closest that a Puritan could come to imagining her unknowable God was as an externalized entity corresponding to the emptiness within her, as he "in whom all fullness dwells," the only object commensurate with human desire.

In another of her prose meditations, Bradstreet uses a more specifically erotic image, that of the maternal body, to describe the process by which the individual discovers the only source that can quench her sensual thirst:

> Some children are hardly weaned; although the teat be rubbed with wormwood or mustard, they will either wipe it off, or else suck down sweet and bitter together. So it is with some Christians: let God embitter all the sweets of this life, that so they might feed upon more substantial food, yet they are so childishly sottish that they are still hugging and sucking these empty breasts, that God is forced to hedge up their way with thorns or lay affliction on their loins that so they might shake hands with the world, before it bid them farewell. (38)

Bradstreet's conceit had a certain currency among the Puritans, who often spoke of "weaned affections" as a hallmark of sainthood; what she brings to the metaphor is the stress on the continuity of desire. The infant's appetite is not simply suppressed: it is transferred to "more substantial food." Likewise, our desire for sensual experience is not to be denied but to be redirected toward an object that can fulfill it more completely than any physical object can: God himself. Bradstreet's elaboration of the breast-feeding analogy resembles Freud's narrative of human development, in that our desire for the world and the pleasure we take in it are seen as the result of an energy that is constant throughout our lives, but constantly displaced, rechanneled, and relocated during our development. The infant in the oral stage identifies the breast as the world, but must find new means of deriving satisfaction from the interaction of its body with the world when this initial source is withdrawn. Bradstreet might be said to append another, final stage to Freud's narrative of human development, a spiritual stage in which we turn to God, not the world, for release. This ultimate reorientation of desire is the subject of Bradstreet's greatest poems.

If this is Bradstreet's great subject, the central problem posed in her poetic canon is convincing the soul that a seemingly absent God offers more "substantial" nourishment than the milk that flows from the physical world. It is not enough to dwell on the deficiencies of worldly pleasures. A greater poetic challenge lies in coaxing God through those "doors of the soul," in making him available to the senses. In other words, God must be *objectified*, that is, "made sensually percepti-ble" and "represented as a focus of desire," in the double sense of the word *object*. Bradstreet's primary strategy for objectifying God is to create parallels between her spiritual life and her sensual and erotic experiences.

The best example of this approach is Bradstreet's "Letter to Her Husband, Absent upon Public Employment." Although God is never explicitly mentioned in the poem, Bradstreet's description of her relation to her husband implicitly recalls the unity that Puritans sought to achieve with Christ:

> My head, my heart, mine eyes, my life, nay more,
> My job, my magazine of earthly store,
> If two be one, as surely thou and I. (226)

The distinction "earthly" establishes the two levels of significance in the poem: the temporal attachment to her husband and the spiritual commitment to God that it mirrors. These two concerns run parallel throughout, creating a kind of thematic rhyme. A Puritan reader would instantly recognize that Bradstreet's language is obliquely referring to God; the modern reader need only compare this verse to a passage from her prose meditations in which she writes, "thy maker is thy husband . . . I am a member of his Body; he, my head" (250). Although Puritan women were expected to see their husbands as resembling God in their authority, Bradstreet does not stress this in her poem; instead, by drawing on the image of the sun, she emphasizes the ways in which her sexual relation to her husband brings her closer to God:

> I, like the earth this season, mourn in black,
> My Sun is gone so far in's zodiac,
> Whom whilst I 'joyed, nor storms, nor frost I felt,
> His warmth such frigid colds did cause to melt.
> My chilled limbs now numbed lie forlorn;
> Return, return, sweet Sol, from Capricorn. . . .
> But when thou northward to me shall return,
> I wish my Sun may never set, but burn
> Within the Cancer of my glowing breast,
> The welcome house of him my dearest guest. (226)

These lines, celebrated for their open expression of erotic longing, also have a religious analogue that readers of Puritan diaries and conversion narratives will recognize. Periods of spiritual emptiness, when God seems to have withdrawn from the writer, are conventional stages in the process of ascertaining one's salvation; longing for God when he seems to have departed is frequently noted as a promising sign of redemption. Even Bradstreet's reference to her children, the products of her sexual union with her husband/sun, supports a religious reading: "In this dead time, alas, what can I more / Than view those fruits which through thy heat I bore?" (226). By referring to her children as the "fruits" of her marriage, she uses a word that Puritans frequently applied to the holy feelings and actions that God's grace inspired in the redeemed individual. Contemplation of these "fruits" often served the Puritan as a means of testing the reality of her redemption in times of God's withdrawal, of consoling herself when spiritually "dead." The identification of Bradstreet's relation to her husband with her relation to God is a theme uniquely suited to poetic expression, which allows her to speak of both with the same words; God is immanent in her sexual experience just as he is implicit in her language and imagery.

In a poem called "Contemplations," Bradstreet again invokes the trinity of sun, lover, and God:

> Thou as a bridegroom from thy chamber rushes,
> And as a strong man, joys to run a race;
> The morn doth usher thee with smiles and blushes;
> The Earth reflects her glances in thy face.
> Birds, insects, animals with vegative,
> Thy heat from death and dullness doth revive,
> And in the darksome womb of nature dive. (205–206)

The simile of the eager bridegroom points in two directions: it refers to the sun, as in Psalm 19, but also to Christ, as in the typological reading of Canticles. This poetic association imitates the process by which God becomes available to the poet's senses, and then becomes the object of her desire. Her sensual enjoyment of the sun's light and warmth leads her to the image of the sun arousing and fertilizing the female earth as a male lover; this in turn leads to thoughts of the Creator who is the source of all life.

By paralleling her erotic yearning for her husband with the earth's seasonal response to the sun's movement through the zodiac, Bradstreet combines the personal and the cosmic, the vast and the intimate in a way that ultimately gains her poetic access to God. The intermittent presence and absence of the sun, Simon Bradstreet, and God himself all serve to heighten and direct the poet's longing. Bradstreet does not believe complete fulfillment to be possible in this life; but the foretastes of it she experiences in nature and sexuality help her to orient her desiring soul toward God. These experiences are transitional, leading her through earthly pleasure to a knowledge of the divine.

Michael Wigglesworth: The Sodom Within and the Sodom Without

Could a male Puritan poet take this same approach to the problem of faith? To some extent, the theology and imagery of his religion encouraged him to do so. Nothing Bradstreet wrote in her prose and poetry is unorthodox, or would be any less applicable to a male believer. But unlike Bradstreet, male Puritans could not use their socially sanctioned experiences of love, marriage, and sexuality as a model for the construction of their religious experience; their relation to God was an anomaly in their lives, lives that could not *legitimately* include passionate, erotic attachments to other men. Furthermore, the idea of the soul as an emptiness yearning to be filled by God suggested a receptive sexual role that may have been required of married women like Bradstreet but was strictly forbidden to Puritan men. The very idea of drawing on their own experience to gain sensual knowledge of God as Bradstreet does would no doubt have excited a variety of complex feelings: anxiety, repulsion, fear, and perhaps a certain element of fascination as well. The poetry of Michael Wigglesworth and Edward Taylor offers striking evidence that contemplating their relation to God often did induce this response—what we would today call "homophobia" or "homosexual panic." These feelings are hardly ahistorical phenomena, but certainly would have existed among men who considered sodomy not only an "abomination" and a capital crime, but a motive for God's violence.

Michael Wigglesworth, although now rarely read, was probably considered the foremost American poet by his contemporaries; he was certainly the most popular and widely disseminated. He composed *The Day of Doom* (1662), a colonial bestseller, and "God's Controversy with New England" (1662), which initiated the first indigenous literary genre, the jeremiad. Although his poetry, unlike Bradstreet's, is resolutely public, with next to nothing in it of a personal nature, he did keep a diary. This spiritual record, so private that parts of it were written in code, describes in scandalous detail the religious and sexual predicament that secretly inspired Wigglesworth's public poetry.

From the very beginning of the diary, Wigglesworth struggles within the paradox of panic and desire. His constantly reiterated complaint is his inability to desire God, his "want of love to God and delight in God" (6), which results in a "deadness of heart" (3). Accompanying this failure of desire, however, is an uncontrollable overflow of lust, which in Wigglesworth's case seems to be directed toward his youthful male pupils at Harvard, where he served as a tutor. "*Such filthy lust flow[s] from my fond affection to my pupils whiles in their presence,*" Wigglesworth writes of feelings he finds so shameful that he records them in code (reprinted in Edmund Morgan's edition as italics), "*that I confess myself an object of God's loathing*" (30–31). Not surprisingly, these longings directly interfere with his attempts to love God: "*I find my spirit so exceeding carried away with love to my pupils that I cant tell how to take up my rest in God*" (11). Although the historian Jonathan Ned Katz sees this conflict as indicating "a concept of love as a scarce and limited good," perhaps a more likely explanation is that Wigglesworth's attempts to arouse his desire for a male God inevitably suggest to him his maddening and "filthy" desire for his male students.[9] For as he admits in another passage, "whilest God is bidding me see his glory I cannot see it; vile and unworthy conceptions concerning god come into my mind" (53). The essential contrast with Bradstreet becomes immediately apparent. Her sexual and spiritual experiences are parallel and mutually enriching; those of Wigglesworth are intrinsically connected but hopelessly at odds, creating seemingly pornographic images of God in his mind. Thus, he finds himself possessed of "a heart that cannot desire great lettings out of Christ's love to me such as some times I have felt which I dreadfully fear" (46). The ambiguity of syntax here aptly expresses Wigglesworth's predicament: does he fear the dreadful tendencies of his own heart? Or is he afraid of the ejaculatory "lettings out of Christ's love" that he is trying to train that heart to desire?

One sees striking evidence of this conflict in one of Wigglesworth's obsessions in the diary: the fact that he is particularly prone to sexual desire when he concentrates most intently on religious obligations. "*Nay I feel my heart apt secretly to give way to my vain thoughts in holy duties and glued as it were to my sensuality or love to the creature*" (10). In one of his poems, he calls these eruptions of sexuality into devotion "satanical injections," and his diary offers several examples.[10] A pleading reference to the sacrament makes divine inspiration sound more like irrumation: "I see a need of whole christ and do desire him, help my want of desires: open thou my mouth wide and then fill it with thy son. I need him" (25). At another point, wishing to commemorate the assistance God has given him in his spiritual development, Wigglesworth decides to "erect a pillar to the prayse of his grace" (93), and so draws a picture that might not be out of place on a bathroom wall (see Figure 7.1). Even Richard Crowder, Wigglesworth's rather reticent biographer, admits that the sketch of this pillar is "strangely phallic."[11] The language and imagery used to illustrate his relation to God leads Wigglesworth almost inevitably from the sacred to the profane, from desire to panic at that which he desires. It is no small wonder that at one point he worries: "do I retain a Sodom within the temple of the holy-ghost?" (104).

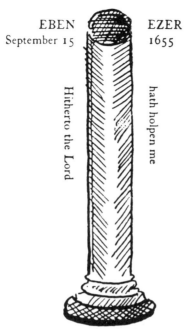

EBEN EZER
September 15   1655

Hitherto the Lord   hath holpen me

Figure 7.1. "Erect[ing] a pillar to the prayse of his grace."

To elucidate Wigglesworth's dilemma here, I should like to draw on the two distinct conceptions of sin, often referred to as "privative" and "positive," involved in Puritan thought.[12] A positive definition of sin means that it exists as an active principle or presence within the individual, whereas in the privative definition sin is the absence or deprivation of some element essential to salvation or belief. These differing constructions are usually indicated by a writer's choice of imagery. Positive sin is represented as some form of corruption or contamination, either disease or filth; privative sin as emptiness, coldness, dryness. The latter imagery pervades the poem in which Bradstreet parallels her husband's absence and God's, an absence that leaves her "chilled," "numbed," and "dead," passively awaiting the return of the "heat" she once felt. This language appears in Wigglesworth's diary as well, when he is lamenting his inability to desire God (the difference is, of course, that Bradstreet's sense of loss increases her yearning for God's return, while Wigglesworth fails to feel this longing at all). However, Wigglesworth also uses the imagery of positive sin, particularly when describing his physical desires. The semen that "escapes him" in his sleep is invariably termed "pollution" or "filthiness"; his predisposition to nocturnal emission is his "disease" or "distemper." This movement from the privative to the positive corresponds to the vicious cycle of desire and panic, as his efforts to arouse desire for God lead to a sense of sexual guilt and contamination. Hence, after the erection of his pillar, Wigglesworth's next entry reports, not surprisingly, a wet dream, which seems to have been brought on by his very efforts to prevent it: "some *night pollution escaped me, notwithstanding my earnest prayer to the contrary which brought to mind my old sins now too much forgotten*" (93).

This complex of anxiety, heightened by the very language with which Wigglesworth attempts to overcome it, creates ambiguities throughout the diary. Katz points out that when Wigglesworth writes about his lust for the "creature," he usually means "earthly comfort in general" but "that seductive 'creature' often turns out to be Wigglesworth's male students."[13] It is frequently difficult to tell whether Wigglesworth is writing about sins that are literally erotic or only figuratively so, because his terminology of positive sin is almost entirely sexualized: he constantly accuses himself of "sensuality," "carnality," "licentiousness," "lust," "wantonness," and "whoarish affections." Even the sin that most often afflicts Wigglesworth, pride, is imbued with sexual connotations: one of its archaic meanings is "a state of sexual arousal or heat," and the language surrounding it usually evokes tumescence (it is a "rising" spirit with which one is "puffed up"). In a short essay on pride that Wigglesworth appends to his diary, he identifies it, significantly enough, as "Sodom's ringleading sin" (104).

It is perhaps a mistake to try to distinguish between overtly erotic uses of these words and figurative ones. Sometimes these words relate directly to Wigglesworth's quite real desire for his students or to his frequent nocturnal emissions and "vile dreams"; but other times they are applied to moments of inattention in church, concern for his economic welfare, or overinvolvement in his studies. Taking his figurative role as a bride of Christ to its limit, Wigglesworth believes that any moment not focused entirely on God is a moment of sexual sin, of "spiritual adultery" with "other lovers" besides his "husband." Since all positive sin involves desire (that is, desire for the world), it is always in some sense sexual. And since all positive sin involves a perversion of desire from its heavenly object (God) to an inappropriately earthly one, it is always in some sense sodomy.

The Calvinist doctrine of total depravity encouraged Puritans to see their sins, no matter how trivial, as inextricably connecting them to the most abominable acts and the most debauched criminals. Sodomy was, in the Puritans' Levitical legal code, punishable by death, and therefore an excessive manifestation of a sinful nature; but it was one of which all sinners were theoretically capable. Katz demonstrates this point by quoting a Puritan minister named Samuel Danforth, who preached that the "holiest man hath as vile and filthy a nature, as the Sodomites."[14] It is therefore not far-fetched to claim that for Wigglesworth, sodomy is the epitome of sin. By turning our attention away from God toward the world, even for a moment, we are committing a sin that bears a remarkable resemblance to sodomy: we are pursuing an illicit object of desire, enjoying pleasures that are unproductive and sterile. Such pleasures do not bear "fruits," in the double sense that Bradstreet evoked in her poem; they do not bear either children or saintly acts and feelings.

Our tendency to such "sensuality" is the result of pride, an overvaluing of the self that leads us arrogantly to choose barren pleasures over those divinely appointed to us. When Wigglesworth associates pride, luxury, and Sodom, he is thinking of biblical statements such as Ezekiel 16:49–50 (where the "iniquity" of Sodom includes "pride," "fullness of bread," and "abomination") and Luke 17:28–29: "they did eat, they drank, they bought, they sold, they planted, they builded; But the same day that Lot went out of Sodom it rained fire and brimstone from heaven, and destroyed them all." The picture of Sodom here is one of a community completely caught up in worldly pursuits, arrogantly indifferent to the wrath of God; it is also the picture of the world on the eve of destruction that Wigglesworth painted in his most popular poem, *The Day of Doom* (1662). By projecting the "Sodom within" onto the world at large and then describing God's fiery punishment in terrifying detail, Wigglesworth succeeded in gripping the popular imagination of his day.[15]

In the same year, Wigglesworth also wrote another poem that externalized the inner state explored in the diary, "God's Controversy with New England." A study of the spiritual malaise of the Puritan commonwealth, it offers a diagnosis that its readers found so compelling that it was ritually reiterated in the election sermon jeremiads of the years that followed. That New England as a whole suffers from the same "disease" as Michael Wigglesworth is not surprising to him, considering the intimate connections the Puritans believed existed between the individual and the community. "Some with the sick converse, till they the sickness catch," frets Wigglesworth in "God's Controversy."[16] Thus his own inability to love God and tendency to love men strike him as epidemic in New England, which he sees in the grip of both "dead-heartedness" and "carnality."

In a curious foreshadowing of the Freudian theory of homosexuality, Wigglesworth attributes the "perverseness" of his homoerotic lusts to a failed relationship with his father. He laments in the diary that because he cannot feel "natural" affection" for his father, he turns to his pupils with "unnatural" love instead; they are, in turn, "unloving" in their response to him, and are frequently "gone after pleasure" among themselves. Thus seeing his own plight reproduced all about him, Wigglesworth wonders how New England can be saved "if this society ly in wickedness, one generation corrupting another" (19). His personal failure to love his father, moreover, becomes paradigmatic of a rebellion against paternal authority endemic to the New World. God, in Wigglesworth's poem, complains that while the Puritan founders of New England "set at nought their fair inheritances" out of "love," their sons have sinfully parodied this admirable rebellion by overthrowing paternal authority out of "carnality." Echoing the fear of Hebrew prophets and English Puritans before the Civil War, Wigglesworth worries that the American Israel is becoming an American Sodom, ripe for "heavy punishment." This fear pervades a diary entry that records the epiphany that clearly inspired "God's Controversy":

wednesday morning, upon the obstinate untowardness of some of my pupils in refusing to read Hebrew, god brings to mind and ashameth me of my own pervers-

ness . . . both to my naturall parents and Achademical: and also I see that this
is the spirit (and I fear . . . wil be the ruin) of the whole country: A spirit of
unbridled licentiousness. (67)

Rather like a seventeenth-century Allan Bloom, Wigglesworth translated his frustration with his students' refusal to learn and to love him into a jeremiad about the
closing of the American soul.

The terms in which Wigglesworth most often phrased this lament derive from his
lifelong interest in medicine: as a young man Wigglesworth had trouble deciding
whether to become a physician or a minister. Although he eventually chose the
ministry, he retained his fascination with the workings of the body in his religious
life and work. He thus strikes one as Chillingsworth to his own Dimmesdale, to use
Hawthorne's *Scarlet Letter* as a paradigm. He is, on the one hand, the doctor of
penetrating insight, fascinated by the bodily manifestations of interior states; but
he is simultaneously the minister whose hidden sense of sexual sinfulness torments
him mentally and physically while, ironically enough, insuring his effectiveness as
a preacher. Ultimately able to diagnose not only his own spiritual affliction but
that of New England, Wigglesworth had the misfortune literally to embody the
contradictions and tensions of Puritan culture.

Wigglesworth's own "unbridled licentiousness" did not manifest itself as a scarlet
letter mysteriously inscribed on his chest, but it did find bodily expression in the
form of frequent nocturnal emissions or "affluxes" of "pollution." This affliction
resembles the homosexual acts he probably only dreamed of committing with his
students: both were fruitless expenses of spirit in a waste of shame. In the diary he
intimates that this "grievous disease" is gonorrhea, which has led some scholars to
assume that he suffered from a venereal infection; it is more probable that the
scholarly physician Wigglesworth had in mind the gonorrhea of classical medical
texts, which was not a sexually transmitted disease, but a chronic, uncontrollable
discharge of semen. Michel Foucault, in his analysis of these texts, points out that
the excess that characterized this kind of gonorrhea was thought to lead ultimately
to dullness, frigidity, sterility, and paralysis.[17] In the classical prognosis we recognize, as no doubt Wigglesworth did, the contrast between the positive and privative
constructions of sin: excess, filth, and disease on the one hand and deadness,
coldness and impotence on the other. It must have struck him also as a precise
physical representation of his inner state, of the alternate superfluity and exhaustion
that resulted from his attempts to discipline desire.

Just as Wigglesworth saw his sins reflected in the people of New England, he
saw the disease that embodied those sins afflicting the landscape. In the diary he
worried that God will "punish my barrenness with publick drought" (29), and just
such a natural disaster was the occasion of "God's Controversy," which is subtitled
"Written in the time of the great drought Anno 1662." In fascinating contrast to
Bradstreet's linking of soul, body, and landscape, Wigglesworth sees his experience

mirrored not in the natural cycle of the seasons but rather in the "unnatural" disruptions of that cycle:

> Our fruitful seasons have been turnd
> Of late to barrenness,
> Sometimes through great & parching drought,
> Sometimes through rain's excess . . .

Divine punishment, as always, fits the crime:

> This O New England hast thou got
> By riot, & excess:
> This hast thou brought upon thy self
> By pride & wantonness. [18]

The specter of Sodom is once again invoked, not only through the now familiar sins that Wigglesworth associates with that city of the plain, but in the form that punishment takes: "God goes on / Our field, & fruits to burn." Sodomy was seen as a sin of excess, the most extreme manifestation of misdirected desire for the world, and the destruction of Sodom by a rain of fire was seen as a fitting punishment for the Sodomites' uncontrolled lust. The images of the aftermath—a pillar of salt, apples that turned to ashes, and the Dead Sea—were all signs of the "barrenness" ultimately associated with such "excess" (much in the manner of Wigglesworth's seminal "afflux"). The other biblical example of divine genocide, Noah's flood, was also, according to historian Alan Bray, thought by some Renaissance writers to be poetic justice for an antediluvian outbreak of sodomy. [19] Wigglesworth includes both fiery and fluid forms of excess in his description of God's judgment on New England and opposes them with the opposite extremes of dryness, coldness, and sterility. The intense desire of the original Puritan immigrants for God led them to found a colony for him, but this desire, Wigglesworth suggests, has overflowed into lust for worldly success and pleasure. A concommitant panic has ravaged the New World, both spiritually and physically. The city on the hill has become the city of the plain.

But did Wigglesworth, the Fisher King whose sexual dysfunction created this wasteland, ever resolve his tormented relation to God? He seems to come close in his later poetic sequence, *Meat Out of the Eater* (1670). These verses attempt to solve "Christian paradoxes" like the collection's title, which refers to God's seemingly contradictory ability to nourish and consume us. Significantly, this Christian paradox also rephrases the cathexis of desire and panic: we turn to God as a lover to nurture and sustain us, but we are confronted by a being both terrifying and voracious. Wigglesworth's solution is to conflate the terms of the paradox, to accept the torment of his relation to God as a form of passionate intensity capable of lifting him from the sensual to the spiritual.

The recurring theme of the poems is the inevitable pain of spiritual life, which Wigglesworth calls "the anguish of the Rod." Because "God doth chastise his own in Love," a Christian must learn to take pleasure in the pain inflicted by God, and "the Rod in Meekness kiss." The joy of God's punishments render him ready to accept God's grace, just "as sharpest Winter Frosts . . . soften the earth / And it for Seed prepare / Making it fruitfuller." This receptivity to God's "Seed" is caused not by divine warmth or beauty, as in Bradstreet's verse, but by the "afflictions" that are "God's plough / Wherewith He breaketh us."[20] Wigglesworth's panic ultimately allows him only masochistic delight in a loving male God; by mixing pleasure with pain, and disguising desire as passivity, he can at last escape the guilt that haunts his spiritual struggles.

Wigglesworth ends *Meat Out of the Eater* with two contrasting images of the individual's relation to God. One is the familiar bride of Christ, a princess dressed for her marriage to God. The other is Jacob, who "took fast hold, and wrestled with the Lord. . . . / Prince-like he wrestled and would not let him go, / Until he had a blessing."[21] Somewhere on the spectrum between these two models—between the heterosexual masquerade and the homosexual clutch, between the erotic and the agonistic—Wigglesworth figures his own troubled relation to God. Modern readers may find a certain irony in the fact that this spectrum prefigures modern stereotypical constructions of gay male identity: as effeminate, psychological drag on the one hand, and hypermasculine sadomasochism on the other. Attempting to imagine possible models for the relation between the male poet and his male God, Wigglesworth produced the same polarized possibilities that American culture was to provide gay men roughly three hundred years later.

While Wigglesworth could not entirely purge "the Sodom within," he could finally accept the anxiety and suffering surrounding it as part of the process of salvation. In one of these later poems, he uses the now familiar imagery of Sodom's excess in a new way: "through fiery flames and water-floods," he claims, "we travel towards Heaven."[22] The pain of privation and excess, which Wigglesworth recorded in such detail in his diary, here becomes our sensual link with God, our assurance of his presence, and we must learn to take pleasure in it. This translation of pain into pleasure is made possible by poetic language; in an undergraduate declamation, "The Prayse of Eloquence," he compares the force of religious language, predictably, to floods and fires, to a "mighty river . . . swelling" with "excessive rains," to "languid sparks . . . blown up to a shining flame." The uncontrollable desire so threatening but so crucial to spiritual devotion finds its parallel in the power of rhetoric to move its audience:

> here to be surprized is nothing dangerous, here to be subject is the best freedom,
> this kind of servitude is more desireable than liberty. For whereas our untractable
> nature refuseth to be drawn, and a stiff will scorns to be compel'd: yet by the

power of wel-composed speech nature is drawn against the stream with delight, and the will after a sort compelled with its owne consent. Altho for a time it struggle and make resistance, yet at length it suffers it self to be vanquish't, and takes a secret contentment in being overcome. . . . Eloquence overturns, overturns, all things that stand in its way, and carries them down with the irresistible stream of it all controuling power . . . with a secret pleasure and delight it stirs men up.[23]

Wigglesworth here shows language functioning precisely as he believes God does when he blesses us with chastisement or ravishes us with his irresistible grace. The pleasure of the text is as perverse as the pleasure of one's relation to God, as each relies on an erotics of domination to translate resistance into consent. For Wigglesworth, poetic or "eloquent" language becomes the indispensable medium of religious experience, because it alone provides an arena in which desire is aroused and panic overcome by force and in which the individual's relation to God can be consummated.

Edward Taylor: The Poetics of Panic

The possibilities of poetic language as a solution to the problem of panic and desire brought on by a male poet's address to a male God were more successfully explored by another, more talented Puritan poet, Edward Taylor. Wigglesworth may seem to be dismissable as an isolated "case," one whose predilection for young men caused a disruption in his spiritual life; but an examination of the poetry of Taylor, another Puritan minister, quite graphically reveals the same pattern of concerns—concerns expressed, however, in a different and more original poetic idiom. Taylor's diary and letters reveal no secret attractions to men, none of the sexual confusion recorded by Wigglesworth; he comes closest to a sexual confession in a love letter to his wife, where he regrets that he cannot offer her his heart because it is already promised to God.[24] And yet his poems, which were private meditations that he did not circulate or publish, speak in terms similar to Wigglesworth's about the anxiety surrounding his relation to God, and ultimately reveal even deeper sources of this panic.

Most of Taylor's poems are what he called "preparatory meditations." They were written to prepare the poet spiritually and emotionally for his participation in the Lord's Supper, a central ritual of the Puritan sabbath and Taylor's lifelong concern. He not only saw the Lord's Supper as the primary pretext for his poetry, but preached a sermon series on it and involved himself in a long controversy over its meaning and proper administration. For Taylor, the sacrament was a wedding feast, both a symbolic consumption of Christ's body and a celebration of Christ's marriage to his spouse, the Church, made up of his individual brides, the elect. The contemplation of these mysteries becomes, predictably, a source of contradictory feelings not unlike those expressed by Wigglesworth when he asked God to open his mouth and fill it with Christ. The note of unrest sounds in the very first of Taylor's meditations:

> What Love is this of thine, that Cannot bee
> In thine Infinity, O Lord, Confinde . . .?
> What, hath thy Godhead, as not satisfide,
> Marri'de our Manhood, making it its Bride? (1.1)

Preparing himself for intimacy with this infinite, insatiable deity is the purpose of Taylor's poetic exercises; but they also reveal a pervasive anxiety about the transformation of his "manhood" into a "bride."

Because these verses were all composed for one specific occasion, they tend to follow a formulaic pattern. Most of the preparatory meditations begin with an expression of the poet's inability to love God, to feel the emotion that would requite his love. Evidences of the overwhelming power and availability of God's love are then considered, only to be followed by protestations of the poet's extreme unworthiness and sinfulness. The poems then end with a plea for God to intervene in some direct way that will force the poet to respond emotionally and enable him to sustain and express that emotion.

The reader is thus presented with something of a poetic anomaly: a sequence of love poems inspired by the *absence* of desire, a series of miniature epithalamia uttered by an admittedly frigid, apprehensive spouse: "Why wantst thou appitite? / Oh! blush to thinke thou hunger dost no more" (1.11). The poems serve Taylor as a means of self-stimulation prior to consummation, a means that ultimately fails and leaves him searching and pleading for another source of arousal: "Lord let thy Gracious hand me chafe, and rub / Til my numbd joynts be quickn'd and compleat" (2.23). The terms are often emphatically phallic. Bewailing his "impotency," he writes that his "Power's down born" (2.38) and begs God to "make Love inflamed rise (2.6)." Once again, panic seems to cause the poet's desire to fail at every turn, a predicament that Taylor addresses in quite straightforward terms in Meditation 36:

> I am asham'd to say I love thee do.
> But dare not for my life, and Soule deny't.
> Yet wonder much Love's Springs should lie so low
> Thy loveliness its Object shines so bright. (1.36)

The source of Taylor's shame reveals itself in imagery we have already seen in Wigglesworth's verse: the fires and floods that embody both excessive human desires and God's retributive wrath. One of Taylor's occasional poems, "Upon the Sweeping Flood," ascribes a recent deluge to God's need to "quench the flame" of New Englanders' "Carnall love." On the other hand, privative sin manifests itself in Taylor's poems as the absence of fire or water. The poet is "as dry, as is a Chip"

(2.64); he laments his "Lifeless Sparke," "Fireless Flame," his "Chilly Love, and Cold" (1.1). His remedy for this frigidity is to beg fire from heaven: "Lord blow the coal: Thy Love inflame in mee" (1.1). If God will not blow the poet's coal, perhaps he will apply his own to the poet's mouth: "a Coale from thy bright Altars Glory sure / Kissing my lips, my lethargy will cure" (2.73). The poet's spiritual dryness leads the poet to ask God to "ope the sluice: let some thing spout on me" (1.37). If aroused, the poet promises to return the ejaculatory favor: God's beauty will "enchant" his "heart . . . till't spout / Out streames of Love refin'd that on thee lie" (2.12). On the level of poetic imagery, the deity's angry aggression and loving grace, the poet's sensual lust and sacred love, have become indistinguishable: Taylor represents them all in terms of the same uncontrollable, overflowing elements. This imagery suggests a continuum of desire, from devotion to passion, from the human to the divine. But, as Wigglesworth demonstrated in his diary, the recognition of this continuity tends to invite an onslaught of panic and the failure of desire.

This panic is increased, moreover, by the suggestive sexual quality of the imagery in several of these passages. The Calvinist doctrine of irresistible grace casts the individual in a passive role, awaiting an infusion of divine love; to Taylor's poetic imagination, this belief requires what Andrew Delbanco has called "the sexually receptive posture of the speaker in his poems."[25] Throughout the meditations, therefore, the poet figures himself as empty, open, and ready for God to fill him with a fluid form of grace:

> O let thy lovely streams of Love distill
>   Upon myselfe and spoute their spirits pure
> Into my Viall, and my Vessel fill
>   With liveliness. (2.32)

> Distill thy Spirit through thy royall Pipe
>   Into my Soule. (2.4)

> Then let thy Sweetspike sweat its liquid Dew
>   Into my Crystall Viall: and there swim. (2.62)

Taylor's reference to the aromatic and phallic grass "sweetspike" is drawn from the erotic imagery of Canticles; it looks forward to the work of a later American poet who would call this same plant "calamus" and use it as a personal symbol of homosexual love.

If many of these passages possess a sensual richness that seems to belie the presence of panic, it is because their imagery of emptiness, coldness, and dryness suggests the privative definition of sin. In contrast, when Taylor is meditating on the positive immediacy of his own sinfulness, the poems take on an intensity of self-loathing. And this intensity is directly inspired by the receptive role he so often takes in his relation to God. "Man marry God? God be a Match for Mud?" (1.23) Taylor asks incredulously; the marriage of the divine and the human is to him as if "Gold" were to "Wed Dung" (2.33). Taylor is not merely imagining himself as a female "bride" here; the scatological imagery he uses strongly suggests that his protestations of unworthiness are in fact expressions of male panic at the prospect of divine sodomy. In the following passage, the image of "ravishment" obstructed by "filth" graphically represents the anality that is the source of Taylor's anxiety:

> Had not my Soule's, thy Conduit Pipe's, stopt bin
> With mud, what Ravishment would'st thou Convay?
> Let Grace's Golden Spade dig till the Spring
> Of tears arise, and clear this filth away. ("The Reflexion")

Or, as Taylor writes in another meditation, "Blesst Lord, my King, where is thy golden Sword? / Oh! Sheath it in the bowells of my Sin." (2.16)

The violence of this last image indicates a still more profound source of Taylor's male panic. He fears the volatility of desire and is at times repulsed by the prospect of its physical embodiment, but most of all he seems to fear that a union between himself and God will annihilate rather than elevate him. Leo Bersani has recently traced the roots of homosexual panic to "the heterosexual association of anal sex with self-annihilation" and with the death of "the masculine ideal . . . of proud subjectivity."[26] This diagnosis seems strikingly applicable to Taylor. "O! what a thing is Love?" he wonders in one meditation, and proceeds to describe its inevitable tendency toward destruction:

> It makes a poother in its Secret Sell
> Mongst the affections: oh! it swells, it's paind,
> Like kernells soked, until it breaks its Shell
> Unless its object be obtained and gain'd.
> Like Caskd wines, jumbled, breake the Cask, this Sparke
> Oft swells when crusht: untill it breakes the Heart.
> O! Strange Strange Love! 'Stroy Life and't selfe thereby. (2.66)

The imagery of the seeds that swell until they burst suggests tumescence and ejaculation; but the images of broken shells and casks indicate an orgasmic experience that is an internally shattering one. Another poem (on the text "Let him kiss me with the Kisse of his mouth") attempts to explain why God gives us such intermittent expressions of his love, why he does not wholly satisfy our desires during earthly life. Bradstreet, in her poem to her husband, showed that periodic absence could heighten longing and thereby sustain desire. Taylor offers a more troubling reason for God's reticence: we may desire more than we can bear to receive. Addressing "man," Taylor explains that God's magnitude could sunder the merely human, or shatter man's "pipkin," to use Taylor's image:

>Maybe thy [man's] measures are above thy [man's] might.
>Desires Crave more than thou canst hold, by far:
>If thou shouldst have but what thou would, if right,
>Thy pipkin soon would run ore, breake, or jar. (2.96)

God's fullness is more than commensurate with human desire; it could not only fill human emptiness, it could rupture the integrity of the individual. To be a receptive vessel before an infinite omnipotent deity is for Taylor a sometimes terrifying thought.

In the face of such threats—sodomy, anality, loss of control, the annihilation of the self—it is perhaps a wonder that Taylor could write about his "marriage" to God at all. And yet he did, in poem after poem, lamenting his lack of desire and trying to arouse it. In so doing, he created a poetics of panic, a literary style that allows him to stimulate his imagination and yet prevent the sexual implications of his own language from silencing him. Critics have often taken Taylor to task for his seeming inability to sustain or develop a single metaphor: in most stanzas, he skitters from image to image with no discernable consistency or direction. Whether or not one judges this poetic restlessness an artistic failing, it aptly expresses Taylor's nervous response to his own subject. In one stanza, Taylor will introduce an image of God's love streaming out of a golden pipe; the next will depict the poet as a tennis ball bouncing up to God (2.142). The connotations of one simile displace the connotations of the previous one, until a third continues the process of displacement. He dances around his meaning, but his frantic choreography often reveals what it seeks to avoid.

Objectification is crucial to this poetics of panic. Everything intangible takes on the physical form of an object, frequently a household one. God and his poet-lover undergo a dizzying series of metamorphoses that rivals anything in Ovid: one or the other becomes a spinning-wheel, a tinderbox, a rose, a loaf of bread, a purse, a key, a bottle, a pair of bellows, or a grape. Taylor derives this technique from the Song of Songs, which provides him with many of the texts upon which his meditations are based: in the double blazon of Canticles, the two lovers compare parts of each other's bodies to plants, animals, and landscapes. The effect, at least in Taylor's poetry, is to disperse the erotic response as widely as possible. Taylor probably intended to spiritualize his imagery by multiplying it to such an extent, but the verse that results can be intoxicating.

By articulating poetic bodies for both God and his own soul out of an endless variety of objects, Taylor not only overcomes his panic and awakens his desire; he ultimately blurs the distinctions of both gender and sexuality in imagining the relation between himself and God. Although, as we have seen, the poet frequently takes the receptive role in the poems, it is by no means the only configuration. Nor is it possible to define either the poet or God as exclusively "feminine" or "masculine." Such boundaries and roles are lost in the myriad images that Taylor uses to figure the consummation of his relation to God. The following suggestive passages from the *Preparatory Meditations* will give some idea of the scope of erotic possibilities Taylor was capable of imagining; his words suggest acts that we might expect to find in Sade *or* Bataille and conjure up images that recall Georgia O'Keefe *and* Robert Mapplethorpe:

> Thou Rose of Heaven, Glory's Blossom Cleare
> Open thy Rosie Leaves, and lodge mee there. (1.4)

> Lord, make my Faith thy golden Quill where through
> I vitall spirits from thy blood may suck. (2.82)

> I bring forth the best of Love to thee
> And poure its purest Streams all reeching Warm. (2.116)

> Christs precious bowells thee Embrace. (2.123)

> I'le in the Circuite of thy Friendship moove,
> So thy Warm Love enspire mine Organs would. (3.31)

> Lord put these nibbles then my mouth into,
> And suckle me therewith I humbly pray. (2.150)

> And both my Mammularies Circumsize. (1.3)

> And Circumsize my Heart, mine Eares and Lips . . .
> Lord bed mee in thy Circumcisions Quilt . . .
> And then these parts, baptisde thine Organs keep. (2.70)

> I'le be thy Tabernacle: thou shalt bee
> My Tabernacle. Lord, thus mutuall wee. (2.24)

It might be fitting to end this catalogue with an example of Taylor's use of the popular Renaissance pun on the "little death" of orgasm:

> Oh! Good, Good, Good, my Lord. What, more Love Yet?
> Thou dy for me! What, am I dead in thee? (2.112)

The protean eros suggested by the permutations of Taylor's imagery finds a correlative only, perhaps, in the polymorphous sexuality celebrated by Freudian Marxists like Herbert Marcuse and Norman O. Brown. The proliferation of images outraces panic, leaves desire without any single construction, and leads the poet to a kaleidoscopic polysexual ecstacy.

For Taylor, poetry creates a kind of privacy that makes such ecstacy possible, even while it emotionally sustains his public role. In fact, all of these poets discover ways in which their art can redefine their private and public worlds by blending the spiritual and the erotic. Bradstreet's seasonal metaphors and divine analogues lend her private life a cosmic significance more vast than that of her husband's "public employment." Thus the voracity of her hungering soul can find fulfillment even in the circumscribed life allowed women by Puritan culture. On the other hand, Wigglesworth and Taylor led eminently public lives: their spiritual experiences had to instruct and inspire the community at large. Although Wigglesworth's guilty secrets made it imperative that he sequester his private life from the world by literally encoding it in his diary, he nevertheless believed that his covert desires spread into the public realm. Poetry thus became a new kind of code in which to write about his own "unbridled licentiousness," a code that universalized his guilt and erased its private origins. It led him to a vision of America as a wilderness of misdirected desire and inexhaustible consumption, a nation that could only find salvation in punishment. Poetry offered Taylor an escape from this America; it created a private paradise, where images could be consumed with reckless abandon, where a mere poet could transform an omnipotent deity into multiform objects of desire. In the medium of language he could experience God's infinite fullness without shattering the fragile membrane of the self.

Once we look at New England culture through this particular lens, the vistas begin opening up rather quickly. How did the possibility of an erotic relation to God inform the rest of the Puritans' literary productions: sermons, autobiography, history? Could this approach illuminate other areas besides literature? Might it help us to explain some of the crises of New England history, particularly those that focused on women, such as the Antinomian crisis or the witchcraft hysteria? For example, might we explain the vindictiveness of Anne Hutchinson's persecutors as an outburst of panic at her demand that they embrace a "naked Christ"?[27] Perhaps still more intriguing is the contrast provided by the next great American poets. In the nineteenth century Walt Whitman writes, without a trace of panic, "I see dance, laugh, sing; / As God comes a loving bedfellow and sleeps at my side all night."[28] Emily Dickinson, on the other hand, addresses God as a "Burglar! Banker-Father!" whose depredations and tyranny she dreads.[29] How did the responses of male and female poets to a male God become reversed? To answer these questions, to trace the process of this reversal, would be to write a new history of New England religious and literary culture.

8

Hester Prynne, *C'est Moi*:
Nathaniel Hawthorne and the
Anxieties of Gender

Robert K. Martin

Serving time as U.S. consul in Liverpool, Nathaniel Hawthorne wrote a now infamous note to his publisher complaining about the competition from "a damned mob of scribbing women"[1]—a much quoted remark that has led some critics to speculate about the conflict between Hawthorne and writers such as Susan Warner or Maria Cummins and others to speculate about Hawthorne's misogyny. But an account of misogyny in Hawthorne that takes no account of his own and his culture's gender anxieties is necessarily inadequate: to assess his conflicting views of women, one must first place them in the context of his anxieties about his own masculinity. For, much like the very women from whom he sought to distance himself, Hawthorne described himself as a "scribbler,"[2] at once trivial (a scribbler, not a writer) and threatening (part of a "mob"). Even as Hawthorne's success as a canonical author increased, he felt that he was not the "man" he ought to be. In part this was a lingering view that art itself was an unmanly, hence trivial, occupation, while in part this anxiety grew out of his own success as a professional author—success that increasingly aligned him with the professional women he scorned and feared. If critics have rarely examined Hawthorne's relationships to women in the light of his own constructions of masculinity,[3] they have also rarely investigated the class implications suggested by that word *mob*, in which a Carlylean fear of the French Revolution conflates the uncontrolled political expression of the lower classes with the threat of an unbridled sexuality—a conflation already evident in "My Kinsman, Major Molineux."

Rather than dwelling with the biographical Hawthorne's attitudes toward women, I want to examine the "scribbling women" *in* Hawthorne's fiction, to look at some of his representations of female artists and their relation to changing patterns of gender and class in nineteenth-century America. By focusing on *The Scarlet Letter* and *The Bithedale Romance*, with their reworkings of the figure of the strong erotic woman artist and their triangulations of desire, I hope to make clear that Hawthorne's anxieties were as much about his intrusion, as a man, into a female world as about women's intrusions into his male world. This exploration of Hawthorne's response to questions of art and gender seeks to locate that response at the precise moment in the history of the construction of gender in which he wrote, a moment well-captured in his apparently indirect-free-discourse rendering of Hester's thoughts on the relationship of gender to historical change: "the very nature of the opposite sex, or of its long hereditary habit, which has become like nature, is to be essentially modified" (1:165). Following Hester's cue, I want to reexamine masculinity in its social and historical contexts—the essential task facing men as feminists, and one made possible by the feminist critique of gender and culture. As Helene Cixous has put the challenge, "woman must write woman. And man, man . . . it's up to him to say where his masculinity and femininity are at."[4]

Hawthorne's career coincided with major changes in the social structures of American life. His early dispossession, through his father's death and his mother's subsequent dependence on her relatives for financial support, and the consequent loss of certainty about his social standing reflect a pattern repeated frequently throughout the 1820s and 1830s as the traditional elite gave way to a new commercial class. These social shifts were closely linked to issues of gender, for the decline of a rural domestic economy, largely self-sufficient and based on home labor, allowed for economic expansion through *men's* work and required the increased seclusion of women and their transformation into objects of display. Thus during this period sexual politics meant the creation of a domestic ideal of women at the moment when the demarcation between "the domestic" and "the economic" was most rigid. Hawthorne might best be seen, in this light, as a child of pre-Jacksonian America who found it difficult to accept the radical reordering of society that made his own later career as a novelist possible. The violent tales of his early years ("Roger Malvin's Burial," "My Kinsman, Major Molineux," "The Gentle Boy") all give some indication of the sense of rupture with the past that dominated the young Hawthorne. All is always lost, they seem to repeat.

As the author of such tales for gift book annuals, Hawthorne's early career was at once genteel and feminine. His future sister-in-law Elizabeth Peabody thought his sister Elizabeth had written the early stories, and Margaret Fuller assumed the author of "The Gentle Boy," whom she had not yet met, "to be a woman."[5] As late as 1843, he published "Drowne's Wooden Image" in *Godey's Lady's Book* for a female audience. Hence, by birth and early professional profile, Hawthorne was still part of the genteel generation of Irving, even if he would continue writing long enough to be the friend and sometime muse for that decidedly "masculine" post-Jacksonian author, Herman Melville. By becoming a writer of novels (even if he called them romances), however, Hawthorne entered another world, a more competitive, public world that by its very professional nature may have seemed more "manly." Yet even though Hawthorne triumphed in this new arena, his triumph came at considerable psychic cost, since it meant betraying the fathers by abandoning the gentility of anonymity and domestic seclusion and by becoming— as publishing author and emblazoned artist—the scarlet woman.

I

Many of these historical tensions are evident in "The Custom-House" preface to *The Scarlet Letter*. Once read largely as a mix of anecdotal background and political revenge, the essay has been increasingly seen as an integral part of the novel, establishing its narrative voice and historical theme. But the essay does much more than that, and in ways that have gone largely unexplored. "The Custom-House" is above all an essay in sexual politics, as implied by Hawthorne's description of the most prominent feature of the building itself—an enormous *female* American eagle over the entrance. This eagle is treacherous precisely because, like Hester's *A*, its meaning is not fixed: although the eagle is "vixenly," she attracts those who imagine "that her bosom has all the softness and snugness of an eider-down pillow." They may soon encounter her ire, however, in the form of "a scratch of her claw, a dab of her beak, or a rankling wound from her barbed arrows" (1:5). Now it may well be that Hawthorne's main purpose here is political revenge, but the language in which he seeks to accomplish it could hardly be more gendered. Underneath the "feminine" exterior there lurks a fantasy of violence rooted in a primitive fear of the empowered woman. So it was, apparently, with the women of Hawthorne's time—that "damned mob" of which he complained to his publisher: you just couldn't count on them always to be ladies. Hawthorne's fiction repeatedly represents the sexual (and cultural) appeal of these "vixens" while regularly deploying plots that require their suppression.

Hawthorne was not, of course, unacquainted with the revolutionary women of his time. He knew Margaret Fuller well enough to express repeated fear and anger; his own wife Sophia was the sister of one of the most important feminists of the period, Elizabeth Peabody; in his Roman years he was associated not only with the Browning circle but also with the noted American sculptress Harriet Hosmer, the center of a lesbian circle of artists termed the "harem (scarem)" by William Wetmore Story. Such strong women found their way into Hawthorne's fictions, where, from Hester Prynne and Zenobia to Miriam, they occupy prominent positions. Hawthorne's works betray an extraordinary ambivalence about these heroines, even as his fictions reflect the cultural plot that will enforce the effacement of such women by the figure of the domestic angel. It is as if Hawthorne wrote over and over again his own choice of the invalid Sophia over her sister, expressing the fears of emasculation that strong women produced in him (and in his culture) while regularly failing to convince us that the sickly maiden was an adequate alternative either in life or art.

The dilemma of the custom-house is one that concerns not only men's relationship to women, but men's relationship to other men, for the custom-house is a male preserve, "a sanctuary into which womankind, with her tools of magic, the broom and mop, has very infrequent access" (1:7). But this separate sphere, like Irving's dream of life in a Dutch genre painting, is already a spoiled Eden, threatened, on the one hand, by the claims of women and, on the other, by Hawthorne's own sense of unworthiness to succeed his male "progenitors." Thinking back over the power of the past and reflecting on the absence of transplantation that might have improved the "stock," Hawthorne laments that the venerable "old trunk" of his family tree should only "have born, as its topmost bough, an idler like myself" (1:10).

These anxieties about sterility mark Hawthorne's career in the custom-house as a return to his ancestors, an attempt to rejoin the "patriarchal body," as he calls it, in "Uncle Sam's brick edifice." His scorn for his colleagues and superiors and his recognition of their uselessness barely conceal his recurring anxiety about filial relationships and authority. The Inspector, for example, is "the father," "the patriarch," but also "a legitimate son" of the revenue system itself as well as of "a Revolutionary colonel" (1:16). As we know from "My Kinsman, Major Molineux," to be the son of a revolutionary officer is to be at once patriarch and parricide. There can be no easy relationship with the past, for all Americans are in some sense "illegitimate" children of "nature" as a result of the revolution, the event that haunts this preface (and the event, not insignificantly, that is indirectly responsible for Hawthorne's discovery of the packet containing Hester's scarlet letter, apparently forgotten in the flight to Halifax by the royal officials). American history, then, is founded upon a violation of authority, a refusal of the king-father's rule; and yet descent from those original parricides, ironically, becomes a mark of legitimating authority, by means of which one becomes a son or daughter of the revolution. In the mid–nineteenth century, the "old families" increasingly drew upon such a claim of descent as a way of marking themselves off from foreign intrusions. If Hawthorne's Inspector is a figure of fun, a comic version of the patriarch, the older man's exaggerated virility nonetheless attests to the anxieties of the fatherless Hawthorne, author now of a fatherless book, of which he claims to be "editor, or very little more" (1:4). Hence the lustiness of the Inspector's voice and laugh, which come "strutting out of his lungs, like the crow of a cock, or the blast of a clarion"; nor are these his only active organs, for he is also "the husband of three wives, all long since dead; [and] the father of twenty children" (1:17).

If such biblical fertility is out of date, the Inspector and the Collector are both remnants of another era, one that Hawthorne prizes in part as a period *before politics* and before the decline from the past. The Collector, for instance, although hopelessly conservative and ruled by habit, has a "fondness for the sight and fragrance of flowers," "a trait . . . seldom seen in the masculine character after childhood or early youth" (1:22). If such figures are "patriarchal," they are not driven by the anxieties of mid–nineteenth-century sexual ideology, with its increasingly rigid division of gender roles. Hawthorne yearns for an older world of gentlemen who can retain their sensibilities, even as he sees their greater marginalization (violently enacted, for instance, in the conflict of the Pyncheons in *The House of the Seven Gables*). He, like Hester, is a victim in part of a changed system and a new *American* cultural identity that allows little place for the aesthetic.

For the custom-house is now the realm of the "man of business," a place where Hawthorne feels he *ought* to be. His sense of manliness requires that he leave behind "the dreamy brethren of Brook Farm," the "fastidious[ness]" and "refinement" of New England literary culture, and return to "[un]lettered intercourse" (1:25). His own fate there, his dismissal from his post, marks a renewed expulsion from patrilineal succession and casts an ironic shadow over the attempt to return to the fathers. Ill at ease among the Transcendentalists and above all unwilling to pursue the implications of their plans for social and sexual reorganization, Hawthorne has retreated to the world of "men," only to find himself judged wanting. " 'What is he?' " Hawthorne imagines the "gray shadow" of one of his "forefathers" murmuring to the other. " 'A writer of storybooks! What kind of business in life . . . may that be? Why, the degenerate fellow might as well have been a fiddler!' " (1:10). As John Irwin has astutely noted, the text's "implied patriarchal censure of the author seems to raise the question of whether masculinity is compatible with the role of the artist."[6] In this preface to a story of a woman scorned by her community for a sexual transgression, Hawthorne dramatizes his own inability to find a place to locate safely both his vocation and his gender.

It is striking that the descent from the past depicted in "The Custom-House" is strictly male. Aside from the eagle that guards the entrance (and the jocular reference to cleaning women), no woman ever enters these precincts—except of course the author of the *A*. In a similar way Hawthorne defines his own descent as a male genealogy, identifying his ancestors only as William and John Hathorne. In calling on "the earliest emigrant of [his] name" (1:8), however, he simultaneously reminds the reader of his willed *difference* from the fathers, his "embroidering" of the family name's spelling. Choosing to be a writer, he now rewrites the name as "Ha*w*thorne," thereby placing his heritage at a distance that he can control. If the fathers have made him a Salemite, Ha(w)thorne alone can claim responsibility for making himself an author.

This exclusively male genealogy serves as the framework for a story that is just the opposite, a story of a mother and a daughter with no visible father. Likewise the narrator of "The Custom-House"—clearly identified in many ways as Hawthorne himself—denies paternity, claiming to be only the editor and not the author of the tale, which is "authorized and authenticated by the [entirely fictive, of course] document of Mr. Surveyor Pue" (1:32). Not unlike the silent Dimmesdale, he disclaims responsibility; he didn't write it, he didn't conceive it. He can't have written it, because patriarchs don't write, they merely record, and because Hester's story is inscribed in a "rag of scarlet cloth" that requires knowledge not available to men. Consistent with her role in a female-authored world, Hester will conclude the novel not only the figurative daughter of Ann Hutchinson but a literal mother (of Pearl) and grandmother as well. We learn that she hears from the grown-up Pearl in a language that is private and unreadable by the community: "Letters came, with armorial seals upon them, though of bearings unknown to English heraldry" (1:262). These signs, known to Pearl and Hester, stand in counterpoint to those that conclude the novel a few pages later, which are written, like the letter, to assign meaning for the community. Hester's woman's tale is framed by men and their meanings, but gains a space within, a space emblematized by her own writing/ embroidering and by the letters of her daughter.

The custom-house is of course the site of Hawthorne's discovery of the mysterious package that contains the scarlet letter. The package, we are told, pertains to the "*private* capacity" of Surveyor Pue, and contains "a certain affair of fine red cloth" (1:30–31; emphasis added). This object is thus associated with the private domain increasingly defined in the nineteenth century with domestic femininity, and it is itself an object of feminine art. Wrought "with wonderful skill of needlework" (a skill associated in Hawthorne's fiction not only with Hester but with Priscilla and Miriam as well), it exemplifies an art form "now forgotten," as "ladies conversant with such mysteries" have informed the narrator. The letter, hence, is not merely of female manufacture but indeed part of a private, mysterious female realm to which one can only have access through the mysterious knowledge of certain "ladies" (1:31). In taking up the task of reading the letter, of reconstituting its secret stitches, Hawthorne thus inscribes himself on the feminine side of the boundary separating male and female "realms," allying himself with those who understand the mysteries of women. And yet this task of telling the tale is given to him not by the "female" letter but by the ghost of the old Surveyor, who appears like Hamlet's father to insist upon "filial duty." But if in his time "a man's office was a life-lease" (1:33), that authority has now been usurped. So, in yet another engendered transgression, in order to be a true son of the Surveyor, Hawthorne, it turns out, must be loyal not to the Custom-House but to his vocation as artist; he must repudiate "Uncle Sam's gold" and "the Devil's wages" (1:39). Only by making art out of gold—not by creating art for gold—can he revive a lost and miraculous skill.

Although the act of authorship is transgressive, telling this tale nonetheless constitutes a curious act of fidelity to the fathers; for it transforms the assignment of the letter by the ancestral fathers into a punishment with ample recompense, an *A* that can be made over into a proclamation of worth rather than a badge of shame. But telling the tale is also the metaphorical equivalent of putting on the letter—an act equivalent, as Hawthorne explains, to branding himself with a "red-hot iron" (1:32). Hawthorne's assumption of the letter aligns him not only with Dimmesdale and his apparent self-administration of the "silent" letter on his chest, but more significantly with Hester, for it is she above all who both wears and "writes" the letter.[7] However much Hawthorne may fear the power of Hester, he is deeply identified with her as an outcast from his own community—publicly humiliated, accused of improper conduct, and expelled from the place of the fathers.

For Hawthorne this outcast state is epitomized when he loses his job (the opposing party has won the presidential election), a state that he likens to decapitation by the guillotine. Deliberately leaving the image hanging between "literal fact" and "metaphor" (1:41), Hawthorne represents himself as at once castrated and assassinated, for the image invites itself to be read both personally and politically. Once more, then, the image of the revolution comes to mean for Hawthorne the death of the fathers, and hence his own, at least threatened, death. For as a "DECAPITATED SURVEYOR," Hawthorne presents himself, humorously to be sure, as one who has assumed the role of his predecessors, figuratively died for it, and now simply "long[s] to buried, as a politically dead man ought" (1:43). Has he not worked in the house of the patriarch? How then is he not guilty? As Hawthorne sketches the inevitable death of the fathers and his own ambivalent relationship to them, he seeks to escape the punishment meted out to them by becoming the daughter-bride, that is, by becoming Hester Prynne. For it is precisely the story of "one Hester Prynne" that begins to fire his imagination upon his dismissal from the custom-house, transforming that "unpleasant" "predicament" into a cause for "congratulations" (1:41) and, indeed, the precondition of the fictional recreation of the wearer of the scarlet letter that now follows.

It is in Hester's voice, therefore, that Hawthorne speaks as a revolutionary, as the parricide he faces execution for being because he is a man. Figuratively resurrected in Hester, he must assume his crime and add to it that of transvestism, both as the author of her tale, which he has "dress[ed] up" (1:33), and as the wearer of the letter. For in a passionate moment of identification, affected by a "deep meaning" that touches his "sensibilities, but evad[es] the analysis of [his] mind," he places the letter "on [his] breast" (1:31–32), thereby re-eroticizing the male body. Wearing her clothes and speaking in her voice, he becomes a hieroglyph of the crime of art by representing that crime precisely as a refusal of the gender boundaries instilled in everyday life, the habits and customs that have overridden the ambiguities of nature.

II

These issues run throughout the narrative of *The Scarlet Letter*, where art is repeatedly presented as a sexual crime, the production of an illegitimate child. Pearl and the letter are, we are often reminded, identical, given that the production of the text and the production of the child both take place outside the law of patriarchy. Who is the father? the ministers ask Hester to confess. But she will not speak; for to speak would be to give the child a father (1:68). The Hawthornean text also refuses acknowledgment of paternity; it almost obsessively insists upon the relativity of reading. The scene before the prison—as the crowd awaits Hester's appearance—"could have betokened" one thing in England, but in New England "an inference of this kind could not so indubitably be drawn"; "it might be" the scene of punishment of a religious heretic or a drunken Indian, then again "it might be, too," the anticipated execution of a witch (1:49). Tokens do not have fixed meanings in Hawthorne, where everything works by metonymy. Perhaps the punishment of Quakers, Indians, and witches can be seen as analogous things, as refusals of otherness. As such Hawthorne's text frustrates the desire for paternity, for certitude, by allowing space only for what "might be"; meaning, like paternity, is rendered putative. Hence, although often discussed as allegory, Hawthorne's art represents a world in which no meanings are fixed, in which everything is always a polysemous surface awaiting interpretation. This is of course precisely the import of his reference to hieroglyphics, and it is stressed one last time in the famous tombstone inscription that closes the work. Although John McWilliams, following a long tradition of Hawthorne criticism in his certainty if not his conclusions, claims that this final inscription is "the conclusive sign that the prevalence of the symbolic letter overwhelms any hope of progress,"[8] in fact it is a signifier without any fixed signified, a set of words requiring "translation" (as the Norton Critical Edition terms its gloss). The reader is left at the end not with a meaning, but with a pointer toward meaning in a language most readers cannot read. It remains another mystery upon which to speculate, like Melville's doubloon, another failure of the belief in the power to interpret Hester's life (or any other) for her.

The artist's function resembles Hester's fantastic embroidery of the letter. Her art may be presented as transgressively criminal, but it is also a response to a crime. Indeed, Hester's artistry is to write her "crime" in a way that disguises it, that makes it no crime at all. Hester does this by embroidering her letter, and hence disguising or displacing the univocal sense assigned to it by the letter of the law. Her embroidered letter is the permanent display of her condemned sexuality that unsettles the terms of her condemnation. At the same time, Hester acts in part out of a need to survive, for her art is also a very material means of producing income: she is, we should not forget, a single mother with a child and few opportunities for self-supporting work. So Hester survives by embroidering, that is, by copying her own story in a disguised form.[9] Her art, Hawthorne notes, "[was] then, as now, almost the only one within a woman's grasp" (1:81). The remark may be taken in a number of ways, but even its most misogynistic implications may be alleviated if we think of them in the context of Judy Chicago's *The Dinner Party* (1979), with its attempt to reclaim the "minor" female arts. Hawthorne clearly sees Hester as an artist, if in a different medium, and he takes her task as central to all art. Hester's art, though, is flawed, for it cannot celebrate passion: "like all other joys, she rejected it as sin" (1:84). But if *her* art cannot celebrate passion, *Hawthorne's* at least occasionally can, especially when he undertakes to speak through her.

And yet Hawthorne's is an art that gives with one hand as it takes with the other. His equivocations about possible meanings are echoed in his alternative plots. Although this double-plotting is especially evident in his treatment of strong women throughout his canon, it is most striking in *The Scarlet Letter*, where he locates all female attributes within a single character. Hester's scene in the woods, when she asserts the power and even sanctity of her love for Dimmesdale, is thus not to be seen either as an ideal or an object of scorn; Hawthorne speaks his Romantic desire through Hester as he also speaks his sense of guilt and shame. She becomes his voice because she speaks so clearly for the kind of freedom that Hawthorne would not allow her *or* himself. As a sexual outlaw, Hester gains a freedom of the imagination, and it is this power that Hawthorne simultaneously seeks to employ and control:

> Her intellect and heart had their home, as it were, in desert places, where she roamed as freely as the wild Indian in his woods. For years past she had looked from this estranged point of view at human institutions, and whatever priests or

> legislators had established; criticizing all with hardly more reverence than the
> Indian would feel for the clerical band, the judicial robe, the pillory, the gallows,
> the fireside, or the church. The tendency of her fate and fortunes had been to set
> her free. The scarlet letter was her passport into regions where other women dared
> not tread. (1:199)

As an "Indian," Hester escapes the social control and surveillance of the community. She has, at least temporarily, access to the forest—not the demonized forest of the Puritans, but the "mother-forest" (1:204) of nature rather than custom.[10] Made into a stranger, she gains the stranger's ability to see the arbitrariness of signs. It is precisely this estrangement that was foreclosed to most American women of Hawthorne's time, who were increasingly bound to the familiar limitations of the domestic. The fallen woman, like the prostitute to whom she is linked, sees into the mystery of the social order and understands at first hand its hypocrisies. Hester has, after all, slept with the minister and suffered the effects of his silence, as well as those of her husband's revenge. Hawthorne knows this and makes Hester know it, but then he takes that knowledge away: the brave paragraph that I have just cited ends, almost piously, "Shame, Despair, Solitude! These had been her teachers,—stern and wild ones,—and they had made her strong, but taught her much amiss." What a dying fall!

Hawthorne's scheme seems to require masochism; he simply will not let the "crime" go unpunished, and so he must ascribe the willingness to suffer to the victim. Hence, to the degree that Hester's embroidered *A* can be seen as the pained writing of her own body, in her own blood, we must also see this "female" masochism as the function of a desperate male need to "authorize" female desire—a need that, figuratively speaking, supplies the needlework that closes and then opens the female body to male possession. The analogy between Hester's bleeding body and her red letter is heightened, of course, by the original description of the letter as a "rag of scarlet cloth," with its associations of menstruation and defloration.[11] But while Hester writes out of her suffering, she does not escape it. Hester's public performance of her sexuality, enacted in the initial scene of the novel and repeated throughout her life by her wearing of the letter, confirms her role, woman's role, as the embodiment of a sexuality that is at once silent and always spoken. As such she becomes a marvelous instance of Foucault's understanding of the transformation of sexuality into discourse. Her every appearance is to speak her story, to repeat almost obsessively the story of her pain and loss, and yet never to complete that story.[12]

For Hester's story has no origins (no visible husband, since Chillingsworth chooses not to reveal himself to anyone but her, and no visible lover to acknowledge the paternity of her child) and is thus always self-made and remakeable. Her work is an art of "fertility" (1:53), her own and that of an endlessly reproducing, self-generating art. Forced to perform a role in the male drama of guilt and sin, Hester simultaneously plays her own part, refusing to speak the lines others have written for her. Her proud assertion of her *A* is an acknowledgment of the fact that even the actor or actress on the stage is always performing his or her own text. In a society that insists that silence surround sexuality, Hester's body becomes the stage on which she constantly refuses silence. What she cannot say is the one thing she is expected to say, to name the father. Hester writes her own text and remains a sign without a transcendent author.

III

The Blithedale Romance complicates the view of the woman artist found in *The Scarlet Letter* by setting up two sets of doubled characters, male and female. This doubling allows Hawthorne to explore two different stereotypes of femininity (and masculinity, although this latter aspect has not been much explored), while making room for a variety of triangular relationships. Instead of simply offering the "redeemed" side of Hester, Hawthorne is now free to present his male characters with two women, half-sisters as it turns out, who can embody opposed views of what it might mean to be a woman in mid–nineteenth-century America. The creation of the Priscilla figure is not simply a matter of proposing a weaker, softer alternative to the strong woman; it represents, as Michael Davitt Bell has argued, a cultural displacement in which sentimentality is praised against the challenge of women's rights and the possibility of social reorganization.[13]

Although Hester acknowledges that the possibility for change in the status of women depends upon a similar change in the cultural construction of masculinity, the subject is not given much attention in that novel. In *The Blithedale Romance*, however, it is a matter of considerable concern. The opposition between the sentimental heroine Priscilla and the Romantic heroine Zenobia is paralleled in the opposition between the genteel, refined minor poet Coverdale and the "massive and brawny" ex-blacksmith, Hollingsworth. Coverdale is the weak man, soft, pampered, a creature of the interior (note his "bachelor-parlor" [3:40] and "bachelor-rooms" [3:145]) and hence of what is increasingly designated as "female space," unable to function in the more open physical and psychological space of Blithedale. Changes in sex roles have implications for both sexes, but they run in complementary rather than in parallel tracks: thus the emergence of the sentimental ideal for women is accompanied by the eclipse of the sentimental ideal for men and its replacement by the muscular "brawn" represented in Hollingsworth.

Simple mention of the names of the two leading male characters in *The Blithedale Romance* should suffice to remind us of the dynamics of male relationship in *The Scarlet Letter*, which in significant ways contains the seeds of the problem posed in the later novel. Chillingsworth's "care" for Dimmesdale brings the two men into "a kind of intimacy" (1:125) that permits the physician to dig "into the poor clergyman's heart, like a miner searching for gold" (1:129). The apparent affection of the older man is but a trap, his motives concealed and intrusive, as he accomplishes by his medicines and his surveillance of Dimmesdale's body an act of penetration he cannot perform on Hester. The "prying" and "probing" of Dimmesdale's "bosom" (1:124) reaches a climax in Chillingsworth's exposure of the male breast, as he "thrust[s] aside the vestment that, hitherto, had always covered it even from the professional eye" (1:138). In this extraordinarily erotic moment, Dimmesdale "shuddered, and slightly stirred" while Chillingsworth displays a "wild look of wonder, joy, and horror!" Although this triangular relationship, replete with suggestions of vicarious sexual fulfillment and possession, is crucial to the novel, the text makes little of it. In *The Blithedale Romance*, in contrast, such matters are much closer to the surface and hence more anxiety-ridden.

Given its basis in the actual experience of Brook Farm's experiments in sexual reorganization, *The Blithedale Romance* not surprisingly recognizes a plurality of desires. Blithedale, Hawthorne writes, "seemed to authorize any individual, of either sex, to fall in love with any other, regardless of what would elsewhere be judged suitable and prudent" (3:72). And indeed almost all combinations do occur, Priscilla with Hollingsworth, Priscilla with Zenobia, Zenobia with Hollingsworth, Hollingsworth with Coverdale, and Coverdale with Priscilla. At the center of this erotic chain, one notes, is Hollingsworth, whose sexual magnetism is represented as transcending typical gender divisions: hence, although bearlike, "there was a tenderness in his voice, eyes, mouth, in his gesture, and in every indescribable manifestation, which few men could resist, and no woman" (3:28). Nor is this tenderness merely abstract; it translates into loving care for the sick Coverdale, who reflects that Hollingsworth's "more than brotherly attendance gave me inexpressible comfort" (3:41). But for Coverdale such a response also goes against the "natural" refusal of feeling between men. Hollingsworth's action thus becomes evidence to Coverdale that "there was something of the woman moulded into [his] great, stalwart frame." Coverdale's thoughts express, of course, an anxiety on his part that originates not so much in Hollingsworth's violation of gender categories as in his own. For it is Coverdale, after all, who lives the life of the "effeminate" aesthete, and it is Coverdale who, as invalid, repeats the situation of Dimmesdale. Finally, it is through Coverdale's paranoid vision—the product of his fears and anxieties about the place of a "minor poet" of leisure in a new world of social change and gender instability—that the reader views the events of Blithedale. Hawthorne's creation of an often unreliable narrator, I would suggest, relieves the authorial voice present in *The Scarlet Letter* of its need to temporize; the creation of Coverdale simultaneously permits Hawthorne to criticize an aspect of himself through a character many readers have taken to be a close likeness of the author. Hawthorne can thus "be" both the mocked Coverdale and the ironizing Zenobia and still "survive" as Coverdale when Zenobia dies.

Through Coverdale's eyes, then, Hollingsworth is made to loom as a type that would become dominant in sexology in two generations' time—the "intermediate being" whose female soul is trapped in a male body. Although Coverdale in his illness responds to Hollingsworth's ministrations, once he has recovered, he is quick to set these embarrassing confidences aside. But his efforts at repression are not altogether successful, as his jealous accusation that Hollingsworth is "wasting all the warmth of his heart" on "a closer friend"—his philanthropic projects— "than ever [I] could be" reveals (3:55). The jealousy that resents Hollingsworth's social theory as if a rival in love will be echoed in Coverdale's similar jealousy of Priscilla and Zenobia; he hates anything that comes between himself and his barely acknowledged desire for Hollingsworth ("I loved Hollingsworth," Coverdale explains, as he determines to "save Priscilla" from the blacksmith [3:70–71]).

Zenobia arouses even greater sexual anxieties in Coverdale than Hester does in her community, perhaps in part because the fears are filtered through the consciousness of Coverdale rather than directly presented by the author/narrator. Figured as the Oriental woman at a time when the Oriental was virtually synonymous with ideas of voluptuousness and feminine evil, Zenobia becomes the repeated object of male spectatorship and desire, as Coverdale's fantasies about her naked body perhaps most vividly attest (his sexual fantasies about Zenobia's "material perfection in its entireness" prompt him to "close [his] eyes, as it were not quite the privilege of modesty to gaze at her"). This voyeuristic gaze is as intrusive, as possessive, as Hollingsworth's more explicit attentions, although in ways that Coverdale disguises in terms of accepted cultural practices of spectatorship: "the stage," he claims, "would have been her proper sphere," since there she could have been a "spectacle" for "the rest of mankind" (3:44). The nineteenth-century actress, as such a passage indicates, offered a way of representing the female body at precisely the time that body was being hidden from public view, in a kind of compensatory cultural shift. In the end Zenobia's sexuality is grotesquely punished in the scene of her death-by-drowning, which transforms her into a kind of dark Ophelia to whom all Pre-Raphaelite sentiment is refused. It is no coincidence that Hollingsworth's iron hook, brought in to retrieve her corpse, mutilates her breast, even as her hands remain "clenched in immitigable defiance" (3:235).

The "demonic" quality of Zenobia's theatricalized sexuality[14] not only stresses her role as orator and political thinker, but her position as artist and thus rival to Coverdale. Hence it is telling that Coverdale dismisses her early on as a merely sentimental artist of magazine fiction—precisely, of course, what Hawthorne himself had been. When, for example, a name is sought to replace "Blithedale," Zenobia proposes "Sunny Glimpse," a suggestion that is rejected, in Coverdale's words, as "rather too fine and sentimental a name (a fault inevitable in literary ladies, in such attempts) for sunburnt men to work under" (3:37). The parenthetical point is repeated in Zenobia's tale of the Veiled Lady, when she says that she calls her hero Theodore "for the sake of a soft and pretty name (such as we of the literary sisterhood invariably bestow upon our heroes)" (3:109). The comment is hardly fair, especially when presented as Zenobia's own thought. Neither Margaret Fuller nor Elizabeth Peabody was a sentimentalist, and Coverdale himself worries about the implications of sentimental self-abasement. But *The Blithedale Romance*, having opened the box of sexual politics, is equally determined to shut it firmly.

If Zenobia represents a threatening feminine literary sentimentality in Coverdale's eyes, Priscilla embodies the age's new ideal of the nonthreatening sentimental woman. Her art is both minor and private—"pretty and unprofitable," as Coverdale calls it. The connection is precise, as Thorstein Veblen would show. Nineteenth-century women's work finds its beauty in its uselessness and, above all, in its exclusion from the market economy. Women's work had not always been "unprofitable"; the frontier housewife of an earlier generation made her family's clothes and contributed in a vital way to the domestic economy. In the cash economy, however, the useless work of women was an outward expression of their own exclusion from utility, of their existence as pure sign. But Priscilla's work cannot be called unprofitable, since her poverty means she *has* to work. It is Priscilla's initial "paleness," "nervousness," and "wretched fragility" that enable Zenobia to deduce that she is "a seamstress from the city," a working woman (3:34, 33); it takes a woman, not insignificantly, to read the signs that indicate Priscilla's poverty and her occupation, since the others like Coverdale, in "the obtuseness of [their] masculine perceptions," read her pallor as a simple sign of her spirituality. Ironically, the weak, fainting woman is assumed to be spiritual when she is merely hungry. Likewise, the text of her body, her "needle-marks," speak for the pain and the trivialization of her bodily anguish. These signs of her masochistic pain contrast sharply to both the sublimity of Zenobia's gestures and the way in which the older woman wears her sexuality, in the form of hothouse flowers. [15]

Priscilla's work is to make silk purses—a rather obvious joke, on a pig farm, about the impossibility of transforming the world. But it is also important to note that this work is performed metaphorically on her own body. "Her aperture," Coverdale says in ostensible reference to one of her silk purses, would "open . . . wide" "to a practiced touch" (3:35)—the touch, for instance, of a man like Moodie, the text's representative employer of seamstresses, who holds a "monopoly in the market" (3:84). Priscilla's fate thus dramatizes the fate of women's art in the nineteenth century, as it is transformed from the individual cottage labor of Hester to industrial labor for the benefit of male owners and taskmasters. Ever the victim of men, Priscilla can only turn her art in upon herself, creating objects that symbolize her status as manipulated organ—a vagina opening at male will—or as empty receptacle for the display of the gold earned by her own unacknowledged labor.

Appearing as the Veiled Lady who speaks in the "riddles of the Sibyl" (3:6) in a mesmeric performance, Priscilla might first appear a modern-day prophetess. Yet, far from celebrating the potential multiplicity and indeterminacy inherent in this Sibyline guise, Coverdale quickly moves to use his fiat, as narrator, to impose the assurance of a unitary meaning on Priscilla's textual significance. In fact, the novel as a whole is the record of Coverdale's attempt to construct a meaning, one meaning, out of the myriad events he observes or imagines. By doubling its female characters, the text has separated the angry feminist voice from the prophetic voice and thus made the latter solely into a conduit for male power. Hawthorne's masculine anxieties and fears, articulated via Coverdale's paranoid narrative strategies, are hence translated into a plot structure designed to reward the dutiful daughter/wife while punishing the independent woman. The fears of castration comically depicted in "The Custom-House" take on more direct significance in this text, as Coverdale's comparison of himself to Sisera, murdered by Jael, vividly attests (3:38).

Sexuality is regularly associated with death in *The Blithedale Romance*. Coverdale's hermitage, or treetop vantage point, is described in terms that emphasize this connection. The space has been created by a wild grape-vine that has "caught hold of" several trees and "married the whole clump with a perfectly inextricable knot of polygamy" (3:98). The fear of polygamy in nineteenth-century America, which reached a peak in the persecution of the Mormons, is the fear of a practice that rendered explicit a sexual politics that was hitherto only implicit. For polygamy makes the underpinnings of patriarchy visible, in a legend of male potency, suggested here by the "wild grave-vine, of unusual size and luxuriance."[16] Likewise, the Blithedale experiment, with its relative openness to sexual arrangements, awakens anxiety about a promiscuous male sexuality released from sexual sanctions; the "feminized" Coverdale no doubt fears how he may measure up among such "luxuriant" displays of phallic potency. Hidden in his hermitage, moreover—from which safe distance he may vent his phallic desires in voyeuristic speculation— Coverdale also signals the inability of romantic love to offer an alternative to the power imbalances entrenched in sanctioned heterosexual relationships: his vine has "lovingly strangled [the pine branches] with its embrace" (3.98). If the text views marriage with hostility at such moments, the reasons are not far to seek; for, as Coverdale explains, "after Hollingsworth failed me, there was no longer the man alive with whom I could think of sharing all" (3:99).

In regard to these ambivalent feelings, Coverdale is not all that different from the villainous magician Westervelt, however much the latter appears to represent the horror of male sexual power. From Hawthorne's earliest tales on, such mysterious figures recur, always imbued with an edge of sexual abnormality. They clearly represent the dark side of the increasingly regularized and tamed male sexuality of a domestic age. Westervelt the gothic villain, however, is also a fop, and Coverdale's response to him is a not fully concealed jealousy of his phallic power: "He carried a stick with a wooden head, carved in vivid imitation of that of a serpent. I hated him, partly, I do believe, from a comparison of my own homely garb with his well-ordered foppishness" (3:92). The figure of the fop reminds us of the slippery line between the feminine and effeminacy, indeed of the cultural and linguistic shift that transforms the word *effeminate* from designating a man who likes women too much to one who is too much like a woman. The power of this fear is suggested by the imagery of Coverdale's description of his view of Westervelt's rooms: a space repeatedly, almost obsessively, linked to anality. What Coverdale sees is a "little portion of the backside of the universe," its "posterior aspect" (3:148–49). But the space between the houses into which he peers is far from being sterile, as one might expect, evincing, rather, a "more than natural fertility" wherein the fruit trees grow "singularly large, luxuriant, and abundant" (3:148–49), not unlike Rappaccini's "fierce, passionate and even unnatural" garden, the "monstrous offspring of man's depraved fancy" (10:110). Having thus provoked Coverdale's forbidden desires, Westervelt's phallic presence reveals the extent to which fantasies of possession may be but the other side of being possessed. The fear *of* Westervelt is in large part a transposed desire *for* Westervelt, the darker, more sexually suspect version of the bestial Hollingsworth and his tender care. Coverdale, the "minor poet," as feminized male, fears that his own art is the means of his loss of potency, even as he fears that for a man to write is always to possess, that the novelist must appropriate his characters' voices if not their bodies and speak through and for women; if Zenobia is the artist of the future, what will remain for him?

Zenobia's art serves above all as warning. Her name suggests her double function in the novel, at once mighty queen and sign of a lost matriarchal authority and trivialized magazine author, like Hawthorne himself. We see her as storyteller in chapter 13, although only after Coverdale's many interventions and repeated reminders of her inadequacies. Zenobia tells "a fanciful little story, off-hand," in Coverdale's condescending phrase, adding that she is not as effective when she writes for publication. Her natural audience is apparently "the young girls" who call out for "a story, a story . . . let it be a ghost story" (3:107). Like Mary Shelley, however, Zenobia does not produce quite what is expected of her. Her story of the Veiled Lady, the story of the women embedded in the male narrative of Coverdale, is one that identifies male fear of the concealed female (genitals) with male anxiety and not with female evil. In her revision of the old story of the disguised woman who must be kissed as a proof of love, Zenobia sees woman as victim, as "sad and lonely prisoner," and man as unbeliever. For Theodore laughs at the tale and insists upon lifting the veil first, at the price of the lady's disappearance. Zenobia's tale, along with her ultimate act of veiling Priscilla, also reveals the extent to which the two women are rivals—not rivals in love but rivals for power. For what is enacted in Zenobia's tale is the battle over a culturally dominant image of woman. Priscilla's maidenly self must be sacrificed if Zenobia's regal, sensual self is to be allowed its play. The two half-sisters are caught up in a cultural and personal drama that can only end in the death of one or the other: Zenobia's death in the master narrative of Coverdale (and to some extent Hawthorne), or Priscilla's death in the (unwritten) Zenobia narrative, which is at least in part, of course, also Hawthorne's.

Whatever alternative plots there may be, that is, the one that would allow the sisters to be reconciled is not so much absent from the text as it is *refused*. There may, Coverdale explains, be "devoted admiration" of a young girl for an older woman, although "we men are too gross to comprehend it." But such affection, which in Coverdale's homophobic explanation approaches that of the "slave," must be attributed to literary effect, to the power of Zenobia's stories or tracts. Alert to the force of female friendship in feminist communities, Coverdale is frightened of its consequences, not only because of what such alliances might mean for women, but because of the fear that their bonds might have an analogue in male friendships. In lines of extraordinary ambivalence, Coverdale reports that there is "nothing

parallel" to women's friendship, at once "foolishly disinterested" and "beautiful."
At this point, however, he strangely hedges his bets by turning to Plato as his
authority and adding that "if there be" a parallel, it would involve the "youth" who
falls in love with an older man and who may expect "a fine and rare development
of character" as the result (3:33). Thus nineteenth-century theories of separate
spheres simultaneously provoked, while they sought to control, the possibility of
same-sex desires and hence the collapse of sharp gender distinctions. Women, like
men, must remain rivals lest they become friends.[17]

However loving Hollingsworth may be capable of being with Coverdale, the
blacksmith too insists upon absolute subordination when it comes to women.
Zenobia's outspoken declarations "in behalf of women's greater liberty" in particular
draw out Hollingsworth's sexism. In response to her heartfelt cry that "when my
sex shall achieve its rights there will be ten eloquent women where there is now
one eloquent man" (3:120), Hollingsworth counters with his view of woman's proper
place: "She is the most admirable handiwork of God, in her true place and character.
Her place is at man's side. Her office, that of the sympathizer; the unreserved,
unquestioning believer" (3:122). Such views make the devotion that both Zenobia
and Priscilla show toward him appalling examples of self-destruction. Although,
as Westervelt's allusion to *As You Like It* suggests, Blithedale is a kind of Forest
of Arden in which true love may be realized, this is a dark version indeed of
pastoral. Gender confusion, however much the source of play and ultimate self-
revelation in Shakespeare, occasions for Hawthorne the deepest anxiety. For the
rules of gender, arbitrary as they are, remain the foundation of male power and
female subordination; without them, Hawthorne hardly dares imagine the consequences. Hence his plot moves to foreclose the very possibilities that the multiple
relationships among his characters have opened up.

And yet Hawthorne keeps returning to scenes that provide a carnivalesque
transgression of boundaries, threatening his sense of the fixity of meaning and
character. As Coverdale spies upon the masqueraders dancing in the forest from
the secrecy of his treetop hermitage, he reports that "their separate incongruities
. . . blended all together, and they became a kind of entanglement that went nigh
to turn one's brain" (3:210). Coverdale wants his personalities, like his sexes,
safely separate, locked into their identities, not subject to change by the mere
shifting of costume. But there is something even more threatening in this scene, as
Coverdale imagines himself "a mad poet hunted by chimeras" (3:211), like Pentheus
murdered by the Bacchae. If it requires a rather large leap of the imagination to
locate Coverdale in a Greek tragedy, the evocation of the primal fear of destruction
by women who have given themselves over to Dionysus is nonetheless appropriate.
Coverdale is one of those who would deny the power of the god, and for this he may
well run the risk of death. His fear is not specifically that of the Bacchae, but of
all that they represent—the "feminine," the disorderly, the intuitive, the wild; and
he, like his culture, will police this fear by replacing the Bacchic woman with the
domestic maiden. In this masquerade he sees a kind of truth that has been concealed

elsewhere, sees Zenobia, for instance, as the armed virgin, as Diana hunting Actaeon, and fears for his survival.

IV

As Mikhail Bakhtin has argued, the carnival is a site of particular anxiety, since it collapses the boundaries of gender, allowing for a literalized realm of possibility and indeterminacy. And the carnival scenes recurring throughout Hawthorne's canon offer what the narrator of *The Marble Faun* calls an "awful freedom" (4:445), a freedom located precisely, as in that novel, in the space between the legs; the carnivalesque threatens the attempt to fix a stable self by revealing gender and sex to be more the products of external signs than of any internal "reality." Hawthorne's response to his strong fictional women is constructed out of a similarly mixed desire and fear, and it is accompanied by anxieties about how to be a "man." From the earliest tales, such as "The Gentle Boy," onward,[18] Hawthorne's sensitive males feel themselves excluded from the worlds of both men and women, see themselves as inhabitating some dangerous liminal space, not unconnected to the "neutral territory" (1:36) of creative inspiration that Hawthorne imagines in "The Custom-House." Part of this anxiety is certainly personal and finds its source in an unacknowledged, or at least denied, desire for intimate male companionship. But Hawthorne's career also coincides with a crucial period in the emergence in North America of heterosexual and homosexual identity, the one dependent on the other.

The construction of male heterosexual identity, in response to a newly independent woman and to the emergence, probably for the first time in history on a wide scale, of homosexual identity in the mid–nineteenth century, meant the increased sequestration and limitation of women[19] and rendered suspect all earlier forms of male intimacy. Both elite and working-class male cultures of the early nineteenth century allowed for widespread homosociality that included the development of ardent same-sex friendships and affection; their gradual replacement by a marketplace and industrial economy meant the replacement of such networks with the figure of the isolated male engulfed by the domestic circle. The domesticity that *The Marble Faun*, for example, so unconvincingly asks its readers to imagine as a bright future is in fact an escape from the dangers of a less rigidly defined system of gender and sexuality, a system represented by Hawthorne's recurring figure of the carnival. The construction of nineteenth-century heterosexual male identity, moreover, is dependent on a parallel construction of a submissive female identity; at the same time, as Michel Foucault has so brilliantly suggested,[20] the emergence of a new homosexual identity in nineteenth-century Western European and North American culture can be seen not so much as a step toward the liberation of a repressed self as a channelling of energies away from a threatening polymorphism.

Hawthorne's threatened sense of self in relation to these new patterns of identity— the new woman and the new gay man—may go a long way in explaining the multiple voices and refusals of certainty in his fiction. Putting the *A* on his breast in "The

Custom-House," Hawthorne is both Dimmesdale *and* Hester, just as he is both the self-ironizing Coverdale *and* the powerful Zenobia. Faced with competition from the women writers of his time, Hawthorne not only feared that they threatened his livelihood, but, more deeply, feared that he was finally one of "them." His anxieties thus bespeak a desire to speak both to and through women, a desire that might have allowed him to say, along with Flaubert, "Hester Prynne, *c'est moi*."

9

The Love-Master

Mark Seltzer

The Anthropology of Boys

The aim of the Woodcraft movement, observed its founder Ernest Thompson Seton, is *"to make a man."* For Seton, a cofounder, along with Baden-Powell, of the boy scouting movement at the turn of the century, the craft of making men was the antidote to anxieties about the *depletion* of agency and virility in consumer and machine culture. As Seton puts it in the first *Boy Scouts of America* handbook (1910), he began the Woodcraft movement in America "to combat the system that has turned such a large proportion of our robust, manly, self-reliant boyhood into a lot of flat-chested cigarette smokers, with shaky nerves and doubtful vitality." In this system, *"degeneracy* is the word." Hence if the scouting "movement is essentially for *recreation,"* this is to understand recreation as re-creation, as "the physical regeneration so needful for continued national existence."[1]

It's not hard to see that such an understanding depends upon a system of analogies between the individual and the national or collective body. "As it is with the individual," Theodore Roosevelt observes in his 1899 men's club speech, "The Strenuous Life," "so is it with the nation." And confronting the wilderness, Roosevelt continues, regenerates "that vigorous manliness for the lack of which in a nation, as in an individual, the possession of no other qualities can possibly atone."[2] Linking together anxieties about the male natural body and the body of the nation— linking together, that is, body-building and nation-building—Seton's or Roosevelt's program for the making of men posits not merely that the individual is something that can be made but that the male natural body and national geography are surrogate terms. The closing of the frontier, announced by Frederick Jackson Turner in 1893, apparently foreclosed the regeneration of men through "the transforming influence of the American wilderness"—a transformation that, Turner argues, makes "a new product that is American."[3] But the closing of the frontier also indicated a three-fold relocation of the making of Americans: a relocation of the topography of masculinity to the surrogate frontier of the natural body, to the newly invented national parks or "nature museums," and to the imperialist frontier that, as the cultural historian Ronald Takaki suggests, took the form of a "masculine thrust" into Asia and Latin America.[4]

What makes such a system of analogies *operational* at the turn of the century is a related, but somewhat different, conflation of the individual and collective body. "The period of Boyhood or the Gang Period corresponds racially to the tribal period," the 1914 *Handbook for Scout Masters* informs us: "The early Adolescent or Chivalry period," the handbook continues, "is racially parallel to the Feudal or Absolute Monarchial period with its chivalric virtues, vices and actions."[5] By 1914 such a correspondence of individual and racial development—the notion that ontogeny repeats phylogeny and that the biological and psychological evolution of the individual recapitulates the evolution of the race—is something of a commonplace.[6] Hence Seton's assertion that the boy is "ontogenetically and essentially a savage" or the prominent psychologist G. Stanley Hall's observation that the male adolescent's activities were analogous to imperialism, an imperialism that Hall described as "the ethnic pedagogy of adolescent races." The invention of adolescence at the turn-of-the-century—most notably in Hall's massive and highly influential *Adolescence* (1904)—is bound up with a more general anthropology of boyhood and pedagogy for the making of boys into men.[7] Such an anthropology and such a pedagogy mobilize the *relays* between the natural and national body I have begun to sketch (see Figure 9.1).

In the pages that follow, I will be concerned with the set of relations that constitute what I have called the topography of masculinity in America at the turn of the century. More specifically, I will be concerned with some of the ways in which anxieties about agency, identity, and the integrity of the natural body are distributed across physical landscapes. I will be concerned, that is, with the relays between individual physiology and physical geography that make up a national geographics. Here my examples are drawn from the popular literature of adolescence and the making of men produced at the turn of the century—specifically, Stephen Crane's novel *Red Badge of Courage* (1895) and the wilderness or "wilding" stories of Jack London.[8] I want to take up as well an apparently opposed, but, I would suggest, fundamentally related countertendency in these accounts of the national body.

These pages form part of a series of case studies in which I have traced the ways in which the body and the machine are coordinated in late nineteenth- and early twentieth-century American culture. I have been examining what the preacher Josiah Strong, in his influential *Our Country* (1885), called "the problems of *The Body*," in what Thorstein Veblen, among others, called "machine culture."[9] It might be argued that nothing typifies the American sense of identity more than the love of nature (nature's nation) except perhaps its love of technology (made in America). It's this double discourse of the natural and the technological that, I have argued, makes up the American "body-machine complex." And I want here to take this account of the traffic between the natural and the technological a step further by looking more closely at the "naturalist" project of making men.

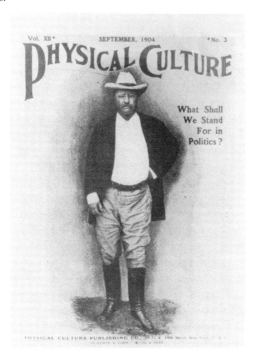

Figure 9.1. Theodore Roosevelt: Body-building and nation-building.

Making Men

The invention of boyhood or "boyology" and adolescence is part of the reasserting of *the natural* in machine culture, and, correlatively, of the modeling of the nation on the male natural body.[10] Yet if the reassertion of the natural and of the natural body in machine culture is generally seen as contradictory or compensatory, such an account is, as may already be clear, somewhat misleading. It's misleading, in part, because it is the very notion of *what counts as natural* that is being negotiated in these practices and discourses. But it's misleading as well because the reassertion of the natural in machine culture is not finally incompatible with the antinatural and antibiological biases that underwrite that culture. If turn-of-the-century American culture is alternatively described as naturalist, as machine culture, and as the culture of consumption, what binds together these apparently alternative descriptions is the notion *that bodies and persons are things that can be made*.

The panic about the natural body in machine culture—the simultaneous invocation and denigration of the natural and biological in "the culture of consumption"—are perhaps clearest in the double logic of *consumption* itself. Stated simply, the notion of consumption depends upon a condensation or conflation of bodily and economic states, of the individual and social body. Such a conflation is made visible in the punning relation between consumption in its bodily senses (as eating or as the body's being eaten away or wasted away by disease) and in its economic senses (as waste or as want that exceeds physical need). Put somewhat differently, one of the most evident paradoxes of the insistently paradoxical notion of a culture of consumption is the manner in which a style of life characterized by its excessiveness or gratuitousness—by its exceeding of, or disavowing physical and natural and bodily needs—is yet understood on the model of the natural body and its needs. The tendency to understand consumption on the model of hunger or eating—in Jean Baudrillard's terms, "as a process of craving and pleasure" or "as an extended metaphor of the digestive tracts"—might be taken to emblematize the simultaneous invocation and transcendence of the natural and bodily in the culture of consumption.[11]

Seton, for instance, understands consumption as a symptom of a perverse turning away from the natural. As he puts it in the first *Boy Scouts of America* handbook, "Consumption, the white man's plague since he has become a house race, is vanquished by the sun and air, and many ills of the mind also are forgotten, when the sufferer boldly takes to the life in tents. Half our diseases are in our minds and half in our houses."[12] Seton's account of the national disease of consumption, its etiology and cure, invokes a familiar opposition of the artificial and female indoor space of domesticity and conspicuous consumption, on the one side, to male and natural outdoor life, on the other. As Missouri Senator George G. Vest put it in his 1883 defense of the founding of the first national park, Yellowstone would serve "as a great breathing-place for the national lungs."[13] The return to nature thus appears as the antidote to consumption conspicuous in body and nation both.

Yet if the naturalist critique of the effects of an "over-civilized" culture of consumption seems clear enough, the return to nature turns out to be a bit more complicated. "Our business," as Baden-Powell put it, "is not merely to keep up smart 'show' troops but to pass as many boys through our character factory as we possibly can."[14] The boy scout character factories, like the "man factories" that Mark Twain's Connecticut Yankee Hank Morgan devises to turn groups of boys into brigades of workers, couple the natural body and the disciplines of machine culture.

For one thing, the scouting organization itself is something of a model of uniform, and uniformed, mass production. As David Macleod has shown, "its appealing and standardized program, its strategy of replicating small units supervised by a promotionally aggressive bureaucracy," made possible a standardized regimen in the building of the American boy. Just as the anthropology of boyhood and adolescence had reoriented the contest between adults and boys from "a few convulsive struggles for autonomy" to a series of grades and "endless little tests along a finely calibrated course," the character factory, like the man factory, standardizes the making of men, coordinating the body and the machine within a single system of regulation and production.[15]

One might instance here the coordination of bodies and standards in the rise of eugenics and euthenics, in movements of scientific motherhood and "physical culture." As the founder of the eugenics movement, Francis Galton, observed in his "Eugenics: Its Definition, Scope and Aim," which appeared in *Nature* in 1904: "Eugenics cooperate with the workings of nature . . . What nature does blindly, slowly and ruthlessly, man may do violently, quickly and kindly." In order to arrest degeneracy, Galton's disciple Karl Pearson argued, it is necessary to "increase the standard, mental and physical, of parentage." One might instance as well the popularity of the body-builder Eugen Sandow, by 1890 one of the most famous athletes in the United States, and of his writings (or ghost-writings) *Body-Building, or Man in the Making* (1905) and *The Construction and Reconstruction of the Human Body* (1907). As Conan Doyle (a friend of Baden-Powell and author of imperialist as well as metropolitan fantasies) wrote in his introduction to the latter: "the man who can raise the standard of physique in any country has done something to raise all other standards as well." These technologies of regeneration, of man in the making, make visible the rewriting of the natural and of the natural body in the idiom of scientific management, systems of measurement and standardization, and the disciplines of the machine process.[16]

What then looks like, from one point of view, a return to nature looks, from another, something like the opposite, a turn against nature. But neither view, it turns out, is adequate to account for the double discourse of the body and the machine in naturalism. In the course of his discussion of the primitivist pursuits that *"make for manhood,"* Seton, for instance, proposes a new standard of evaluation for these pursuits—proposes, in fact, what he calls *"Honors by Standards"*:

> The competitive principle is responsible for much that is evil. We see it rampant in our colleges to-day, where every effort is made to discover and develop a champion, while the great body of students is neglected. That is, the ones who are in need of physical development do not get it, and those who do not need it are over-developed. The result is much unsoundness of many kinds. A great deal of this would be avoided if we strove to bring all individuals up to a certain standard. In our non-competitive tests the enemies are not *"the other fellows"* but *time and space*, the forces of Nature.[17]

Seton's account of "honors by standards" enacts in miniature the rewriting of the natural body in the idiom of machine culture that concerns us here. What this passage registers, I will be suggesting, is the transition from *competitive individualism* and market culture to what we might call *disciplinary individualism* and machine culture.[18] The replacement of unregulated competition by abstract and impersonal standards is also imagined as the replacement of the individual and organic body by the collective body of the organization—here concisely registered in the bridge-making phrase "the great body of students." This is not, however, to replace individuality with standards (honors *versus* standards) but to make the achievement of the standard the measure of individuality (honors *by* standards)—to make individuals as *statistical persons*. But if statistical persons here are imagined as *un*natural or anti-natural (the competition among persons has become the competition between persons and "the forces of Nature"), the translation of the natural into abstract and disembodied laws of force ("*time and space*, the forces of Nature") points not merely to the unnaturalness of persons but to the unnaturalness of nature itself. Indeed, since persons are here personations, the personification of the natural as "Nature" indicates precisely Nature's unnaturalness.

Living Diagrams

The notion of the unnaturalness of nature has, of course, become something of an interpretive standard in recent cultural criticism. The rule-of-thumb that has guided much recent criticism might be restated in these terms: when confronted by the nature/culture opposition, choose the culture side. This criticism has thus proceeded as if the deconstruction of the traditional dichotomy of the natural and the cultural indicated merely the elimination of the first term and the inflation of the second. Rather than mapping how the relays between what counts as natural and what counts as cultural are differentially articulated, invested, and regulated, and rather than reconsidering the terms of the nature/culture antinomy and the account of agency that antinomy entails, the tendency has been to discover again and again that what seemed to be natural is in fact cultural.

What has sponsored this choice are, of course, the political benefits that seem to accrue from it: if persons and things are constructed, they could, at least in principle, be constructed differently. The choice of the culture side thus seems guided by the anxieties about choice and agency—by the melodramas of uncertain agency—that have marked a good deal of recent cultural criticism.

But as the examples I have to this point given may already suggest, this virtually automatic anti-naturalism or sheer culturalism does not come with a specific political program "hard-wired" into it. And the panic about agency—the "sublime" melodrama of agency suspended and recovered—reenacted in recent cultural criticism has something of a resemblance to the rituals of agency depletion and regeneration that, for example, "make for manhood" in naturalist discourse. The resolutely abstract account of "agency" in recent cultural work, like the resolutely abstract account of "force" that governs the emphatically male genre of naturalism, has the effect of guaranteeing the restaging of the drama of agency-in-crisis and the choice of the culture side. I am suggesting that these recent, allegedly "postrealist," accounts continue to inhabit, and to conserve, the forms and tensions of the realist body-machine complex.

More specifically, the tension between honors and standards registers what the historian of technological systems James R. Beniger has called "a crucial transition in human thought about programming and control between the 1870s and 1930s." This transition involves, in part, the shift from the "untrammelled market economy" of the mid–nineteenth century to the modern economy of systematic management.

The transformation of the market by increasing systematic and administrative control may be seen as the progressive replacement of the "invisible hand" of the market economy by what Alfred Chandler describes as the "visible hand" of the managerial economy—the general achievement of standardization, programming, and processing of materials, persons, and information. The "levelling of times and places" in a culture of standardization is part of the progressive replacement of animate or naturally occurring sources of energy (animal power and water power, for instance) with inanimate sources of energy; of living or naturally occurring styles of motion by mechanisms and by "mechanical prime movers"; and, most generally, by (in Beniger's terms) "the transcendence of the information-processing capabilities of the individual organism by a much greater technological system."[19]

These transformations in the forms of energy, motion, and organization are part of the process that Thorstein Veblen, for example, advocated as the replacement of what he invidiously called "the radiant body" by "dispassionate sequences of cause and effect."[20] The shifts from animate to inanimate forms of energy and motion, and technological "transcendence" of the natural body—these transformations, I will be suggesting in my considerations of naturalist fiction, make for the renegotiation of what Veblen calls the "vague and shifting" line between the animate and the inanimate in machine culture, the "discrimination between the inert and the animate" by which "a line is . . . drawn between mankind and brute creation."[21] But before turning to the manner in which Crane and London represent such a renegotiation, I want to consider briefly several instances that epitomize what such a redrawing of the line looks like.

The first is a brief fantasy that appears in Henry Ford's autobiographical *My Life and Work* (1923). The production of the Model T required 7,882 distinct work operations, but, Ford noted, only 12 percent of these tasks—only 949 operations—required "strong, able-bodied, and practically physically perfect men." Of the remainder—and this is clearly what he sees as the major achievement of his method of production—"we found that 670 could be filled by legless men, 2,637 by one-legged men, two by armless men, 715 by one-armed men and ten by blind men."[22] If from one point of view, such a fantasy projects a violent dismemberment of the natural body and an emptying out of human agency, from another it projects a transcendence of the natural body and the extension of human agency through the forms of technology that represent it. This is precisely the double logic of prosthesis, and it is also the double logic of a sheer culturalism that posits that the individual is something that can be made (see Figure 9.2).

The replacement of the natural body by the artificial body of the organization entails a transformation in production that is also a politics of reproduction. That is, the technologies for the making of men devised in naturalist discourse provide an anti-natural and anti-biological alternative to biological production and reproduction: the mother and the machine are, in the naturalist text, linked but rival principles of creation. These technologies of reproduction make up what I have elsewhere described as the "naturalist machine." One form of this competition

Figure 9.2. "Education of the Movements
of the Wounded Soldier," from Jules Amar,
The Physiology of Industrial Organization
(1918).

between principles of production takes appears in the redefining of the category of
production itself. Such a redefinition, in the naturalist discourse of force, displays
in part a compensatory male response to a threatening female productivity—a
compensation already implicit in such a counterposing of "male" and "female"
powers or principles. It displays also the "culturalist" desire to devise an antinatural
and antibiological countermode of making, a desire to "manage" production and
reproduction.

Not surprisingly, such a desire is clearest in the work of Frederick Winslow
Taylor, "the *father* of scientific management." The real achievement of taylorization
is not the invention of a system of industrial discipline. As Michel Foucault, among
others, has shown, the invention of disciplinary practices, in the army, the hospital,
the factory, the school, has a long history, extending throughout the social body,
from the late eighteenth century on. The real innovation of taylorization was the
redescription of managerialism and supervision in the idiom of production. That
is, the real innovation of taylorization becomes visible in the incorporation of the
representation of the work process into the work process itself—or, better, the

incorporation of the representation of the work process *as* the work process itself. Taylor, in effect, rationalized rationalization.

What this amounts to is in part a system of supervision by representation: as James Howard Bridge put it in his *Inside History of the Carnegie Steel Company* (1903), "The men felt and often remarked that the eyes of the company were always on them through the books."[23] Systematic management indeed involves a coordination of production and representation: "the process of production is replicated in paper form before, as, and after it takes place in physical form."[24] But it is finally just this distance between physical processes and processes of representation that systematic management manages to eliminate.

In brief, the radical transformation in the thinking about programming and control from the 1870s to the 1930s that James Beniger has called "the control revolution" involved, above all, a rethinking of the problem of representation, communication, and information-processing: that is, the understanding of processes of representation—the always-material forms of information-processing—as production, and the understanding of production as processing, programming, and systematic communication. As the systems theorist Niklas Luhmann has recently summarized: "The system of society consists of communications. There are no other elements, no further substance than communications."[25] One reason Maxwell's famous sorting demon (the hypothetical being that sorted fast and slow molecules so as perpetually to maintain energy in a closed system) seemed so paradoxical at the time was the basic difficulty in understanding sorting—information-processing—as work. And one reason such a paradox now seems so commonplace is the basic difficulty in understanding work as anything other than as a process of sorting, representing, or programming.

One effect of such a collapsing of the distinction between production and processing is a collapsing of the distinction between the life process and the machine process. Taylor's application of the principles of scientific management to the work process (in *The Principles of Scientific Management* [1911]) closely paralleled Jacques Loeb's application of the principles of scientific engineering to the life process (in, for instance, *The Mechanistic Conception of Life* [1912]). Both processes appear as control-technologies, as self-reproducing programs: "information processing and communication, insofar as they distinguish living systems from the inorganic universe, might be said to define life itself—except for a few recent artifacts of our own species."[26] And it's precisely that exception—the invention of the technological system—that redraws the vague and shifting line between the animate and the inanimate and draws into relation a transformation in production and a politics of reproduction. For if the modern engineer-manager "does not create, but moderates and adjusts," this is because creation, production, and agency are themselves to be seen as processes of adjustment, replication, and systemic regulation.[27] These are some of the ways in which the appeal of systematic management is neither reducible to nor separable from anxieties about the gender of production and reproduction.

It should by now be clear, however, that naturalist discourse registers such a transformation in production in terms of what I have called the double logic of prosthesis: in terms, at once, of panic and of exhilaration. The discourse of naturalism is situated at the crux of this transformation: at the excruciated moment of confrontation between bodies and machines. Such a confrontation is richly emblematized in the fascination with forms of representation—with maps, diagrams, grids, models, and pictures—and with the fascinated juxtaposition of bodies and representations. We might consider, for example, the well-known photographic work of Eadweard Muybridge, with its juxtaposition of bodies in motion against gridded backgrounds (see Figure 9.3). Muybridge's fascination with the technological replication of "the natural" appears also in the model he was building in his backyard at the time of his death—a scale model of the Great Lakes.[28] It is such a renegotiation of bodies, technologies, and landscapes that I want next to look at, very briefly, in the work of Stephen Crane.

But such a moment of confrontation might also be emblematized by a somewhat different set of relays among representation, discipline, and the transcendence of the male natural body. The calibration of bodily movements, the conversion of bodies into living diagrams, the practices of corporeal discipline that appear at once as a violation of the natural body and its transcendence: there is something like a resemblance between the mechanisms of scientific management and the invention of sadomasochism, also at the turn of the century. As Gilles Deleuze has argued in his study of Sacher-Masoch, *Coldness and Cruelty*, one discovers in these systems of discipline and punishment "a naturalistic and mechanistic approach imbued with the mathematical spirit" and also an obsessive imperative to represent: "Everything must be stated, promised, announced, and carefully described before being accomplished." One discovers, above all, a "transmutation" of animal nature and the natural body into the human and the artifactual, a redrawing of the line between the human and brute creation, a line here drawn by the whip.[29] There is

Figure 9.3. Eadweard Muybridge, *Animals in Motion* (1899).

perhaps something of a resemblance among Sacher-Masoch's fantasies of discipline in such writings as *Venus in Furs, The Wolf,* and *The She-Wolf;* Seton's cub scouts, den mothers, and wolf packs; and the accounts of discipline and bondage in Jack London's stories of coldness and cruelty, stories of men in furs such as *The Sea-Wolf, White Fang,* and *The Call of the Wild.* Following a discussion of Crane's work, it is the pleasures of systematic management and man in the making, that I will be looking at, in conclusion, by way of the work of London.

National Geographics

Perhaps the best known American story of the anthropology of boyhood and the making of men at the turn of the century is Crane's *Red Badge of Courage* (1895).[30] It might be argued that *Red Badge* in effect tells two stories at once, a love story and a war story. On the one side, there is an "inside" story of the "quiver of war desire" (55), of male hysteria and the renegotiation of bodily and sexual boundaries and identities. These insecurities about boundaries are registered, for instance, in the "bloody minglings" (104) that give the soldiers a "purchase on the bodies of their foes" (79) and in the "potent . . . battle brotherhood" (31) of an eroticized violence, of body-machines rhythmically "thrusting away the rejoicing body of the enemy" (101). These insecurities are registered also in the fears of unmanning and infantilization that make up this inside narrative: the threats of bodily dismemberment that are frequently localized (if that is the right word) in well-marked scenarios of castration (battle fields "peopled with short, deformed stumps" [71]) and fantasies of maternal engulfment ("as a babe being smothered" [31]). On the other side, there is an "outside" story of social discipline and mechanization, of territory taken and lost, of body counts and the industrial and corporate disarticulation of natural bodies and the production of the disciplined, collective "body of the corps."

It's not quite a matter of equating these twin stories, the psychological and the sociological. Nor is it, certainly, a matter of choosing between them. If the inside story and the outside story seem interchangeable, this is precisely because it is the boundaries between inside and outside that are violently being renegotiated, transgressed, and reaffirmed. This is what scenes of battle look like in Crane's story:

> Wild yells came from behind the walls of smoke. A sketch in grey and red dissolved into a moblike body of men who galloped like wild horses. . . .
>
> The youth shot a swift glance along the blue ranks of the regiment. The profiles were motionless, carven, and afterward he remembered that the color sergeant was standing with his legs apart, as if he expected to be pushed to the ground.
>
> The following throng went whirling around the flank. Here and there were officers carried along on the stream like exasperated chips . . . A mounted officer displayed the furious anger of a spoiled child. He raged with his head, his arms, and his legs . . . The battle reflection that shone for an instant in the faces on the

mad current made the youth feel that forceful hands from heaven would not have held him in place if he could have got intelligent control of his legs.

There was an appalling imprint on these faces. The struggle in the smoke had pictured an exaggeration of itself on the bleached cheeks and in the eyes wild with one desire.

The sight of this stampede exerted a floodlike force that seemed able to drag sticks and stones and men from the ground. They of the reserves had to hold on. They grew pale and firm, and red and quaking. (28–29)

The transgression of boundaries involves not merely the bloody mingling of bodies of individuals and the "moblike body of men" but also the "floodlike force" merging bodies and landscapes (assaulted "flanks," and, elsewhere, forming fronts and protecting rears). The "dissolving" of men into artifacts (sketches and imprints, "motionless, carven") also marks the uncertain relation between surface "reflection" and interior states: the "fitting" of inside and outside in the struggles of individual and regimental bodies to pull themselves together ("*in* the faces *on* the mad current," "*in* the smoke . . . *on* the bleached cheeks"). The fit of bodily and group identities is signaled by redundancy or tautology ("They of the reserves had to hold on") and by the erotics of a body of men "wild with one desire" ("They grew pale and firm, and red and quaking").

The becoming artifactual of persons, in these descriptions, is perfectly compatible with the substitution of the regimental and regimented body for the natural body—the military "making of men." And the "drilling and training" that makes men into members, components of the war "machine," also substitutes the invulnerable and artificial skin of the uniform-armor for the vulnerable and torn natural body ("He held the wounded member carefully away from his side so that the blood would not drip upon his trousers" [28].)

These primal scenes of battle are, finally, struggles to make interior states visible: to gain knowledge of and mastery over bodies and interiors by tearing them open to view. This is what the "shock of contact" (103) with the male natural body and between male bodies looks like, as it is enacted in the not socially unacceptable context of battle.

There is a good deal more that might be said about scenes such as these. For now, it may be noted that if anxieties about identity and virility are distributed across natural landscapes; if it seems possible to work out the transgression of bodily boundaries through the transgression of geographical boundaries; if it seems possible to restore or subtract agency or manhood through the annexing or subtraction of pieces of territory—then it's precisely the coordination of interior states and exterior and territorial states that makes such excruciated crossings thinkable. "The terrain of their rage," as Klaus Theweleit observes, albeit of a different body of men, "is always at the same time their own body."[31]

From one point of view, the description of such social processes in terms of natural processes appears as a form of *naturalization* of the social. But to the extent that the notion of naturalization has become virtually synonymous with mystification or disguise, such a notion is inadequate to describe these actions—actions that are at once identified with *and realized through* the reworking of natural processes and landscapes. That is, the channeling of "floodlike forces" describes at once the regulation of bodily flows and identities and the work of civil engineering. I have in mind here the range of work that includes, for instance, the culture-work of channeling, bridge-building, and canalization ("the roads . . . were growing from long troughs of liquid mud to proper thoroughfares" [5]); the strenuous exploit of Roosevelt and the building of the Panama Canal ("The land divided, the world united"); the emergence of the civil engineer as culture hero in the literature of the 1890s (in the novels of Richard Harding Davis, for instance). Freud's model for the mechanisms of sublimation that extend the culture-work of the ego into the territory of the id is, not surprisingly, the draining of the Zuider Zee.[32] Put simply, to the extent that the anti-biological and anti-natural biases of naturalism involve, as we have seen, the transcendence of "the natural" and "the female" both, they involve the transcendence of a female/nature, identified with liquid interiors and flows. Such a channeling of natural floods into orderly movements thus forms part of the technologies for the making of men we have been tracing here (see Figure 9.4).

Figure 9.4. "I took the canal zone." Theodore Roosevelt, at the Culebra Cut, Panama, 1906.

It might even be said that the processes of man-in-the-making assume something like the form of a continuous "flow technology." The effect of drilling and training ("he was drilled and drilled and reviewed, and drilled and drilled and reviewed" [10]) is to transform interior states, such as seeing, thinking, planning, and feeling, into visible and measurable movements of the body. (That is, to channel interior states into *esprit de corps*.) The disciplines of organized bodily movement that make up systematic management are made visible not merely in the military corps or in the time-motion studies of Taylor and the Gilbreths but, more generally, in the identification of the life process and the work process with the imperative of keeping things and bodies in directed motion.

This is in part because "physical movement, processes, and speed, present the most pressing problems of control" for industrial production. But it is also because the dream of directed and nonstop flow forms part of the psychotopography of machine culture. As the historian Daniel Boorstin puts it, "If Ford had succeeded perfectly, a piece of iron would never have stopped moving, from the moment it was mined until it appeared in the dealer's showroom as part of a completed car"— not that, if he had succeeded perfectly, the automobile would quite stop there, in the still life of the display room. "The watchword, then, was 'Flow!' "[33]

Or, as Jack London expresses it, "life is movement; and the Wild aims always to destroy movement":

> It freezes the water to prevent it from running to the sea; it drives the sap out of the trees until they are frozen to their mighty hearts; and most ferociously and terribly of all does the Wild harry and crush into submission man—man, who is the most restless of life, ever in revolt against the dictum that all movements must in the end come to the cessation of movement.

Hence the mastery of men—the *un*natural mastery that revolts against the natural law of "the Wild" that freezes motion—consists in technologies of flow and continuous motion. The mastery of men consists in "their capacity to communicate motion to unmoving things; their capacity to change the very face of the world."[34]

Men in Furs

There is perhaps no more compelling exploration of the cluster of relations I have been examining here than in the work of a writer who seems as far from the concerns of either machine culture or the culture of consumption as one could possibly be. But the violent confrontations between the natural and the cultural, between the wants of the body and the disciplines of correct training, and, most fundamentally, between the life of motion and the threat of a cessation of life and motion—all are nowhere more powerfully represented than in the writings of Jack London. London's work reduces these conflicts to their most rudimentary forms: the culture of consumption to "the law of the meat" and the disciplines of machine culture to "the toil of trace and trail." The difference between life and death in London is the difference between the body staying in motion and the freezing of bodies and motion. And the difference between what counts as an agent and what doesn't is the difference between eating and being eaten. London's writings enact both the fascinations of the body-machine complex ("Body and brain, his was a more perfected mechanism" [*WF* 203]) and the violence registered in such crossings or *miscegenation of nature and culture*— a miscegenation of the natural and the cultural most apparent, of course, in the figure of the wolf-dog and other men in furs.

The abstract and zero-degree white zones that London's persons, or personations, move across are governed by the dispassionate laws of force that London, in *John Barleycorn* (1913), calls the "White Logic": "the antithesis of life, cruel and bleak as interstellar space, pulseless and frozen as absolute zero" (*JB* 1094).[35] The abstract and emblematic character of this landscape makes explicit the links between bodies and territories, and the struggle to stabilize the uncertain relations between inner and outer states: the struggle, for example, of men who are "all equally as mad to get to the Outside as they had been originally to get to the Inside" (*WF* 253). It makes explicit also the paradoxical economy of London's call of the wild, what I have been describing as the unnaturalness of Nature in naturalism. That is, if "the Wild" and its White Logic are "the antithesis of life" (the enemy of motion), this is to indicate the unnatural or "beyond the natural" (*WF* 172) character of life (motion) itself. Such a turning away from the natural makes for what might be described as the compulsory unnaturalness or compulsory perversity of naturalist discourse. This perversity is revealed, on the one side, in the unnatural disciplines of the machine process and, on the other, in the unnatural disciplines of naturalist sexuality.

The twin principles of gold and the machine are the economic principles that put bodies in motion across the landscape of the great white male North: "Because men, groping in the Arctic darkness, had found a yellow metal, and because steamship and transportation companies were booming the find, thousands of men were rushing into the Northland" (*CW* 21). The delivery of men here indicates something more than transportation technologies. It registers as well what I have elsewhere called the perverse *accouchements* of the naturalist text: the antibiological and technological making of men and the replacement of the mother by the machine. If, as London puts it in *White Fang* (1906), "the white men came from off these steamers" (204–5), this is because the mechanical reproduction of men is explicitly counterposed to the biological reproduction of persons.

Hence London, in *The Sea-Wolf* (1904), describes Wolf Larsen's men in these terms: "They are a company of celibates, grinding harshly against one another . . . It seems to me impossible that they ever had mothers . . . they are hatched out by the sun like turtle eggs, or receive life in some such similar and sordid fashion." These celibate machines are "a race apart, wherein there is no such thing as sex"

(*SW* 583). Hence Baden-Powell, in *Young Knights of the Empire* (1916), describes the engine room of the steamship *Orsova* in these terms:

> And it is indeed an impressive sight to stand below these great monsters of steel and watch them faithfully and untiringly pounding out their work, all in order and exactly in agreement with each other, taking no notice of night or day, or storm or calm, but slinging along at all times, doing their duty with an energetic goodwill which makes them seem almost human—almost like gigantic Boy Scouts.[36]

The mechanical process of producing men is thus a process of systematic management—the formation of the disciplinary individual. And the system of *disciplinary individualism* involves not merely the individualization and specialization of work and workers (the "division of labor" and "special knowledge" that London takes up, for example, at the opening of *The Sea-Wolf*). It involves also the taylorization of bodies and interiors: what London calls the "achieve[ment of] an internal as well as external economy" (*CW* 25). It involves, most fundamentally, the identification of the life process and the machine process, the "coordination" of the body and the machine.

Not merely does the toil of trace and trail transform "sullen brutes" into ideal workers—"straining, eager, ambitious creatures" (*CW* 33). ("So he worked hard, learned discipline, and was obedient" [*WF* 196].) Bodily processes are identified with efficient machine processes, internal and external economies all in order and precisely coordinated.[37] For London, as for Seton, what this means, finally, is the bringing of individuals up to efficient standards through a mastery of the laws of "time and space, the forces of Nature."[38] London's accounts of the wild often resemble time-motion studies, and "the sounding of the call" appears as a "time-card . . . drawn on the limitless future" (*CW* 73). This is the unnatural Nature that Veblen neatly condenses in his notion of "the instinct of workmanship."

But the disciplines of Systematic Management are bound up with another form of S/M in the Klondike. One achievement of disciplinary individualism is, we have seen, the transformation of interior states and natural bodies into supervisable and finely calibrated spatial movements. Another and correlative technique is the rigorous segregation or partitioning of working bodies, spaces, times, and functions: the rank-and-file of bodies side by side, without promiscuous contact. One effect of these technologies is to rule out what Crane calls "the shock of contact"—the flooding of physical and individual boundaries. Or, as London writes of one of his masters of time and space: "He could not endure a prolonged contact with another body. It smacked of danger. It made him frantic" (*WF* 202).

Yet if these figures display again and again "the panicky impulses to avoid contact" (*WF* 248), they display as well the desire for the "smack" of contact. Multiplying at once the system of differences and (therefore) the possibilities of transgression, systematic management makes possible the hidden desires for a contact at once proximate and proscribed, a contact eroticized and rendered violent by this combination of proximity and proscription. Not surprisingly, the workplace in naturalist discourse is an arena at once of discipline and of eroticism, of segregation and of a promiscuous mixing across sexual, class, and rank boundaries.[39]

Such an erotics of discipline is nowhere clearer than in London's stories of discipline and bonding, of coldness and of cruelty. The counterside of the fear of contact is "the deliberate act of putting himself into a position of hopeless helplessness"—the initiate's self-surrender to "the love-master." He was, London observes, "in the process of finding himself":

> There was a burgeoning within him of strange feelings and unwonted impulses . . . In the past he had liked comfort and surcease from pain, disliked discomfort and pain . . . But now it was different. Because of this new feeling within him, he ofttimes elected discomfort and pain for the sake of his god . . . It was an expression of perfect confidence, of absolute self-surrender, as though he said: 'I put myself into thy hands. Work thou thy will with me.' " (*WF* 244, 248)

Learning to love pain and the godlike hand of his master, White Fang learns to love at once the pleasure of unnatural acts (acts contrary to every "mandate of his instinct") and the pain of turning from "the natural" to "the cultural." And since the notion of a turning away or perversion from the natural to the cultural can scarcely be separated from modern sexuality "as such," what White Fang learns in learning to love pain are the culturalist possibilities of love "as such."[40]

Which is not to say that London merely represents the compulsory perversity of naturalist sexuality in the disguised and acceptable form of the animal fable. The "naturalization" of the disciplines of machine culture is, I have argued, inseparable from the redrawing of the uncertain line between the human and the animal, between "mankind" and "brute creation." Along the same lines, London's stories of men in furs make utterly explicit what I have been describing as the transcendence of the natural body in the naturalist project of making men. I want to close by taking up, very briefly, a somewhat different implication of such stories of men in furs and of what might be called naturalist *skin games* generally.

Writing in 1859 about the recent technological achievement of photography, Oliver Wendell Holmes described that achievement in these startling terms:

> Form is henceforth divorced from matter . . . We have got the fruit of creation now, and need not trouble ourselves with the core. Every conceivable object of Nature and Art will soon scale off its surface for us. Men will hunt all curious, beautiful, grand objects, as they hunt cattle in South America, for their skins and leave the carcasses as of little worth.[41]

It might be suggested that if photography is the realist form of representation par excellence, taxidermy is the form of representation proper to naturalism. There is something of a continuity between Holmes' celebration of the ruthlessly superficial hunting and skinning with a camera and the dioramas of stilled life that make up, for example, the visual communion between "man" and "nature" in the Roosevelt Memorial of the American Museum of Natural History.[42] And there is something of a continuity between these exhibitions of typical Nature captured by the naturalist art of taxidermy—visual displays that seem to hover midway between the *tableau vivant* and the *nature morte*—and the representation of the panic about virility and generation in Hemingway's novel *The Sun Also Rises* (1926). I have in mind in particular the scene in that novel which reads that panic through the display of stuffed dogs in a taxidermist's shop window, a scene that concisely draws into relation the still life of the market and the skin games of naturalism: "Simple exchange of values. You give them money. They give you a stuffed dog."[43]

Jack London's *The Sea-Wolf* tells the story of the regeneration of the effeminate writer, Humprey Van Weyden, through his trials aboard the ship captained by the eponymous Wolf Larsen. The work of the ship is the taking of skins. Following the migration of the rookeries or breeding colonies, the ship "travelled with it, ravaging and destroying, flinging the naked carcasses to the shark and salting down the skins so that they might later adorn the fair shoulders of the women of the cities" (*SW* 603). The making of Van Weyden into a man ("a master of matter") involves not merely the slaughter of breeding seals ("a flank attack on the nearest harem" [*SW* 709]) but, above all, the solution to a problem in mechanics—the resetting of the fallen masts of the ship. As Van Weyden expresses it:

> But where were we to begin? If there had been one mast standing, something high up to which to fasten blocks and tackles! But there was nothing. It reminded me of the problem of lifting oneself by one's bootstraps. I understood the mechanics of levers; but where was I to get a fulcrum? (*SW* 732)

Not surprisingly, the Archimedean paradox is also the paradox of the *self-made man*. The problem in mechanics is the appropriate form of the making of men in machine culture, the form of virgin birth proper to that culture. As Van Weyden's "mate" Maud declares: "I can scarcely bring myself to realize that that great mast is really up and in; that you have lifted it from the water, swung it through the air, and deposited it here where it belongs" (*SW* 758). This is, that is, what sex in machine culture looks like.

But the making of Van Weyden parallels what seems to be the *un*making of Wolf Larsen. Larsen is at once sadistic (his command was "like the lash of a whip" [*SW* 497]) and the perfect specimen of the natural body of man ("I had never before seen him stripped, and the sight of his body quite took my breath away" [*SW* 593]). Larsen's power, however, is "a thing apart from his physical semblance" (*SW* 494). Stricken blind and progressively motionless in a process of physical degeneration that parallels Van Weyden's regeneration, Larsen is at once "imprisoned somewhere within that flesh" and in the process of "rising above the flesh" (*SW* 754). London's rudimentary lessons in the mind-body problem thus make visible the reduction of life to motion and to the natural body *and* the transcendence of the natural that "proved our mastery over matter" (*SW* 767). If the flesh was quite dead, yet "the man of him was not changed" (*SW* 754): "it was disembodied . . . It knew no body" (*SW* 764).

This process of transcendence is a process of transcending the natural and the female both. It is, finally, a matter of mechanics. "His body," London writes of Larsen, "thanks to his Scandinavian stock, was fair as the fairest woman's" (*SW* 593). But this fair and womanly skin is a natural cover that barely conceals something else entirely: "I remember him putting his hand up . . . and my watching the biceps move like a living thing under its white sheath" (*SW* 593). The power that moves "like" a living thing, under the white male skin, is thus only the semblance or reproduction of life. This male reproduction of life is thus revealed with the stripping off of that semblance of natural life and natural motion and with the achievement of unnatural life and unnatural motion: "I did not argue. I had seen the mechanism of the primitive fighting beast, and I was as strongly impressed as if I had seen the engines of a great battleship or Atlantic liner" (*SW* 594). This is, that is, what the unnatural body of man looks like. The stripping away of skins is thus the perpetual reminder of the difference between the natural and the technological. But it is ultimately and more powerfully the rewriting of this difference: the perpetual redemonstration of the unnaturalness of Nature—of "the mechanism of the primitive." "Under the skin," Artaud writes, "the body is an overheated factory."[44]

III

Cleaning Out the Closet(s)

10

Are We (Not) What We Are Becoming? "Gay" "Identity," "Gay Studies," and the Disciplining of Knowledge

Ed Cohen

(New York, Summer, 1989)

As I sit down to elaborate the text of a paper I gave last fall at the Second Annual Conference of the Lesbian and Gay Studies Center at Yale for this collection of critical essays, I am confounded by how quickly things have changed so much—for me as a gay man, for the profession of literary studies in America, for me as a professional academic, for gay professors, and especially for academics professing "gayness." Reflecting back on the months since that paper was first written, I am highly conscious that these personal and historical dynamics have become so thoroughly foregrounded in my own life that were I not a well-versed critical (though optimistic) "skeptic," I might be lulled into believing in "progress" again. During the last twelve months, I have turned thirty; moved from San Francisco to New York City; completed a highly enjoyable first year as a tenure-track assistant professor; managed to write a number of talks and articles, all well received if not (yet) published; been solicited to write this as well as several other new "gay studies" pieces; and garnered not one but three contracts for my first book. Furthermore, all this occurred in the shadow of the most emotionally demanding part of my life, where in therapy, body work, meditation, yoga, and especially among friends and colleagues, I am attempting to imagine and create for myself an urban male sexuality that affirms the desirability of my "gayness" in late twentieth-century, postmodern, "postfeminist," post-Reagan, post-AIDS America. But let's not talk only about me.

The reason I am beginning here with my own life story is only partly narcissistic. Indeed, I am somewhat embarrassed by this rhetorical strategy, for I fear being thought boastful or immodest. However, by way of apology I will claim (and hope you will discern) that my public acts of self-reflection also serve as an acknowledgment of gratitude. Since if "I" know anything, *I know* that what I perceive as my incredible good fortune is itself largely indebted to the struggle of those who, both before and along with me, struggle to make heretofore "ec-centric" experiences not only visible but intelligible. In this historical context, my emerging, Jewish, academic, gay male "I" is necessarily part of a larger configuration of shifting power relations that over the last one hundred years have made and are making "experiences" such as mine possible to imagine, let alone write about or publish. Specific to the narratives of gay men, my ability to write about sexuality *as a gay man who is accorded the legitimacy if not the authority of academic privilege* is so novel that I still sometimes wake up in fear that it is really only a dream. For, as the text of my Yale talk—revised and reprised below—attempts to illustrate, such fear is not only oneiric but historical. It is in order to begin to work through this fear, then, that I take this occasion of re-vision to engage with and to question both the parameters of my own work as a "gay" academic and the emerging frameworks for "gay studies" more generally.

In the two and a half years since I first (unsuccessfully) sought an academic job as an openly gay man writing and teaching about the historical articulations of gender, class, age, and nationality, my work and work like mine has moved from institutional obscurity and obliquity to, if not (yet) legitimacy, at least tolerability. During this time several major research institutions in the United States (Yale, the City University of New York, and Duke having the highest profile) have created epistemological as well as bureaucratic and organizational spaces for what is being openly called "gay" or "lesbian and gay" studies. A number of "respectable" journals whose contents effectively define the "acceptable" terrain of critical debate within American literary studies (e.g., *PMLA, Critical Inquiry, South Atlantic Quarterly*) have begun to include articles or issues devoted to examining the cultural manifestations and transformations of emotional and erotic relations between people of the same sex.[1] The recent hirings of gay and lesbian junior faculty working on issues of gender as gay men and lesbians appear to signal the penetration of such work into the institutional rubrics that constitute our disciplines—although the "reality" of this appearance will be ascertained only as these assistant professors move towards and, I hope, through the tenure process. Perhaps most promising, academic publishers have begun to recognize both the legitimacy and marketability of books about gay and lesbian lives, artifacts, and meanings, thereby making such texts widely accessible (if not affordable) and concomitantly affirming the viability of future projects. As welcome as these changes may be, however, if we recognize that they simultaneously frame and define the processes through which "lesbian and gay studies" seem to be/coming in American universities today, we will find that they also raise difficult questions about what it is "we" are "becoming."

Since such prospective questions are often least effectively posed in the abstract, being better considered in their—painful as well as pleasurable—concreteness, I will take as a heuristic example one of my favorite (and most hated) self-obsessions: getting published. Certainly those of us playing the academic game today know only too well that this obsession is not just personal but also structural. However, for those of us recently entering and working in the profession as gay men and lesbians, the current, extraordinarily high, professional expectations for written "productivity," combined with the difficulties of publishing in a not (yet) fully legitimated field—whose legitimation ironically derives in large part from publica-tion—compounds the practical, political, and symbolic stakes of the famous dictum "publish or perish." Necessarily, then, this stressful context both consciously and unconsciously frames the choices we make concerning what and how we research, write, and teach. Hence, the specific practices (not to mention ambitions, fears, beliefs, and desires) through which we go about constituting what seems to be coalescing as a newly discernable field of inquiry are inextricably linked to the creation of our personal and professional "selves." What we are beginning to call "gay and lesbian studies" is constantly constrained and enabled by the exigencies of those institutional formations of knowledge along, between, and around which we are moving. Publishing is certainly only one of many such formations, but given its significance both for the dissemination of new information and critical frameworks and for the creation and perpetuation of gay and lesbian academics qua academics, its importance cannot be underestimated.

As a way of specifying the kinds of issues raised by the necessity to publish for the "becoming" of "lesbian and gay studies," let me recount a personal story concerning the trials leading up to the appearance of my first "major" article, an event that was crucial to my becoming a viable job candidate. Between April 1986 and October 1987, I had the good fortune as a graduate student to survive the process of submission, revision, acceptance, and publication for one of the first "gay" articles to appear in that American bastion of literary legitimation, *PMLA*.[2] An incredible academic rite of passage, this process generated a plethora of frustrations, insights, and questions about the possibilities of being and working "out" in the profession. Allow me to be clear from the start: I am grateful to all those who made it possible for me to have my essay appear in this context. The staff and the board of *PMLA* were consistently encouraging and understanding of my difficulties in complying with arduous and confusing editorial demands. Yet while acknowledging the generosity of the individuals who worked with me and the real improvements they helped to achieve in my essay, I also want to point to the structural constraints that delimited how "gay" my piece could appear in this (con)text.

PMLA's process of "blind submission" requires that all articles offered to the journal be read anonymously by two scholars in the field in which they are written. In this case, since my essay focused on two books associated with Oscar Wilde (*The Picture of Dorian Gray* and *Teleny*), it was first sent to a "Victorianist" and then to a gay male reviewer whose professional "expertise" is in nineteenth-century American literature. Both readers provided wonderful advice for revision and recommended that the revised essay be considered further by the editorial board. At this point, as a barely published graduate student who was facing the upcoming job market for the first time, my joy at passing this initial stage of *PMLA*'s acceptance process was hardly containable. However, even at such an exuberant moment the dissymmetry between the categories ascribed to my readers' institutional "identities" gave me pause. What did it mean for my essay—which examines the strategic polyvalence of a late nineteenth-century text written for the dominant literary market by a "subcultural" author whose sexual subculture existed neither legally nor licitly—to be considered first from the dominant perspective of the contemporary literary studies market (i.e., historical periodization within national literatures) and then subsequently from the perspective of an emergent "subcultural" professional identity? In other words, how did my essay's movement through the process of institutional legitimation (which was the immediate effect of its publication, as I will recount below) position it at/as the intersection of canonical and ec-centric frameworks? And moreover did such positioning (re)produce, interrupt, or fail to disturb the inevitable privileging of center over margins?

While the significance of these questions was at first obscured by the immediate task of rewriting my article for *PMLA*'s editorial board, their import was ultimately reiterated by this next level of editorial consideration. For, after discussing the appropriateness of including my essay in a forthcoming issue, the editorial board decided it was unable to achieve a consensus and sent the article back to me with a thoroughly contradictory list of suggested revisions, asking me to rewrite and resubmit my piece a second time. The frustrations I experienced upon receiving this request were multiple. While some members of the board suggested expanding the historical implications of my argument, others wished I would be more narrowly literary. While some seemed to like the theoretical orientation towards gender, others balked at what they called the "false hype of discourse." While some approved the implicit address to a gay literary audience, others felt excluded by this purview. Yet not the least frustrating was that while some recognized the political implications of both my subtitle (which was *then* "Towards a Gay Literary Interpretation of *The Picture of Dorian Gray*") and conclusion (which attempted to explore what it meant to do such a "gay" reading), others strongly preferred that I drop both the operative adjective and the larger theoretical inquiry. At this point my intuition suggested that underlying the board's conflicting assessments of my work lurked the highly mediated language of homophobia. Certainly there was no outright statement of discomfort with the appropriateness or the import of my analysis; however, I could not help but be piqued by how vague many of the critical comments were, *except* when it came to the "political" dimensions of my text. Nevertheless, since I was in the middle of a job search that was demonstrating to me that being professionally "out" might mean being professionally unemployed, I felt powerless to object. So I compromised: among many other changes, I took "gay" out of the title, while leaving the conclusion intact.

In their second round of consideration, the editorial board responded somewhat more approvingly: they accepted my article "conditionally." One condition was rather forthright: since the essay exceeded the journal's specified word limit, it would need pruning. The second condition was less routine: referring to my essay's polemical "coda," *PMLA*'s editor wrote:

> we all felt that the coda should be dropped and replaced with a new conclusion.
> Although we recognize that you may have included the coda because you wished
> to make a political statement, we believe that the text stands on its own (in effect,

accomplished the same purpose more forcefully). All of us agreed that you should, in fact, provide an appropriate conclusion and that your essay would be best served if it ended with Wilde and your literary argument.

Given the "literary" focus of *PMLA*'s editorial policy, I wasn't entirely surprised by this condition of acceptance, although I was disturbed by it. While noting the possibility that I might be trying to make a "political" statement, the board concurred that such a statement was best said by being left unsaid. Invoking their authority as the arbiters of legitimacy for literary studies, they decided that an "appropriate" conclusion (at least if I wished my essay to appear in *PMLA*) was a "literary" one. The decisiveness of this distinction, "political" versus "literary," was upsetting to me because in my view, and indeed in the terms of the very argument that they were conditionally accepting, such an opposition could be understood only as a strategic defense of a particular, *highly political* deployment of "the literary"—one that had heretofore excluded the possibility of "gay" interpretation *per se*. Nevertheless, having by this time found that for a variety of reasons I was not a credible candidate for an academic job (the circumstances of which I will recount at length below) and knowing that my essay's appearance in *PMLA* could well make me one, I needless to say rewrote the conclusion to my article so that it was "acceptable."

I am now retrospectively trying to make the considerable psychic pain that accompanied this "compromise" meaningful in two ways. Personally, as I was forced to address the possibility that my own idealism (or perhaps naiveté) was grounded in the privilege accorded to me as a highly educated, white, middle-class male, I developed a new somatic and emotional understanding of the materiality of such privilege. Heretofore I thought "I" "knew" that my belief in my entitlement not just to speak but to be heard *on my own terms* was a product of a "self-identity" nurtured and supported by multiple technologies of class, gender, culture, and ethnicity that more globally participate in excluding, silencing, or obscuring others who are not accorded such privilege. However, my self-"knowing" now became anything but "intellectual." At the very moment that I sought to use my privileged positioning in order to envision and to voice a different configuration of middle-class maleness, I was confronted by the "other" within my "self": that is, by the sociohistorical contingency of my most intimate "sense of identity" as a privileged, white, middle-class male. Indeed, perhaps the most productive aspect of my psychic distress was that it called my attention to the ongoing pain and limitation through which my illusory perceptions of self-authoring "oneness" (implied by this "identity") had been and continued to be wrought. It was, as Adrienne Rich describes it, "a moment of psychic disequilibrium, as if you looked into a mirror and saw nothing. Yet you know you exist and others like you, that this is a game with mirrors."[3] Furthermore, Rich's trope, "a game with mirrors," reminded me of Jacques Lacan's more famous "mirror," while providing a new social, historical, and political context in which to understand it.[4] For if, as the strategically opaque

French psychoanalyst seems to suggest, my infant "self's" recognition of itself as a coherent, unified psycho-physical organism is "in fact" a critical misrecognition (*méconnaissance*) predicated on mistaking the mirror's "image" for the "real," then my momentary inability "to see" myself in this social and historical "mirror" might help me to cognize my misrecognition and thereby attempt to imagine and articulate a more effective (if not more consonant) constellation of self.

Institutionally, my difficulty in complying with *PMLA*'s editorial demands made me acutely aware of the multiple and conflicting processes of knowledge formation and the attendant power relations that shape and take shape by and through these concrete practices. Again moving from an abstract to a physical knowledge of an earlier "intellectual" insight, I came to interpret the emotional distress occasioned by my inability to accept PMLA's prepublication requirements placidly as the bodily manifestations of a material contestation of power whereby my institutional vulnerability subjected me to the somatic effects of "normalization." At an epistemological level, I learned that the unfolding of a "gay" literary analysis is circumscribed by the conditions for producing if not a "true," then at least a recognizably "acceptable" text—defined in this case by the suppression of its own "gayness." However, even if this condition is only a transitory moment preceding the emergence of practices that will make it possible to articulate gay "ec-centricity" as a positive rather than an unvoiced "politics" in the bastions of institutional authority, such articulations will, for the foreseeable future, continue to be produced in relation to these larger coordinates of legitimation. As a consequence, how we come to imagine and give voice to such positivities will almost necessarily contradict the implicit unity desired by movements towards constituting institutional gay or lesbian "identities." For, while the emergence of "lesbian" and "gay" paradigms will certainly afford us the opportunity to begin to make heretofore obscure(d) practices visible, they cannot be defined solely on our own terms. The inexorability of this dynamic was suggested to me by a letter I received in response to my *PMLA* essay from a gay man who teaches at a small state college in the Midwest.

> With the publication of your article "Writing Gone Wilde" in *PMLA,* I find an antique weight lifted from my shoulders. The vocabulary to say what you said did not exist in 1971 when I completed my doctorate. For the first time I see my gay side in the critical terminology I am accustomed to using professionally and, at last, I can verbalize the reality of my place in the gay subculture in a vocabulary that the dominant hetero-tyranny can understand. What a wonderful breakthrough!

Here the terms in which the warm praise for my article is couched underscore the multiple and perhaps conflicting representations of self that constitute my "gay" "professional" "identity." Beginning with the historical recognition that fifteen years earlier the "vocabulary" to undertake such an analysis was not yet available, my correspondent goes on to foreground the conflict between his gay and professional "side[s]." Thus, when defining the "breakthrough" that my essay constituted for him, the writer quite rightly describes my undertaking as an act of translation, of bespeaking "my gay side in the critical terminology I am accustomed to using professionally." My painful but ultimately rewarding experience with *PMLA* made me conscious that it is this relational activity of articulating ourselves to ourselves and to "others" that will constitute the initial project of "gay studies"—at least as it emerges through the practices of professional academics.

While I want to return to this constellation of "identity," "discipline," "profession," and "knowledge" in the final, more theoretical, section of this essay, I will turn now from one set of personal reflections to another. What follows is the revised text of the talk I gave last fall at Yale's Lesbian and Gay Studies Conference called "Politics and Pedagogy." Unlike my experience with *PMLA*, this rite of passage was one of unmitigated pleasure for me: not only because it was the first time I'd spoken to a group of academics about the problems of being "out" in the profession without having to explain that the "problem" isn't that I am gay, but also because it was the first time that I was so openly affirmed for attempting to synthesize my personal, professional, and political beliefs. For me, then, the process of writing and presenting this paper interrupted the rules of the academic "game with mirrors"; it was as if, when I looked again into the mirror to find my missing self, "I" was surrounded by many supportive and caring friends.

Different Strokes (New Haven, October, 1988)
Some Autobiographical Reflections on Teaching
Writing Across Gender

As a prologue to this paper's attempt to address the topic of "Pedagogy and Politics," I would like to begin by recounting my own rather painful prologue to the politics *of* pedagogy: that is, to the difficult process of securing an academic job in a literature department of an American university.

It all began for me in the fall of 1986, when I first went "on the market"—as the profession's self-commoditizing metaphors so aptly put it. As an overeducated, white, middle-class male with a bouquet of academic awards, a few publications, and, perhaps most importantly, the support of one of the nation's more "prestigious" academic institutions, I might have been supposed to have been a credible candidate for a number of university teaching positions. Indeed, I was so supposed by the large number of faculty who advised me to apply for jobs that year: *"Considering the quality of your work and the timeliness of your project,"* they told me, *"you should be highly desirable this year."* There was only one hitch: I had chosen to write my dissertation on a subject that was not only far from being legitimated, but could not in all probability be openly discussed by at least *some* individuals on any given job search. For my title, which was *then* "Talk on the Wilde Side: Towards a Genealogy of the Discourse on Male *Homo*sexuality," and my self-representation as the writer of a "gay history project" quickly revealed that I was trying to explore the transformations among the terms within which we continue to come to terms with the experience of men's physical, emotional, and intellectual intimacies with other men.

To cut an excruciatingly long story very short, I was *not* a desirable commodity in the intellectual marketplace that year. Of the almost thirty jobs I applied for, only one was interested enough even to look at my writing sample, and none was interested enough to interview me. *"I could have taken it if I just hadn't gotten a job,"* I told myself, *"but why wouldn't anyone even talk to me?"* It was never clear from the many rejection letters what my specific deficiencies were, and certainly they could have been plural: I had not completed my dissertation, my publications were not yet all in print, my area of specialization was not *quite* what was being sought, and to top it off, I had "on principle" refused to waive my right to see my recommendations. Yet even given this plurality of irregularities—or perhaps eccentricities—the ultimately monolithic character of the negative responses made it seem as if there might also be another, *more political*, "logic" at work in the decision-making process.

In the following year, as I attempted to make sense out of my own sense of abjection—if only in order not to repeat the previous year's devastating experience—I consulted with almost everyone who would listen to me. Some people gave me excellent insights: they pointed out that in my desire to be professionally "out," I had adopted a defensive posture so that I was continually attempting to establish the credibility of my project by overemphasizing its placement within an already accepted set of theoretical paradigms. In this game of critical overkill, they suggested, I presumed the fear that I feared to meet and thus sought unsuccessfully to outmaneuver it, while in fact conjuring it. Other advisers were much less psychological and much more blunt. One very supportive and well-meaning senior professor succinctly told me, "You just can't use the word *gay* in your application." (And I should say parenthetically that he also suggested very strongly that I cut my "long" hair.) Pondering this range of advice, I decided that what I needed to do was to represent my work in a way that was respectful of the project I had undertaken and yet accessible to people who might not necessarily be sympathetic to the undertaking. As a result, I recast the description of my dissertation—*without* using the word *gay* and dropping *homo* from the title—so that the project now appeared in my job letters as "an inquiry into the historical construction of the opposition between 'heterosexual' and 'homosexual' in late Victorian culture" and was framed as "drawing upon and extending the analysis of the relation between the 'sexual' and the 'textual' undertaken by feminist literary critics and historians." In some respects this was actually a more accurate characterization of my thesis, since my claim was indeed that the pathologization of the "homosexual" was predicted on an earlier problematization of "normal" masculinity. However, the experience of my own self-silencing—especially on a subject that it had taken me years to learn to speak and write about publicly—was acutely painful. Yet the pay-off was clear. Of the almost forty jobs I applied for in 1987, twenty-three requested writing samples, and eleven arranged MLA Convention interviews, and two offered me jobs.

Which brings me rather circuitously to the ostensible topic of this paper: the question of how to conceptualize teaching and writing about experiences of intimacy between individuals of the same sex in varying historical and cultural (con)texts. The problem as I—rather abstractly—phrase it here first arose for me concretely and not abstractly, as I prepared for these job interviews. In considering my perspective on teaching and writing about the social constructions of gender and wondering how I could articulate this perspective to an unknown but apparently interested audience (they had, after all, decided to interview me), I realized that I was not very certain about what it would mean for me to say to them that I was interested in working on "gay literature," "gay criticism," or "gay culture." Not that I'm not interested in all three, whatever they "are"—or, perhaps more accurately, are becoming. However, I wasn't sure what it would mean for *me* to say it to *them:* that is, to a hiring committee for an English department in a major American research university. For clearly, if I were to articulate my focus in this manner, I would not just be specifying a certain, highly overdetermined, and, at this point, ridiculously self-divided, personal, political, sexual, aesthetic, and ethical "identity." I would simultaneously be situating this "identity" on an epistemological terrain across which the institutional mappings of disciplinary boundaries are continually drawn and redrawn. Or, in other words, I would be attempting to deploy a strategy derived from the "identity politics" of the new social movements (e.g., civil rights, black consciousness, feminism, gay liberation, the liberation struggles of subaltern cultures, etc.) within a context that was not fundamentally concerned with "rights," "liberation," or "identity" except insofar as they might become objects of intellectual inquiry. Hence, it was not clear to me that a political intervention in behalf of "gay studies" would necessarily speak directly to or—even more utopianly—interrupt the institutional configuring of power and knowledge that English departments specifically and universities more globally both effect and legitimate.

Reviewing my own work on late nineteenth-century British representations of gender, I began to wonder then if, rather than establishing a critical framework in terms of my personal and political "identity," there might not be some way to locate a point of intellectual entrée in terms of a "relation" or, more dynamically, a "process." My hope in so doing was that it might afford the local effectiveness of an "identity"—that is, provide a positioning from which to organize and channel movements of knowledge—while not confining the mobility of this positioning within any self-unified epistemological boundaries. What I sought to interrogate, then, was the possibility of *politically* situating an academic consideration of gender as part of the process of constituting and transforming genders as they are historically produced and reproduced. For, clearly, as part of the concrete institutional arrangements that self-consciously organize and channel socially legitimated forms of visibility and intelligibility, the humanities and the human sciences are privileged sites for articulating those highly imbricated processes of meaning production through which we come to represent—both to ourselves and to each other—the "reality" of our experience. In this light, my project seemed to move away from rather than towards an "identity" (gay or otherwise) in much the same way that Teresa de Lauretis has recently suggested à propos of feminism's critique of subjectivity: "identity is not the goal but rather the point of departure of the process of self consciousness, a process by which one begins to know that and how the personal is political, that and how the subject is specifically and materially en-gendered in its social conditions and possibilities of existence."[5]

Now in retrospect it seems almost ironic that the most legitimating credential on my vita, and indeed the reason I became a viable candidate for a teaching position in English at all, was an article I wrote to historicize the notion of "identity" called "Writing Gone Wilde: Homoerotic Desire in the Closet of Representation," which appeared in *PMLA*. This essay took as its point of departure a question that had long confused me about interpretations of *The Picture of Dorian Gray:* how was it that from the moment of its publication and subsequently through the almost one hundred years of critical reception, this book has been branded as "homosexual" and yet does not contain one representation or even one specific intimation of physical intimacies between men? Or as I more succinctly phrased it there, "What if someone wrote a novel 'about' homosexuality and no body came?" In attempting to answer this question, I was forced to recognize that rather than *being* a novel about "homosexuality," Wilde's novel was an integral part of the *process whereby "homosexuality" came to be.* Writing in 1890, several years before the translation of Krafft-Ebing's *Psychopathia Sexualis* would make the words *homo*sexual and *hetero*sexual current in English usage, Wilde fashioned a text that crystalized the multiple currents whereby the context of "masculinity" (or "manliness," as it was more often called then) was made meaningful. By playing upon the "pleasure" of the aesthetic, Wilde effectively en-gendered the highly ironic and unstable signifieds of his sexually marginal, subcultural experience so that the text necessarily articulates—if only *sotto voce*—the counterpoint between the incessant reproduction of hegemonic sexual positionings and the painful-yet-pleasurable emergence of that soon-to-be "other," the male homosexual. In contrast to this widely read, manifestly "straight" book (which did, after all, first appear in an American "family" magazine), another novel, this one pornographic, also appeared in 1890 and has been posthumously—though perhaps apocryphally—associated with Wilde. Entitled *Teleny, or the Reverse of the Medal* and reputedly written serially by a group of men with Wilde acting as both instigator and editor, this pornographic text is one of the earliest examples I know that represents positively both love *and* sex between men. Indeed, the novel contains one of the most explicit, eloquent, and sustained apologies for intimacies between men to have appeared during the nineteenth century. Taken together, the two texts illustrate both the range of possibilities within which male intimacies could be configured during the last decades of the nineteenth century and the extent to which such configurations were predicated upon a subcultural interruption of normative sexual discourses. Thus, they also underscore the process whereby literary and nonliterary texts transform the cultural meanings that imbue specific forms of human—in this case male—relations. For as the eloquence of the pornographic text suggests, the meanings that were being produced by and for its audience made accessible positive interpretations whereby experiences that were nominally "unspeakable" in the dominant culture could be not only articulated but enjoyed.

The point of such an interpretation, it seems to me, is not to circumscribe the activity of texts like these within any personal or political "identity"—that is, to define them as "homosexual" or even "gay." Rather it is to take them as points of departure for a more sustained inquiry into the historical production of the concepts of identity whereby certain sexually marginal practices are made meaningful to different and yet overlapping audiences. In this way, we do not look to history to confirm us in our own historically determinant forms of self-presence, but instead locate our intellectual practice as a process whereby we engage in the reproduction and/or transformation of our own self-representations. To return for a moment to the literary terrain in which I am employed: such a strategy could be usefully deployed not just to interrogate the mobility of gender categories within both canonical and non- (or not yet-) canonical works, but also to examine the ways gender enters into and indeed crystalizes the categories through which disciplines constitute their authority and legitimacy, thereby reciprocally—if implicitly—authorizing and legitimating certain normative concepts of gender.

For example, the title of this paper, "Different Strokes," first referred to a course I designed to explore the dynamic of "masculinity" and "modernism." Here I felt that more than being an extrinsic or epiphenomenal relationship, the constitution of literary modernity in Britain—or at least in the British novel—was predicated on actively distinguishing the artifacts of "high" culture from the domesticated forms of popular fiction. While the latter were usually deemed to be "feminine," denoting the diminution of both their formal organization and their producers and consumers, the former were constituted as "masculine" precisely because they reiterated the authority or even autonomy of textual production itself. Yet as this reiteration coincided with the larger reconfiguring of adult middle-class masculinity in the wake of trade unionism, the incipient failure of the imperial project, first-wave feminism, the emergence of "new women," and the popular representation of male homosexuality, among many, many other transforming events and movements, the aesthetic ideologies of literary modernism produced and consolidated new forms of male authority and subjectivity. More than providing just a series of texts, literary modernism offered up frames for intelligibility and narrativity that constituted the acts of perceiving and articulating as *always already gendered*. It is only within such frames, then, that the "difference" of texts by writers like Wilde, Gide, Proust, Woolf, and Stein can be posited, since the effective determination of such "eccentric" positions can only be seen as part of the reproduction and contestation of literary subjectivity and authority. Moreover, by describing the relation between the margin and the center as a dynamic one, this interpretation of modernism opens up the possibility for reexamining the en-gendering works of such "high" modernists as Conrad, James, Lawrence, and Joyce, for it underscores the extent to which these texts themselves are critically refiguring the constellations of masculinity.

In challenging the efficacy of categories of analysis predicated upon "sexual identity," I am not trying to deny or discount the political importance that articulating such identities within the academy can have. Rather, I am trying to suggest that while individually or collectively we may want to claim or create positions from which to make visible and intelligible diverse bodies of practices (or practices of bodies) that have historically been excluded from intellectual inquiry, to do so in the name of any one such position will ultimately repeat the problematic oppositions of sameness and difference that have plagued earlier attempts to institutionalize identity politics. However, if we begin to conceive of our intellectual practices as part of the processes whereby such identities are reproduced and transformed, then we can begin to address the "technologies of gender" through which we articulate and are articulated by institutional formations.[6] In other words, if rather than taking ourselves to be gay or lesbian academics whose fields of inquiry are marked out by the assumption of our own self-identical authority, we can undertake to inquire into the ways that our fields and disciplines necessarily effect our own self-difference, then we will be able to affirm our intellectual endeavors as articulating new possibilities for personal and political self-representation. By explicitly situating intellectual undertakings as political narratives, this affirmation opens the possibility, as de Lauretis has suggested, of moving away from "identity" and entering into the unfolding of what Michel Foucault has called "becoming gay." Using this concept to address the difficulty of articulating the "identity" in "identity politics," Foucault suggests that the orientation of gay politics should be one of process and creation rather than disclosure and truth. I will in closing leave you with what has become for me one of his most compelling suggestions:

> we must be aware of . . . the tendency to reduce being gay to the question: 'Who am I?' and 'What is the secret of my desire?' Might it not be better if we asked ourselves what sort of relationships we can set up, invent, multiply or modify through our homosexuality? The problem is not trying to find out the truth of one's sexuality within oneself, but rather nowadays, trying to use our sexuality to achieve a variety of different types of relationships. And this is why homosexuality is probably not a form of desire but something to be desired. We must therefore insist on *becoming* truly gay, rather than persisting in defining ourselves as such.[7]

(New York, Summer, 1989)

By now you will probably have recognized that I am somewhat obsessed with questions of "identity" these days. This is no doubt due partly to the fact that, having undergone so many changes during the last two years, I present the classic symptoms of what Erik Erickson called an "identity crisis." Indeed, given the relative uniqueness of my historical position—that is, my ability both to be accorded institutional legitimacy and to earn a living as an "out" gay man teaching and writing about gay men—I am hard pressed to take either my professional or personal "identity" for granted. As I ponder such practical decisions as "Do I want to teach a 'gay literature' course?" "Do I want to foment a 'gay studies' program where I teach?" "Do I want my work categorized as 'gay'?" I find increasingly that "I" *am* a contradiction, that I can only answer myself honestly by saying, "Yes and no." Yes, I want to affirm the meaning and value of my own self-difference and through this act of affirmation encourage and support others to do the same for themselves. No, I don't want to reify and reduce my multiple contradictions and distinctions to a single category predicated on any defined "identity," sexual or otherwise. The more I think about it, the more I realize that my "identity crisis" is not so much a crisis about "my identity" but rather my crisis with identity *per se*.

Yet, beyond this microlevel of personal analysis, there lurks a larger set of theoretical issues that reciprocally shape the quality of my "crisis." Framed by the emergence in late twentieth-century, post-AIDS America of a self-conscious epistemological and institutional space called "lesbian and gay studies," my movement into the academy raises questions for me about the ways that we come to represent ourselves to ourselves and to each other. While our desire to delimit an arena of inquiry that will legitimate the fusion of personal, political, and professional concerns has led some gay and lesbian academics to attempt to position ourselves within this space, these multiple and often conflicting identifications might preclude the possibility of our (my?) always being entirely at home here. Perhaps at a level of higher generalization this observation can be applied to the ways various forms of "identity politics" have entered into the configurations of institutional knowledge. In each case, the problems of definition—of what constitutes the domain and range of the inquiry, of what methodologies obtain, of what goals are sought, of what can be properly included or excluded from consideration—have riven the putative "identity" around which the emergent institutional space was initially constituted. Yet, given the belated appearance of "gay and lesbian studies" and its concomitant coincidence with the post-AIDS rearticulations of gay identities (both in the mass media and in gay and lesbian communities), it seems that we may have a historically unique opportunity for self-consciously reflecting upon the conditions of possibility that underwrite our own projects even as we begin to embark upon them.

Whereas "women's studies," "black studies," "Chicano studies," "Native American studies," and "Asian studies" all entered the academy at historical moments when the limiting conditions introduced by the assertion of sexual, racial, or ethnic "identity" were qualified by the effects of larger political movements predicated on these identities, "gay and lesbian studies" does not have such a well-defined political context. Indeed, not only has "lesbian and gay studies" emerged at a time when "gay identity" is increasingly problematic both personally and politically (especially, in the wake of AIDS, for gay men), but the initial attempts to define a coherent object of inquiry have also generated a heated opposition ("essentialism" versus "constructivism") undermining the very possibility of positing "identity" as a stable epistemological ground. Compounding these difficulties, the recognition that "gay" and "lesbian" are not symmetrical categories, that "our" commonality of difference is itself cut across by the very real dissymmetries of gender, race, age, and ethnicity that obtain both inside and outside the academy, and that in attempting to assert the coherence of a recognizable academic field, we are circumscribed by all of the power differentials that imbue such institutional spaces, has made the process of birthing "lesbian and gay studies" both painful and problematic. But how, then, in this our infancy, can we begin to take our first steps if we are already engaged in dredging up the ground beneath our collective feet? How do we go about the business of getting ourselves in business if we can't agree who "we" are?

My inclination in answering both these rhetorical questions is to say—equally rhetorically, of course—"fuck identity." Or perhaps more accurately, let's not make an "identity" out of whom we fuck. Since the multiplicity of sexual practices that are engaged in by those who lay claim to the nominations "gay" and "lesbian," much less "bisexual," unquestionably boggles the mind, why not allow ourselves to take these varied sexual pleasures for our points of departure? In fact, if we belabor the analogy a little, why not take this plurality of pleasurable somatic, psychic, emotional, intellectual, and spiritual *movements* as our "ground"? What if we begin to think of "gay" and "lesbian" not as "identities" but as processes? Or, to trope on Foucault, "becomings"? Perhaps then we can begin to articulate our "differences" a bit differently. What if we stop trying to start from who "we" are" and instead begin by imagining where we want to go and how we can get there? Of course, such a beginning (which is not an origin, mind you) will also entail an inquiry into who "we" are, but the "we" will now only be an effect of the question, not a limit on its domain. To this end, "we" might begin by abjuring our hard-won gay and lesbian "identities" in favor of more relational, more mobile categories: "gay dis-positions" or "lesbian attitudes," for example.

While recognizing that this call to abdicate our claim to coherent "identity" entails a real loss that many are as yet unwilling or unable to make, it seems important to consider briefly the strategic advantages afforded by imagining "gay" and "lesbian" as dynamic categories. Initially, such a conceptualization might obviate the need to pose "essentialist" and "constructivist" descriptions as antitheses. Instead, we could begin to consider them as culturally and historically specific moments in a process of development and growth through which we are creating new ways to represent the contradictory experiences of sexual difference both to ourselves and to others. Focusing on the contingency rather than the historical immutability of "ec-centric" sexualities, we engage ourselves and our intellectual practices as critical elements in their articulations, allowing ourselves to enjoy the pleasures of "knowing" (in both the biblical and academic senses) as sexual. To take a somewhat facetious example, in graduate school I was inducted into an ad hoc group of "fem"-men-ists, both gay and straight, who were dubbed by our dyke friends and colleagues, "male lesbians." We were united under the motto "We fuck with categories." Although at the time it was mostly an "in" joke, it now seems to me that the force of the pun was precisely on target. For, to the extent that we can transform our ec-centricities into our strengths, utilizing our "off-center" positions to challenge the concrete institutional arrangements whereby the "center" is both defined and produced, then we create the possibility for interrupting these defining practices even as they reiterate our specific marginalities—all the while, *enjoying ourselves in the process*.

Whether or not "Lesbian/Gay Studies Programs" become common/places in American academic institutions, the project of "becoming" gay and lesbian academics can no longer be in doubt. In our writings, in our classrooms, on committees and panels, we are assiduously negotiating the precarious professional pathways that simultaneously (re)produce and transform epistemological, institutional, psychological and political distinctions and discourses. Through this process we both materially engender new institutional dynamics among faculty, students and administrators and concomitantly create new ways of "being ourselves" in these relations. Which brings me once again back to the problem of identity: Who is it that "we" are being here when we are "being ourselves"? To which I can only respond with my opening question: Are we (not) what we are becoming?

11

Wilde's Hard Labor and the
Birth of Gay Reading

Wayne Koestenbaum

Gay reading as a critical term may seem indefensible. Potentially oppressive, it is attractive only if considered part of a reverse discourse, elective and not imposed. Since recent histories of sexuality have shown that gay identity evolved from classifying, medical, and legal impulses, I threaten to gild the lily of homosexuality's roots in punishment by invoking, in this essay, an interpretive community founded on desire for the same gender.[1] Embracing without thought of consequence the dominant culture's assumption that sexualities are, like social security numbers, valid nodes of power and control, I risk submitting to a dangerously comfortable essentialism—as if gayness transcended gender, class, race, nationality, or epoch.

Although the notion of a "gay reader" may be fraught, I want to construct such a reader. The interpretive position I describe may be occupied by a woman, but it is most historically precise to speak of it as a gay man's. By referring only to men, I oversimplify. And yet this urge to warp evidence to fit the perimeters of wish is itself part of my subject: I acquiesce to "camp," to the grand urge to make irresponsible claims in the name of a self that, dreading erasure, writes itself in too bold a hand. Exaggerated masquerade helps the drag queen invent "identity"; he broadcasts an imagined and essential self through luridness, paint, and posing. My description of a limited point of view— mine—as if it were universal, shares with the drag queen a taste for absolute gesture, a desire to wear socially constructed identities (showgirl, secretary, prostitute, diva) as if they were god-given and natural.

Male feminist criticism means to articulate maleness as strange, outcast, and impermissible; gayness *is* outcast, and so I may discuss my reading of Oscar Wilde without apologizing for its partiality. Hedging bets—"what I describe here applies only to a small group of privileged gay men"—capitulates to homophobia. Assuming the prerogatives of *écriture feminine*, I will map gay reading as if it were a continent, though it may be only a peninsula.

The (male twentieth-century first world) gay reader, like the female spectator, knows the rewards of looking from the outside in. He reads resistantly for inscriptions of his condition, for texts that will confirm a social and private identity founded on a desire for other men—an urge strong enough that it seems a vocation and defines him and his kind as a separate world. Reading becomes a hunt for histories that deliberately foreknow or unwittingly trace a desire felt not by author but by reader, who is most acute when searching for signs of himself.

Two critics have begun to describe such a reader. Roland Barthes, under the guise of methodology-as-eros (*S/Z*), asks what other gay critics have been shy to answer: are there undermining and refiguring styles of reading that have either an imagined or actual connection to gay desires?[2] And D. A. Miller, in *The Novel and the Police*, closes with an essay on *David Copperfield* that playfully gestures toward David Miller reading Dickens: the importance of being David.[3]

On the one hand, I am invoking something as pedestrian as gay male reader-response criticism. (How do specific gay men read? What difference does it make if we postulate a gay male reader?) On the other, more provocative hand, I am hypothesizing that there are connections between gay identity and prison (both are enclosures established by social codes) and that a certain kind of involved, implicated reader is a gay man in the prison of his identity: the way we read now, our hunger to place ourselves in texts, began, in part, with Oscar Wilde in Reading Gaol, sentenced in 1895 to two years of "hard labour" for "gross indecency" with men. In the letter he wrote from prison to his lover, Lord Alfred Douglas (Bosie), "In Carcere et Vinculis" (posthumously titled *De Profundis*), and in the poem he wrote after release, "The Ballad of Reading Gaol," Wilde gestured toward such a gay male reader and suggested that "gay identity" is constructed through reading, although once it has been located on the page, it glows like an essence that already existed *before* a reader's glance brought it to life.

It is strange that Oscar Wilde, hardly addicted to eternal verities, invented an essentialist gay reader. Recent studies of Wilde by Ed Cohen, Jonathan Dollimore, and Regenia Gagnier, among others, have shown Wilde's detachment from the intrinsic paradisaical "nature" that thrilled André Gide; a gay Satan, radically reversing the dominant logos, Wilde was precursor to such postmodernists as Andy Warhol.[4] Wilde, like Warhol, understood publicity to be modern art's preeminent genre and saw himself as part of a literary and cultural marketplace; he recognized that mechanical reproduction was the empowering, if sometimes disenfranchising, fact of his age. When art can be copied, writes Walter Benjamin, the "aura" of an original is lost. Wilde, however, reclaimed aura for gay purposes by redefining mechanical reproduction *as* aura and insisting that the copy bears the original's transcendence.[5] Dollimore argues that Wilde, in his prison writings, retreated from anti-essentialism into the quietism of earnestness; on the contrary, I claim that, in *De Profundis* and "The Ballad of Reading Gaol," Wilde posits an essential "gay identity" in order to develop gay writing and gay reading as reverse discourses.

Obsessed with copying, cannily undermining essences, Wilde entertained the glittering, seductive, and centerless play of surfaces and refused to take essences earnestly. Though he celebrated the aura's degradation, Wilde, in fact, did not pledge strict allegiance to the copy; his texts acknowledge their status as reproductions, but they also feign, or contain, an aura. And the aura that Wilde's prison writings hide, beneath the sparkle of the secondhand, the derivative, and the stereotyped, is a "gay" essence. Because his imprisonment created, in a suffering instant, modern gayness—enough so that homosexuals became, in E. M. Forster's memorable phrase, "unspeakables of the Oscar Wilde sort"[6]—Wilde in jail could hardly avoid the knowledge that his name had become, like an instantly memorable advertising logo for a new product, the aura of gayness.

Although the "gayness" in a text may be merely an illusion of essence, a trope, a reflection, not a tangibility, the reader's hunger for textual gayness *as if it were real* is no different than the longing of any reader in a world saturated with copies for the original. Wilde took seriously this longing and satisfied it. He invented a reader who finds palpable gayness by unearthing Wilde's spirit—his figure—from the text's letter. Though essentialist, this postulated "gay reader" never abandons historical knowledge, never forgets that an actual man, Oscar Wilde, did two years of hard labor in prison; this reader (whether holding a work of Wilde's or a later gay text) is always searching for "Oscar Wilde" as the origin of an imprisoned indecency that contemporary gay men must recognize as their own. Wilde justified his incarceration by imagining a new kind of elucidator/disciple, in love with him enough to accord his "nature"—his sexuality—the status of an essence. Wilde's imprisonment taught a century the costs of being gay; the letter he wrote in prison preaches the rewards of using gayness to form a reverse discourse based on reading, a *vita nuova* founded, ironically, on the very name of his jail.

De Profundis: The Gaol of Reading

De Profundis, like many novels, warns that tragedies come from misreading, miswriting, or mishandling letters; but Wilde's letter is unique among self-conscious epistles because its writer and its implied reader are gay. This document asks: what difference does one new term—*gay*—make in reading a letter?

The "you" supplicated and denounced in *De Profundis* is Bosie (Wilde's lover) and the reader of the posthumously published letter. Bosie was a specific recalcitrant gay reader. Wilde, addressing him, made him emblematic. The fact that gay identity was born from Wilde's trial forces us to take this scene of reading between Bosie and Wilde seriously and to generalize from Bosie's position to the stance of post-Wilde gay readers. According to *De Profundis*, the reader is a young, attractive, indolent boy implored to perform something—to address the writer. The reader is a traitor, a boy who has been intimate with a famous man and has abused that privilege.[7] Not every reader of *De Profundis* is a lazy, indifferent ephebe. But Bosie's silence seems representative: the gay reader as imagined by Wilde is a querulous wordless presence, a renegade disciple, a disloyal fan, whose lack of fealty and whose silence make the writer write.

Bosie's silence forces Wilde to compose:

> Dear Bosie,—After long and fruitless waiting I have determined to write to you myself, as much for your sake as for mine, as I would not like to think that I had

passed through two long years of imprisonment without ever having received a single line from you, or any news or message even, except such as gave me pain.[8]

Wilde's entire miraculous *De Profundis* is an answer to an unwritten letter, to a desired text's absence—as if he were indirectly bemoaning the absence of a tradition of gay belle letters to which he can respond. Wilde sends his epistle into the void that precedes the invention of gay writing.

If Bosie's silence infuriates Wilde, the youth's greater sin is that he has *tried* to write: Bosie, whom Wilde calls "the true author of the hideous tragedy" (130), has dared to publish the elder man's private love letters in the *Mercure de France* and to dedicate a volume of verse to him. The gay reader projected by *De Profundis* hubristically overreaches and claims a writer's prerogatives. Overinterpreting, throwing himself, like the hysteric, too fully into what he reads, he crosses, without the writer's permission, the boundary between private and public; throughout the letter, Wilde anxiously repairs those veils of privacy that he spent his career methodically rending. He denounces Bosie's use of the "open postcard"—as if in response to the indignity of having letters read in court and seeing them treated not as mediated representations but as damning realities. Ronald Firbank composed his novels on postcards—an emblematic space for openly gay writing; unlike the closet of sealed envelopes, postcards preclude privacy. Wilde, jailed, regretted the exposed page that seemed to unincarcerated Firbank a source of play. *De Profundis* is unhappy to resemble a postcard, open to the censoring eyes of prison officials, and inscribed with the message "Wish you were here."

In prison, Wilde was permitted to read before he was permitted to write.[9] The book lists that he gave the gaol officials do more than document his longing for imaginative liberty. They confirm that reading, as an act of will and pleasure, may take writing's place and that certain styles of reading, performed under strict, punitive circumstances (whether the prison or the closet), *are* writing and counteract servitude. Wilde's prison reading stands for elucidations that take place inside the closet. It is fair to treat Reading Gaol as figurative as well as literal, for Wilde himself turned it into trope: "on the day of my release, I shall be merely passing from one prison into another."[10] Thus the paradigmatic gay reader sketched by *De Profundis* is not simply Bosie, but the imprisoned writer, reduced by jailkeepers to mere reading and learning to find in the reader's position the seeds of a finer disobedience. "Better than Wordsworth himself I know what Wordsworth meant" (152), says Wilde, and "if I may not write beautiful books, I may at least read beautiful books" (153). The fear that *De Profundis* will never reach its intended reader or that language itself is fated by its elusive differential nature never to span the distance between speaker and listener empowers one to read beautiful books but not write them and to read beauty into them—to read even an ugly book as if it were beautiful.

De Profundis separates into two tonalities. The first is manic and particular: Wilde recites Bosie's sins, and compiles a minute, exacting history of various letters—their transmission, receipt, and consequence. He spends much of *De Profundis* recounting "revolting and loathsome letters" (103), "no less loathsome letters" (105), "one of your most offensive letters" (107), "one of the violent letters you wrote to me on the point" (107), "some equally unpleasant telegrams" (108), "passionate telegrams" (111), "a most pathetic and charming letter" (119), "a letter of fantastic literary conceits" (121), "dreadful letters, abusive telegrams, and insulting postcards" (124). Wilde claims, in fact, that he was imprisoned as a result of writing Bosie a "charming letter" (120). These letters evoke the world of mechanical reproduction—of repetitions so painful and numbing that Wilde in prison faces a shadow "that wakes me up at night to tell me the same story over and over till its wearisome iteration makes all sleep abandon me till dawn: at dawn it begins again" (125). This reiterative Wilde is a prisoner who has stumbled, newly stereotyped as gay, into literature's bloody arena, uncertain what to say, uncertain who is listening—acknowledging, by his confusion, that being, or becoming, gay changes everything textual and makes letter-writing a different act.

The second tonality is the blurred realm of the aura. Wilde compares himself to Christ and forgives Bosie. The two lovers hardly require letters because nothing separates them—as if Wilde's fanciful dictum "There was no difference at all between the lives of others and one's own life" (170) had come true. When the gap between writer and reader vanishes, so does the gap between word and meaning; Wilde seeks signs thoroughly drenched with their referents—like a divinity's words untranslated, "the actual terms, the *ipsissima verba*, used by Christ" (174). Wilde wants a reader, like an enamored fan, to winnow *De Profundis* for traces of the writer's original mark. His ideal gay reader is like Bette Davis' vulture/protégé, Eve Harrington, who, loving the star, ruins her. The Wildean gay reader is a fan who longs to sleep with the beloved writer and who reads in order to wear, figuratively, the author's outfits.

Towards the end of *De Profundis*, Wilde describes his own page as a body. Indeed, *De Profundis* is a scarified body, whose every bleeding wound the reader should suck for the ichor of the writer's aura. If the woman has been compared to the blank page,[11] then the Wildean gay male may be called a wounded, stabbed page—a St. Sebastian marked by arrows, redeemed by gaping gashes. (Affairs between United States congressmen and their adolescent male pages is a more recent instance of the word "page" bearing homoerotic freight.) Wilde, describing *De Profundis*, invites the reader-as-Bosie to enjoy the gashed male textual body:

> I cannot reconstruct my letter or rewrite it. You must take it as it stands, blotted in many places with tears, in some with the signs of passion or pain, and make it out as best you can, blots, corrections, and all. As for the corrections and errata, I have made them in order that my words should be an absolute expression of my thoughts, and err neither through surplusage nor through being inadequate. . . . As it stands, at any rate, my letter has its definite meaning behind every phrase. There is in it nothing of rhetoric. Whenever there is erasion or substitution,

however slight, however elaborate, it is because I am seeking to render my real impression, to find for my mood its exact equivalent. Whatever is first in feeling comes away last in form. (197–98)

Wilde, describing the flawed, tear-smudged letter, asks for the reader's forgiveness, but knows that erasures and emendations attest to originality. No mere copy, the letter is an authentic prison document. Its blots are signs of aura that the reader should treasure as stigmata. Thus Wilde succumbs to or invents Pound's modernist poetics of absolute rhythm—where every phrase faithfully represents, in a one-to-one correspondence, some essential emotion.

But is the page the writer's body or the reader's? The letter's rheumy accuracy portrays not its writer, but Bosie, its reader: "if you have read this letter carefully as you should have done you have met yourself face to face" (197). The reader is invited to study *De Profundis* in order to see himself—his moral ugliness—more clearly. The text as mirror is a portrait of the reader as a young man, and its true subject is the reader's body experiencing Wilde's white-hot mark:

> you will let the reading of this terrible letter—for such I know it is—prove to you
> as important a crisis and turning-point of your life as the writing of it is to me.
> Your pale face used to flush easily with wine or pleasure. If, as you read what is
> here written, it from time to time becomes scorched as though by a furnace blast,
> with shame, it will be all the better for you. (130)

The lacerated page is Bosie's body, licked by the flames of Wilde's faithful portraiture.

In sum, *De Profundis* is a liminal, revolutionary document, a primary invocation to a historically constituted gay reader; it is the first text that Wilde wrote after he had been publicly branded as gay and one of the first texts ever written with the knowledge that it would be seen as the work of an "exposed" gay man. *De Profundis*, though composed in a prison cell, is uncloseted. Handing over its no longer secret preference, it coins a new gesture: it asks to be read as a document of a gay man's position and supposes that its canniest reader will be gay. Written as a private letter destined to be published posthumously, the epistle's central, burning problematic is the obsolescent distinction between public and private, the regrettable death of the division between commercial and domestic, open postcard and sealed missive.

Privacy lost, Wilde is reduced to the anonymous status of a letter:

> I myself, at that time, had no name at all. In the great prison where I was then
> incarcerated, I was merely the figure and *letter* of a little cell in a long gallery; one
> of a thousand lifeless numbers, as of a thousand lifeless lives. (136; emphasis
> added)

A letter is a private communication between writer and reader. But it is also a piece of alphabet—an *A*, for example, as in *The Scarlet Letter*, where *letter* implied, as it did for Wilde, a stigma, a fixed, blazoned identity, legible to strangers. Every reader of Wilde necessarily accuses him, remarks his sin. But the gay reader, himself scarlet, sees that the scarlet *A* means something other than its proscribed, punitive denotation.

When placed beside *figure*, *letter* refers to literality—the letter of the law. The question of letter in *De Profundis* is, finally, how literally we should take Bosie: Wilde's angry invocation to his lover is the document's loudest rhetorical gesture, and yet is the letter solely directed at the real, historical boyfriend? Isn't Bosie simply the disobedient lacuna where the post-Wilde gay reader finds himself—a reader who exists, in the first place, *because* a typology of homosexuality arose from Wilde's trial? *Letter* also denotes a bit of typeface, used to print. *De Profundis* balances the two meanings of *letter*—a communication between writer and reader, and a puncturing, imprinting fragment of typeface that can replicate itself, that generates unoriginal and inauthentic copies, but that has the power to wound the reader's conscience by reminding him of his own essential nature.

The Reproduction of Wilde's Prison Writings

Wilde gave fetishistic attention to the typing, printing, and publication of "The Ballad of Reading Gaol" and *De Profundis*. His fastidious, mannered interest in surface as opposed to depth seems to contradict my claim that certain texts possess gay "essences" that a reader can intuit and interpret. However, I would argue that Wilde's self-conscious commodification of his prison experience deepens, rather than flattens, the figure of his suffering. Attention to type, to publication, to the mechanics of a letter's spread, to language as a series of differences drifting away from a phantasmal source, needn't drain "life" from the image or negate an essential "gay identity." By commodifying his prison experience, Wilde tried to perpetuate, through the mechanics of modern publicity and publication, "imprisoned homosexuality" as an essential identity. "Gay reading" can live inside the copy as if it were the original because it has the knack of finding nature or essence within the copy reproduced unnaturally, by cloning.

Clone, a disparaging term for muscled gay men who dress and groom themselves stereotypically, signifies a mechanically reproduced masculinity inhabited as if it were real. One can acquire reality only by faking it. Men can acquire masculinity only by mimicking it. Because the word *clone* evokes laboratories, it also subtly derides a gay male's nonprocreative sexuality; it defines homosexuality as replication of the same. Gay men may father children, but homosexuality has often seemed equal to mechanical, not sexual, reproduction. Against this assumption that gay men are, at best, Petri dishes, gay criticism needs to develop a theory of typing or copying that wipes the tarnish off clones. Mechanical reproduction is *not* second-rate: there is nothing wrong with becoming a clone, wanting to be famous for fifteen minutes, striving to be sexy through mimicry, or commodifying one's life, body, and work. To consider replication degrading is, literally, homophobic: *afraid of the same*. If the patriarchal male pen is, figuratively, a fertilizing penis, let us enjoy the fact that the gay male instrument of textual dissemination may well be a xerox machine—or, in Wilde's time, a typewriter.

Indeed, *type* refers both to typeface and, in French, to a guy, a chap, a fellow. How do guys resemble typeface? When a man looks like a man, he possesses a reproducible, imitable essence of "maleness." Wilde, aware of masculinity and language as replicable properties, was obsessed with the word *type*. In his dialogue "The Decay of Lying," he wrote that "a great artist invents a type, and Life tries to copy it, to reproduce it in a popular form, like an enterprising publisher."[12] In *De Profundis*, Wilde describes Christ as having "the essentials of the supreme romantic type" (176) and condemns Lord Alfred Douglas as "a very complete specimen of a very modern type" (198); further, he admonishes Bosie, "you had better quote from it. It is set up in type" (209). Of course, Wilde was "stereo*typed*" (105) as a homosexual, and even described himself as "a specially typical example" of degeneration's "fatal law."[13] Wilde was content to be a type of the homosexual not because he enjoyed being stigmatized, but because he wished to puncture the future, to influence.[14]

To print successfully, moveable type must be, like Wilde's sexuality, inverted: the *Chicago Manual of Style* defines *type* as "individual bits of metal with the images of letters cast in reverse on their ends."[15] Letters, like *De Profundis*, have most hope of influencing when they come from reversal (of fortune, of sexual preference). Type makes impressions on a page: it is striking that Wilde should have titled several poems "Impressions" and that, after his death, Robert Ross should have remarked that "Wilde left curiously different impressions on professing judges."[16] Wilde's concern with "type" conceals a skewed query into the etiology of homosexuality (is it imprinted or chosen?) and the radical claim that one typesets, as it were, the page of one's own psyche.

With "The Ballad of Reading Gaol," Wilde monitored exactness and density of type and complained particularly about the weak impression made by his pseudonym, "C.3.3." Leonard Smithers, the publisher, wrote to Wilde:

> It has been a somewhat awkward title page to set with satisfaction, and even now, owing to the lightness of the impression of the 'C.3.3.' it does not look perfectly satisfactory. But this will be set quite right when the sheet is properly made ready for the press, which is a matter which takes several hours careful coaxing of the type to accomplish properly.[17]

Wilde was equally fastidious about the copying and typing of *De Profundis*. Exclaiming that Ross "must read it carefully and *copy it out carefully every word* for me," he longed to see the work typed.[18] Giving Ross the manuscript, Wilde was particular about the typewriter as the crucible through which this text must pass: "the only thing to do is to be thoroughly modern and have it typewritten."[19] Wilde mockingly described the typewriter as feminine: "I assure you that the typewriting machine, when played with expression, is not more annoying than the piano when played by a sister or near relation. Indeed many among those most devoted to domesticity prefer it."[20] It is significant that Wilde should call for a woman—and a modern contraption associated with female labor—to commit to print his messianic message. Homosexuality, in its earlier incarnation as sodomy, implied an alienation from procreative sex; and yet Wilde was a father, although he lost title to his children and to his literary estate while in prison. Oddly, his son, Vyvyan Holland, whom we might call an original and not a mechanically reproduced impression, became the custodian of what he terms "the original (if I may so call it) carbon copy" of *De Profundis*.[21] Wilde's son, Vyvyan, continues his father's struggle, through *De Profundis*, to redefine the meaning of reproduction. Even Wilde's punishment— called "hard labour" by the law—conceals a verdict on the relationship between homosexuality and reproduction. Parliament effected a pun: Wilde's labor gave birth to nothing. His punishment, which was literally oakum-picking, seems a metaphor for capitalism's alienated labor, for modern publication (mechanical reproduction), and for the "barrenness" of gay sex.

De Profundis invents a gay reader berated by the text into equivalence with the writer; appropriately, Wilde's contemporaries considered it a durance to read his prison works. Editions of "The Ballad of Reading Gaol" depicted the book as a jail. The leather cover of a 1937 limited edition reproduced a prison wall, down to the grilled window; a 1907 American edition, on its cover, invited the public to "Read the Greatest Tragical Poem in Literature," as if of first importance were not the poem itself but the reader's entrance into its imprisoning magnitude. This cover's mysterious insignia—a spirit lamp—implied that reading the poem might magically bring Wilde back (see Figure 11.1).[22] When in 1907 Doubleday advertised its "Patrons' Edition De Luxe of Oscar Wilde," it lured the reader into an even more punitive proximity to the text: "Your name will be beautifully engrossed on the title page of the first volume of the set you own . . . To be identified with one's books has always been the truest mark of the book-lover. . . . It associates one more closely with the Masters one loves."[23] Reading a beloved author's books, one is pressed, like Bosie, into typeface, name sadistically "engrossed" on the book's cover—as in Kafka's story "In the Penal Colony," where letters are written on the prisoner's flesh. Wilde, angry that Bosie dedicated a book to him, understood that being tattooed on another man's page could be torment. Doubleday's 1907 edition pursues suggestions made by *De Profundis* itself—that the reader is no ordinary passive spectator, but a disciple whose body must sympathetically take on the writer's pains.

When parts of *De Profundis* were published after Wilde's death, readers fell under the spell of a man who seemed legibly alive. His readers obeyed the logic of "type," of cloning: they felt compelled to read Wilde twice. Laurence Housman wrote of *De Profundis*, "I read it once with great and almost entire admiration, and am now reading it again."[24] This repetition was exactly what Wilde, in the letter, demanded of Bosie: "you must read this letter right through," must "read the letter

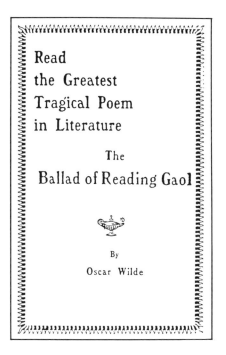

Figure 11.1 [Boston, no publisher, after August 1907.] Cover of the copy in the Clark Library, Los Angeles.

over and over again till it kills your vanity" (97–98). A reviewer in the *Times Literary Supplement* commented that "everything which Wilde says of Christ in this little book is worth reading and considering and reading again."[25] By reading Wilde twice, readers engineered his resurrection: according to one reviewer, Wilde was a "revisiting shade of immortal Glamour" that fell "athwart every part of the poem."[26] Wilde's shade appeared to the automatic writer and medium Hester Travers Smith, who recorded Wilde's after-death pronouncements in her book, *Oscar Wilde from Purgatory*, and even André Gide was visited by the dead master in seances.[27] A homophobic reviewer of *De Profundis*, who commented "I refuse to forget that [Wilde] is most fearfully alive,"[28] inadvertently revealed that modern gayness may be defined as Wilde's posthumous persistence, and that the gay reader is constituted by the prison of *imitatio Oscar*—by the compulsion to fill Wilde's shoes. Leonard Smithers, first publisher of the "Ballad," continued until 1907 (seven years after Wilde's death) to use the date 1899 for new printings of the poem[29]—evading a new copyright and century, maintaining Wilde's perpetual presence, and feigning that every copy, further removed from Wilde's living, tear-stained page, retained some intrinsic connection to the original. But Wilde understood that cloning—

mechanical reproduction—was useful to gay identity. When a difficult, new, rarefied, illegal pleasure repeatedly appears, it grows familiar; it enters the dictionary. Reading a copy of "The Ballad of Reading Gaol" is like caressing a saint's bone and feeling it to be the calcified origin of one's own seemingly immutable "gay identity"—rock-hard, contingent, textual.

"The Ballad of Reading Gaol": The Interpreted Cock

The gay reader is not merely a responder to printed matter. He is a commiserator. In Wilde's "The Ballad of Reading Gaol," the last thing he wrote for publication, there are two criminals. One is Wilde, in prison. He speaks of himself infrequently: "And I trembled as I groped my way / Into my numbered tomb."[30] He usually reverts to the plural ("We sewed the sacks, we broke the stones, / We turned the dusty drill" [238]), a "we" of prisoners united by the oppression of repetitive tasks and by a shared discursive position: they are each remonstrated to feel empathy with a greater, more emblematic criminal in their midst—a Christlike "He," whose execution they mourn. (This "He" is a man Wilde saw executed in Reading Gaol—Charles Thomas Wooldridge, who had murdered his wife, slitting her throat three times.[31] Does a pact between gay male writer and reader depend on erasing the slain wife and justifying her death? Women are missing from my paradigm of gay male reading. Has something actual and feminine been figuratively slain to make room for this bucolic practice of gay male interpretation? Or is this parenthetical shudder homophobic?) If Wilde is the first criminal, the second is C. T. W., to whom the Ballad is dedicated. As Wilde mourns C. T. W., we, reading the poem, mourn Wilde, our greatest "He." Thus the poem does for gay community what a mass does for Christendom: it enacts, in little, the spectacle that started the "church." "God's son died for all" (247): Wilde died for the sins of us outcast men. Gay community begins around the vicarious experience of a Passion: the reader becomes gay—joins a community of outcast men—by reading Wilde, as Wilde became gay by commiserating with C. T. W. Cloned, the reader is remade in the image of the convict's type; cloning is not a lonely experience, because confessing outcast status enfolds one in a nation of others who are also like Wilde.

Reading the poem, we cross the space between ourselves and Wilde, as Wilde, commiserating, closed the gap between himself and C. T. W. The poem's subject is the distance between two outcast men, Wilde and the reader, who collide by crossing: "Like two doomed ships that pass in storm / We had crossed each other's way" (236). Wilde and the reader, after all, are alike: "A prison wall was round us both, / Two outcast men we were" (236). Both reader and writer are potentially criminals: "Yet each man kills the thing he loves, / By each let this be heard" (232). The words on Wilde's grave at Père-Lachaisse come from the "Ballad":

And alien tears will fill for him
  Pity's long-broken urn,
For his mourners will be outcast men,
  And outcasts always mourn. (248)

These lines predict the constituency of mourners who will arrive there and read the memorial as a mirror; this inscription projects gay identity forming around Wilde's emblematic imprisonment. The chiasmus in the lines "For his *mourners* will be *outcast* men, / And *outcasts* always *mourn*"—the way that the two words, *mourners* and *outcasts*, change relative places from one line to the next—further reflects gay identity's formation. The outcast identity grows to be independent of and prior to the act of mourning that originally constituted it: reading Wilde's grave creates a gay subjectivity empowered to read the grave. This chiasmus is the *cross* on which Wilde expired, a Calvary. Post-Wilde gay readers discover they are gay as if it were a fact already there, when it is precisely their mourning of Wilde, their acknowledgment of a likeness, that guides them toward that identity.

The verb *read* is a homonym for the color *red*, a word prominent in the Ballad. The poem's title, "The Ballad of *Reading* Gaol," underscores, by macabre exploited coincidence, this homonym, which conflates Christ's blood, communion wine, Wilde's suffering in Reading Gaol, and our reading of the poem. The poem plays with the word: "For none of us can tell to what *red* Hell / His sightless soul may stray" (236); "He did not wear his scarlet coat, / For blood and wine are *red*" (231); "He does not bend his head to hear / The Burial Office *read*" (233); "The grey cock crew, the *red* cock crew, / But never came the day" (240); "God's dreadful dawn was *red*" (242); "In *Reading* Gaol by *Reading* Town / There is a pit of shame" (252). The two meanings, red and read, most palpably intersect here: "The man in *red* who *reads* the Law" (251). Does the man who reads the Law write it, too, or just absently intone what another man has decreed? Wilde discovers the possibility of reading the Law against itself—through reading, opening up a rift within the Law and finding a sexual surprise.[32]

The surprise is Wilde's resurrection: the persistence of his reputation and of the homosexual "type" molded in his image.

For three long years they will not sow
  Or root or seedling there:
For three long years the unblessed spot
  Will sterile be and bare,
And look upon the wondering sky
  With unreproachful stare. (246)

For a mythic three years (Christ died at 33, and Wilde was prisoner C.3.3.), no signs of him will appear above his outcast grave; his legacy will be "sterile"—

unreproductive. But then, he predicts his own return; he imagines his revarnished reputation, as well as a new self-designation arising—the ability to choose "outcast" as a pleasing identity. With a new identity comes a new language, an eccentric prison argot at which "the Ballad" marvels:

> I never saw a man who looked
> With such a wistful eye
> Upon that little tent of blue
> Which prisoners call the sky . . . (231)

Prisoners, as if perversely, affix the word *sky* to a paltry tent of *blue*—a word infused, at the turn of the century, with gay meanings;[33] outcast men name the objects of their world unconventionally, and it is Wilde's fall and hard labor that gave birth to this new, potentially enfranchising, lexicon.

Here, Wilde describes the "reading" that will sprout from his fall, making it, like Satan's in *Paradise Lost,* fortunate:

> Out of his mouth a red, red rose!
> Out of his heart a white!
> For who can say by what strange way,
> Christ brings His will to light,
> Since the barren staff the pilgrim bore
> Bloomed in the great Pope's sight? (246–47)

Reading arose: the rose that comes out of his mouth is red, and we must read it. What rises from Wilde's mouth, from Wilde's work, is the possibility of a barren typology—"homosexual"—bringing about new ways of assigning meaning. In *De Profundis,* Wilde said that "everything to be true must become a religion" (154). For gayness to be more than a mere lifestyle or recreational choice—for it to be an encyclopedia, a geography, a wealth of routes and signs—it must acknowledge its own capacious interpretive mannerisms as more than manner, as matter; it must recognize that gay men, at least since Wilde, have known themselves through mourning and cloning—noting a likeness between the plights of two outcasts. Outcast identity is particularly incarcerating, but any identity is a prison—an enclosure, whether fashion or flesh, over which we have little control, but that helps us to read.

I dwell on "reading," of course, because I am a literary critic—interested in styles of interpretation that accommodate readers like myself. My glance at Wilde in Reading Gaol takes place within the limited frame of a revisionary literary critical project. But reading is more than a private traffic with printed matter. It is an engagement, achieved through the imagination, across a distance; a tightly knit affair between a speaker and a listener; a survivor's gesture of reconnaissance and affection toward the past. Reading is mourning—a community forming around a likeness, around a death or a fall. In "The Ballad," Wilde wrote, "The red cock crew": he meant that the cock was red. But I mean something else: the read cock. The cock is Wilde's. And we must interpret it; we must try to read what his cock cries. The read cock—the interpreted penis—elucidated desire—*gay identity as Wilde imagined it*—is something worth reading, interpreting, inventing. If Wilde did not write it, let us write it for him.

12

Homo-Narcissism; or, Heterosexuality

Michael Warner

The modern system of sex and gender would not be possible without a disposition to interpret the difference between genders as the difference between self and Other. This elementary structure has been a subject for feminist theory at least since 1949, when Simone de Beauvoir posed it as the central problem of *The Second Sex:* how does it happen that man is constituted as the subject, and woman is constituted as the Other? For de Beauvoir, this is not just what men would like to believe, but the psychic structure of gender. Femininity is learned as a way of constructing oneself as object, a way of attributing full subjectivity only to the masculine. This identification of the male as subject and the female as Other, she argues, underwrites all the asymmetries of gender throughout history.

But the same insidious identification also has a more specially modern variant.[1] In the modern West, having a sexual object of the opposite gender is taken to be the normal and paradigmatic form of an interest either in the Other or, more generally, in others. That is why in our own century it has acquired the name *heterosexuality*—a sexuality of otherness. In this organization of sexuality, heteroerotics can be understood as the opposite *either* of homoerotics *or,* in the more general extension, of autoerotics. Indeed, according to this logic homoerotics is an unrecognized version of autoerotics, or more precisely of narcissism; both are seen as essentially an interest in self rather than in the other. The perverse options are therefore the exceptions that prove the rule, since both are overcome in the otherness of heterosexuality. The very categories of hetero-, homo-, and auto-erotics are jointly defined by the same understanding of gender as simple alterity.

In *The Second Sex,* for instance, de Beauvoir herself writes a sentence that is both bland and startling: "When the boy reaches the genital phase, his evolution is completed, though he must pass from the autoerotic inclination, in which pleasure is subjective, to the heteroerotic inclination, in which pleasure is bound up with an object, normally woman."[2] As a summary of Freud, this is quite bland. But in the context of de Beauvoir's argument, this way of opposing interest in others simultaneously to autoerotics and to homoerotics is startling. As she shows so eloquently, there is nothing innocent about the slippage from interest in "an object" to the assumption that such an interest is "normally" in woman. Nothing guarantees such an outcome other than the boy's discovery that women are defined as objects to him in a way that other men are not. And since the girl discovers at the same time that her destiny is to be an object of desire, her encounter with alterity is very different from the boy's. She is not offered the same simple distinction between her own subjectivity and the other's objectivity. The discovery of otherness in the other gender, therefore, is neither neutral nor symmetrical. In de Beauvoir's argument, as in the work of other feminists who continue her Hegelian tradition, this construction of gendered otherness is seen as the structure of domination.[3]

If the scenario of gender difference is difficult to imagine without the asymmetries of domination, it is also true that all of our accounts of this scenario bear the stamp of the modern organization of sexuality. Every description of the subject's access to gender and alterity, beginning with Freud's account of the Oedipus complex, seems already to be oriented by the poles of hetero- and homosexuality. Could the modern system of hetero- and homosexualities be imagined without this ideological core, or vice versa? By shifting the question in this way, I mean to indicate how difficult it is to analyze a discourse of sexuality, when our own tools of analysis already *are* that discourse. But I also mean to indicate ways in which gender domination presents problems besides the obvious one that it poses for women.

Where women are "normally" defined by otherness, the transition from autoerotics to heteroerotics entails a peculiar problem for men. To cite de Beauvoir once more, a key feature of male subjectivity comes about as a corollary of the subjugation of women: "For the male it is always another male who is the fellow being, the other who is also the same, with whom reciprocal relations are established."[4] The point of this for feminism is clear: insofar as woman is Other, she stands outside of reciprocity. But an important question for the male subject is less clear. Since sexual desire is directed toward an object, male desire will be directed only toward women, rather than toward the men who are fellow beings, subjects, the same. But what if this does not take place? And well it might not: for the man values other men as fellow beings and will accordingly seek their recognition and desire. At the same time, no matter how much he wants to think of the Other as woman, it remains true that men are others to him as well, just as women are fellow beings. When another man, this "other who is also the same," becomes the object of desire, has the male subject failed to distinguish self and other?

It may sound absurd, but that is just what psychoanalysis classically concludes. Psychoanalytic theory has from the beginning described homosexuality—especially among men—as a version of narcissism. Freud, for example, declares that the homosexual chooses "not another of the same sex, but himself in the guise of another."[5] This is not a simple judgment. And it would certainly not hold much intuitive force outside of the modern West, where erotic relations either among men or among women are imagined by most cultures as something other than relations of mere sameness.[6] But there has never been a sustained critique of the premises behind Freud's judgment, on this issue so widely taken as common sense. The gay movement has either ignored it or tried to reject it out of hand, no doubt because its invidious consequences are so easy to apprehend. Yet we need not wave away this powerful tradition, nor even deny that one kind of homoerotics in the modern West has the logic of a relation to self. It is imperative, though immensely difficult, for us to retheorize that relation.

The first difficulty lies in appropriating psychoanalysis. Although it is uniquely equipped to analyze the slippage in our culture between understandings of gender and understandings of self and other, traditionally psychoanalysis has been the principal site of that slippage. "Psychoanalysis," de Beauvoir concludes, "fails to explain why woman is the *Other*."⁷ Of course, different directions have been taken by psychoanalytic theory since 1949, and one would not offer so simple a conclusion today. But the related problems of heterosexuality remain as unclear—indeed, ideologically clouded—as they were then. What guarantees that a transition from autoerotics will or should lead to heteroerotics? How does it come to be taken as self-evident that homoerotics is really an arrested form of interest in oneself? Why do we find it so difficult to think about sex and gender without these ideological categories and their teleological narratives? And why do these questions seem linked to the structure of modern liberal society? Only modern liberal society, after all, understands sexuality as a choice between hetero- and homosexualities, conceiving them as sexualities of difference and sameness. The only way to pose such large questions is by examining the theory of narcissism, where the issue of gender and alterity arises with peculiar insistence.

Freud postulated a connection between homosexuality and narcissism before the notion of narcissism was even fully developed. He went so far as to argue that the existence of the link between the two is "the strongest of the reasons which have led us to adopt the hypothesis of narcissism."⁸ In the same essay, "On Narcissism," Freud argues that homosexuals express something different from what he calls primary narcissism. In primary narcissism, a child cathects itself in a unity with its parent, without differentiation, without a developed ego. This narcissistic love of the parent-child dyad is what the later love of the parent as a separate person will be propped on. Homosexuality, by contrast, is described by Freud as coming about in the later stage, when the subject's original narcissism encounters "the admonitions of others" and the awakening of his [sic] own critical judgement."⁹ The subject's primary attachment to itself, suddenly broken and troubled by criticism, is recuperated in the development of the ego ideals. It then happens, says Freud, that the individual seeks in another some ideal excellence missing from his own ego. And this is the type of narcissistic choice made by the homosexual, by which Freud generally means the male homosexual: the choice of what he himself would like to be.

Without reconstructing any more of the difficulties raised by Freud's problematic essay, I would like to make two observations about his argument. The first is that the two kinds of narcissism are very different. One is residual, an effect of infancy that lingers into later life. The other is proleptic and utopian. The homosexual (male), according to Freud, develops his narcissism not simply because of the residual attachment to the parent-child dyad, but because of a developmentally advanced ego ideal that is difficult to realize. I will return to this point later; it is important because Freud's thinking here leads him close to breaking his usual frame of reference. Indeed, by foregrounding the development of critical judgment and the admonitions of others, Freud places the subject in a context much larger than that of the restricted family. And by indicating the relation between narcissism and ideals, Freud works no longer in the realm of simple pathology. What is puzzling, then, is that Freud continues to treat homosexuality as regressive. Although one important criticism of Freud's account is that his narrative is rather arbitrarily committed to a hypotactic logic of linear development, an equally important one is that his own analysis, in this essay, does not necessarily show the homosexual's narcissism as a developmental regression.

A second observation then follows: Freud cannot account for the normative implications of his analysis. It is not a neutral analysis. He speaks with an unmistakable tone of condescension toward the homosexuals who are really seeking themselves. He does not imagine that one might speak of narcissism other than pejoratively in this context, though he does in others.[10] Nor does he acknowledge that to describe homosexuality as *merely* a version of narcissism is counterintuitive. The homosexual, after all, is by definition interested in others in a way that is not true of the narcissist in general. Ovid tells us that Narcissus rejects not just the girls who love him, but also the boys. Those boys, then, have an interest in other persons, if not in the other gender, and the myth of Narcissus does not collapse the two. What warrants the forgetting of this difference, which becomes a nondifference, sameness? Why should gender amount to alterity *tout court?*

Freud's secondary narcissism does not preclude a recognition of alterity. Everyone undergoes—and indeed requires—the kind of narcissism Freud describes. Everyone makes identifications with others on the basis of ego ideals. But we call them ideals only insofar as identification is accompanied by alienation and longing. The act of taking up ego ideals therefore does not foreclose a sense of the other's otherness, no matter how much we might like to eliminate that otherness. Indeed, in the last section of "On Narcissism" Freud suggests that this double movement of identification and desire is what makes the subject truly social. In the very action of taking an ideal, the subject apprehends a difference between the ideal and the actual ego. And that difference is just what produces our sense of longing and our search for the recognition of others. Because the ideals remain alien, insofar as they are ideals at all, they drive the subject to the pursuit of the other.

Identification in this sense is not a satisfactory unity; Freud shows that the ideals of identification have a critical relation to the self that the ego will continue to feel as dissonance, especially in the form of guilt.[11] It follows—though this does not always remain clear in Freud—that they are both identifications and objects of longing. And that can be true even of the ideals that are most critical and guilt-inducing. As Kaja Silverman points out, the most normally Oedipal boy in the world is placed in a relation of longing with the image of the father; insofar as the father's image is taken as an ideal, or superego, it remains "susceptible to sexualization."[12] Identification, in short, does not result in a relation of identity, and this is especially the case where another subject is involved. The difference that is therefore inevitably involved in taking the other as a sexual object, an other, cannot entirely be elided—even where the desire is founded on an identification. But that is what Freud does when he claims that homosexuals "are plainly seeking *themselves* as a love object."

Freud here imagines, in effect, that the dialectic of desire could not continue beyond the first moment of alienated identification. The figure of Narcissus represents that blockage; in Jacqueline Rose's phrase, Narcissus shows how "an apparent reciprocity reveals itself as *no more than* the return of an image to itself."[13] But it is not so easy to explain any erotic attachment as merely the reflexive attachment of a self to itself. Even the apparent return of an image reveals also some forms of reciprocity. When the subject chooses another on the basis of a desired ego ideal, he or she is already engaged in dialogue with others and in multiple perspectives on self. In Freud's account, the individual is encountering the admonitions of others and the development of his or her own critical judgment. As a result, the subject adopts the position of the other toward him- or herself. This kind of narcissism, therefore, already involves the subject in the negativity of speech.[14] If desire arises in these alienated identifications, it by the same token must always reactivate the potential for mutual recognition. Freud does not imagine this possibility long enough to argue against it. He concludes that homosexual desire *reduces* to narcissism without significant remainder and hence is a developmental misdirection.

Freud's conclusion here has hardly proven to be idiosyncratic. It remains the most powerful way of treating homoerotics as a symptomology, and some version of it still dominates every major branch of psychoanalytic theory.[15] Though the DSM III no longer lists homosexuality as a disease, the theoretical tradition continues to reveal it in the light of pathology. Professional psychology and psychoanalysis continue to understand themselves as explaining homosexuality, as giving its causes. But the entire discourse is possible at all only if the pathological status of the homosexual is assumed from the outset. If homosexuality is taken to be a symptom, then etiology provides a logic for saying that it reduces to narcissism. But if the symptomatic character of homosexuality is not simply taken for granted, then it would be necessary to theorize its dialectical and interactive character— precisely that which would prevent a reductive etiology. It is not surprising to find such ideological effects in the medical and scientific institutions that have, after all, generated the modern discourse of hetero- and homosexualities. It is more surprising to find the normalizing conclusion in Freud, since his own account demonstrates the dialectical and interactive movement that leads from the ego to homoerotics. (And back: one more reason Freud might have avoided his normalizing conclusion is that he was intermittently conscious of his own investment in homoerotics, particularly with Josef Breuer and Wilhelm Fliess. After his break with Fliess, Freud wrote to Sandor Ferenczi about his "overcoming" the trauma of the break: "A part of homosexual cathexis has been withdrawn and made use of to enlarge my own ego.")[16]

My point, however, is not simply that we should depathologize the homosexual. There is also a further, equally unremarked problem in the argument. If normal development leads from autoerotics to narcissism to heterosexuality, how would heterosexuality transcend its sources in narcissism more than homosexuality does? Freud assumes, as does psychoanalytic discourse generally, that the heterosexual (male) is a better realist than the homosexual (male). The heterosexual male chooses the Other—woman—but the homosexual male only *thinks* he chooses another. Yet it is not difficult to read Freud's essay as showing that all erotic life—not just the pathology of homosexuals—takes its form from the search for the ego ideal in the position of the other. (This of course is the direction in which Jacques Lacan will push the inquiry.) When Freud initially describes how the investment of the ego ideal can be transferred into a sexual desire for another, he is describing the pathology of homosexuals. By the end of the essay, he is using the same language to interpret a form of heterosexual romance. The lover, says Freud, overvalues the other in whose eyes he sees *himself* ideally desired. Yet Freud does not draw the obvious inference that it might not be so easy as first appeared to construct a normative hierarchy of hetero- and homosexuality by showing the function of the ego ideal in generating desire.

What, then, is developmental in the development from narcissism to heterosexuality? Or at least, what is developmental here that is not equally characteristic of homosexuality? Freud's various solutions to this problem come to grief because they are in the last analysis based on an *a priori* opposition of the genders as subject and Other. Nowhere are the difficulties of the project more clear than in *The Ego and the Id*, a text in which Freud returns to the unstable problems of the narcissism essay. In the earlier essay, identification and the ego ideals stemmed from the admonitions of others and the development of the subject's critical judgment. Now, in the later work, Freud writes that the "origin of the ego-ideal" lies in "an individual's first and most important identification, his [sic] identification with the father in his own personal prehistory."[17] The difference is that Freud has now introduced the Oedipus complex in an attempt to explain the developmental path that leads to heterosexuality. But why have the male subject and the male parent been singled out as the primary axis of identification?

In an astonishing footnote to this sentence, Freud acknowledges that there is no good reason at all: "Perhaps it would be safer to say 'with the parents'; for before a child has arrived at definite knowledge of the difference between the sexes, the lack of a penis, it does not distinguish in value between its father and its mother. . . . In order to simplify my presentation I shall discuss only identification with the father." According to the footnote, identification with the father has been emphasized only arbitrarily, for convenience. But the text that it glosses shows that the father must not be just any identification, but "the first and most important" one. That is what guarantees the Oedipalized heterosexual outcome. If nothing naturally makes this axis of identification the primary one, then the heterosexual resolution will be no more of a development than a homosexual one. Without this ideological support, Freud's derivation of heterosexual norms is subject to narrative incoherence.

The footnote admits, in effect, that the father has primacy only in his symbolic cultural value, which is learned later; he has no primacy in the simple development of the child's identification. Both parents are subjects of identification, and both are objects of attachment. This leads Freud to postulate both "positive" and "negative" forms of the Oedipal situation. Again, however, he presupposes the chiastic axes of heterosexuality that the model is designed to derive. Freud assumes that an identification with the mother will retain an attachment to the father and vice versa. He does not imagine that one might identify with the mother and yet have an attachment to other women or identity with the father and yet have an attachment to other men. Nor can he justify the primacy of one axis over another. In an especially striking moment of circularity, Freud writes that only the child's "sexual disposition"—i.e., its "masculine" or "feminine" bent—will determine the relative weight of these identification axes.[18] At this point, nothing establishes which axis— if indeed we can assume their constitution as axes—will be primary, or "positive" rather than "negative."

Freud maintains the normative character of Oedipal resolution only by ignoring these qualifications in a rather blunt declaration that the male child identifies with the father and takes the mother as object. In *Group Psychology and the Analysis of the Ego*, published two years before *The Ego and the Id*, Freud presents this declaration in its most normalized form:

> A little boy will exhibit a special interest in his father; he would like to grow like him and be like him, and take his place everywhere. We may say simply that he takes his father as his ideal. This behaviour has nothing to do with a passive or feminine attitude toward his father (and towards males in general); it is on the contrary typically masculine. It fits very well with the Oedipus complex, for which it helps to prepare the way.
>
> At the same time as this identification with his father, or a little later, the boy has begun to develop a true object cathexis towards his mother according to the attachment [anaclitic] type.[19]

As we know from Freud's qualifications in *The Ego and the Id*, nothing in this narrative can be assumed. The child takes both parents as ideals and has object attachments to both parents. Why does Freud so insist, despite his own observations, on the primacy of this "positive" form of what has already been assumed as a chiastic structure? Both the supremacy of the father and the goal of heterosexuality seem to derive from the Oedipal scene as it is summarized here. If this is the moment when de Beauvoir's mastery relation has been established, it is also the moment when the available object choices have been resolved into hetero- and homosexualities. The father's supremacy is assured since, for children of both sexes, he will be identified with as subject, while the mother's nurturing role will result in an object attachment to her.

But what is easier to miss is that Freud has presupposed that the child's identification and its object attachment will be assigned to different genders. Hence Freud's anxious haste to deny that identification with the father results in a "passive or feminine" attitude toward him. Freud consistently supposes that identification desexualizes the parental image, that the positive Oedipus complex cancels out the object choice of the negative complex and vice versa.[20] This is partly because he presupposes that the parents' heterosexual choices will be internalized along with their images, so that identification with the father will simply transfer the father's gendered desire to the boy. (To explain himself in this way, however, would amount to an admission that heterosexual desire is only a status quo.) But it is also partly because Freud's entire account is based on the exclusiveness of identification and attachment.

Identification and attachment are the structuring moments in psychoanalysis that correspond to subject and object. Identification constructs a feature of the world as a feature of the subject; attachment constructs its features as objects. But the opposition is unstable. As Mikkel Borch-Jacobsen shows, the two operations can be read as mutual forms of denial. If identification denies the radical alterity of the other, attachment-desire "is organized as a vehement rejection of all resemblance, all mimesis."[21] Freud's deepest commitment, throughout the changes in his position on the subject, is that these two operations will be exclusive, and one will be reserved for each gender. An admission that it would be possible both to identify with *and* to desire a gendered image would be the most troubling of all. If Freud implies in "On Narcissism" that the homosexual narcissist does just that, he has a very different account in the later works.

Here it is striking that Freud has two entirely different pathologies for homosexuality, and they accompany entirely different accounts of the ego ideal. Both *Group Psychology* and *The Ego and the Id* attempt to explain the homosexual by means of the chiasmus of gender identification and desire. The ego ideal with which the child identifies is a gendered parental image, and the child's sexual object will accordingly be the parental image of the opposite sex. In both of these later texts, the homosexual is said simply to choose the "negative" axis—for the male child, identifying with the mother and taking on her desire for the father. But in the earliest essay, the sources of the ego ideals had been much more general. They had not necessarily entailed the gendered parental images, with the chiastic Oedipal teleology of those images.

What if it is possible, as Freud implied in the earlier essay, that the boy might both identify with the father and yet desire his image? This possibility is implied insofar as the boy's identification would still not close the gap between himself and the gendered ideal. Indeed, identification could result in a longing because of that gap between actual and ideal. But subject and object would not be distributed to different genders. Freud is therefore obliged in this essay to regard the relation as one of mere sameness. Freud explains homosexuality alternately as sameness (in the earlier essay) or as inverted difference (in the later works). No matter which route of explanation Freud takes, he does not infer from his own insights that difference and sameness might coexist, in both desire and identification, without being reducible to the difference or sameness of gender.

It is only the more striking that Lacan never makes this inference either, since it is he who radicalizes the function of the ego ideal in a way only suggested by Freud. Lacan's analysis of the *imago* of the ego shows it to be *both* the site of identification *and* the source of desire. "We call libidinal investment," he says, "that which makes an object desirable, that is to say, the way it becomes confused with the image we carry within us."[22] Where Freud initially argued that an intricate confusion of the desired object with the image of what one would like to be is just the pathological derivation of homosexuality, Lacan shows that such an investment always structures the erotic. Lacan cites Goethe's Werther as an example of the way heterosexual investment is based not only on anaclitic parental cathexis but also on the reflective function of the ego ideal. When Werther first sees Lotte, he writes,

> No, I do not deceive myself! In her dark eyes I have read a genuine sympathy for me and my destiny. Yes, I feel . . . that she loves me! Loves me!—And how precious I become in my own eyes, how I—to you as an understanding person I may say it—how I admire myself since she loves me.

With this passage in mind, Lacan says, "That's what love is. It's one's own ego that one loves in love, one's own ego made real on the imaginary level."[23] Of course, there are other things that one could say about Werther; his is not the only form of "what love is." My point is simply that Lacan made it one of the central projects of his career to critique our elementary assumptions about the difference between identification and desire, subject and object. In so doing, he definitively removed any possibility of making narcissism a basis for a normative hierarchy between hetero- and homosexuality. Homosexuality may indeed be a way of loving one's own ego, but so is heterosexual romance.

Yet however radical and subtle Lacan's analysis of the imaginary might be, it seems never to have occurred to him that it might now be unnecessary to pathologize the homosexual's relation to narcissim. Quite the contrary. In a passage from the seminars of the very same year (1954), Lacan takes it on himself to describe homosexuality as a perversion, not because of the contingency of morals, nor because of the supposed needs of biology, but because of the narcissistic structure of homosexual desire. "It is himself," Lacan says of the homosexual," "whom he pursues." What I find especially incomprehensible about this classical assertion is that it appears as a gloss on one of Lacan's most Hegelian formulations: "the [homosexual] subject exhausts himself in pursuing the desire of the other, which he will never be able to grasp as his own desire, because his own desire is the desire of the other."[24] This, as Lacan notes, is the form of "the imaginary intersubjective relation." Nothing about it is peculiar to homosexuality. Moreover, when he is pursuing the Hegelian logic of his analysis, Lacan is capable of treating this same imaginary intersubjectivity as opening onto a dialectic of recognition.[25] In this case, he does not do so.

Compare the tone of his account with the tone of the equally Hegelian description that de Beauvoir had given five years earlier of the logic of lesbianism:

> To be willing to be changed into a passive object is not to renounce all claim to subjectivity: woman hopes in this way to find self-realization under the aspect of herself as a thing; but then she will be trying to find herself in her otherness, her alterity. When alone she does not succeed in really creating her double; if she caresses her own bosom, she still does not know how her breasts seem to a strange hand, nor how they are felt to react under a strange hand; a man can reveal to her the existence of her flesh *for herself*—that is to say, as she herself perceives it, but not what it is *to others*. It is only when her fingers trace the body of a woman whose fingers in turn trace her body that the miracle of the mirror is accomplished.

But de Beauvoir does not mean, by "the miracle of the mirror," an entrapment in a circuit of sameness. Far from it. Because she understands the problem of alterity sketched here as one taking place in a setting of domination, the dialectic of lesbianism is a model of how the imaginary transcends its limitations: "in exact reciprocity each is at once subject and object, sovereign and slave; duality becomes mutuality."[26] This is exactly what Lacan denies. Though he offers no reason for this belief, he asserts that the homosexual is perverse because the recognition of the other's desire remains closed to him. Lacan goes so far as to say that it is "not without reason" that homosexuality is called "a desire which dare not speak its name." (Of course, however, Lacan like Freud assumes that only male homosexuality is in question. If the lesbian dialectic allows women access to their subjectivity in addition to their normal objectivity, we might say the reverse for male homosexuals: they seek access to their objectivity in addition to their normal subjectivity. And because that means that would imply a compromise of privilege, a feminization, it is more unthinkable.)

Lacan's position in this respect is not as different as one would like to think from that of the reactionary Christopher Lasch. Lasch's writings on the subject have infinitely less subtlety and intelligence than Lacan's. But partly for that reason they lay bare the politics of the analytic tradition from which Lacan, less understandably, could not free himself. In a complimentary preface to a book by Chasseguet-Smirgel, Lasch claims that by eradicating differences of gender, the homosexual pervert "erases the more fundamental distinction between the self and the not-self, the source of every other distinction."[27] One hardly knows where to begin with this kind of comment. In the first place, it would simply be absurd to think that homosexuals eradicate gender; the very logic of homosexuality as a category is impossible without gender and its utopian identifications. Equally foolish is the rather crude form of heterosexist ideology in which it is supposed that people who have homosexual relations do not also have other kinds.

More deceptive, however, is the assumption that gender is the phenomenology of difference itself. This is the core of the psychoanalytic tradition I am trying to map. It is a staggeringly primitive confusion. Can it actually be imagined that people in homosexual relations have no other way of distinguishing between self and not-self? That no other marker of difference, such as race, could intervene; or that the pragmatics of dialogue would not render alterity meaningful, even in the minimal imaginary intersubjectivity of cruising? Why is gender assumed to be our only access to alterity? It is not even the only line of sameness and difference that structures erotic images. Race, age, and class are capable of doing that as well. Sexuality has any number of forms of the dialectic between identification and desire. But we do not say of people whose erotic objects are chosen partly on the basis of racial identity or of generation or of class that they have eradicated the distinction between self and not-self. We say that only of gender. The difference between hetero- and homosexualities is not, in fact, a difference between sexualities of otherness and sameness. It is an allegory about gender.

We have only to consider the breathtaking simplicity of the premises for the whole argument to dissolve. But let me emphasize that I am not making a point about Lasch's blindness. He merely reproduces an ideological confusion that is axiomatic for the modern sex/gender system. Even Lacan ascribes to what he calls "the cosmic polarity of male and female"[28] nothing less than the transition from ego-identification to dialogue:

> For it is a truth of experience for analysis that the subject is presented with the question of his [sic] existence, not in terms of the anxiety that it arouses at the level of the ego, and which is only one element in the series, but as an articulated question: 'What am I there?', concerning his sex and his contingency in being, namely, that, on the one hand, he is a man or a woman, and, on the other, that he might not be, the two conjugating their mystery, and binding it in the symbols of procreation and death.[29]

This passage appears exactly as an explanation of how alterity can be grasped within the narcissistic structure of subjectivity. Lacan is explaining the so-called "schema L," which describes the mediations between the subject and the Other, by which Lacan means "the locus from which the question of his existence may be presented to him." He here proposes that it is the otherness of gender that allows the subject to apprehend his or her own ego as an other. If we are to read Lacan generously here, we will emphasize the qualifier "it is a truth *of experience for analysis*" as meaning that the situation he depicts is only a nonnormative description of how gender operates in the present culture. We could then make these assumptions the subject of critique, as does de Beauvoir. But Lacan does not take that step, and it is just as possible to read the emphasis differently: "it is a *truth* of experience for analysis."

The passage is not without a sentimental and mystifying element. Lacan implies that the realization "I am this individual and not that one" not only does but *should* come in the form "I am this gender and not that one." He further assumes that a recognition of gender implicitly contains the particular form of mortality-transcendence found in the myths and rituals of heterosexual conjugality. But the dialectic of identification does not lead without mediation to procreative, genital sexuality. Indeed, Lacan often paints a very different picture himself:

> What is my desire? What is my position in the imaginary structuration? This position is only conceivable in so far as one finds a guide beyond the imaginary, on the level of the symbolic plane, of the legal exchange which can only be embodied in the verbal exchange between human beings. This guide governing the subject is the ego-ideal.[30]

Here, as elsewhere, Lacan argues that the narcissism of desire is transcended only by the rule-governed multiple perspectives of symbolic interaction. Language in general brings about forms of difference and norms of reciprocity and thus allows the subject the negativity with which to consider his or her identity in the role of another. Yet no absolute break with narcissistic identification has occurred, since the subject's ability to do this continues to be regulated by the ego ideals. As a picture of the development of subjectivity, Lacan's scene here resembles the "admonitions" and "critical judgment" referred to by Freud as the origin of the ego ideals in "On Narcissism." The subject has encountered the Other, "the locus from which the question of his existence may be presented to him." But significantly, that locus and its questioning do not imply the gender of an object choice.

Lacan moves between this account, in which the decisive factor is symbolic interaction, and another account, closer to the so-called second topography of Freud's later work, in which the ego ideal is specifically the paternal image. Again, the generous reading is that Lacan's analysis is descriptive of the way the father's authority stands for the subjective function he describes in our culture. But again, Lacan is not critical of that cultural equation, and he does not analyze the ways in which it is possible for subjects to interact without the prescribed relation to the paternal image. Instead, as we have seen, he adheres to models of pathology that incorporate and presuppose the normative role of gender defined as the simple apprehension of alterity. Because of this elision, the fundamental phenomenology of gender in Lacan's account often has an ideological character, though his most radical (and most Hegelian) arguments work in another direction. Indeed, if the equation between homosexuality and narcissism in psychoanalysis tells us anything, it is that the central premises and vocabulary of psychoanalysis have been designed for a heterosexist self-understanding. They have totalized gender as an allegory of difference, leaving little analytic space between the development of subjectivity and the production of heterosexual norms.

How does this mystification get sustained? When Lasch declares homosexuality perverse because it eradicates the distinction between self and not-self, does he not realize that many of his readers will come to the passage with the experience that must inevitably disclose its falseness? In fact, I think he does not. The entire psychoanalytic heritage on this subject does not imagine itself in dialogue with those it describes.[31] If I have taken some pains to show this, it is because I consider it a *tactical* necessity to have a better understanding of what the sources of this discourse's power are. If the tradition I have described simply reflects the illiberal intolerance of a few homophobic theorists, then we need not sweat it any more. If it is structural to the premises of psychoanalysis, then we need more of an attack on modern psychoanalysis. If it lies in the heart of modern social organization, then we should consider how, and in what institutions, and where a more organized resistance should begin.

That is not to say that we need a theory of homosexuality in the usual sense. There may be any number of logics lumped together under this heading, from the "lesbian continuum" theorized by Adrienne Rich to the more recent phenomenon of gay communities organized through a discourse of rights. Both for women and for men in our culture there are probably as many ways of cathecting other women or men as there are ways in other cultures, where the discourse of homosexuality remains so foreign. Indeed, part of the oppressiveness of the modern formation is that all forms of erotics among men or among women get classified by the same logic. We might begin to clarify the question by saying that the theorization of homosexuality as narcissism is itself a form of narcissism peculiar to modern heterosexuality. The central imperative of heterosexist ideology is that the homosexual be supposed to be out of dialogue on the subject of his being. Imagining that the homosexual is narcissistically contained in an unbreakable fixation on himself serves two functions at once: it allows a self-confirming pathology by declaring homosexuals' speech, their interrelations, to be an illusion; *and more fundamentally it allows the constitution of heterosexuality as such.*

If that sounds like a strong claim, let me repeat that by heterosexuality I mean the modern discursive organization of sex that treats gender difference as difference in general. It is a sexuality organized by its self-understanding as *hetero*sexuality and therefore also includes the categories of homo- and autoerotics against which it defines itself. What I would like to suggest is that it is possible to read this historically recent discourse as, in part, a reaction formation. The allegory of gender protects against a recognition of the role of the imaginary in the formation of the erotic. It provides reassurance that imaginary intersubjectivity has been transcended. To the extent that our culture relies on the allegorization of gender to disguise from itself its own ego erotics, it will recognize those ego erotics only in the person of the homosexual, apparently bereft of the master trope of difference. If it were possible to admit that any relevant forms of otherness operate in homosexuality, then the main feature of heterosexual self-understanding would be lost. The heterosexual would be no longer be able to interpret the gendered, binary form of his or her own captation in desire as already being the transcendence of that captation.

But there is a broader issue at stake here, and one that could be raised as an objection. What if we are to return to the more generous reading of Lacan, seeing the psychoanalytic account not only as an ideological rationalization, but as an essentially accurate description of the *cultural* mechanisms whereby gender and alterity are equated? For surely Lacan is correct to point out that the equation takes place not just in psychoanalytic theory, but on very elementary levels of subjective experience. It *is* a truth of experience for analysis, in our society, that the subject is presented with the question of his or her existence through the problematic alterity of gender. That is why the *psychoanalytic* tradition of linking narcissism and homosexuality has been so easy to confirm. And although the categories and norms of that tradition can be shown to be ideological and incoherent, they are the categories and norms of subjective experience in our culture, rather than simply the prejudices of a few theorists. The argument that I have made here therefore raises a whole new problem: what is the social and historical character of this organization of sexuality and gender?

This issue challenges us to separate the two problematics that I have brought together in this essay: on the one hand the problem of women's construction as the Other, with its prehistoric sources in phallocentrism; on the other hand, a sex/ gender system in which object choice is posed as an apprehension of alterity *tout court*. These two structures of power are currently coarticulated as a unity of experience, but they have different histories. The system of hetero- and homosexual- ities is a much more recent phenomenon, codified in discourse only for the past century. Through most of Western history erotics among men in particular have been understood precisely along axes of difference: the active/passive difference in the discourse of sodomy, for instance, or the pedagogic difference of generations in the classical discourse of pederasty. If suddenly it has become necessary and common-sensical to imagine erotics among men or among women as homosexuality, a sexuality of sameness, we might ask how that has come about. We might also ask what relation there might be between this recent organization of sexuality and the longer history of phallocentrism that constructs woman as Other. Indeed, one reason it is so hard for us to imagine hetero- and homosexualities as recent developments is that they have been articulated so closely with that phallocentric construction of Otherness.

Unfortunately, if the organization of sexuality around the axis of the hetero and the homo is the result of historical change, we have virtually no social theory of why its organization in this form should have been so recent or what kind of historical narrative it would call for. The account typically given in the wake of Michel Foucault has been to attribute the system of heterosexuality to its discourse, beginning roughly with the naming of *homosexuality* in the late nineteenth century.[32]

The Foucauldian account has an undeniable force in showing that the discourse of sexuality is a form of biotechnical power, not a superstructural effect. Nevertheless, I think my argument suggests, in effect, a different strategy of historicizing the whole organization of sexuality. If I am correct that the ideology of gender as alterity is a special way of not recognizing the imaginary sources of desire, then why should Western society have developed that need for misrecognition so recently? Why should there have been an imperative for such a massive displacement of ego erotics?

To pose the question in this way is to link the problem of heterosexuality not simply to modern society in the sense of recent society, but to the force of modernity. A full critique of heterosexism would involve questions about the role of the ego in post-Enlightenment capitalist society. That debate is a complex one, but I can at least indicate its relevance here. On one side Christopher Lasch, in *The Culture of Narcissism*, laments the ego orientation of consumer society as producing debased forms of individualism and symptomatic perversions such as the gay rights movement.[33] On the other side, Jürgen Habermas can argue that the self-reflection of the autonomous ego is the source of a still progressive modernity. And he can show in a fairly nuanced way that ego-identity becomes both necessary and problematic in a whole new range of social contexts.[34] Both sides agree that a tension between the ego and its ideals has become newly important in post-Enlightenment Western capitalism. In response to that debate, could we speculate that the ego erotics coded in homosexuality is a special feature of this social history?

Obviously, that subject is too large to be treated here. But I should note that the possibility of such an account is already implicit in the way Freud imagines an erotics of the ego ideal. In the essay on narcissism, Freud takes a broad social view. Having once stated that secondary narcissism is possible only after the development of critical judgment and the encountering of the admonitions of others, he returns with an even more general description:

> For what prompted the subject to form an ego ideal, on whose behalf his conscience acts as watchman, arose from the critical influence of his parents (conveyed to him by the medium of the voice), to whom were added, as time went on, those who trained and taught him and the innumerable and indefinable host of all the other people in his environment—his fellow men—and public opinion.
>
> In this way large amounts of libido of an essentially homosexual kind are drawn into the formation of the narcissistic ego ideal and find outlet and satisfaction in maintaining it.

Here Freud advances a notion to which he returned often, especially in the *Group Psychology*—the notion that sociality itself is in some essential way a desexualized homosexuality. But when Freud describes the environment to which the subject must relate in such a homosexual way, he depicts an essentially modern society. It is defined by the critical force of training and teaching. It is made up of an "innumerable and indefinable host" of people. And at its limits it finds expression in a highly generalized perspective of criticism: public opinion. This set of social pressures on the ego may also be what Freud has in mind when he links his developmental narrative with the historical transition from traditional to modern. He claims, for instance, that "primitive peoples," like children, orient themselves to the world through primary narcissism rather than secondary.[35] One doesn't have to be uncritical of Freud's ethnocentrism here to imagine that a special role for critical judgment in modern Western societies might also mean that the subject of those societies might be structured by a correspondingly special ego erotics.

Lacan's account also suggests as much, and Lacan in fact often asserts that social modernity has brought about a general pathology of ego erotics.[36] His example of Werther's narcissistic love, we might note, is already articulated within the normative subjectivity of modernity. We can see how that articulated relation works by taking a strikingly similar example from an American admirer and contemporary of Goethe, Charles Brockden Brown, also writing in the context of the late Enlightenment:

> Good God! You say she loves; loves *me!* me, a boy in age; bred in clownish ignorance; scarcely ushered into the world; more than childishly unlearned and raw; a barn-door simpleton; a plow-tail, kitchen-hearth, turnip-hoeing novice![37]

Arthur Mervyn here encounters his heterosexual love as a relation between his ego ideals and his actual ego. Several things follow. First, it is a moment of narcissistic ego erotics ("loves *me!* me . . ."), but the affective charge is attached to what seems like an unbridgable gulf of difference ("Good God!"). The extravagant otherness of his beloved—she is, in fact, older, foreign, and Jewish—allows her to be the fulcrum of Mervyn's desire-laden self-relation. The passage therefore marks the mutual involvement of a conspicuous *hetero*sexuality with a potentially homoerotic fixation on a reflexive ego erotics. And in fact, its usual charge, both in this novel and in Brown's work generally, is decisively, even sensationally homoerotic. Mervyn's awakening here might be constructed as the origin of heterosexuality, but that only shows how closely linked heterosexuality and homosexuality are in the erotics of the ego.

Mervyn's desirous self-relation, however, is also a moment of critical self-consciousness. In the very act of focusing on himself as a possible object of desire, he confronts the difference between his ideals and his actual ego. He occupies the vantage of a critical public opinion, defining an image of himself there: "a boy in age; bred in clownish ignorance; scarcely ushered into the world; more than childishly unlearned and raw; a barn-door simpleton; a plow-tail, kitchen-hearth, turnip-hoeing novice!" This is exactly the sort of role-detached, posttraditional self-consciousness that Habermas identifies with the normative content of modernity. If this sort of ego erotics seems to bear the stamp of the special social contexts of modernity, with its norm of critical self-consciousness in an environment of equals, then both hetero- and homosexuality share its essential structure.

But I do not wish to emphasize only the normative, critical content of modernity. It should also be possible to specify a whole range of social and historical institutions in which the subject is called on to take an evaluative/desirous posture toward his or her ego ideal. The imaginary register will be important, albeit in different ways, for the discourse of rights, the forms of exchange in capitalism, the role-detachment that comes with a system-differentiated society, the mass imaginary of video capitalism, rituals and markets of adolescence, and the like. The work of analyzing the subjectivity of these interarticulated contexts has only begun.

The possibility I'm trying to indicate is that homosexuality, encoded as such, takes these multiple sites of ego-reflection in modern liberal capitalism as multiple sites of erotic play and interaction. Heterosexuality deploys an understanding of gender as alterity in order to mobilize, but also to obscure, a self-reflexive erotics of the actual ego measured against its ideals. In a modernity constituted by multiple sites of ego erotics, sex ceases to be complacently patriarchal and becomes heterosexual, mystifying its own imaginary register with its liberal logic of difference. Homosexuality, however, engages the same self-reflexive erotics, without the mechanism of obscuring it. The homosexual who makes the choice of "what he himself would like to be" expresses the utopian erotics of modern subjectivity. This utopian self-relation, far from being the pathology of the homosexual, could instead be seen as a historical condition and, in the perverse and unrecuperated mode of homosexual subjectivity, the source of a critical potential. This is why modern heterosexuality needs a discourse about homosexuality as a displacement of its own narcissistic sources. The psychoanalytic tradition enacts and justifies that displacement.

13

Rebel Without a Closet
Christopher Castiglia

In her study of "male homosocial desire" in English literature, Eve Kosofsky Sedgwick argues that, in an erotic triangle, through their competition for, their "traffic in," a shared female object of desire, two male rivals bond "homosocially," establishing and ensuring "the structures for maintaining and transmitting patriarchal power."[1] Sedgwick's paradigm, however, depends on the repression of the homosexual into the homosocial. The "closet cases" Sedgwick examines appear as the misogynists they are because they are unable to let go of the letter, if not the spirit, of heterosexual desire. Sedgwick's model works admirably in her study of these texts, because it is heterosexually, if homosocially, oriented (that is, it still centers on the boy-meets-girl plot, even if to deconstruct it). But what happens when the boys get together without the girl? What might *their* triangle look like? What concerns me in this discussion is a paradigm applicable to texts in which the homosexual—as opposed to the homosocial—content of the rivalry is more explicit.

Robert K. Martin, in his study of Melville, *Hero, Captain, and Stranger*, provides a model for applying Sedgwick's paradigm to a more homosexually oriented erotic triangle. Martin traces a triangle in Melville's sea novels involving the Captain (Ahab, for instance), who represents "the imposition of the male on the female" and therefore sexual, political, and economic power; the Dark Stranger (Queequeg), who "offers the possibility of an alternate sexuality, one that is less dependent upon performance and conquest"; and the Hero (Ishmael), who must choose between them. "The novels may be distinguished," Martin writes, "precisely by the degree to which the hero is able to make the choice for the Dark Stranger and to accomplish his act of rebellion against the Captain."[2]

I want to modify the triangle one more time by suggesting that the figures Martin establishes—the Captain, the Dark Stranger, and the Hero—are translated in recent popular film culture into another obvious figure of authority (the father), another threat to the father's authority (a homosexual man), and a kind of hero, to a greater or lesser degree (the son), who must negotiate between the patriarchal privilege offered by his father (and consequently heterosexual convention) and the Otherness, the alienation from male heterosexual privilege, embodied in the son's potential acceptance of a homosexual lover, signifying an acknowledgment of his own homosexuality. The power struggle among father, son, and lover is, of course, implicit in the figures Martin describes, as it will be in narratives where homosexuality emerges from the depths to which it is repressed in the novels studied by Sedgwick. The difference between the triangle examined by Sedgwick and that studied by Martin is that while the former is concerned with the transmission of patriarchal power, the latter threatens to disrupt that transmission altogether. The films under discussion here, like Melville's sea novels, raise the question of how patriarchal power can be achieved by the son—how it can be deeded by the father—once homosexuality threatens to place the son outside the sphere of patriarchal prescription. What is ultimately in question in the triangles under discussion is the father's power to name and therefore to control.

By drawing attention to a father's right to prescribe the sexual, social, political, and economic subjectivity of his son, I am also foregrounding the ways in which the father-son-lover triangle in American film has inscribed the cultural "policing" of desire and of discourse. Policing—the dissemination and reinforcement of hegemonic ideology through every layer of a culture's discourse—has been most elaborately theorized by Michel Foucault in his discussions of discipline.[3] The most "pertinent general propagations" of Foucauldian discipline, as they are characterized by D. A. Miller, include

> (1) an ideal of unseen but all-seeing surveillance, which, though partly realized in several, often interconnected institutions, is identified with none; (2) a regime of the norm, in which normalizing perceptions, prescriptions, and sanctions are diffused in discourses and practices throughout the social fabric; and (3) various technologies of the self and its sexuality, which administer the subject's own contribution to the intensive and continuous "pastoral" care that liberal society proposes to take of each and every one of its charges.

The films under discussion represent striking examples of Foucauldian discipline. Each film is explicitly and centrally concerned with "the self and its sexuality," as well as with the technologies—psychiatry, law, peer pressure—through which they are regulated. Moreover, the examination of sexual identity is intrinsically connected with "a regime of the norm" within the setting of each film—the traditional domesticity of white, middle-class suburbia. In this analysis, then, I join Miller in "moving the question of policing out of the streets, as it were, into the closet—I mean, into the private and domestic space on which the very identity of the liberal subject depends."[4] But once within that "private and domestic space"—depicted as the ultimate "technology" for "normalizing perceptions, prescriptions, and sanctions"—the subject must also come "out of the closet," bringing home the uncanny, forcing normality to a moment of crisis that necessarily reveals the faults upon which it is constructed. Finally, because the texts under discussion are *films*, they provide a particularly problematic representation of/through "surveillance." A film necessarily positions its viewer in a patrol car—nothing that happens escapes one's view. Film gives its viewer the sensation, however illusory, of (super)vision. Nominally, the viewer is identified with the dominant ideology—the Law—represented by the police. But when a film "identifies" with—privileges, sympathizes with—the "outlaw," can the filmic paradox of controlling medium and resisting subject be resolved, even reversed?

The father-son-lover triangle is nowhere more evident than in Nicholas Ray's 1955 classic, *Rebel Without a Cause*. As the film begins, Jim Stark (James Dean) is alienated from his family as a whole but particularly from his father, Frank (Jim Backus). The apparent problem with Mr. Stark is that he—like the fathers of countless sissies in American film—doesn't wear the pants in the family, letting his wife and his mother walk all over him. Left without a masculine "role model," Jim begins the allegorical search for his "proper" sexual identity that constitutes the overarching subject of *Rebel*'s plot.

At the moment of greatest crisis between Jim and his father—the opening sequence at (appropriately enough) the police station, where Jim has been brought for drunken disorderliness—he meets the two characters who will pull his sexual identity in opposite directions: Judy (Natalie Wood) and Plato (Sal Mineo). Jim feels an instant affinity with Plato, offering the shivering boy his jacket. The jacket becomes, in the course of the film, the dominant trope for Jim's self-image, and for reasons that become clear in time, Plato at first rejects Jim's offer. At the same time as Jim establishes connection with Plato, he recovers the compact Judy has left behind. Jim is, from the start, caught between two separate narratives: the fairly traditional boy-meets-girl plot offered by Judy and a somewhat less well-defined option represented by Plato. Introduced within the precinct station, Jim's erotic choice is what the film—and the society it represents—seeks to police.

In the course of the film, Plato's sexuality becomes an issue of increasing intrigue, as well as increasing gloom. When Plato opens his school locker, instead of revealing a cheesecake glossy, the door bears a photo of Alan Ladd.[5] Plato becomes more and more solicitous of Jim's attention, to the point of obsession, even inviting Jim to spend the night at his place. And, as Plato's homosexuality becomes clear (his name is significant), so does his mental instability. Plato is at best neurotic (he is initially in the police station for shooting a litter of puppies, an act that highlights his "unnatural" character), and the closer he gets to Jim, the more unhinged he becomes. The film sets up an implicit connection, then, between homoerotic bonding and insanity.

The cause of Plato's insanity, apart from his implied homosexuality, is his failure to attain a markedly different kind of Platonic ideal: the traditional nuclear family. Plato is marked as excluded from traditional domesticity by virtue of having been abandoned by his wealthy, gallivanting parents (in a distinctly middle-class universe, his wealth also signifies his difference). He is further identified as an outsider in that he is raised by the film's only black character, his nurse and guardian. Plato tries to make Jim and Judy his surrogate parents, implying that his erotic relationship with Jim is also a paternal-filial one, but Plato is no more successful with one relationship than he is with the other. Homosexuality, through the character of Plato, is associated not only with insanity, then, but with a complete alienation from the family—a position that, one should recall, Jim himself approaches at the beginning of the film. To give up on Daddy's love—or worse, to literalize that love in a physical male-male relationship—is just plain crazy.

As Plato becomes more interested in Jim, the latter's sexual identity changes. When the film starts, Jim is quite traditionally dressed, wearing a jacket and tie. But as the film progresses, he becomes increasingly androgynous. In a film that defines manhood in terms of active choice—Frank Stark tells his son, "Be careful about choosing your pals; don't let them choose you"—Jim is strikingly passive, functioning more as the object of Plato's desire than as the subject of his own. Signaling his increased "feminization," in the course of the film Jim exchanges his traditional suit jacket for the now famous red one. The color red, associated with Judy's "wild" sexuality, is quite significant in the film. In the initial sequence at the police station, Judy (who has been brought in for wandering the streets alone late at night) wears a red coat. And it is her bright red lipstick that ensures *her* alienation from her father, who calls her a tramp. When Jim dons his flaming red jacket, then, he exchanges his traditional garb for one that subtly links him to Judy and her defiant femininity. That Plato is in some way responsible for Jim's androgynization is undeniable: it is Plato, after all, who nicknames Jim "Jamie" (a nickname that, for no apparent reason, startles Judy).

The decisive battle over Jim—a conflict between Plato's desires and the policed enforcement of traditional masculinity—occurs in the sequence at the abandoned mansion, close to the end of the film (a sequence redolent—in retrospect—with the ambient sexuality of 1980s Calvin Klein advertising). Jim, Judy, and Plato lie together, making it occasionally unclear who is touching whom, again conflating the traditionally separated realms of the familial—the three are posing as a mock family—and the sexual. Jim's alienation from his own father in this scene is indicated when, in the oddest moment of the film, he suddenly begins to speak in the voice of Mr. Magoo, the cartoon character whose voice since 1949 was supplied by Jim Backus. This intertextual reference renders Frank Stark both comic and fictional, robbing him of his authority as father. But at this moment of crisis in Frank's authority—a crisis as well for the authority of the film, insofar as it rests on a representation of apparently unconstructed, hegemonic "reality"—Plato's newfound family is disrupted by the appearance of the Boys. In a literalization of the Freudian model of the return of the repressed, the macho boys arrive to terrorize poor Plato at the very minute that Jim and Judy go off "to be alone." Plato escapes to the planetarium, where he is surrounded by police, and, despite the fact that Jim has unloaded Plato's gun, Plato is still shot to death as he attempts to run from the bright lights of the police cars.

One might expect to see in *Rebel* a triangle in which Jim and Plato bond over

Judy, but such is not the case. Judy is important to the narrative, both as the apparent object of Jim's desire and as the mother in Plato's surrogate family. Yet Plato does not figure as a rival for Judy's affections, being more explicit in his choice of a masculine love-object than the characters studied by Sedgwick (the relationship between Jim and Buzz more closely resembles Sedgwick's model). If, as Sedgwick argues, the male-female-male triangle is established for the transmission of patriarchal privilege, then such a triangle involving Jim, Plato, and Judy— none of whom possesses such power—would be useless indeed. Rather, if one can argue that the difficulty of resolution is equal to the centrality of its significance, the more important triangle in *Rebel* exists among Jim, Plato, and Frank Stark. Through this triangle, the father is returned to his "rightful" position of authority within his family, while his "rebel" son is brought back within the purlieu of paternal authority.[6] Telling Jim, "Stand up and I'll stand up with you," Frank Stark signals both the new bond between father and son and the phallic authority that bond "erects."

The patriarchal—and erotic—bonding of father and son depends upon the elimination of the father's rival, Plato, who at the same time as he yearns for a family, represents illogic, nontraditional sexuality, the fascination of life outside the realm of the "normal." What allows the completion of Jim's bond with patriarchy is the trade in—the literal sacrifice of—Jim's homosexual counterpart. It is only with Plato's death—through the agency of the police—that Jim is reconciled with his family, and is placed firmly within a heterosexual relationship with Judy (although he introduces her, in an oddly unromantic moment, as his "friend"—a euphemism often reserved for gay lovers). The last words of the film come from Mrs. Stark, who exclaims, "He is . . ." before she is silenced by her newly empowered husband. But what is shut up at the film's end is the process of (re)inscribing masculinity. It's clear to everyone by the end of the film what a "he" is, and the final ellipses signal the tragedy of Plato's death. The end of Plato's influence is signified when Jim zips up Plato's corpse in his old red jacket. The symbol of ambiguous or "rebellious" sexuality need no longer be Jim's mantle; it is now buried with its inspiration. Mr. Stark tells Jim, "You did everything a man could," placing his own jacket on his son's shoulders. In this final exchange of jackets, Jim is re-covered by the patriarchal power to name and to transmit "manhood."

Frank Stark's newfound authority over Jim marks the resolution of the film's second significant triangle. In the film's opening sequence at the police station, the juvenile detective hands Jim over to his father, who in turns offers the detective a cigar (which, in the context of *Rebel*, is surely not just a cigar). Its humor aside, this scene marks the more serious competitive alliance between the two representatives of phallic authority in the family and in society at large. This triangle, too, has concerned the fate of Jim's sexuality from the film's start, and, from the outset, the deck has been stacked. Frank Stark assumes his authority from the one father figure who is strong and powerful and not at odds with the younger generation: the juvenile detective, Ray. Of course, *Rebel* was written and directed by Nicholas Ray. The author here is both father and policeman, steering his characters/children towards the one satisfactory ending: a heterosexual, nuclear family.

The policed establishment of the traditional family is one of the many ideologies and fashions the 1980s have borrowed from the 1950s. In both decades, the family standard closely resembles the Andersons of *Father Knows Best*, with any mate other than a girl like Mom perceived as a dire threat to the Buds of America. The ultimate 1980s family fantasy, *Dynasty*, for instance, borrows one of its central triangles intact from *Rebel Without a Cause*. A son of ambivalent sexuality is reconciled with his father, who represents the patriarchy more unabashedly in the person of oil tycoon Blake Carrington. The bonding of father and son is again accomplished through the traffic in (the murder of) the third male: the lover—who threatens to separate father and son, to put at risk men's positions in a rigid social and economic structure. With *Dynasty*, however, the art of reconciliation-through-death, seemingly the best scenario for acting out the erotic triangle, takes on a more threatening aspect through its grisly repetition—*two* of Stephen's lovers are murdered. One lover is shot by guerrillas at a wedding; a previous lover has been killed by Blake himself, who is "let off" by a jury of his peers, again highlighting the complicit relationship between heterosexual privilege and legal (lack of) discipline. Homosexuality is represented in both narratives as a metonym for insanity and death: the obvious heroes are the police/fathers—Blake or Ray.

But the 1980s have also generated variations on the father-son-lover dynamic of *Rebel*, for better and for worse. More original—and more encouraging for gay viewers—is ABC's *Consenting Adults* (Gilbert Cates, 1985),[7] which depicts the disruption of the "perfect family": affluent, suburban, affectionate but not intimate. When attractive, athletic, intelligent Jeff Lynn informs his parents, Ken and Tess, that he believes himself to be homosexual, his mother arranges for Jeff to see a psychiatrist who will attempt a "cure"; his father reacts less positively, tolerating his son's presence as long as Jeff remains a virgin. Once Jeff has a sexual experience, however, Ken explodes, threatening to cut off monetary support to his undergraduate son. The threat further alienates Jeff, who moves in with his sister and brother-in-law and eventually with a lover. Parents and son refuse to communicate. But when Ken dies suddenly of a second stroke, Tess, afraid that she too may let time run out, breaks the ice and reconciles with Jeff. Clearly the erotic triangle in *Consenting Adult* reaches a radically different resolution than in *Rebel Without a Cause*. The homosexual son or lover is no longer sacrificed; instead, the father goes. Through a number of subtle strategies, Ken Lynn, the patriarchal center of the film, is decentered and finally removed altogether.

The film undermines Ken's position primarily through the subversion of the jokes and stories he tells to gain control over his family and to retain center stage. As the film begins, Ken celebrates his recovery from a near-fatal stroke. With the exception of his son, Jeff, who is away at the University of Washington, the entire family is present. The party is interrupted when Jeff phones to tell Ken that he loves him, thereby rendering his father silent for the first time since the film's start. To cover his embarrassment, Ken tells the following joke:

> A man goes into a restaurant and he tells the waiter, "I want cold eggs, bitter coffee, and burnt toast." The waiter says, "Sir, I can't serve you that." The man says, "Why not? You did yesterday."

In telling this joke, Ken successfully recaptures his narrative control. He is again at the center of attention. Ken's second joke, told later in the film, is racier:

> So the guy slips the gal around the back, up the fire-escape, and into this sleazy hotel room. I mean, we're talking sleazy here. There's nothing in the room but a bed, a table, a telephone, and a Bible. So they settle down. They're making the best possible use of the bed and suddenly the phone rings. The man tries to ignore it. It rings again. "Hello?" It's the night clerk. "Hey, didn't I rent you a single room?" The guy says, "Yeah, you did." The desk clerk says, "Well, do you have a woman up there with you?" The guy says, "Yeah, I'm afraid I do." The desk clerk says, "Well, what are you going to do about that?" The guy thinks a minute and says, "Maybe you should send up another Bible."

Finally, when his doctor tells Ken that his health has once again deteriorated, Ken tells his third joke:

> The priest says, "Life begins at the moment of conception." The minister says, "No, no. Life begins at the moment of birth." The rabbi thinks a minute and says, "You're both wrong. Life begins when the last kid goes to college and the dog dies."

Ken's investment in these jokes may be best understood in light of Freud's theory of humor. Described by Freud as a mode of cathexis, humor "signifies the triumph not only of the ego, but also of the pleasure principle, which is strong enough to assert itself here in the face of the adverse real circumstances." In its "repudiation of the possibility of suffering," the superego allows the ego a narrative that anticipates emotion, only to diffuse that emotion.[8] The realities and their attendant emotions, distanced and diffused by Ken's jokes, are reflected both by their content and by the context in which he tells them. Ken's first joke registers his displeasure at not "getting what he wants" in general. One notes in the second joke—Ken's first to deal, albeit coyly, with sex—a shift in emphasis, reflecting the most important narrative event to occur between the first joke and the second: Jeff's first sexual encounter with another man. As physicality forces its way into Ken's quotidian control, he, through the joke, attempts to objectify, repress, force the physical out. As Jeff's action questions the primacy of heterosexual union (and hence of his father's privileged status), Ken's second joke invokes religion to excuse a petty crime done in the name of heterosexual hanky-panky. God and (straight) men are, on some level, in cahoots. Finally, an awareness that the heterosexual marriage Ken has held up to his son as the epitome of "natural" union is in fact riddled with tension and dishonesty—Ken's marriage is devoid of intimacy because of his inability to "open himself up" to his wife—is diffused by Ken's last joke, which asserts that "life begins" exactly where the Lynn marriage dies. That Ken, whose status as father and husband is called into question by the challenging desires of his son and of his wife, chooses the joke as his privileged discourse is not surprising. Freud, describing the psychic operations of humor, notes that "the humorist acquires his superiority by assuming the role of the grown-up, identifying himself to some extent with the father, while he reduces the other people to the position of the children."[9] Ken, who is literally losing his authority over his children, turns instinctively to the discourse of humor to reassert his "superiority."

Yet his family resists Ken's efforts at control, as one scene demonstrates particularly well. When Jeff comes home from college on Christmas Eve in a last attempt to make amends with his father, he initiates conversation by asking Ken:

> Jeff: Do you remember that year you decided that we should raise our own turkey?
> Tess: Oh yeah! Tom the Terrible!
> Ken: You chased him around the yard so much he was all muscle.
> Jeff: No, he chased me. That turkey thought he was an eagle!

Ken attempts to fictionalize Jeff's childhood as that of a "normal" boy: active and aggressive. But Jeff refuses to allow his father to write his history, insisting on his own story: the myth of Ganymede. In the *Metamorphoses*, Ovid writes, "The king of the gods once loved a Trojan boy named Ganymede; for once, there was something found that Jove would rather have been than what he was. He made himself an eagle, the only bird able to bear his thunderbolts, went flying on his false wings, and carried off the youngster."[10] Jeff exchanges his father's myth of normal heterosexual adolescence for his own homosexual myth. Furthermore, whereas Zeus, the archetypal Father, successfully carries Ganymede away, Tom the Terrible is incapable of capturing Jeff. The eagle/father of Ovid becomes, in Jeff's revision, the turkey/father, Zeus' sexual mastery of Ganymede ironically transformed into Ken's failure to "capture" Jeff either within his narrative of Jeff's youth or within the more general narrative of heterosexual success. The final irony lies in the fact that Zeus, the father, wishes to *be* Ganymede; viewers familiar with Ovid's myth may therefore deduce that Ken's reaction to Jeff's sexuality might conceal a fair amount of repression or, at best, jealousy of his son's homosexuality.

Even more striking is the degree to which the film itself takes Jeff's part by undermining the narratives upon which Ken's authority rests. The sequence leading to Jeff's first sexual experience, for instance, neatly undercuts Ken's first joke. Having left his parents' home after a fight with his father, Jeff stops on his way back to school to get a bite to eat. He orders a cup of soup and then, changing his mind, returns the soup and orders coffee. As all this occurs, Jeff makes eye contact with a young man, with whom he eventually leaves to make love. By making love to the man, Jeff ensures his exclusion from the familial unit, the domain of his father's narrative. Yet the scene of exclusion from the patriarchal narrative occurs precisely within that narrative. For in picking up a man *in a diner*, Jeff subverts Ken's first joke. Ken's trope is sarcasm, Jeff's is irony, turning the scene of his father's security into a scene of rupture and subversion. The heavy-handed sarcasm of Ken's narrative is undermined by the subtle communication between the men, and, in a final irony, Jeff is incapable of the very nastiness that Ken's joke expresses. When he gets up to leave the diner, Jeff tells the waiter, "It wasn't the soup. I'm just not hungry."

Ken's second joke is revised by Tess, who demonstrates the repression involved in Ken's alliance with God. When she tries to discuss Jeff's sexuality, Ken refuses to listen. He retreats to his room and shuts the door, as Tess yells after him:

> "I have a lot to say. You just don't want to hear it. All right, fine! This has been your answer to all our problems for how long? Go on! Walk down that hall, go in that bedroom and close that door. Climb into that empty bed, and go to sleep asking yourself, 'Why has God done this to Ken Lynn?' "

Ken cannot make "the best possible use" (as he puts it in his joke) of his bed, because, physically and emotionally impotent, he isolates himself from his wife. He has defined the relationship between a man and a woman in terms of sex, and, since he is sexually impotent, his definition turns against him. Even God forsakes him, sending an heir who is queer. The benign alliance between Bed and Bible seems to have turned malicious, as Ken's narrative supercedes the limits set by its author.

If Ken's narratives represent an effort to gain control over a distanced—and infantalized—Other, his final joke represents Ken's final loss of that control. At the very moment that, according to Ken's joke, "life begins," Ken himself dies. In his earlier jokes, Ken frames narratives in which he, as the subject and not the object, is in his eyes obviously not implicated. Yet in his last joke—told when he knows he hasn't long to live—Ken lets himself become the object, the brunt, having apparently internalized the irony previously imposed on him from without. In a narrative in which an acceptance of the physical makes Ken's superiority ironic, Ken's wit can only seem, in the end, sardonic and desperate. The film's ironic twist on Ken's joke is that while, according to Ken, a parent's life begins when the children leave, Jeff's "life" (meaning both his sexual life and his life enabled by a sense of privacy, as Ken's joke implies) begins with Ken's departure. For Freud, joke-telling established the subject as a father figure; but in *Consenting Adult*, the joke backfires, ultimately leaving Ken the child, Jeff the parent.

The irony that Jeff's homosexuality gives to his father's attempts to construct the perfect family is perpetuated by the changing nature of frames in *Consenting Adult*.

During the opening credits, the camera pans across a row of framed photographs of the Lynns, establishing the "family" as a definable unit, a construct that can be fixed. But there are two absences from the initial "frame" of the family. The first, of course, is Jeff. But a second absence becomes apparent when Ken's son-in-law, taking a picture of Tess and Ken, cries, "More passion! More passion!" The two absences—Jeff and passion—become linked for the viewer. From the start, the problem with this unit as framed is that it lacks an awareness of passion, of desire—in short, of the body.

After the opening sequence, the film's frames grow increasingly more narrow. Clusters of twos—binaries almost always in tension—mark the second half of the film. Displayed in Ken's office, for instance, is a picture of father and son that Ken, unable to exist within the same "frame" as his son, removes from sight. The most tense scene of the film—in which Jeff is ostracized from the family for having had sex with another man—is shot in "separation"; that is, no two characters are shown within the same frame at the same time.

As definitions of sexuality change, however, the film's frames re-enlarge, as an exchange between Ken and Tess makes clear. Ken comes to Tess' bedroom to say good-night but is, once again, unwilling to sleep with his wife. Tess, who has previously borne her husband's neglect in silence, now presses Ken for an explanation. He tries to blame Jeff's homosexuality, and then his stroke, but finally admits that he is embarrassed about his sexual impotence. Tess explains that she loves him because of a bond deeper than that established in sex, and he is finally able to join her in bed. We watch Ken negotiate his way from a definition of his relationship based on reproduction, phallocentricism, and power to one based on tenderness, mutuality, and caring. He must move from his own definition of sexuality, in short, to that of Tess and Jeff, who understand in different ways that sexuality is finally undefinable, either by act or by speech. Ken's move from his old definition of sexuality (always implicitly "enacted"—like his jokes—upon an other) is marked by the expansion of frames. When Ken first comes to Tess' bedroom, he is seen within the frame of the doorway, while Tess is seen beside him, framed in a mirror. But Ken and Tess walk out of their frames, meeting halfway to embrace, thereby signifying the redefining that is about to occur.

Consenting Adult ends, it would seem, where it begins: a family gathering. Tess invites Jeff and his lover to spend Christmas with the rest of the family, and thus the stage is set for another family (re)union. Yet we are not, in the end, where we began, for an important reason. The family, by the end of the film, has done away with frames, just as Ken and Tess do in the bedroom scene. While the film begins with photographs, it ends with a nonphotograph. That is, it specifically ends with an event projected but not seen. What allows this avoidance of "framing" is precisely what marks the first gathering from the second. In the first, the father is the dominant narrative authority, excluding, by his presence, sexuality as represented by Jeff. In the projected final gathering, it is the father who will be absent, his monolithic narrative control giving way to the dialogic narrative of mother and son. Freed from the frames, from the definitions, set by the father, the family can see itself, not as a reified unit, but as a fluid collection of individuals. In effect, the construct of "the American family" has dissolved before the force of a son's acceptance of his body.

Although some critics were disappointed by *Consenting Adult*, arguing that the parents' heterosexual worries eclipse the homosexual plot, I would argue that Jeff becomes entirely omnipresent, even if as a character he begins to seem of secondary importance. Through a manipulation of narrative order, *mise-en-scène*, and the frames of the camera itself, the film continually enacts the unwriting of Ken's narrative that Jeff and Tess, through their acceptance of alternative definitions of sexuality, initiate within the narrative. The narrative "becomes" Jeff, as it were, its presence filling in for his on-screen absence. Surveillance comes into the hands of the outlaw. The final irony of *Consenting Adult* is that the proponents of heterosexual social hegemony who try to exclude gay presence are unaware that they, as characters, exist within a kind of gay narrative hegemony. In *Consenting Adult*, the slogan "we are everywhere" takes on a new, textual significance.

Consenting Adult changes the original paradigm of the homosexual triangle to privilege the homo- over the heterosexual male. But there's still a problem with any plot requiring a ritual violence for resolution or advocating the establishment of any hegemony at all. The presence of death in this film problematically eliminates the potential for critique, for political change. Whether it's the father or son who's killed, the myth that the two cannot exist simultaneously, each providing a helpful critique of the other, persists. The paradigm never functions progressively.

The closest a film has come to using the male triangle without requiring a ritual death (or a symbolic death—the cooptation of the son into the patriarchy) is *Welcome Home, Bobby* (1986), CBS's contribution to the deluge of gay-related films. *Bobby* at first seems to be yet another film about a boy's attempt to win his father's pleasure at whatever cost. And like his filmic predecessors, Bobby comes up against an oppressive cop-father. When Bobby goes to confront his father (in the garage, where men go to be men), his father tells him, "The men in this family are men. You'll abide by that rule," again implying that masculinity can be enforced, policed. But the film quickly takes a turn for the better. Soon after the scene in the garage, Bobby appears at the dinner table in full drag and, in no uncertain terms, tells his father to take his expectations and go to hell. Because of this speech, Bobby earns his father's respect—on Bobby's terms. The film ends with Bobby's father coming out to the shack where Bobby has been living to tell his son he wants him to come home. Happy ending. No deaths. A minimum of selling out.

There are two reasons *Bobby* can use the paradigm in ways the other films couldn't. First, *Bobby* offers a community, a support network including gays and straights that gives Bobby helpful advice and no-strings-attached affection. This network also presents a new character: the Good Father. Bobby gets help and support both from a straight psychiatrist (who is also, oddly, a Catholic priest—a Father) and from a gay high school teacher. The gay son is faced not with only Bad

Fathers and Good Policemen. Second, *Bobby* finally comes out on the side of education and change. Death is the only resolution in a plot that doesn't allow for dialogue, except as a mode of cooptation. But in *Welcome Home, Bobby*, the father finally learns the lesson one of his sons tried to teach him earlier in the film: "Prejudice, Pop—it's terrible."

Postscript: Nightsweats on Elm Street; or, Optimism Without a Cause

When I wrote "Rebel Without a Closet" in 1986, I was comfortably convinced that representations of gays in the media were changing for the better. My optimism was, of course, ludicrous, especially in the face of the proliferation of homophobic representations surrounding, circumscribing, constituting the AIDS epidemic. I should have better heeded—as I since have—my assessment that "AIDS provides filmmakers with an easy metaphor, an easy out."

Soon after writing "Rebel Without a Closet," I was watching *Nightmare on Elm Street 2: Freddy's Revenge* (Jack Sholder, 1985) with some gay friends. When one leaned over and, referring to the film's protagonist, asked me, "Why is that boy swishing like that?" I was startled, for I had been thinking that in one of the opening sequences, in which the boy wakes from a nightmare soaked to the skin, he seemed to be experiencing "night sweats," an AIDS symptom. The rest of the film confirmed my sense that *Freddy's Revenge* was "about," if not AIDS exactly, then the murderous consequences of homoeroticism and of homosexuality. That the film also resurrects the classic father-son-lover triangle of *Rebel* therefore came as no surprise.

The second installment of the *Nightmare on Elm Street* sequence differs from the others (there are five, to date) in two important ways. First, all the victims in *Freddy's Revenge* are men, in contrast to the misogynistic violence at the core of the contemporary slasher film. Second, in the others, Freddy, a child-murderer who has been burnt to death by vigilante parents, returns in the dreams of the remaining children of the otherwise quiet suburban Elm Street, and, killing them in their dreams, he kills them in reality as well. One of the principal horrors of *Nightmare on Elm Street* is that death comes through no physical agency, but as it were from the subconscious itself. In *Freddy's Revenge*, however, the teenaged protagonist, Jesse Walsh, murders for Freddy, who is somehow inside him, not just psychically as in the other films, but physically (in a particularly gruesome scene, Freddy appears, following *Alien*, from Jesse's stomach). The connection between the insistence on male objects of violence—who are also, as I shall argue, objects of *desire*—and the rendering of murderous agency within the body of the film's protagonist together make *Freddy's Revenge* an ingenious, if ignorant, allegory of the fate of homoeroticism in the age of AIDS.

Freddy's Revenge has three sequentially repeated narrative components: first, an argument between Jesse and his father; second, an implicit or explicit erotic exchange between Jesse and another man; and third, the murder of that man. Mr. Walsh is a caricature of a bad movie father: ineffectual yet bossy, a petty domestic tyrant. Jesse and his father have an argument right at the film's outset, ending when Mr. Walsh tells his son, "Nobody likes a smart ass, buddy boy." Paternal wisdom notwithstanding, it soon appears that Jesse's "smart ass" is precisely what everyone likes. In the next scene, during a baseball game in gym class, Jesse gets in a fight with another boy, Grady, who pulls Jesse's sweatpants down, exposing his ass to view. Jesse and Grady proceed to roll around on the ground, Jesse's pants around his knees, until the gym teacher, Schneider, breaks the fight up, telling the boys, "Assume the position!"—meaning, do push-ups. The sexual undercurrent of this scene becomes explicit when, as they pump up and down, Grady tells Jesse, "[Schneider] gets his rocks off like this. Hangs around queer S & M joints downtown. He likes pretty-boys like you." That night Freddy first comes to Jesse, apparently, as in the other movies, in a dream. Rather than murdering Jesse, however, Freddy propositions him. When Jesse yells for his father's protection, Freddy responds, "Daddy can't help you now. I need you, Jesse. We got special work to do here, you and me. You've got the body and I've got the brains"—removing his hat to show his exposed brain to the terrified boy. Next day, when we again see Jesse, he is conforming to Grady's claim that he is a "pretty boy" and to Freddy's reduction of him to a body. For as the tape player blasts "Touch Me All Night Long" (an ironic selection, given the meeting of Freddy and Jesse at night, not to mention that Freddy kills with his razor-tipped fingertips), Jesse lip-synchs to the female vocalist and dances around his room in a strangely femme version of Tom Cruise's BVD-clad dance in *Risky Business*. Throughout this sequence, the camera focuses first on Jesse's ass, then on his crotch, ensuring his representation as a sexual object.

The connection of alienation from the father, feminization, homoeroticism, and murder is repeated in the next series of events. When the family's pet canary goes mad and finally explodes, Mr. Walsh accuses Jesse of rigging the bird with a cherry bomb. Jesse screams, "You can't talk to me like that!" and storms off. That night, apparently in a dream, Jesse goes to the "queer S & M joint downtown" and, sure enough, gets picked up by Schneider, now decked out in leather and chains. In a parody of gay porn, Schneider takes Jesse back to the gym, has him run laps, and then tells him to hit the showers. The camera shows first Jesse, naked in a spray of water, then Schneider who (in a slightly different gay fantasy) is attacked by the sports equipment in his office. Two jumpropes drag Schneider into the shower room and tie him to the nozzle, as he is supernaturally stripped naked. Suddenly the razor hand appears and cuts Schneider to ribbons. When the camera pulls back, we see that the razored hand belongs, not to Freddy, but to Jesse. Soon Grady, the other boy in the phys. ed. *ménage-à-trois*, is done in too. Afraid of going to sleep (for some reason, the movie maintains the standard storyline that Freddy comes to Jesse in his dreams, although we've seen this not to be the case), Jesse goes to Grady's house late at night and asks if he can stay there. "Something is trying to get inside my body," Jesse tells Grady, who responds, "Yeah and she's female . . ., and you want to sleep with me!" Although told he must by no means take his eyes off Jesse, Grady soon falls asleep, Freddy emerges, and Grady is killed. Again the film sexualizes Grady's death. When Jesse runs to his girlfriend, Lisa, to tell her what has happened, he explains in oddly sexual terms, "He's inside of me, and he wants to take me again." Lisa responds in words characteristic of the paranoid discussions of promiscuity and AIDS, "It's got to be everything you've taken in."

In the face of these murderous homoerotic/filial skirmishes, heterosexuality arrives to save the day. In the film's one attempt at heterosexual representation, at a pool party the night after he kills Schneider, Jesse and Lisa begin to make love. As Jesse licks his way down Lisa's torso, his tongue suddenly becomes monstrous (revealing, among other things, that his transformations are not occurring in dreams). Yet Jesse is unable to kill Lisa (as, in an earlier menacing scene, he has been unable to kill his little sister). Whatever murderous monster is inside Jesse, the film suggests that heterosexual women are immune from its actions. Therefore, despite his terrifying "history" (everything he's taken in), Lisa is able to save Jesse. When Freddy again takes over Jesse's body, Lisa follows him to the abandoned factory where Freddy lives and tells him, "[Jesse's] in there and I want him back. I'm going to take him away from you." With a final triumphant, "I love you, Jesse," Lisa forces herself to kiss Freddy, who loses his hold on Jesse and disappears in a pool of slime. With Jesse's final placement within a heterosexual couple—as with Jim's in *Rebel*—familial order is restored as well. In a final scene, as Mrs. Walsh walks her son out to the school bus, she says, "It's good to have you home again."[11]

In the ending of *Nightmare on Elm Street 2*, as in that of *Rebel Without a Cause*, "normality"—heterosexuality in the context of the traditional (white, suburban) nuclear family—is reinscribed over the corpse of the threatening sexual Other. With the reinscription of "normality" also returns the authority of the father. (Freddy is a particularly potent threat to paternity in general—his birth is the result of a gang-rape, so he has no identifiable father; furthermore, he murders to avenge his mother, placing him firmly within the grasp of the maternal will.[12]) The "policing" of sexuality as a mode of controlling domesticity—and vice versa—is clear in a scene following the murder of Schneider. When the police, who find Jesse walking the streets naked, return him to Elm Street, one officer tells Mr. Walsh, "I'd keep a short leash on him, if I were you," conflating the S & M sexuality of Schneider, the domestic tyranny of Mr. Walsh, and the supervisional prerogatives of the police, all of whom are invested in objectifying and regulating the young man's desires. Insofar as it equates homoeroticism, the dissolution of the family, and a horrible threat to the "general community," *Nightmare on Elm Street 2* represents recent efforts, discussed by Simon Watney,[13] to blur boundaries between private and public. The media manipulations of AIDS, as Watney demonstrates, is preliminary to the "policing of desire" and becomes increasingly dangerous in an age when the regulation of privacy in the name of public morality and of public behavior in the name of "respectable" privacy (a paradox embodied by the Supreme Court's *Hardwick* decision, which in effect claimed that a gay person's private acts offended public sensibilities, while his public identity threatened the sanctity of the family, leaving him excluded from both the public and the private spheres that, under the court's jurisdiction, become one and the same) threatens to leave gay men and lesbians with no safe house, nowhere to escape the moralizing scrutiny of the Law. *Freddy's Revenge* represents a particularly dangerous version of the blurring of the private and the public because the Other who threatens the domestic stability of suburban America is particularly monstrous. Even when the will of the father cannot be defended on its own merits, it can be enforced through representations of the hideous consequences of alternative alliances. As AIDS-phobia grows without any remarkable increase in public education on the disease, the erotic triangle of earlier films promises to become more central, more gruesome, more policed.

IV

Revolutionary Alliances:
Call and Response Across Gender

14

Caged Birds: Race and
Gender in The Sonnet

Marcellus Blount

> I know why the caged bird sings, ah me,
>> When his wing is bruised and his bosom sore,—
> When he beats his bars and he would be free;
> It is not a carol of joy or glee,
>> But a prayer that he sends from his heart's deep core,
> But a plea, that upward to Heaven he flings—
> I know why the caged bird sings
>>> —Paul Laurence Dunbar, "Sympathy"

Borrowing from the insights of Anna Julia Cooper, a late nineteenth-century black woman writer, teacher, and intellectual, I should like to choose the phrase "when and where I enter" as my access to the subject of engendering men and to the debate over the position of Afro-American men in feminist literary and cultural studies. In *A Voice From the South* (1892), Cooper bemoaned the desire of black male leaders to speak for the entire black race, and she posited instead the centrality of her black female consciousness: "Only the BLACK WOMAN can say 'when and where I enter, in the quiet undisputed dignity of my womanhood, without violence and without suing or special patronage, then and there the whole *Negro race enters with me.*' "[1] This bold statement, fascinating in its conception of female authority, revises the words of Martin R. Delany, author of *The Condition, Elevation, and Destiny of the Colored People of the United States, Politically Considered* (1852), who remarked that—as a black *man*—the entire race entered with him. Yet Cooper's stance as feminist repeats the rhetorical and ideological posture of Delany as masculinist. Both rely upon their gendered selves as the means of constructing the social and political agendas for their own racial constituencies. Both speak for the race through their sense of gender.

When W. E. B. Du Bois, considered the primary turn-of-the-century Afro-American spokes*man*, later expropriates Cooper's famous statement in his essay "The Damnation of Women" (1920), he demonstrates why black women have fought to wrestle from black men the responsibility for representing themselves and their race.[2] Du Bois takes Cooper's remarks without attributing them to her, instead identifying the quotation merely as the words of "one of our women."[3] As a result, Du Bois achieves his voice by assuming hers; Cooper is rendered anonymous. He concludes his essay on a note of unbridled optimism that nonetheless turns on a troublesome panegyric "to [the] memory and inspiration" of black women:

> I have known the women of many lands and nations,—I have known and seen and lived beside them, but none have I known more sweetly feminine, more unswervingly loyal, more desperately earnest, and more instinctively pure in body and in soul than the daughters of my black mothers.[4]

While it is important to note that he seeks to deliver the reputations of black women from sexist and racist myths about black female morality and sexuality and to rescue them from the fantasies and exploitation of white men, Du Bois risks harnessing black women with the prevailing gender conventions that have trapped other groups of women in this country. It is also true that, no matter how conventional his codes, Du Bois was struggling to engender black women in order to reaffirm his experience of race as a coherent subjectivity. In his male imagination, however, these women become "sweet," "feminine," "unswerving," "loyal," "earnest," "instinctive," and "pure": admirable qualities all for the idealized, mythical black goddess, but not for race leaders and black intellectuals like Cooper and Du Bois.

Likewise, Du Bois's praise for black women is both set in motion and rendered problematic by his need to filter his representations of black women through the lens of his own masculine imperatives. Speaking for black women as a way of talking about his own experience of gender, they become "the daughters" of *his* "black mothers." In spite of the distortion that comes when he engenders himself in this way, Du Bois's essay does manage to portray effectively the aspirations of black women to uphold the legacy of such racial figures as Harriet Tubman and Sojourner Truth. What we have learned all too well is that black women themselves must fight to control how they are represented. While Du Bois and Cooper disagreed on tactical strategies, it is crucial for an understanding of the inseparability of "race" and "gender" that we remember that as Cooper achieves her voice by revising the work of black men, she nonetheless inherits a responsibility to engender her sense of race, which necessarily includes engendering black men.

I choose to begin with the struggles of Cooper and Du Bois as a way of historicizing our present critical debates. Yet rather than continuing to explicate the gender dynamics in Cooper and Du Bois's treatment of race, I intend to examine some of the various strategies that black male and female artists use to represent themselves and each other within dominant institutions of Euro-American culture. I hope to develop as well a means of reading the works of Afro-American writers that highlights the centrality of gender within racial constructions without reducing the diverse relations among "race," "gender," and "ideology" to issues of perpetual antagonism between black male and female authors, characters, and critics. The "war of words" between black men and women need not entail continual skirmishes across an unbridgeable divide of sexual difference, even though relevant statements, figures, and characters in our literature and criticism may at times resemble such military maneuvers. There is much in this interchange of what Afro-Americanists like to portray as the "call and response" aesthetic that, in this context, involves an understanding of the necessity—for the sake of the race and against those who would make "others" of both black men and women—of being mutually engendering, no matter how tentative, awkward, and uncomfortable some of these racial and gender positions may be. Indeed, what demands further critical study is the extent to which black men and women engender each other in ways that are mutually beneficial and sustaining.

Whatever the present position of black men in black feminism, we need to begin to theorize how questions of gender, usually focused on black women, enable us to reexamine the nature of black male subjectivity. In the hands of such skillful practitioners as Hazel Carby, Mae Henderson, Deborah McDowell, Valerie Smith, and Hortense Spillers, the black feminist enterprise has liberated black female writers and characters from what Mary Helen Washington has called the "little spaces men have allotted women."[5] What remains to be seen is if black men can be liberated from the tiny spaces they have alloted themselves. Now that black female artists and critics have assumed their rightful status as the most compelling voices of contemporary Afro-American culture, one of our present goals must be the engendering of black men within the context of gender ideologies that encourage a range of possibilities for male selfhood. In this sense, black feminism may provide real alternatives for black men as we redefine our notions of black masculinity. By exploring the possibilities of feminism, we can revise our sense of what it means to be men.

In locating ways of engendering black men, we need to draw upon feminist methodologies *and* the texts of black women themselves. The complex relations among gender, race, and representation are especially visible, I would propose, in the writings of black men and women in traditional literary forms. These forms necessarily involve the Afro-American writer's participation in the larger cultural discourses that have represented race and gender as terms of "otherness" within a battle zone for repeating and revising forms of cultural oppression. In representing themselves within these literary rituals, Afro-American writers have had to rewrite them from the point of view of their own individual and community needs and expectations. Male and female Afro-Americanist critics must continue to study how black men and women have attempted to define themselves within and against the confines of white and black patriarchal structures. With the help of black feminist criticism and black women writers, we need to rethink how black men negotiate their sense of themselves as blacks and as men.

Within this context of constructing race and gender through the languages of a literary tradition associated with white and mostly male privilege, I would like to explore some of the possibilities for mutual engendering in the sonnets of Afro-American poets. In particular, I will use the poems of Henrietta Cordelia Ray, Paul Laurence Dunbar, Claude McKay, and Gwendolyn Brooks as paradigms for reading the relative position of black men and women in American society and thereby depicting the progressive engendering of the Afro-American literary tradition. The sonnet is an ideal form for these purposes because of its strict conventions of representation. It provides an ideal forum for affirmation and contestation, as poets define themselves within and against the terms of what Wordsworth called the sonnet's "scanty plot of ground." As contested ground, these sonnets enact the racial and gendered struggles for identity in Afro-American art. As a stage for lyric voice, these poems represent the terms of the black writer's subjectivity.

Many of our most talented black poets have written sonnets, from Henrietta

Cordelia Ray to June Jordan, including along the way Paul Laurence Dunbar, Claude McKay, Countee Cullen, Alice Dunbar-Nelson, Langston Hughes, Sterling Brown, Margaret Walker, Melvin B. Tolson, Robert Hayden, and, most expertly, Gwendolyn Brooks. This roll call of black sonneteers suggests the diversity of the black poetic project. The persistence of the sonnet as a mode of lyric subjectivity suggests both the centrality of the black poet's preoccupation with traditional literary form as a means of achieving literary voice *and* the multiplicity of creative solutions to the vicissitudes of engendering the black lyric subject. The pursuit of form in the Afro-American sonnet has measured the participation of black poets in Euro-American cultural traditions while testing the individual poet's claim to originality and authenticity. For black poets, the sonnet has served as a zone of entrapment and liberation, mediation and self-possession. These poets have turned to the sonnet as an alternative space for performance, one that demonstrates the poet's craft while calling into question the marginality of black men and women in Euro-American discourse. Fettered within the fourteen lines of the sonnet, black poets have subverted their legacy of voicelessness as Afro-Americans, as men, and as women. As Dunbar tells us, they have somehow managed to sing.

The origins of the sonnet in Europe are emblematic of the distinctive features of the sonnet as a literary form. Contrary to what one might expect, historically the sonnet has been a form of revision and rebellion, encoding race, gender, sexuality, class, and national origins as the very terms of difference that constitute and render problematic its ideological dynamics. Even though the sonnet's origins as a literary form are located within the discourse of elite white men of the thirteenth century, by the time of the Renaissance, white women poets had begun to figure the sonnet as contested ground. In her essay "Assimilation with a Difference," Ann Rosalind Jones maintains that women as "objects of love in male-authored poetry spoke as the lovers of men in female-authored texts," writing "within but against the center of the traditions that surrounded them, using Neoplatonic and Petrarchan discourse in revisionary and interrogatory ways."[6] In this regard, it is useful to remember Petrarch's beloved Laura of blond hair and black eyes, the woman whom, as Sandra Bermann tells us, this Italian poet of courtly love "does not represent so much as continually distance, displace, and fragment."[7] As Bermann argues, the beloved Laura "is but the condition of possibility that allows the poet speaker to develop his quest for self"—or rather, his masculine self. Two women poets who subverted their inherited female role as the silent, idealized beloved, Pernette du Guillet and Louise Labé, challenged "the rhetorical and symbolic order on which love poetry was based."[8] Louise Labé, in particular, attempted to assert the extent to which Laura was not a woman but a gendered convention, and in Labé's love poems written to a man who was not her husband, she reverses the gender polarities of the sonnet as a received genre by laureling her male lover.

Even men have found the need for playing at the margins of the sonnet. For example, Shakespeare borrows Surrey's revisions of Petrarch only to reinvest the figure of the beloved—his young male friend and dark mistress—with his own perplexing, and for some critics vexing, differences. Milton binds himself to the early political discourses of the sonnet, skillfully using the form as a vehicle for public elegy and political voice. Finding his way back to the heroic sonnets of Petrarch and Dante, Tasso and della Casa, Milton adopted and then personalized what James Mueller describes as the so-called "magnificent style" of "involuted syntax, recondite allusions, and bold rhythmic modulations" whose "proper subjects were specified as philosophical reflection or contemporary issues and personages of requisite grandeur."[9] Both Shakespeare and Milton reveal, in different ways, the extent to which the sonnet as a genre has itself reveled in the productive tensions of the social and cultural context of its construction. Even writers at the center of literary history have found solace within the contests of its poetic margins.

By appropriating this conventional and potentially conservative form for their own particular use, nineteenth- and twentieth-century Afro-American writers, both male and female, have extended the sonnet's debates over its figurations of race and gender. In the late nineteenth century, Henrietta Cordelia Ray and Paul Laurence Dunbar were the major black sonneteers. Both extended racial and gender boundaries in their depiction of blacks and women in their sonnets. Recently resurrected in *The Schomburg Library of Nineteenth-Century Writers* (1988), Ray published two volumes, *Sonnets* (1893) and *Poems* (1910), including well over a hundred poems.[10] She has been previously ignored for many reasons: the inaccessibility of her work; her marginalized cultural status as a black woman; the resistance of the American literary culture to the elite accomplishments of the black bourgeoisie; the current tendency to eschew nineteenth-century poets working in traditional verse forms; and the ways in which she disrupts received notions of Afro-American poetry. Nonetheless, Ray distinguished herself through her subtle revisions of the gender politics of the sonnet and her insistent challenge to the Europeanist canon of literary authority.

Like Cooper, Ray is concerned with the "undisputed dignity" of womanhood. By writing sonnets on such elevated figures as "Milton," "Shakespeare," and "Beethoven," Ray positioned herself as a black woman within the cultural discourses that symbolized and helped to maintain the terms of her racial and gender oppression. Rather than simply imitating white poets, her sonnets contest the authority of previously exclusive traditions by clearing a space for herself as a black woman poet. The mere act of apostrophizing Milton—"O poet gifted with the sight divine!"—clarifies her position as a black intellectual who has mastered elite, cultural discourses that she might manipulate for her own ends. Du Bois is perhaps more direct in his famous challenge to Euro-American cultural authority in *The Souls of Black Folk*—"I sit with Shakespeare and he winces not"—yet Ray is sufficiently audacious in her own display of learnedness. Appropriating Milton through the conventions of the elegy, only to revise the gender dynamics of its "male" conventions, Ray renders the great poet the object of her own poetic intentions, idealizing him as though he were *her* beloved:

>   thou couldst trace
> The rich outpourings of celestial grace
> Mingled with argument, around the shrine
> Where thou didst linger, vision-rapt, intent
> To catch the sacred mystery of Heaven.
> Nor was thy longing vain: a soul resolved
> To ponder truth supreme to thee was lent;
> For thy not *sightless* eyes the veil was riv'n,
> Redemption's problems unto thee well solved.[11]

Inscribing herself into the sonnet's codes of expression and concealment, Ray mingles praise with desire. She thus conjoins the traditions of heroic remembrance and courtly love in a poem whose literary authority at once reaffirms and undermines the conventionality of its utterances.

In her sonnet "To Laura," Ray demonstrates her disregard for the structures of address that have marked women as objects, even in the midst of appearing to abide by them. The poem memorializes Laura, no longer as Petrarch's beloved, but as Ray's "sister outsider." Listen to the poem's treacherous sestet:

> Dear sister, in those realms of radiant light
> Where thou hast grown to know a richer lore
> Than that of earth, sometimes rememb'rest thou
> The hours of our companionship so bright
> With joyance? Ay, but we shall meet once more,
> And at God's throne in praise together bow.[12]

Like Cooper, Ray writes "without violence." While she does not seek to incite a feminist or black revolution, she has given us a sonnet that turns with a difference. For Petrarch, Laura was an unattainable ideal. For Ray, she has become a figure for their shared possibility. Beyond "The fret / And turmoil of the world," in a subtle allusion to Wordsworth's sonnet "Nuns Fret Not at Their Convent's Narrow Room," Ray locates her ideal of "self-mastery" in the unbridled space of "Mem'ry's fairest court": her own poetic imagination. Unlike Petrarch, Ray addresses Laura directly, likening herself to this woman of Neo-Platonic beauty, implicitly subverting her own status as object *and* as necessarily disinherited from the symbolic economy that produces "those realms of radiant light" and "richer lore." She writes herself into the possibilities of the freedom of idealized form at the same time that she revises the ways in which such forms should be realized. Whatever its apparent subject, the sonnet "To Laura" is clearly *about* Henrietta Cordelia Ray.

Although several of Ray's sonnets, including "William Lloyd Garrison," "Wendell Phillips," and "Robert G. Shaw," are heroic portraitures of modern subjects, only one, "Toussaint L'Overture," depicts a black historical figure. None portrays a black American. Evenly balanced between male and female heroes, Ray's sonnets create a pantheon of private and public figures as forebears in whom she invests anew the possibilities of their own valor without confronting directly the relationship between heroism and race. Dunbar had a slightly different agenda as black artist. Recognizing more than Ray the viability of the sonnet as a mode of personal *and* racial subjectivity, Dunbar furthers the fight for black self-determination by writing the first sonnets on Afro-American men. In such poems as "Douglass," "Booker T. Washington," and "Robert Gould Shaw," he memorializes black and abolitionist heroes of the struggle for freedom from American slavery. As well, his sonnets on black men contest dominant nineteenth-century American notions of racial inferiority by representing black male leadership in heroic proportions. Emphasizing the extent to which black leaders belong to an identifiable tradition of racial progress that subverts American ideologies of racial difference, his sonnets are triumphs of racial memory and political activism. Dunbar invokes leaders from the historical past in order to help to guide race progress for the future.

While Dunbar wrote one long poem on Frederick Douglass shortly after his death, he later wrote the sonnet "Douglass" as a lament for the passing of Douglass' leadership:

> Ah, Douglass, we have fall'n on evil days,
> Such days as thou, not even thou didst know,
> When thee, the eyes of that harsh long ago
> Saw, salient, at the cross of devious ways,
> And all the country heard thee with amaze.
> Not ended then, the passionate ebb and flow,
> The awful tide that battled to and fro;
> We ride amid a tempest of dispraise.
>
> Now, when the waves of swift dissension swarm,
> And Honor, the strong pilot, lieth stark,
> Oh, for thy voice high-sounding o'er the storm,
> For thy strong arm to guide the shivering bark,
> The blast-defying power of thy form,
> To give us comfort through the lonely dark.[13]

By writing this stately Petrarchan sonnet about contemporary American racial politics, Dunbar underscores Douglass' legacy as an Afro-American statesman. He calls upon Douglass as a black man to be the beacon of clarity and understanding that characterized his leadership in the nineteenth century, not simply as escaped slave but free *man*, a black man dedicated to the advancement of the black race. Consistently throughout the sonnet, Dunbar's encomium privileges Douglass' talents of vision and voice. By way of synecdoche, Douglass is represented by his eyes; his historical significance, by his gift of prescience at the crossroads of slavery and freedom. Yet, at its most masculine, the poem reaches for Douglass' "strong arm" and the security of his "blast-defying power." By declaring Douglass' absence (a veiled call for his presence), Dunbar represents contemporary blacks as a race beset by "swift dissension," beseiged in stormy darkness, and in this respect the poem widens the scope of historical vision and power and their necessity to the racial struggle.

The poem begins and ends with the presumption of black masculinity. Steeped in paternal metaphors, Dunbar's representation of Douglass invests him with the omnipotence of the "Father," his present absence with the anticipation of his Second Coming. Yet male physicality, not spirituality, lies at the heart of Dunbar's historical memory. In the absence of honor, the poem's sestet turns on the activation of Douglass' force and unassailable form, as contemporary black leaders have become Douglass' children in the struggle for Afro-American selfhood. When Dunbar recreates Douglass, he has already been constituted as a contemporary personality and a historical figure. Indeed, after his death in 1895 the act of praising Douglass in a variety of elite and popular forms had become conventional. In the poem, Dunbar combines the a priori male subject with the conventions of the heroic sonnet to *perform* racial subjectivity as it has already been constructed. In the process, Dunbar projects Douglass' voice, clarifies for us the necessity of his vision, and remembers his personal and collective strength. Yet in underscoring the possibilities of a representative Afro-American self, he limits himself to figures whom others have already invested with racial authority.

For Ray and Dunbar, the sonnet provided a set of conventions that allowed them to give form to gendered and racial selves. Although it has become commonplace to discuss the quest for freedom and literacy in nineteenth-century Afro-American narrative, this paradigm also applies to the black poets of the time, and it helps us to understand the gender, racial, and political dynamics of the sonnets of these two people. In the process of authenticating their right to speak to black and white audiences, Dunbar and Ray revel in their cultural literacy as defined in the terms of both Euro-American culture and the Afro-American tradition. Still, even the most daring of their poems are cautious; the freedom they achieve, somewhat constrained. Although they insinuate their individuality into the folds of their sonnets, they rely perhaps too heavily upon the racial conventions they inherit from Afro-American political discourse and the gender conventions they acquire from Euro-American cultural discourse. Twentieth-century black sonneteers have been more experimental, yet it is important to remember that they were able to draw upon the example of their black literary precursors, refining and extending their stops along the way.

While nineteenth-century Afro-American sonneteers relied almost exclusively upon subjects whose authority had clearly been established in historical, literary, and cultural discursive forms, Claude McKay and Gwendolyn Brooks have explored the mutual possibilities of racial and gendered experience in the heroism of the heretofore unsung black masses. They derive their authority as spokespersons for their race and genders from the daily life and sentiments of their newly constructed subjects. Indeed, by giving representational status to anonymous subjects, they interrogate just what it means to stand for and to be among the people. Heroism finds its way into uncommon places, and Brooks even calls into question the very notion of the heroism in which

Claude McKay remains invested, subverting the gender distinctions that linger in the sonnet tradition. In this respect, ironically, it is she who is the more successful in engendering her sonnets about Afro-American men.

One of McKay's early unpublished sonnets, "In Memoriam: Booker T. Washington," repeats and no doubt is influenced by the nineteenth-century strategy of representing the already-constituted Afro-American subject. Written after Washington's death in 1915, the Petrarchan sonnet eulogizes the great race leader as McKay remembers having once seen him; for the young McKay, he was " A splendid tower / of strength," suffused with "subtle tact and power":

> O how I loved, adored your furrowed face!
> And fondly hoped, before your days were done,
> You would look in mine too with paternal grace.
> But vain are hopes and dreams!—gone: you are gone,
> Death's hand has torn you from your trusting race,
> And O! We feel so utterly alone.[14]

Although the sentiments remind us of Dunbar, here McKay is more personal, and the elegy is fixed in the performance context of an auditorium at Tuskegee Institute. Whereas Dunbar's relationship to Douglass is public, McKay's Washington, perceived through memory, is fittingly his own. The figure of Washington for the young fatherless McKay, depicted in terms of paternal affection, is a personal icon for the race leader whom he would like to be. Hence McKay feels this loss as a wounding of his own racial body. In this sense, Washington has been a masculine "tower" for the race, but also an important element of the young writer's racial identity.

Many of McKay's published sonnets betray the terms of his search for an ideal racial self. He fixes his own dilemma in the context of the black *man's* insistent quest for racial authority. Feeling his own increasing burdens as a representative of the race in literature, he engenders himself as a black man who speaks for his race in general and to other black men in particular. His most famous sonnet, "If We Must Die," demonstrates the tension between racial and gendered utterances. The poem presents a traditional ideal of black masculinity:

> If we must die, let it not be like hogs
> Hunted and penned in an inglorious spot,
> While round us bark the mad and hungry dogs,
> Making their mock at our accursed lot.
> If we must die, O Let us nobly die,
> So that our precious blood may not be shed
> In vain; then even the monsters we defy
> Shall be constrained to honor us though dead!
> O kinsmen! we must meet the common foe!
> Though far outnumbered let us show us brave,
> And for their thousand blows deal one deathblow!
> What though before us lies the open grave?
> Like men we'll face the murderous, cowardly pack,
> Pressed to the wall, dying, but fighting back![15]

Written in 1919, in the wake of the Red Scare and the Red Summer of race riots throughout the urban centers of the United States, "If We Must Die" is McKay's bold statement of a masculine, racial strategy. The nobility of his chosen form reaffirmed the conventions of dignity and the structures of address to which the poem's personae aspire. Etched into the consciousness of literate black Americans for generations to come as a model of Afro-American heroism, this poem has become a point of reference for the entire racial experience and a touchstone of the Afro-American entry into subjectivity. As Winston Churchill used it as a rallying cry to call the British into sustained battle against the Nazis, this single poem of renunciation earned McKay an international reputation even beyond his race.

While they speak for the entire race, the militant selves of the poem are in fact explicitly "male." The phrase "If we must die" utters the poem's call to participation, and it gathers meaning through its repetition in the first and second quatrains. The phrase "O kinsmen!" makes that call to participation explicit; the poem's would-be warriors are men. McKay fails to explicate the unique position of women within this embattled black community, choosing instead to talk about the race by imagining the aspirations of black men. The contest for black humanity in the poem is waged exclusively through the battle for black masculinity. Within the poem's rhetoric of pursuing honor and dignity, maleness is one of the spoils of the racial battle. In relation to white men, it is the ultimate mark of heroism. Whatever the position of women, for McKay this battle is between men.

Following Dunbar's footsteps by placing Afro-Americans in the heroic sonnet, McKay is the first to represent a collective Afro-American self within the slender technical boundaries of the sonnet form. In "If We Must Die," McKay gives public voice to other black men who might speak privately for all black people. The poem enacts McKay's powerful struggle for a masculine identity as a black writer in the midst of racial oppression. From the vantage point of his vocation as black writer, he turns to language to relieve the dissonance of his perception of what his life has become upon emigrating from Jamaica and his realization that his native culture of class distinction and apparent civility has ill prepared him for the viciousness of the racism that surrounded him daily. In the poem, McKay ultimately retreats to the social order of his youth with its values of personal honor. Death might come, be it not "inglorious."

"If We Must Die" builds its contrasts not between man and woman but rather man and beast, both terms variously construed. In an essay entitled "A Negro Poet Writes," the Jamaican-born McKay had written earlier of his initiation into American racism: "I ceased to think of people and things in the mass—why should I fight with mad dogs only to be bitten and probably transformed into a mad dog myself?"[16] The resonant figures of bestiality here and in the poem underscore the extent to which McKay was haunted by the terms of his own dehumanization: the hostility and "ignoble cruelty" of what he witnessed in the United States. With his sense of nobility, McKay inherits a good deal of what Wayne Cooper, McKay's biographer, calls "the heroic sentimentalism of Victorian England."[17] British imperialism left its mark on the British West Indies in many ways, and clearly McKay's experience of transplanted Victorian culture informed his writing. In part through his "special friendship" with his British patron, Walter Jekyll, he learned to internalize Victorian myths about male behavior in an aristocratic society. The sonnet form becomes an appropriate battlefield for the contest between McKay's sense of himself as a gentleman and the need to respond to racial violence. The gentlemanly form of the sonnet girds the language of warfare within the codes of nineteenth-century combat. Such codes allow McKay to fight racism on his own terms. With its heroic sentimentality, "If We Must Die" is for McKay the black male "deathblow" that will assure his possession of the rigid ideal of masculinity that comes as the poem's prize.

When Brooks began to write her famous sonnet sequence in her first volume, *A Street in Bronzeville* (1945), she must have had McKay's poetry in mind. Brooks plays her role in the mutual engendering of black men and women by providing a revision of McKay that becomes for black men a place to enter into gendered status without the trappings of rigid codes of masculinity. In "Gay Chaps at the Bar," Brooks challenges the gender assumptions of McKay's call to male arms by subverting the male ideal of war, only to breathe life into the actual letters of black soldiers in World War II written to Brooks from the front. By re-engendering male racial discourse, she brings herself and other black women into Afro-American political identity, ironically, by speaking honestly about what it means to be black men. Brooks begins:

> We knew how to order. Just the dash
> Necessary. The lengthy of gaiety in good taste.
> Whether the raillery should be slightly iced
> And given green, or served up hot and lush.
> And we knew beautifully how to give to women
> The summer spread, the tropics, of our love.
> When to persist, or hold a hunger off.
> Knew white speech. How to make a look an omen.
> But nothing ever taught us to be islands
> And smart, athletic language for this hour
> Was not in the curriculum. No stout
> Lesson showed how to chat with death. We brought
> No brass fortissimo, among our talents,
> To holler down the lions in this air.[18]

Although Brooks' male speaker, writing about the war zones, begins with McKay's masculine bravado, his voice crinkles with anxiety, even from the beginning. Yes, the black soldiers could order drinks from the bar, thereby demonstrating their sense of power and control, but as black men they could not order other troops. Instead, *they* were ordered. Yet order is precisely what their world now lacks, and within the dislocation of battle, its hierarchies of gender have begun to erode as they fret over their identities as men. For while these troops may be adept at female seduction, war has rendered superfluous this point of masculine reference. However "stout" the lessons of their maleness, they have no language for conquering death with their flirtations. They do not want to die nobly, like McKay's speaker; they simply, understandably, do not want to die. The martial accents of the octave, along with its self-confident assertions and blustering swagger, give way in the poem's final lines to the incompatibility of dominant heroic male ideals and the real experience of war. In this sense, Brooks takes McKay to the Front and back as a way of showing him that the battle for male gendered selfhood must be waged with black women against the patriarchal imperatives of other men.

Just as Brooks insinuates her own female voice within the confines of the male "Gay Chaps" sonnets, she struggles to assert a coherent Afro-American identity within the destructive forces of American racism. By revising previous Afro-American sonnets, she does indeed find a vehicle for expressing the particular experience of black men and women. Within the subjective terms of her lyric "I"/"eye," Brooks witnesses and gives voice to the shared perspective of black men and women, setting it against the hypocrisy of a decidedly white male order. Brooks feminizes her black male subjects as a way of distinguishing and rescuing them from the authority of the social and political realm that generates both racism *and* sexism. By giving voice to their private desires, she pits their individuality against the public, patriarchal orders that her poems work to unsettle in devious ways. Rather than having black men imitate the problematic gender codes of white heterosexual men, Brooks liberates them from the phallocentric conventions of the heroic sonnet. In the process, her representations of black men refine and clarify the terms of their masculinity within a community bound by race *and* gender.

By embodying the male voices of her soldiers within the tiny boundaries of her feminized sonnets, Brooks clears a space for her later poems on womanhood and the female struggle for identity. She writes herself into the canon of Western literary history by "seizing" a poetic form steeped in male conquest and political struggle, then progressively remakes its racial and gender associations as her career as a poet develops. In "Gay Chaps at the Bar," Brooks demonstrates that she can speak about men directly, without hesitation. In her sonnets published in *Annie Allen* (1949) and *The Bean Eaters* (1960), she stakes her claim to female authority based upon female subjectivity. Yet she makes it clear that black men are included within her discourse on womanhood. Ironically, Brooks reveals that the liberation of black woman is the secret to achieving a more realistic, democratic notion of black masculinity.

From this perspective, her sonnet sequence "The Womanhood" responds to her call for authentic black male identity in "Gay Chaps at the Bar." Among these poems of 1949, "First Fight. Then Fiddle" in particular must be located within the context of her earlier call to black male warriors:

First fight. Then fiddle. Ply the slipping string
With feathery sorcery; muzzle the note
With hurting love; the music that they wrote
Bewitch, bewilder. Qualify to sing
Threadwise. Devise no salt, no hempen thing
For the dear instrument to bear. Devote
The bow to silks and honey. Be remote
A while from malice and from murdering.
But first to arms, to armor. Carry hate
In front of you and harmony behind.
Be deaf to music and to beauty blind.
Win war. Rise bloody, maybe not too late
For having first to civilize a space
Wherein to play your violin with grace.[19]

"First fight. Then fiddle." These are "orders" to be sure, issued without anxiety of
audience or authorship, to Brooks' poetic sisters *and* brothers. Like Cooper and
Ray, Brooks posits the "undisputed dignity" of her womanhood, which is, as she
realizes, really no different in intention from the quests for nobility of Dunbar and
McKay. Her realization of this unity of purpose informs her understanding that,
like Cooper, the whole race enters with her. Therefore, she gathers into this poem
about artful selfhood the terms of gender difference, figured in the poem's initial
distinction between fighting and fiddling, only to disrupt the binary oppositions that
ensue by suggesting that because her battle plans involve racial strategies they apply
equally to black women and men. Like the black women in "The Womanhood," the
black men in "Gay Chaps at the Bar" are both fighters and fiddlers. Fiddling, of
course, is a wonderful figure for poetic voice, the expert manipulations of the
instrument of poetry itself. However, poetry comes not without battle; this poem is
an emblem of Brooks's struggle for poetic voice as a black woman in an attempt to
speak for the entire race. She begins the fight—literally and figuratively—in "Gay
Chaps at the Bar" by demonstrating the shrewdness of her knowledge of masculine
and racial warfare. In "The Womanhood," she shows us that she has scored a
definitive victory. By merging the identities of black men and women, she has
managed to get them to fight for the same thing.

With this sonnet as her instrument, she betrays the codes of her poetic technique
and political ideology. Insisting upon the simultaneity of voice and silence as the
basic ontology of her poetry (c.f. her famous line from the poem "In the Mecca":
"Silence is a place in which to scream"), she confronts the terms of her "muzzling,"
figuring the threat to her creative aspirations of her marginality as a black woman
and figuring the aesthetic strategies available to her precisely because of that
marginality. Although the conventions in which she writes are not exclusively hers,
and indeed they have represented her silencing as "the other" in traditional sonnet
discourse, here she "bewitches and bewilders" these forms, singing "threadwise"

through the bars—not simply *within* the bars of Euro-American poetry. Cataloguing her repertoire of deception and subversion, she highlights the continuity between writing poetry and political activism, as the thing represented becomes the thing itself. Armed with her violins, Brooks makes her sonnet world a privileged space and a creative place for the dangerous indirections of Afrocentric and woman-centered rhetoric. By fiddling, she teaches black women and men how to fight the same fight, investing these gendered tropes of "dignity" and "nobility" with the black aesthetic of doing it right.

Like many other sonnets written by black Americans, Brooks' poems show us why the caged birds of nineteenth- and twentieth-century Afro-American poetry have been able to sing as black men and women. Rather than always falling prey to the discourses of racism and sexism that pervade European and American poetic traditions, and by recognizing the inseparability of these two patriarchal forces, black poets have learned to appropriate the conventions of these literary forms without being coopted by their dominant racial and gender attributions. In liberating black men and women, the sonnets of Ray, Dunbar, McKay, and Brooks have represented the very terrain of the battle for racial and gendered identity. Yet these black poets have entered the grounds of the sonnet, not to gain entrance to the master's house, but rather, by fiddling with its foundations, to bring it down. In its place, they have "civilized a space" for celebrating their representations of race and gender.

Needless to say, our present struggles to engender black men and women within the surprisingly intractable boundaries of contemporary criticism must be informed by the persistence of black writers themselves who, like McKay and Brooks, recognize the utter necessity of articulating a coherent black subjectivity. In order to fight against the historical forces that imprison both black men and women, we must learn as critics to fiddle with the institutional structures that govern our lives and our work as a way of exploiting them for our own ends. By setting our own agenda as Afro-Americanists and feminists, we must be prepared to write within *and* against the dominant critical voices of our profession, using whatever means at our disposal to get what we want. Above all, we must be clear about what it is that we *do* want, and here again Brooks is instructive. By brilliantly engendering black men within the context of her feminist endeavors, she shows us how to people a new community of black feminist scholars—mutually engendered and all the more powerful. By choosing carefully when and where we enter, we can hone the weapons of our battle for authority and selfhood. By reaffirming what we share, we can win.

15

Homelessness at Home: Placing Emily Dickinson in (Women's) History

Thomas Foster

In a letter written to her close friend and future sister-in-law, Susan Gilbert, Emily Dickinson anticipates the challenges that her poetry continues to pose for contemporary feminist critics at the same time that she prefigures important themes that would reappear later in the poetry. Dated 11 June 1852, when Dickinson was twenty-two and about ten years before she began to produce the body of her poetic work, this letter closes with an important warning to its reader and to Dickinson's readers generally:[1]

> Now, farewell, Susie, and Vinnie sends her love, and mother her's, and I add a kiss shyly, lest there is somebody there! Dont let them see, *will* you Susie?
>
> Emilie—

> Why cant *I* be a Delegate to the great Whig Convention—dont I know all about Daniel Webster, and the Tariff, and the Law? Then, Susie I could see you, during a pause in the session—but I dont like this country at all, and I shant stay here any longer! "Delenda est" America, Massachusetts and all!
>
> open me carefully

While the topic of this essay is the relation that appears in Dickinson's poetry between the ideology of domesticity and women's claims to historical agency, I will begin by establishing how a series of issues raised in this letter are relevant to that topic. First, the letter provides all the terms necessary to understand the relationship between Dickinson's situation as a woman writer and her seeming lack of interest in historical and social issues, as attested by her self-enforced seclusion within her father's home.[2] Second, the letter's injunction to "open me carefully" suggests that the perennial debate over Dickinson as "private poet" can be understood in terms of our habits of reading rather than the author's individual eccentricities or any external historical determination of her life's choices. Finally, in its address to another woman, this letter enacts the dynamics of identification between women in the construction of feminine subjectivity. But the letter goes further, to confront dramatically the difficulties women writers face in finding a *space*, both a social position and a textual position of enunciation, where women can speak and have their speech legitimated as a historical event.

My concern here will be with how in her poetry Dickinson conceptualizes this space as specifically domestic, while at the same time she resists the dominant representation of the home as a separate and subordinate feminine "sphere." I would like to suggest that implicitly in this letter and more explicitly in the poems, Dickinson uses domestic space to figure the contradictions between her assignment to a bounded subject position, one that limits public recognition of women's various activities, and her capacity as a woman to resist that assignment. As a site of contradiction, the home becomes a space of possibility for Dickinson. By turning first to this letter as an introduction to the problems of reading Dickinson and to the demands for interpretation that she makes on her readers, we can then more fully understand the relevance of nineteenth-century representations of domestic space to Dickinson's poetry and finally see how the poems demand to be read against the context of those dominant discourses.

"Open Me Carefully"

Dickinson's letter to Susan Gilbert shows the writer becoming progressively more aware of how the act of writing creates possibilities for public discourse—that is, possibilities for this discourse to be read by persons other than the letter's individual addressee—while at the same time the conflation of femininity and domesticity functions to contain and privatize those possibilities. Perhaps most striking is the sense of exclusion from the public world of politics, law, and finance dominated by men voiced in the letter's postscript. The knowledge of law Dickinson claims reflects the self-consciousness of someone who has been subjected to its strictures, not the perspective of one who has had a role in writing the law or even in electing the officials who do. Dickinson reacts to her exclusion by imagining herself in her father's role as delegate to the national Whig convention, but she subverts her appropriation of masculine prerogatives by inverting the usual priorities: she wants to get to the presidential convention primarily in order to spend time with another woman, not to enjoy the exercise of political power. Even in Dickinson's imagination, Susan Gilbert remains excluded from the convention, so that if Dickinson were a delegate she could only see the other woman in the time she has off from her official duties. A recognition of gender identity and the limitations placed on women as a group underlie Dickinson's comments in this letter, even as she imagines a movement beyond those limitations that would not require her to repudiate her gender.

Before Dickinson creates a textual space of defiant opposition in the form of this postscript, the woman-identified character of both her social awareness and her imagination becomes apparent in the ending to the letter proper, with the playfully and self-consciously erotic overtones of the kiss Dickinson asks Susan Gilbert to be sure to keep secret.[3] Those overtones become more explicit in the final fragmentary caution, "open me carefully," which marks a convergence of sexuality and textuality. This final phrase indicates the need for interpretation to "open" a text whose meaning may not be exhausted by the immediate message it conveys; the phrase implies a need to go beyond the letter—the object in Susan Gilbert's hand as well as the literal denotation of its words—to reach that "me," the figure of the woman as author, produced and mediated by her own textual practices.

But "open me carefully" also raises the possibility of interpretive violence as sexual violence, violence against women. In other words, Dickinson ends her letter in the hope that Susan Gilbert will not take the potentially hostile position of a male reader in relation to her text. In contrast to the emphatic "*I*" of the postscript, Dickinson's addition of that final "me" points to the way that she claims autonomy by self-consciously making herself and her own subjectivity the object of her discourse. At the same time, this lapse into the status of grammatical object suggests Dickinson's insight into the nature of discursive power itself, by implying that ultimately there is no escape, no way to avoid exposure to the interpretations of others. Interpretive violence always remains a possibility. Nevertheless, that final phrase also leaves open the possibility that discursive appropriation can be countered by another act of interpretation, a different, more "careful" form of inquiry.

Now, after the publication of Dickinson's letters and poems, I believe the phrase "open me carefully" should also be understood as a warning to the male critic of her work. The letter's final enigmatic phrase extends the plea that Gilbert protect the privacy of the women's figurative kiss ("Dont let them see"), to ask that the same protection be given to the body of the letter itself. But the phrase also anticipates the letter's exposure to a possibly voyeuristic intruder who nevertheless forms part of the textual scene of the kiss.[4] The previous reference to not letting "them" see encodes this intruder as a male figure who is at once excluded from the physical circuit of the women's intimacy and included, to the extent that his existence is acknowledged. The possibility of applying the phrase "open me carefully" to a reader other than the letter's addressee shows Dickinson's awareness of how writing practices can transgress the boundaries of the public and the private, in a social context where public and private correspond to the gendered spaces of the marketplace and the home.[5] As a male reader of Dickinson, then, her letter positions me by exclusion. But it also includes me by addressing the possibility of my gaze, if indirectly. The letter thus provides an allegory of my responsibility to women's texts, while at the same time it clearly indicates that its primary concern is with relations and possible conflicts among women. The letter provides a textual model that retains sexual difference as well as differences within both gender identities, setting a standard for my own critical practice.

Dickinson's letter therefore makes it clear that its writer does not simply identify with her gender and with other women like Gilbert. Dickinson also rejects, in the strongest possible terms, the limitations imposed on her by that identity, especially confinement within a horizon of domesticity and a teleology of motherhood, both associated with the social and cultural hegemonies she names "America" and

"Massachusetts." Julia Kristeva suggests that "when evoking the name and destiny of women, one thinks more of the *space* generating and forming the human species than of *time*, becoming, or history."[6] Dickinson's poems rewrite this ideological conflation of domestic space and an inevitably maternal femininity; home comes to figure the instability or double gesture that both affirms and negates a gender identity founded on the idea that women's social isolation can be empirically determined and thereby taken as a given fact.[7] Dickinson's use of domestic imagery makes possible a materialist reading of her poetry, while it also redefines oppositional practice in terms of a poststructuralist thematics of displacement and undecidability. The home is reinscribed as a contradictory and textualized social space. Gayatri Spivak locates this same double necessity at the base of all forms of oppositional identity, when she describes the strategic formation of a political consciousness whose interest requires the disappearance of that very identity, since it has been formed in response to specific, oppressive conditions of existence. This double gesture, I will argue, also underlies Dickinson's designation of women's contradictory social position as "homelessness at home."[8]

When Dickinson uses this phrase to represent her contradictory relationship to domesticity as the hegemonic site of feminine identity, she constitutes the figure of home as a crucial test of the power of male-dominated discourses to objectify women, to assign identity and circumscribe women's social existences. Dickinson, however, refuses to remain within the boundaries of the modern Western discourses that define the home as an essentially feminine space. Those imposed limitations oblige the male critic like myself, in the very performance of his critical practice, to work through the ideological privilege of the male subject of knowledge with respect to women and their cultural productions.[9] Therefore, to Dickinson's double gesture, I attempt to respond with my own. As Sandra Harding points out, "once essential and universal man dissolves, so does his hidden companion woman. We have, instead, myriads of women living in elaborate historical complexes of class, race, and culture."[10] But this defetishization of male privilege is only one form that my responsibility takes. The corollary to Harding's statement is that traditional gender categories mystify both male power and differences among women. But it seems to me impossible for critics like myself to resist the appropriation of women's writing and feminist cultural work, heedless to the political basis for such work, unless we also remain attentive to the effects of sexual difference, of the ways we are excluded and positioned by the texts we study. In this context, Dickinson's expropriation of the figure of home as a metonymy for women's identity and women's differences from men is exemplary.[11]

Home Economies

The moment of Dickinson's greatest poetic production, the decade of the 1860s, is important in both American and American women's history; those years mark one of the central intersections between the two genealogies, as feminist historians have pointed out. Yet most critics of Dickinson have failed to remark that the beginning of her career in the late 1850s and the period immediately following coincide with the completion of the transition to industrial capitalism in the Northeast.[12] It was during this period that the institution of a separate "woman's sphere" gained legitimacy; the redefinition of gender roles and gendered spaces not only was the main event in women's history during the years 1820–1865 but was also crucial "in the making of American industrial capitalism," in Mary Ryan's words. With the increasing importance of the factory as the site of wage-labor and the ensuing separation of home and workplace, "gender created its own geography" of public and private spheres, so that the concept of womanhood took on "a distinctive spatial character during the early stages of industrial capitalism."[13] The ideological conflation of femininity with generative or maternal spaces that Kristeva analyzes must be historicized in terms of these processes of modernization and their effect on women's lives.[14]

Middle-class women reacted to these changes by attempting to transform their enforced separation from the marketplace and productive labor into a position of moral superiority, and the program of widening "woman's sphere" became a powerful feminist trope for social reform in general. The primary literary vehicle for this trope in the United States was the nineteenth-century domestic novel. Noting that "the cult of domesticity is a social concept that replaces the marketplace with the home," Nina Baym writes that domestic novelists, like domestic feminists, "were thinking about a social reorganization wherein their special concept of home was projected out into the world."[15] Baym's goal is to reveal the progressive political content of this deployment of domesticity. In contrast, Mary Kelley defines the limitations of such a program by showing how the projection of the inner circle of the home onto the larger social order by these women novelists resulted only in a public staging of the restrictions and contradictions imposed on women's lives.[16] Dickinson's poetry raises those contradictions to the level of textual self-consciousness; she implies that any extension of the domestic sphere in the attempt to redefine social life will also necessarily involve a radical redefinition of domesticity and the character of women's lives, a step the domestic novelists could not yet envision.[17]

In life, Dickinson realized an alternative outlet for the historical agency that she imagined in her 1852 letter to Susan Gilbert only by remaining inside her family home and making it a site of poetic production. But the 1852 letter also suggests that Dickinson's action in situating herself within those four literal walls actually constitutes a rejection of "home," given the definition of *home* as "one's own country" that is included in Dickinson's cherished lexicon, fellow Amherst resident Noah Webster's *American Dictionary of the English Language*. For Dickinson's declaration that America has been destroyed (" 'Delenda est' America, Massachusetts and all!") reveals the violent effacement of gender that underlies the elevation of a masculine privilege, full rights of citizenship, to the neutral universality of the pronoun "one." However, Dickinson's lexicon also defines home as "the present state of existence," glossed as being "at home in the body."[18] To be "at home" in a female body was to be dispossessed metaphorically, in terms of political participation, and literally, in terms of property rights and home ownership. By dramatizing these contradictions, Dickinson transforms her own internal exile—her choice to remain at home—into a counterhegemonic space that both functions in the present *and* embodies the promise of a different future: the textual space of the poems.

In her poetry and in contrast to the domestic novelists of her time, Dickinson realized what it would mean genuinely to make herself at home in a feminine space and subject position, to seize it as her "own country" where she could be "at home in the body." She would have no place in either public or private spheres as they were presently constituted. "The very success of the literary domestics" may have "made them displaced people" in spite of themselves, as Kelley argues, "unable in their own minds to leave the home" but still "in many significant respects placed beyond the home, beyond female boundaries."[19] In contrast, Dickinson's poems are structured by what Spivak calls a determination "to operate from displacement as such," and in foregrounding the contradictions of that position, they are able to contest the limitations on women's lives that were taken for granted by the domestic novelists of the time.[20]

On the one hand, the importance of "home" in nineteenth-century America's ideological construction of gender forms a necessary background for understanding the images of home and domestic work that appear in Dickinson's poems. On the other hand, however, Dickinson's poetic discourse is not strictly determined by the discursive conventions that were dominant at the time she was writing. Rather, Dickinson's use of the figure of home intersects with the struggle of the early feminist movement to constitute women as recognized historical agents without allowing that political program to be assimilated within existing structures of dominance. Hence, for Dickinson, the home functions as a position both inside and outside dominant social structures, and she thereby reveals the contradictions on which modern capitalist society is founded and which capitalism's vision of domesticity attempts to resolve. The establishment of a canon of domesticity during the early modern transition to industrial capitalism made it possible for the bourgeois home to function as a central image anchoring the elaboration of capital's "ordering principles" and their installation at the base of social relations; as Fox-Genovese and Genovese observe, "in both theory and practice, domestic economy offered a social representation of the internal and the external, public and private, ordering principles derived from an acceptance of absolute property." Consequently, to the degree that they refuse containment within those "ordering principles" and the gendered spaces they map, the alternative domestic economies explored in Dickinson's poems hold out the possibility of resisting the antimonies of bourgeois thought and suggest the disruptive potential of women's emergence as subjects of history.[22]

The thematics of the home in Dickinson's poetry invites comparison to these "ordering principles" of capitalist society and makes it possible to see how Dickinson's poems attempt to restructure radically the typical relations between time and space, inside and outside, public and private spaces, within modern industrial societies. One way that Dickinson resists the spatialization of women's lives within the home is by insisting on the temporality of women's experience of domesticity. Dickinson's concept of the female subject in its relation to the social order is characterized by the trope of prolepsis, or anticipation, in which the future is represented as already present in some form, as when Dickinson declares that "America, Massachusetts and all" has already been destroyed in the 1852 letter. For Dickinson, this trope functions critically and negatively to delegitimate existing conditions by suggesting alternatives and raising the possibility of change. For example, in *P* 1489, "A Dimple in the Tomb / Makes that ferocious Room / A Home," a future state after death is presented in terms of the social role of homemaker that was presumed to constitute womanhood in general, while the poem simultaneously implies that the canon of domesticity will find the full realization of its values only in a different future—a future whose difference would be as absolute as the boundary between life and death.[23] In this example, simultaneously conceiving the future in terms of the present and conceiving the present as not yet fully present combines commitment to traditional feminine values and rejection of the limitations placed on them. The use of death as an image for this future measures the negativity of Dickinson's critique; a society reorganized on the basis of feminine values was not possible within women's lives as they were structured at that time. But as Sharon Cameron has shown in her analysis of poems structured proleptically by a speaker recounting the story of her death in the past tense, Dickinson's poems continually attempt to enter a space beyond her own (domestic) life and to define the positive value and social content of such a space.[24] In the more detailed readings that follow, I will try to show how the trajectory of these attempts can be reconstructed.

Homelessness at Home

In a poem written after the death of her mother in 1882, according to Thomas Johnson's attribution, Dickinson presents the result of her loss as an existential transience:

> Fashioning what she is,
> Fathoming what she was,
> We deem we dream—
> And that dissolves the days
> Through which existence strays
> Homeless at home. (*P* 1573)

These final lines of the elegy demonstrate a self-consciousness about the position shared by Dickinson and her mother within the home as constructed by both patriarchal and capitalist social relations. The speaker's life repeats the confinement from which the mother has flown "To the bright east," "Fashioning" herself in the mother's image as if the older woman were still a presence, as the generations wander like ghosts or sleepwalkers within a space not their own and through a series of days dissolving into one changeless Now. But Dickinson also implicitly draws on and critiques the masculine privilege of life on the open road (of which Whitman was the great poet), a way of life based on detachment from the mother and the domestic space associated with her. For the woman poet's bonding with her mother does not necessarily result in a reproduction of mothering; that same bonding holds the promise of dissolving the boundaries circumscribing the speaker's life and those of women generally, to make possible a transgressive and negative "straying." The historicity of temporal transience points toward a spatial freedom conceptualized in the present as vagrancy and internal exile. But the "freedom" here is not that of the autonomous ego, and to wander does not mean separation from a female-identified location or subject position in language. It is identification with other women that underlies both the internalization and the liberation of that position from its fixed limits.

Dickinson had already affirmed a similar sense of homelessness and transience in the early 1860s, as attested by "Forever—is composed of Nows" (*P* 624). This poem refers to a "different time" characterized by a "Latitude of Home" in which "Months dissolve in further Months." A later poem elaborates the phrase "Latitude of Home":

> Up Life's Hill with my little Bundle
> If I prove it steep—
> If a Discouragement withhold me—
> If my newest step
>
> Older feel than the Hope that prompted
> Spotless be from blame
> Heart that proposed as Heart that accepted
> Homelessness, for Home—　　　(*P* 1010)

The final line revises the traditional marriage plot: the speaker gains maturity by leaving her parents' home for "Homelessness" rather than a household of her own to control. To accept the latter would be to take a "newest step" that only repeats an old story of women's dependence on men. The poem is about the difficulty, the "Discouragement," of thinking women's agency in terms external to that story. The final lines draw on marriage imagery—"Heart that proposed as Heart that accepted"—to redefine it as women's own particular form of alienation from the home, as the implied space of connection between the daughter who speaks in the poem and her mother.

However, the combination of old and new in the steps the speaker is taking also raises the possibility that the two hearts in the penultimate line both belong to the speaker but at different times, in a potentially different future that yet remains yoked to an oppressive present. She would then be wedded to the idea of women's autonomy, as a personal and political goal. This political reading is also suggested by the speaker's refusal to "blame" or disown the impulse, the "Heart," that motivated her exchange of home for homelessness; that refusal hardly makes sense in the context of a narrative where transcendence or departure from the speaker's childhood home and family is presented in overwhelmingly negative terms, as in the poem's first stanza. Though Dickinson never literally and physically traded home for homelessness, through the act of writing this poem and expropriating vagrancy as a trope for a woman's life struggle, she literally assumes the position of the "Heart that propose[s]," while acceptance or realization on any large scale still lies in the future of the women's movement.

"How many times these low feet staggered" (*P* 187) more directly shows how any imagined alternative to the boundaries on women's lives represented by the home must remain trapped within the present impossibility of acknowledging that freedom of movement as viable. That impossibility in fact points to the oppressive effects of existing social relations and suggests a critical perspective on them. The first stanza of the poem describes the dead body of a woman in terms that emphasize her inaccessibility to our desire for knowledge of her everyday life. The second stanza of "How many times" implies that death places the woman beyond the traditional home industries; her "adamantine fingers" "Never a thimble—more—shall wear." The epithet "adamantine" might refer to the rigor of a dead body or to the quality of endurance demanded of such a worker during her lifetime; thus her condition starts to prefigure a living death, buried within the space of the body described after death as a condemned, locked-up building ("soldered mouth," "awful rivet," "hasps of steel"). The implicit critique sets the stage for the reversal in the third stanza, when death appears as an escape from household labor:

> Buzz the dull flies—on the chamber window—
> Brave—shines the sun through the freckled pane—
> Fearless—the cobweb swings from the ceiling—
> Indolent Housewife—in Daisies—lain!

This "escape" necessarily renders inaccessible to both speaker and reader the unrecorded history of "how many times [her] low feet staggered," a story "Only the soldered mouth can tell." But the poem implies that the speaker's inability to understand the housewife's story from the inside is the result only of the woman's death, and in the final stanza the poem moves toward a satiric tone as this woman's death makes it possible for the speaker to assume a perspective usually encoded as masculine, a perspective external to women's work and lives. From that male perspective, even death is no excuse for a woman's departure from an identity defined by adherence to or neglect of her household duties. The final reference to the dead woman as an "Indolent Housewife" points to the possibility of women redefining their lives in terms external to domesticity as presently constituted, a redefinition that can appear only negatively, as "indolence," from a perspective that remains confined within the assumptions about both femininity and domesticity that were current at the time Dickinson was writing. That same final line also demonstrates the speaker's ability to distance herself from a male perspective even as she assumes it, just as the poem ends with a more than satiric assertion that feminine identity persists even outside the boundaries of domestic life. The ending risks being taken as a reassertion of domestic standards, but it also raises the possibility of women transgressing the traditional boundaries of the feminine without conforming to the paradigm of the "sprightly gentlemen" in *P* 54, who keep the external world of both commerce and nature "bustling" even "When we with Daisies lie." One mark of that nonconformity would be "indolence" as a measure of the incommensurability between an economy based on use or need and one based on profit and exchange, the different aims of the former appearing as a failure to produce when placed in the context of the latter.

Significantly, the possibility of transgression in this poem is linked to an undecidability between interior and exterior spaces, figured by the flies on the window in the final stanza. Are they inside, like the cobwebs, buzzing to get out, or are they outside, like the sun, trying to get in? Are they "dull" because they are dying, trapped in the house, or is their sound dulled because the speaker hears it only through the window, from the inside? In both cases, the speaker continues to locate herself *within* the housewifely space even as she blurs its boundaries.

In a more comic mode, a similar inversion and transgression occur in "Alone and in a Circumstance" (*P* 1167).[25] In that poem, the speaker tells us a spider "on my reticence" grew "so much more at Home than I" that "I felt myself a visitor / And hurriedly withdrew." While the speaker's "reticence" is presumably the result of her domestic location, that silence is figured as a "Home" in which she is made to feel like a visitor—made aware that her relation to the home is not inevitable but contingent on social determinations. The speaker's "withdrawal" or dispossession by the spider leads her into the public sphere, the "street" where "the Law" applies and legal "redress" can be found. Her departure from the metaphorical "Home" of her imposed silence represents a refusal to be limited to domestic work, indicated by the fact that her leaving permits the spider to fill the house with webs, like the cobwebs left by the "Indolent Housewife" of the earlier poem. The poem's comic effect is produced by reversing this causal relation, so that the spider's filling the house with webs is presented as the cause of the speaker's sense of estrangement from her "Home." The very fact that the poem confronts us with a *speaker* reveals an inherent instability in the condition of both female "reticence" and female domesticity, an instability already structurally present even before the poem narrates how the speaker became conscious of it. This instability appears as a function of women's capacities for both independent speech and historical action.

"None can experience stint" (*P* 771) supports a reading of "Indolent" as marking both the principle of exclusion underlying domestic economy and the potential for disruption when that exclusion is challenged. The poem implies that there can be a position outside the opposition between exchange and use, an opposition which devalues domestic labor as nonproductive indolence, as impoverished, in comparison to profitable work:

> None can experience stint
> Who Bounty—have not known—
> The fact of Famine—could not be
> Except for Fact of Corn—
>
> Want—is a meagre Art
> Acquired by Reverse—
> The Poverty that was not Wealth—
> Cannot be Indigence.

The poverty of the unsalaried housewife is not a "Reverse," the absence of "Wealth." Instead it is both a lack of wealth and a positive thing in itself, like Derrida's originary absence or arche-writing, an absence already in existence before there was anything, any presence, to become absent.[26] Women or others who are excluded from business concerns and profit, or "Bounty," cannot be defined as impoverished in the terms used by those concerns, even though there may be no other terms available to designate their condition. The same argument can be applied to the home, since "Indigence" connotes homelessness or vagrancy as well as poverty. Women's poverty "Cannot be Indigence" because it was their position within a household upon marriage which excluded the vast majority of nineteenth-century women from ownership or control of their wages, if they had any. This sense of the final lines supports a reading of the poem's subject as *women's* "Want." But they also imply that women's rejection of traditional confinements is not a detachment from the feminine; home is not simply traded for a homelessness that would duplicate the conditions of men's lives.

It is in relation to this second interpretation that Dickinson's poems about wandering outside and looking in at scenes of abundance must be read. In "I had been hungry, all the Years—" (P 579), for example, the speaker is unable to partake of food when invited in to dine on "Tables" instead of in "Nature's—Dining Room" because she has become too accustomed to doing without. Like many others, this poem inverts distinctions between inside and outside in a way that makes those distinctions impossible to draw definitively, engendering an undecidability that also manifests itself in the problem of whether to interpret certain key terms as literal or figurative. Only if the speaker's hunger is taken as literal does she situate herself outside the home; otherwise both hunger and food or home become tropes for what the speaker lacks and what she needs to satisfy that lack. If the lack is precisely her inability to participate in public life, to attend the national Whig convention for example, then when she speaks of trying to enter and eat she is referring to leaving home. Interior and exterior are reversed. But the poem states that even if she were offered such participation, she would be unable to make a new "home" for herself in the public sphere where only *men* are free to feel "at home": "The Plenty hurt me—'twas so new— / Myself felt ill—and odd." Through the metaphor of wandering outside and looking in, the speaker lays claim to the right to move beyond the boundaries of the home, a reading that would move toward the literal. It is in this sense that the speaker can say she has learned "Hunger— was a way / Of Persons outside Windows— / That Entering—takes away —." The speaker's hunger to move beyond the constraints of gender has already begun to be satisfied by her choice of a vehicle to express that hunger; full assimilation is not only unnecessary but undesirable, literally, just as the speaker loses her desire for food when she is invited inside the preserve of wealth. She finally remains neither securely within the home nor willing simply to transcend it.

The window often figures the simultaneous possibility and impossibility of such textual inversions of public and private spaces. That figure remains implicit in the opening lines of an early poem:

> At last, to be identified!
> At last, the lamps upon thy side
> The rest of life to see!   (*P* 174)

The transposition of an article of household furniture (the lamps are later revealed as a trope for the dawn) into the outside world effects a reversal of inside and outside. The poem achieves this effect by alluding to the way a person inside a lighted room can see only her reflection in a window when looking out, but someone on the darkened side can see in, a trope for the masculine privilege of moving from the public world into the home while the inverse movement is denied to women. The lines imply that women's identity will be realized publicly only when that inverse movement becomes an option for them; here, though it is a prospect to which the speaker has access only through sight, not through physical contact.

The significance of the window as an image for a physical confinement that can be overcome through imagination or vision and thereby holds out the promise of physical release is often invoked in Dickinson's poems through the point of view of a fly or insect. After the initial comparison of "It would have starved a Gnat" (*P* 612), the speaker contrasts her condition to the insect's, since she does not have

> the Art
> Upon the Window Pane
> To gad my little Being out
> And not begin—again—

She cannot stop trying to get through a boundary that cannot be seen (like the symbolic or ideological definition of separate spheres), no matter how many times she is repulsed. Unlike the gnat, the speaker's death in this attempt is only metaphorical and not final, which implies two things: first, that if she could get her "Being" outside she would be beginning a new life, and second, that perhaps even the attempt is enough to generate a new beginning.

The constellation of fly, window, and death appears again, in a slightly different configuration, at the end of "I heard a Fly buzz—when I died" (*P* 465). A speaker who tells us in the first line that she is already dead retraces the events leading up to her demise:

> There interposed a Fly—
>
> With Blue—uncertain stumbling Buzz—
> Between the light—and me—
> And then the Windows failed—and then
> I could not see to see—

As Sharon Cameron notes, the doubling of darkened windows and the darkness that falls over the eyes in death, accounting for the repetition of *see*, suggests that some form of perception and consciousness or interiority might survive death, that it might somehow be possible to still see within the darkness that is death, since it remains necessary to close the eyes even within that darkness. Though that possibility is negated in this particular case, the whole poem has implied such a possibility, since the speaker is narrating the events leading up to her death using the past tense, the only indication that the death is merely figurative, as in "It would have starved a Gnat."[27]

However, as in the earlier poem, the phrase "the windows failed" can also be read as a failure to shut the speaker *in* any longer, hence as an image of release from confinement, and the doubleness Cameron specifies might function as part of that release since it distinguishes one interiority (the consciousness in the body) from another (the domestic space of the home) and implies that they are not necessarily linked as content to container. The ending leaves open the question of whether this death is to be taken literally (meaning that the speaker's voice would be emanating from beyond the grave) or whether it functions as a metaphor for a possible *liberation into* the public world. This undecidability operates, then, to combine a radically critical perspective on the exclusion of women with the anticipation of possibilities for change.

The contradiction between death as a vehicle of change through the absolute refusal of hegemonic norms and death as a finality after which no change is possible pervades Dickinson's poetry, and the very fact that it is never resolved indicates the extent to which she escapes the ideological limitations of the period. Dickinson's poems lay bare the violence with which a social order attempts to justify or conceal the gender relations structuring a division of labor oppressive to women. *P* 1489, "A Dimple in the Tomb / Makes that ferocious Room / A Home," exemplifies this exposure of the violence underlying social taxonomies. The effect of the poem depends on the indeterminate status of its central categories: is "Tomb" a metaphor for "Home" or vice-versa? Is the poem a critique of the deadening effects of domestic confinement on women, or does the poem enact the difficulties of redefining domesticity by showing how the concept of home is capable of containing and appropriating to itself even a condition—death—that might seem entirely external to domestic life? Does the trope on tomb and home mean that confinement in the home is no more constricting than resistance, when death is the only option for resistance? Or does it mean that the ability to transform the tomb, as the speaker does in utilizing this trope, implies the possibility of transforming the social world external to the family in some homologous way? Such textual oscillations encode the contradictions of domesticity itself, contradictions that both form the basis for the gender identity of Dickinson's poetic personae and make it possible to conceive that identity as a disruption of nineteenth-century representations of home as "woman's" proper "place."

"I lingered with Before—"

Dickinson is notorious for never literally expanding the circumference of her values and consciousness beyond the "feminine" confines of her father's home in Amherst. Her rejection of that limitation took the form of "homelessness at home." Only in her poems does Dickinson follow the line of flight articulated in her 1852 letter to Susan Gilbert ("I shant stay here any longer!"). Finding herself located within a domestic perspective, in her poems she proleptically treated a future state of greater freedom as if it were already present and by doing so foregrounded the contradictions and potential for resistance already present in women's lives. She also strategically asserted the inseparability of any future changes from an identification with the feminine values and female subject position that the ideology of separate spheres worked to contain.

Dickinson's poems demonstrate the prefigurative potential Sheila Rowbotham locates in feminist organizational forms, which are not utopian, she writes, because they "seek both to consolidate existing practice and release the imagination of what could be."[28] In Dickinson's "What shall I do when the Summer troubles" (P 956), the time of the speaker's discontent is also the proleptic anticipation of a time "when the Eggs fly off in Music." This figuration of a future condition of freedom combines the speaker's desire to leave the nest of domestic confinement with her desire to resist separation from that feminine space of connection to the mother. The same characteristic gesture and the same temporal structure appear again when a speaker declares both "I lingered with Before—" and "I Years had been from Home" (P 609).

This trope of "homelessness at home" opens a textual space where the acceptable narratives of women's lives could begin to come into contact with the stories of persons positioned outside of middle-class domesticity, since the trope implicitly rejects the enclosure of women's lives and histories within the boundaries of the home. Dickinson's representation of home thereby mediates between the dichotomies that Sandra Gilbert and Susan Gubar locate in nineteenth-century women's writing. The poems search for an alternative to the position of "the lady who submits to male dicta" by accepting her "proper" place and the position of the madwoman, denied any social space in which to operate. They also negotiate the perceived necessity for a woman writer "to choose between admitting she was 'only a woman' or protesting that she was 'as good as a man' " and accepting separation from a domestic role as the precondition for public life.[29] Dickinson's poems resist placement within either an ideological definition of femininity as true womanhood or the representations of female transgression, madness, and masculinization available at the time of her writing.

The critical implications of this choice emerge in *P* 1645, where Dickinson refuses to deplore the condition of a male vagrant and so also refuses the role of moral arbiter and the job of "social" or "enlarged housekeeping." The poem breaks with the conventional representation of femininity in the act of redefining "home":

> The Ditch is dear to the Drunken man
> For is it not his Bed—
> His Advocate—his Edifice?
> How safe his fallen Head
>
> In her disheveled Sanctity—
> Above him is the sky—
> Oblivion bending over him
> And Honor leagues away.

The poem invokes the standard ideology of domesticity and playfully alters its meaning by carrying it to a logical extreme, treating even a makeshift home in a ditch as a feminine space. The "Sanctity" of domestic values is not rejected, but they are no longer placed on a pedestal above public life. Instead, those values and their bearers have a chance to get their hands dirty in history. Rather than taking the topic of the poem as a pretext for reformist rhetoric and thereby accepting a position within the home as the basis for claims of moral superiority, Dickinson's treatment of this homeless figure reflects critically on her own position as a white, middle-class woman. It is by bringing to light the contradictions of that position that Dickinson lingers in the "before" of a feminine identity that would define itself outside the structures of dominance characterizing nineteenth-century American society, leaving her homeless at home.

16

Celibate Sisters-in-Revolution: Towards Reading Sylvia Townsend Warner

Robert L. Caserio

The English writer Sylvia Townsend Warner is celebrated and popular among nonacademic readers; but in spite of this and in spite of the fact that her novel *Lolly Willowes* (1928) is a feminist manifesto deserving a place in the curriculum no less than Virginia Woolf's texts, Warner has received virtually no attention in American studies of modern fiction. Yet her work is of great literary and theoretical interest. Her novels make plain the need for an approach to feminist-oriented fiction that sees such fiction in terms of a tradition in which some male writers are creatively implicated. Even more importantly, Warner's fiction represents a development in the English novel of a Marxist-oriented but Marxist-revisionist materialist analysis of history, in tandem with a radical challenge to realist traditions of representation, with which feminist and Marxist critics alike might well want to come to terms.

The pivot of the interest is Warner's consummation of more than a half-century of fiction that pictures chaste or celibate pairs of (so to speak) sisters-in-revolution. While *Lolly Willowes* represents a fierce female solitary self-possession, *Summer Will Show* (1936) and *The Corner That Held Them* (1948) dramatize such self-possession in its relation to other women. The result is two novels about "sisterhood," about a chaste bond of relation between or among women that is political and that is related to revolution. Among avatars of this sororal icon in Warner are Rhoda Nunn and Mary Barfoot in George Gissing's *The Odd Women* (1893), Madge and Clara Hopgood in Mark Rutherford's *Clara Hopgood* (1896), and Sophia and Constance Baines in Arnold Bennett's *The Old Wives' Tale* (1908). These pairings are of course late developments of Charlotte Brontë's Shirley and Caroline, of George Eliot's Dorothea and Rosamund; and they are extended in the representation of celibate sisters in Woolf's *The Years* (1937). As such, Warner and her creations loom as figures at the end of a long vista lined with other writers, both female and male.

Among Warner's modernist contemporaries, the politically charged possibilities of chaste sisterhood appear in Woolf's idea, in *Three Guineas*, of a society of outsiders devoted to an interidentified "mental chastity" and intellectual liberty.[1] Jane Marcus has noted how the mental chastity called for by *Three Guineas* "take[s] the Victorian ideal of female chastity, which was patriarchal culture's . . . imprisonment of women's bodies and minds," and transforms that mode of imprisonment into a "deeply feminist" possibility. One can understand the ideological justice of Marcus' claim that "we need search no further for the origins of . . . Woolf's pacifism and mysticism" once we have referred the latter to the inspiration of her aunt Caroline Emilia Stephen, who wrote about the history of sisterhoods and about Quaker mysticism and pictured herself as "a nunnery of one." But if Marcus' persuasively historicized picture of Woolf, under her aunt's influence, as "a rational mystic who calls for human community from her cloistered imagination"[2] is something we need search no further for the origins of, one might still wonder how the transformation of a patriarchal ideal into a feminist possibility works. With what gain and what cost does it reorder woman's economy of pleasure? What does the feminist recovery of an ideal of chastity mean for our historical moment, for a vision of contemporary history or politics? Is it really possible that men may have helped in this transformation from patriarchal to feminist ideal? Turning from Woolf and Warner to the male pictures of "rational mystic cloisterhood" implicated in Gissing, Rutherford, and Bennett, we indeed find under way the metamorphosis of an imprisoning Victorian notion of chastity into something allied with liberty.

I want to attempt to dispel much of the uneasy sense, which may be provoked by the male-authored sororal icons to which Warner is allied, that the proposed virtue of women's chastity remains tainted by patriarchal coercions. But I need first to set out a second and even more problematic aspect of why Warner might interest contemporary criticism. Already by the 1860s English fiction, according to Catherine Gallagher, was dissolving "the realist's project . . . to discover the really real"[3]—which is to say that English fiction was dissolving assumptions that "the really real" is a matter grounded in material history and in historical specificity. Clearly Warner, who was a decades-long member of the English Communist Party, was inspired by Marx; but although her work, with all its fidelity to historical concreteness, shares in the realist and the Marxist project, it shares no less in a tradition that attempts to dissolve realism and realism's representational probabilities. The result is that Warner's fictions compound Marxism's interest in the specific determinations and differentiations of any cultural formation with an antirepresentational bias; and they mix the feminist traditions crystalized in *A Room of One's Own* and *Three Guineas* with antihuman, even inhuman, apolitical mysticism and supernaturalism. This compound, uniquely synthesized and accented, has a potential importance for feminist and nonfeminist readers alike; and I shall be arguing that both politics and history are relocated by Warner in ways that are *valuable* even if they don't strike us as politically and historically *immediate*. But it appears that our criticism does not yet have in play the terms best to comprehend and to value Warner's achievement. Our desire for a political correctness of method and stance is part of the problem: we assume, realist fashion, that we have a fail-safe basis for political liberation in referring political questions to the concretely experienced immediacies of history.

An example of such a fail-safe strategy, an adversarial criticism of a compound of elements very close to those I have described in Warner, can be found in Anglo-American feminism's repeated questionings of the French theorist Luce Irigaray.[4] Toril Moi's reservations about Irigaray, for example, could easily be applied to Warner's *Lolly Willowes*, half of which is what we call fantasy, and even to her *Summer Will Show*, a blatantly "historical" novel: "The material conditions of women's oppression," Moi writes, "are spectacularly absent from [Irigaray's] work. But without specific material analysis, a feminist account of power cannot transcend the simplistic and defeatist vision of male power pitted against female helplessness that underpins Irigaray's theoretical investigations."[5] Now this is the ground-note of a generally expressed discontent with Irigaray: her theory lacks specificity and precision; her theory falls away from history, which is to be thought of as the realm of an ever-changing set of precise material practices, be it in the construction of gender or in the act of writing.[6] But one has doubts about these repeated criticisms. Where Moi is concerned, the plea for historical specificity and material analysis sits side by side oddly—not to say incoherently—with Moi's deconstructionism. How can the deconstructionist anchor herself, or find a fail-safe centrality, in an appeal to the *materiality* and *specificity* of this or that practice?

Warner's power, I would argue, like Irigaray's, results from a more flexible and complex understanding of history and historical materialism than is present in Moi's critique. This is due precisely to Warner's tendency to dramatize the disjunction between feminist theory and concrete experience, and, consequently, to her falling away from the realm of history into that of vision. And there are, I submit, more complexities of response and historical analysis in Gissing's, Rutherford's, and Bennett's comprehension of feminist issues than in Moi's. This is precisely because both in their fictions and Warner's—whose common saturating element is the specificity and material analysis dear to realism and naturalism—there is *already* a steady revision of this very element. Moreover, there appears to be a correlation between this revision and the focus in these texts on celibate sister-figures, each of whom is intimate with revolutionary impulse and praxis. And the very possibility of arguing that the male-authored of these novels might *not* reinforce patriarchal norms of virginal chastity is related to the persistence of similar plots in female authors both preceding and following these male texts—plots reaching back to Lucy Snowe's story in *Villette*, repeated in Woolf's *The Years*, and continued in such fiction as Iris Murdoch's *The Bell* and Muriel Spark's *The Girls of Slender Means*. This persistent picturing of a celibate ideal of woman's life must argue for more than the cultural stubbornness of what is tainted by patriarchy.

Thus, in spite of our century's liberal and radical attempts to recover and release sexual desires and pleasures—especially women's—from patriarchal repression; and in spite of our patriarchal churches' repressive emphasis on chastity and celibacy as cure-alls for deviations from the order of heterosexual monogamy, I suggest that we will find a live tradition of fiction-writing by women and men that has attempted to extend the cultural life of celibacy and chastity, to make them carry on ascetic ideals and at the same time transfer to them liberal and radical political meanings. But it is not just the surprising extension of this ascetic ideal that is at issue. It appears that in the course of transformative continuation and transfer, chastity and celibacy stand for a new address in fiction to the representation of society and history.

I

Instead of giving the male authors the benefit of the doubt, I'd first like to examine the unease we may feel at the late-Victorian male pictures of the "ideal" of woman's chastity. Gissing's *The Odd Women*, for example, represents heterosexual erotic jealousy and marriage as near-fatal temptations for Rhoda Nunn's feminist mission, concretized in the business school she and her partner, Mary Barfoot, run in order to free women from their dependence on patriarchy. Rescue from the temptation lies in Rhoda's breaking with the suitor who offers her a conventional union. But does Rhoda's triumph imply a punishment for feminist virtue—a new version of the wages of sin? Rhoda never "falls"; but her sexual desire apparently must be martyred to her feminism. The same suspicions reassert themselves in response to Rutherford's and Bennett's texts. In *Clara Hopgood* we literally have two sisters: Madge, who with dignified self-possession bears a child out of wedlock (and then goes on to marry a Spinoza-like London Jew), and Clara, who denies herself marriage, then enlists (as a spy) and martyrs herself in the cause of Mazzini's revolutionary efforts against Austria. Although both sisters are revolutionists— the one against sexual morality's punitive address to desire, the other against imperialism's oppression of a people—Clara becomes the novel's cynosure. For Rutherford seems to turn away from Madge's successful rebellion, and its access to sexual pleasure and satisfaction, in order to make Clara the novel's nun and thereby to renew Victorian patriarchy's favored figure, the virgin. In the case of Bennett's well-known Baines sisters in *The Old Wives' Tale*, it is Sophia, the more revolutionary of the two, who conforms—once again—to the image of the virgin. For her attempt to free herself from her patriarchal family by securing her sexual pleasure with Gerald Scales and by eloping to Paris—to a Paris whose revolution against the Empire is a macrocosmic image of Sophia's against Bursley—scarcely lasts; after Gerald's loss Sophia reverts to a life of celibacy. In all three of these male representations, then, patriarchy's "death" ironically results, it would seem, in the resurrection of patriarchy's ideal of woman as chaste nun.

Yet such suspicious readings are inadequate. They do not take into account the way in which the topos of chastity is torn away from its patriarchal site by a dynamic involvement with a new representation of society and history. Let us turn first to *The Odd Women*. As John Goode has brilliantly argued, Gissing's novelistic form represents a struggle with the sociological mode of analysis implicit in fictional realism's—and in Marxism's—attachment to an organic link between specificity and representational typicality and totality. The organic link had been based in the experience of "declassment," whereby an individual's movement from one class to another reveals the shape of the social totality. But Gissing observes that something in the lived interrelation of individual and totality has come to a halt, and that this implies a halt for what the classic realist novel can do. For, as Goode shows, being *de*classed has been replaced in the uncertain world of Gissing's novels with the experience of being *un*classed, of finding oneself so radically "emancipated" from the social totality that one enters "a place that has no bearing on a potential function."[7] This "place" of the unclassed is for Gissing suspended between a specific, limited experience, enacted in a specific zone or enclosure, and a theoretical everywhere and nowhere, a place of abstract vision wherein the individual "locates" an extended, alternative, and better life. *The Odd Women* is a formal mimesis of this gap. History and ideology are components of the novel that comment on the novel's foreground drama—and vice versa—but the components and the comments remain on different planes. The novel and the ideology portrayed by the novel are both at odds with—not matched with—the typical and specific situations they seem to portray. What exists in classed or classifiable terms is disjoined from what can be identified in terms that are unclassed—and unclassifiable.

Gissing numbers feminists—and women in the light of feminism—among the ranks of the unclassed. Women in feminism's light, that is, are seen to have a double existence. They have an identity located in typical and specific functions and places, in situations and class that are not in the least "odd." But the feminist *vision* of this class function and location, claiming with Mary Barfoot that "the old types of womanly perfection are no longer helpful to us,"[8] opens up an ideological alternative to what is both typical and specifically situated. What is important here is that the alternative reveals itself as a *theoretic* possibility, which, as Goode says, is "an ideology which can have no concrete elaboration" (80). The resulting disjunction is figured by the sororal pair at *The Odd Women*'s center. The novel presents these two as a pair and as no-pair, even though they are so much alike that they have struggled against desire for the same man. In their desire they are, however, typical—yet Rhoda Nunn shudders to think of her own temptation to enter normative life. "Type of a whole class . . . in missing love and marriage she had missed everything. So thought the average woman, and in [Rhoda's] darkest hours she . . . had fallen among those." She now makes "no vows to crush the natural instincts" (334), but she turns her back on marriage for the sake of her work, her students, and Mary.

In the novel's finale Gissing represents with odd indirectness Rhoda's constancy in her pairing with Mary. He displaces any narrative potential for a consummatory scene between the two heroines onto a scene of rapprochement between Rhoda and another female character—Monica Widdowson—who has brought Rhoda's wedding plan to its crisis. This is a rapprochement that is also a parting: what begins in mutual coldness for the women ends in a kiss, but this pair will never see each other again, because of the death in childbirth that is the culmination of Monica's miserable marriage. It is thus a scene structured by conjunction and separation. And because it appears to be standing in the place of another potential ending— the "marriage" of Rhoda and Mary—the scene suggests itself as an illustration of Rhoda's and Mary's relation. This passionate but celibate attachment—which Rhoda describes on the novel's last page as "flourishing like the green bay-tree"— we are made to think is a union and separation, a pairing not easily specifiable or classifiable as one, first because it is more intense than friendship and yet not a marriage of the flesh, and then because of the theoretic implications it has for a social order that will be beyond all pairings. Yet it is also a pairing whose zoned intimacy and limited practical ends are as it were at a chaste remove from an all-inspiring theoretical horizon.

In an 1895 preface to the reissue of *The Unclassed* (1884), Gissing describes his characters as dwelling "in a limbo external to society. They refuse the statistic badge—will not . . . 'be classed and done with.' "[9] The obliquity of Gissing's final representation of Mary and Rhoda together is partly a refusal of the statistic badge for them. Their partnership has reference to a particular class—a subset of already educated but still educable women—whom Rhoda sharply opposes to "the uneducated classes," "the profitless average" (58, 63). This seems to show absolute attachment on the heroine's part to the statistical badge. Yet how is her and her partner's union to be classed? Statistically and specifically they are business associates; but the statistic badge leaves out the radically visionary theory that Mary, in chapter 13, propounds as the basis of the business. Moreover, were they to be even hinted at by Gissing as carnally coupled, they would be all the more eligible for a badge, an official classification. Here even if we suppose that Rhoda's celibacy is the product of the patriarchal virgin-ideal combined in Gissing with a taboo against picturing lesbianism, what we would catch in the combination is the metamorphosis of a repressive patriarchal motif into a motif suitable for *Three Guineas*.

The celibacy that is also a pairing intensifies Gissing's communication of what resists classifications and representations of the world that have been found handy for patriarchal interests. Significantly the one "happily" married man in *The Odd Women* is a mathematician planning (on the approach of his wedding) to write a book about probability, which will be based no doubt on statistical procedures and averages. But the narrative gives the man of probable numbers short shrift. The curtness is a sign to the reader of Gissing's turn away from typicality and representational averages. For these are *male* averages, the narrative seems to indicate. Seeing the world in the light of statistics and types is a male tradition that the unclassed invade and evade.

What if feminism is, as Gissing suggests, an ideology whose power lies in its ability to outdistance or to contradict its particular concrete elaborations and even our habitual ways of representing or classifying the concrete practices that are supplemented by typifying ideological elaborations?[10] The pursuit of feminism so as to question a habitual way of classifying and calculating the world is echoed by Rutherford's representational strategies in *Clara Hopgood*. The compositional logic of Clara and Madge originates in a specificity of time and place—a concrete historical representation of the era of Chartism—but moves away from that specificity and indeed makes heroic an aspect of life that disappears from any concrete viewpoint. Each of the sisters—Madge, the more impulsive sister who conceives her child in a moment of consensual ecstasy and then adamantly refuses to marry the dutiful father, and Clara, who denies herself marriage with the Jew who becomes in turn her sister's lover—represents a successive phase of remove from sociologically typical or representative class; each travels a path that, unlike declassment, does not reveal a sociological or historical totality, but does lead to an unclassed corner of existence; and Clara's ultimate dedication to the *risorgimento*—and her disappearance and death—symptomizes an ideological horizon whose purity resists concrete elaboration. This is why, it appears, Rutherford chooses not to have Clara join the movement at home—Chartism—to which the urban intellectuals of her circle have attached themselves; the novel's sympathy is with mystical visions not so much of historical conditions and human betterment as of an unflinching principle of rectitude and self-suppression illustrated by Clara's celibacy. The service Clara undertakes to a foreign cause is also a kind of meditation on feminism. For the novel suggests that women suffer under conventions that are more general and diffused than what a specific class suffers—even though the social plight of nineteenth-century workers and women overlap. But in the case of women, the struggle is more generalized even if no less urgent than a specifiable class struggle.

I am speaking here of a resistance to historical specificity or situation that nevertheless seeks to be taken into account by historical-mindedness and not to be dismissed by history as mere ideological delusion, as false consciousness. The resistance enters Rutherford's narrative in the form of a disruptive embedding of excerpts from a curious collection of essays. The few excerpts of a copy of this collection read by Clara compose the exact middle of the novel; they echo Gissing's opposing of oddness to probability. One excerpt declares that what is "of most value to us is often obtained in defiance of the laws of probability"; another insists that "the interaction of human forces" is "incalculable"; others emphasize "the preliminary stillness" of mystic experience, "the closure against other voices and the reduction of the mind to a condition in which it can *listen*," and the "determinative" nature, not of material reality, but of "a mere dream, a vague hope, [which] ought in some cases to be more potent than a certainty in regulating our action."[11] The narrative assigns to Clara traits matching these aphorisms. The match subverts the assumptions that historical agencies are concretely determinate and identical with environing material circumstance. *Pace* Moi, there *is* determination here, but it is associated with an oppression-lifting mystical environment, of which Madge and Clara are the bearers. The women bear in interesting ways: out of wedlock, in Madge's case, and celibately, in Clara's. As such, the sisters together repeat Rhoda Nunn's refusal to crush her passions and her simultaneous surmounting of passion's pleasures.

In Gissing and Rutherford, then, a male picture of female celibacy moves a patriarchal classification of female virtue, chastity, into an antipatriarchal political position. But while the persona of the virgin is left intact by this picture, the narrative form of sociological analysis to which the persona had belonged is emphatically not. This is so even for Arnold Bennett, whom Virginia Woolf criticized for relying upon oppressive materialist naturalism, and hence for relying upon conventional sociological typifications. But *The Old Wives' Tale*—pace Woolf's self-enabling misprision of Bennett—also dramatizes its sisters as the bearers of a revolutionary impulse and praxis that are shown by the novel to unclass them, even as they remain to conventional eyes "types" of their time, station, and place.

To read *The Old Wives' Tale* in this light requires a decidedly revisionary perspective. The habitual response to the novel has summed it up in terms of the thoughts assigned to the novel's sisters, first when Sophia, after thirty-six years of separation, confronts the dead body of her ex-husband and then as Constance later confronts the dead body of Sophia. Both sisters' thoughts share in Sophia's stupefaction at the sight of Gerald's corpse: "That was all . . . Youth and vigour always came to that. Everything came to that . . . 'And what shall I have lived for? What is the meaning of it?' The riddle of life . . . was killing her."[12] But the stupefied unknowing here is not the novel's point. For Bennett the impact of the fact of death on "what life is" *has changed*, precisely because of a shift Bennett documents in social and historical forces and then exemplifies in his novelistic analysis of them.

Although Bennett's characters don't grasp the fact that since the mid–nineteenth century patriarchy has been moribund and that conventional life is now saturated by revolutionary tendency, Bennett's construction of the narrative attests to this truth: in *The Old Wives' Tale* no experience can escape revolutionary change. Constance Baines treats her husband, Sam Povey, and her son as if they were middle-class patriarchy's heirs-apparent, but she doesn't recognize—nor do they— that the middle-class patriarchal role has been evacuated. It is to demonstrate indirectly this evacuation that Bennett shows how Sam's death results from his efforts to mobilize mass action in support of his cousin Daniel, who is guilty of the manslaughter of an oppressive wife. On the surface the political machinery Sam uses exemplifies Bursley's middle-class solidarity and paternalist self-righteousness. Yet the narrative implies that Sam's motive for defending Daniel lies in a negation of familial virtues. Sam in the past has been initiated by Daniel into "the great Pan tradition" (187)—which presumably is not mere priapianism, but a proto-Freudian devotion to sexuality as the revolutionary mover of all things. Sam's public cause has no conscious connection with ideas about Pan; yet clearly what the public machinery of the defense of Daniel means for Sam is at root anarchic Eros, a politically chaotic inspiration, unconsciously subversive of the middle-class conventions which are the basis of the representational machinery.

In this way Bennett exhibits Sam as a class type whose representational action expresses a blind desire to escape typical representativeness, and whose vision— the Pan ideology—finds no concrete elaboration. Sam's conventional class life is an unacknowledged form of "unclassment." To become unclassed, moreover, is the fate of all the major actors in *The Old Wives' Tale*. Political engagement, in terms of class movement or mass action, is inescapably the lot of the two sisters. But these politics hide no less than they represent or express their class constituents.[13] For example, Constance seems true to type—to Baines' patriarchy, to the solid economic and domestic virtues of her class. Yet the type itself is vanishing and is the cliché of the novel's title. A compositional logic in Rutherford's sororal pair shows itself again: here the one sister is used by Bennett as a representative type or class, as a type of representation; Constance joins the sociologically general to the specific, lived instance. The other sister is used to confound the type, to exhibit an unclassed, unclassifiable alternative. And Sophia compounds paradoxes, in a way that eludes specification no less than typification. She is the fallen woman and rebel who, in the neighborhood of French prostitutes, revives celibacy; she is the politically reactionary conservative who, in the midst of the Siege of Paris and the Commune, enacts a revolutionary female economic independence. As the French patriarchal empire falls, Sophia's postmarital chastity seems to revive a patriarchal ideal—only to move it onto a line of protofeminist self-sufficiency. Perhaps inevitably, the protofeminist ideology floats above the narrative horizon; it cannot be concretely elaborated because the social order appears to close its radical potential in on an inescapably restricted zone. Sophia's ultimate return to Bursley emphasizes the modern obstruction of mobility and the stubborn endurance of the typical. But what endures is also hollow. The typical encloses what is odd, which lurks within, undoing typicality by measuring the "nature" of woman at the point where "woman" is no longer sustained by the artifices of incorporation or of representative instance.[14] Sophia's "odd" return to Bursley and chastity represents the hollowing-out of typifying representations of middle-class womanhood.

On the one hand, then, history is seen by *The Old Wives' Tale* as the track of representative classes matched with specific instances of life; on the other hand, history (it appears) is—or is becoming—a revolutionary collapse of classifications, a refusal on all fronts of the statistical badge. This disjunctive vision is the heart of the narrative conjunction of Constance and Sophia. Bennett's narrative makes this disjunctive, double vision a way of knowing, in contrast to the riddling meaninglessness felt by Sophia. Nevertheless, there seems to be even in this double vision itself a potential for heightening the fact of an all-environing mortality. Why might this heightening occur? Why alongside, of all things, the heightening of writers' interest in sexual abstinence? And how can a renewed emphasis on chastity and mortality be allied with Marxist revolutionary inspirations? Since both heightenings

appear in Warner, in and through the sororal motif and structure, it is time to turn
to her address to these questions and their answers.

II

Warner has not been absent until now: I have been redacting the male novelists
as her work makes it possible to see them—reading them as if they are tending
towards what she makes of them. What she makes of them has everything to do
with what *Lolly Willowes* makes of representational and sociological typicality and
specificity.

For most of the brief *Lolly Willowes*, the reader is saturated in a hundred years
of the historical specificity—and typicality—of the Willowes family, with Lolly as
the focus of the century-long view. But in its final third, the narrative turns against
the historical typicality and specificity. The fantasy Lolly has long entertained of
being a witch, the ally of Satan, comes to be literally true. At first, the reader
cannot believe his or her eyes concerning this development. Lolly, the spinster
aunt, feels a call to leave London and her relatives to live in the secluded hamlet
of Great Mop. But the financial independence Lolly thinks she has turns out to be
illusory when she finds that her brother has invested and lost her trust funds without
consulting her. The sociological analysis here, matching specific instance and
representative type, is classic. The specific virginal spinster is a middle-class
creation, the typical product of privilege accorded to fathers and brothers and
distrained from daughters and sisters, especially unmarried ones, in a late, high
imperialist phase of capitalist development.

So, given the sociological and historical plausibility and probability of events,
when Lolly at Great Mop begins to fancy that the hamlet is a coven and that its
citizens are visited by the Devil, we are still reading in the light of realist plausibility
and can only assume that Lolly is losing her mind. And even when appearances at
Great Mop begin to suggest—in spite of our doubts—that Lolly's theory is sound
after all, we might assume that the narrative is cultivating a modernist or postmod-
ernist suspension of certainty. But this is not the case. Satan makes a personal
appearance to Lolly several times, and he and the heroine converse to great self-
justifying—and feminist—effect. The narrative cancels our doubts about the actual
fact of this alliance, and it asks us not to read the Satanic episodes as merely a
political parable.

To be sure, when we read that "it had pleased Satan to come to [Lolly's] aid.
Considering carefully, she did not see who else would have done so. Custom, public
opinion, law, church, and state—all would have . . . sent her back to bondage,"[15]
it is tempting to consider Satan's function as only a parabolic convenience for
the illustration of feminist polemic. But the narrative elements supplement the
polemic—they don't just illustrate or decorate it—by giving the polemic a finality
that resists, on the one hand, the indeterminacy we associate with imaginative
arbitrariness and, on the other hand, the determinacy we associate with historical

specificity and typicality. The most fantastic element of the novel, the intimacy with Satan, is presented as unequivocally continuous with verisimilar historical specificity; and yet the typicality of Lolly Willowes, her claim to stand for every woman of her (upper middle) class and for Everywoman as well, is undermined by the novel's violation of historical specificity via the novel's "realization" of history as fantasy. The result is an uncanny mix that is sociologically expressive and that at the same time undermines sociologically expressive specification and typification. The novel's fantasy element represents a disjunction between feminist theory and concretely lived elaborations of the theory, because an individual life like Lolly's cannot encompass the elaboration concretely.

The impossible encompassment is correlated with Warner's characterization of Lolly's form of desire. When Lolly's nephew pursues her to Great Mop, his affection exudes a possessiveness that makes his aunt feel "she has not been allowed to love in her own way" (87). What her way of loving is is consonant with all the curious apartness, all the chaste desire implicit in the celibate sisters of the tradition I have been citing. Lolly is so self-possessed, so apparently fulfilled by herself, that her love appears to be of a paradoxically nondesiring kind. In Lolly Willowes the more desirous and more class-situated of the sisters in the sororal tradition is eliminated and replaced by a Satan who is summed up as "imperturbable, inscrutable, enormous with the dignity of natural behavior and untrammeled self-fulfillment" (132). Through Lolly Willowes, the double of this Satanic character, Warner makes us see that celibacy can take on the dignity of natural behavior—and even of untrammeled self-fulfillment. To see in this way diabolically inverts, of course, our cultural assumptions (as well as semantic ones) about chastity and celibacy. Perhaps even more diabolical is Warner's use of celibacy in the works that follow Lolly Willowes to turn upside down not just the Pan-consciousness with which we have come to misprize celibacy but the security of our political ways—even our radical political ways—of knowing the world.

One might see Warner's Summer Will Show, in which the coupling of spinster-heroine and Satan is replaced by the coupling of sisters-in-revolution, as an attempt to spell out more clearly the involvement of the earlier novel's fascination with practical female freedom and of the earlier novel's simultaneous engagement with history and class and disengagement from history and class's categorical centrality. It appears, given the ending of Summer Will Show, that Warner—on the eve of her departure for Spain with her lover, Valentine Ackland, to fight against fascism—is using the novel to underwrite the centrality of Marxist class conflict in the representation of history and therefore perhaps to reverse the deviations from such analysis in Lolly Willowes. Indeed, the last page of Summer Will Show presents itself as being literally in the process of absorption by The Communist Manifesto. The novel's heroine, Sophia Willoughby, is reading, in Paris in 1848, Marx's pamphlet, the beginning of which, quoted in full, becomes Warner's last page of narrative. The homage paid the Manifesto in this concluding gesture is profound: the novel might be said to erase itself for the sake of the polemical tract.

But there are more ways to read this ending than as Warner's submission of this novel—even of the novel form in general—to Marx. The heroine is an English aristocrat, a wife and mother whose separation from her husband is succeeded by her children's death from the smallpox they contract from a worker on their estate. Sophia sets out for Paris to recover her husband, so that she can bear children again. But in Paris, Sophia's sudden passion for Minna Lemuel—a Jewish storyteller and actress who is her husband's ex-mistress—draws her into revolutionary activity; in the end she is recruited by communists to deliver the first printing of the *Manifesto* to its distribution points in the city. The narrative thereby shows how Sophia, having set out for Paris to initiate her further bearing and delivery of children, exchanges this project for bearing and delivering the offspring of Marx and Engels. The plot thereby suggests that the latter are enwombed in a woman's story, that Sophia's narrative is impregnated with the *Manifesto*, so that the latter grows out of female experience.

In reading this way, we must not forget the subtlety with which Warner plays with narrative, especially when her work appears to be saturated in realistic convention. Just as *Lolly Willowes'* disjunction of realistic and supernatural modes constitutes a narrative whose face looks innocent of the disjunction, so too the route whereby *Summer Will Show* ends by delivering *The Communist Manifesto* to the reader at once illustrates Marx *and* evades Marxist analysis of a classic kind. The narrative illustrates Marx, of course, when it shows that the life-and-death economic and hence *social* intimacy of landed aristocrat and rural peasant will *force* its way upon aristocratic consciousness—which is what the deaths of Sophia's children illustrate. In the separation and the failed pursuit of her husband, moreover, Sophia confirms the feminist deductions drawn by Engels out of Lewis Morgan: in the development of capitalism and of its corollary, the monogamous family, woman is the first proletariat, the slave whose bondage under patriarchy exhibits the contradictions of liberty in the capitalist formation that depends on her enslavement. And there is above all—where classic Marxism is concerned—the potential Stalinism of the segment of plotline identified with the revolutionary named Ingelbrecht, who is writing a treatise "on the proper management of revolutions." The portions of his treatise embedded in *Summer Will Show* deride a type of revolutionary who "seem[s] incapable of feeling a durable anger against the conditions which they seek to overthrow. . . .When they have finished their speech, or poignarded their tyrant, they are in such a mood of satisfied excitement that they are almost ready to forgive the state of society which allows them such abuses on which to avenge themselves."[16] It appears that Minna Lemuel, the Jewish bohemian artist, is such a character. She is wounded (probably fatally) as the result of her extending a moment of forgiveness to a representative of the reactionary state. In arriving at Minna's probable death the narrative might seem especially to be endorsing Ingelbrecht's character analysis, and in this light Sophia's absorption in *The Communist Manifesto* equally seems to be a critique of Minna.

Since Warner's novel both follows Marx *and* departs from him, let us first see how Warner follows, by reading the narrative in the light of the proto-Marxist Ingelbrecht. Isn't it indisputable that when Minna is bayonetted at the barricades, she illustrates Ingelbrecht's analysis of incapacity for durable anger? Minna invites the wound, because the guardsman who delivers it is a young boy—a West Indian mulatto—whom she has known through Sophia and whom she kindly and forgivingly welcomes across the line of defense. We can read this denouement in an orthodox Marxist way as a scene of workers destroying each other because they cultivate bourgeois sympathies and thereby become the puppets of patriarchal capitalism: the young guardsman, one of the colonial wretched of the earth, has been delivered into military service by Sophia's ex-husband. It is the latter, not Minna, whom the guardsman should be "poignarding."

Marxist reading of the typifying kind—or of the kind that unites the concrete and the typical—would emphasize what the guardsman *should* do, because such reading trusts the historical intelligibility of the merest contingency. Even what the guardsman *does* do to Minna in the narrative—even the internecine battle among the world's dispossessed—exhibits the intelligibility of historical capitalist structure. Now of course Warner's narrative cultivates and instances such intelligibility. One might argue that Sophia's alliance with and passion for Minna is meant to illustrate Engels' equation of women with workers: Sophia, the aristocrat, in finding Minna, finds the working class along with her own place in it. And it is highly arguable that Ingelbrecht's criteria for an adequate revolutionary psychology, which is intransigent towards both defeatism and utopism, which emphasizes the unique specificity of the present material moment of history, is the flinty anchor of hope that saves Sophia from despair over Minna's loss (and probable death).

But if the correctness of Ingelbrecht is all that *Summer Will Show* made manifest, it would do so at a high cost. It would mean Warner in 1936 would have to be read as turning against the reality of the fantastic in *Lolly Willowes*—for the spell of Satan there is equivalent to Minna's storytelling talents, which Ingelbrecht thinks are a sign of the amateurish revolutionist. Even more importantly, if Ingelbrecht is to be the measure of Minna's meaning, the narrative's Marxism would be at the expense of the inherited sororal icon Warner foregrounds. Sophia's absorption in Marx after Minna's loss would have to be read as a critique of a misguided antirevolutionary essence in Minna and in Sophia's passion for her. Worse yet, the critique of Minna by Ingelbrecht would compel us to read the chastity of Sophia and Minna's attachment as a vulgar bourgeois repression of lesbianism by Warner in the name of a "higher," anti-emotional—and antibourgeois!—political correctness.

I would turn such a reading aside by trusting Warner's intelligence and the elements encoded in the sister pairing. The narrative's embedding of excerpts from Ingelbrecht and Marx does not indicate that the fable of Sophia and Minna exemplifies only those excerpts. The female figures bear—and deliver—disruptions of meanings they only partly illustrate. The embedded excerpts are offered, it is possible to see, as purely theoretic visions, equivalent in their function in *Summer Will Show* to the function of the embedded aphorisms in *Clara Hopgood*. These embedded commentaries in Warner are no less apart from than intimate with their narrative form. *Summer Will Show*'s interest for us is that it uses the Sophia-Minna coupling to assert the primarily *theoretical* nature of Marxist principles for making the world intelligible. The novel makes the assertion without derogation, without suggesting that theory is inferior to pragmatic specificity. *Summer Will Show* holds up the honor of Marxism as a *theoretical* enterprise. At the same time Warner does not evade the disjunction between theory and the circumstances it cannot penetrate. (And such circumstances are not just specifics: they are other theories too.) It is significant that Sophia cannot find Minna's body among the revolutionary dead, for Sophia is left alone with the dignity attached to a theoretical vision of things that evades concrete embodiment. Ingelbrecht's theorizing of Minna's character is powerful because it is theoretical, not consummated by foolproof applicability. But Warner allows Minna to have the last laugh on Ingelbrecht. When Minna declares the superiority of justice over charity, another character recognizes this as an expression of Ingelbrecht's aversion to charitable bourgeois cessations of anger. Minna rejoins, "He got it from me" (375). Minna thus is the source of the narrative agency that criticizes her; *she* follows Marx because she originates Marxist ideas; and yet she inhabits a dimension that makes Marxist ideas and analysis secondary.

So Minna's final action is not legible exclusively in the light of Ingelbrecht's theory of Minna's character type—unless her final action is a momentary slip in the theory that is, after all, not his but hers. And the theory which is hers—and which must have to do with the narrative logic of Sophia's love for *her* rather than for the man Ingelbrecht—amounts to more, we may assume, in Warner's book than in Ingelbrecht's or Marx's. What is of course "more" in Warner's book is not the alliance of the women but their passionate mutual love. But since the love is chaste, not bodily, we might read the passion as a theoretic one, as—so to speak—the figure-theory of a passion, as Ingelbrecht's and Marx's thought are figure-theories of revolutionary psychology and revolution. The representation of the passion of the heroines, withheld from a picturing of intercourse and so referring to the body and yet evading the body, projects the same self-possession, the virtually nondesirous love, one sees in Lolly Willowes. Accordingly, the representation gives us another play of contraries like the one between fantasy and plausibility in the earlier work. Only here the play is given a more direct motivation in terms of women's relation to class-centered historical analysis. The theory-passion is a reaction, it appears, to the way Ingelbrecht and Marx leave out of account women's passion for each other; it is a passion that cannot deliver Marx's manifesto as the exclusive fruit of its womb.

Like Rhoda Nunn, Clara Hopgood, and Sophia Baines, Warner's heroines, who come from opposite ends of the class spectrum (and of Europe), escape their class backgrounds but not in a way that transfers them from one class to another—to, say, the working class. Together the women live hand-to-mouth, are performance artists on the Parisian streets; they are not workers, but are *like* workers. They are presented by the narrative as metaphors for the proletariat, no less than their love is a metaphor for a carnal passion that is virtual rather than realized. In the *likeness* to workers of the women, we find another way in which the heroine's concrete life is presented by Warner as a theoretical matter, reality-cum-speculation. The life that surrounds the heroines bases itself in the fact and representation of material class distinctions as if the distinctions were secure ground, were the solidity against which all speculation—and every discrimination between fact and theory, reality and fantasy—can be measured. We know from *Lolly Willowes* how Warner takes from us the security we feel in holding on to such distinctions. In *Summer Will Show*, it is the drama of the women together that takes this security away from us.

What is remarkable in the loss of security thus effected is that Warner uses the sororal pair to endorse historical materialism and its ramifications, and nevertheless to be skeptical of it, in the name not just of what it leaves out, but also in the name of what it does not recognize about its own ungrounded speculativeness. Warner certainly seems to realize the risks run by her double intentions: she can be accused of hypostatizing a bohemian response to the world, or of idealizing theory and fantasy. But the bohemian response, as *Summer Will Show* represents it, is more widespread than bohemian and bourgeois, or even worker and Communist, know or acknowledge. That Sophia and Minna are *like* this or that class rather than *of* one class or another means that they have become unclassed. Shunted aside by what is sociologically typical, they are at once liberated and enclosed—cornered in bohemia—which is where, judging from the novel's last pages, Sophia will remain. The advantage of this, Warner's revisionary feminist-Marxism suggests, is that it is an appropriate corner in which to read Marx. For it is a social site from which society appears to be a purely theoretical horizon, not an inert, incontrovertible reality or fact. And this is an appropriate vantage point from which to read Marx—the Marx for whom society *is* a speculative order rather than an inert fact, and the Marxism that is self-conscious of its having one foot always in theory.

What, then, of the idealizing tendency of this emphasis in Warner—symptomized, I think, by the cultivation of fantasy mixed in with the historical probability equally cultivated by her work? We must come back to the presence of death in Warner. Sophia's loss of Minna can be read as Sophia's politically correct separation from Minna's allegedly amateurish revolutionism. But Sophia's sustainment of Minna's loss can mean something else: the contingency of reality and theory, the constant demiseability of both. Alone with Marx in Minna's corner, Sophia is not protected from death, because even the *Manifesto* absorbing her attention is mortal. The *Manifesto* speaks, no doubt with more irony than it intends, of communism as a haunting specter, as that which is already dead; but of course it calls the specter "a nursery tale," which it will lay to rest by uncovering the live body of the thing. But the live body is also already lost, neither dead nor alive for sure. The intermingling of fantasy, historical materialism, and speculative theory in Warner's work signals their intermingling in a medium of mortal fragility. The idealizing tendency is a mere appearance, because Warner submits it to this fragility.

Minna's unrecovered body is like the communist pamphlet: her body has a spectral vitality whose specific and typical history is inseparable from abstract speculation and from dying. One of the autobiographical stories Minna tells in *Summer Will Show* describes her first view of a frozen river thawing in the spring: the oppressed Jewish child thinks the river is a theory-likeness of liberty. When in the following year she returns to see the frozen river break up once more, she discovers encased in the ice the bodies of slain men and horses. This for her is a revelation not of liberty but of history: the freezing-thawing domain in which the dead live and the living are specters. On the advent of summer what shows is mortality. So with Warner's narrative as a whole. In traversing the route from class to unclass, in discovering that every arrangement of social order is an argument and a theory, Sophia's story brings death into the foreground of attention. By at once endorsing Marxism and criticizing Marxism for the way it cannot come to theoretical terms with the unclassed—especially with the unclassed who are women and who passionately love women—it seems as if Warner's narrative can come only to an abyss of mortality as its ground. Its certainty is the certainty of what will fall away.

This uncertainty is an ancient topos: the vanity of human wishes because of the omnipotence of death. But the topos is revitalized by the way Warner historicizes and sociologizes it, even as she holds up to view the vulnerability to demise of historical and sociological knowing. Women are for Warner the nearest relatives to this demise; they are not the wives and mothers symbolizing and bearing the immortality of the race. The passionate celibacy that pushes them closer to the mortal verge, making them especially able to see history as the history of death, results from their reaction to being left out of historical account. Naturally, it is not a total leaving out: woman is accounted for eternally and, in Marx and Engels too, by specification, classification, typification. But the idea of unaccountability Warner pursues is the idea of the sororal tradition: that woman is a double being, that her other half, the revolutionary sister mysteriously self-possessed in her desire and pleasure (like Lolly Willowes) reduces all accountings of history, and of herself in history, to the status of mortally fragile speculations.

But *can* there be any plausible connection, we might ask, between this novelist's Marx-inspired revolutionary impulse and her emphasis on human vanity? Marx founds himself on a trust that economic and social liberty is even more empowering and enduring than capitalism. The classic Marxist revolutionary makes his first move by revealing the inalienable power of human productivity. By means of this revelation those who are presently powerless are returned to the sources of power in themselves. But the figure of the revolutionary projected by Minna and Sophia is not the classic one. They suggest that the best revolutionist, even as he or she works in the service of renewed empowerments, subverts the idea that any personal or collective order can defend against power's inevitable loss. For Warner, Marx's analytic road to liberty is superior to any other; yet when she follows the road to its end, she reverses Marx's ultimate evaluations. Marx ends with a reallocation of capitalist powers that values the phenomenon of power itself and makes power identical with freedom. In contrast, Warner suggests that the value of the liberty Marx alone leads us to is that it frees us to face an inevitable vulnerability in human affairs and orders.

It is notable that collective life in Warner's fiction appears as no more a fortress against demise than is any single self-possession or any passionate pairing. In *The Corner That Held Them* the sororal bond between two women is exchanged for an entire convent of "sisters." Warner wants to show that single persons and pairs do not exist independently of communities of endeavor. Yet much as Warner celebrates communal endeavor in her picture of the convent's noble striving to build a better order for itself, and much as she clarifies the specific historical conditions of the striving, she also suggests that communities of endeavor are always on the verge of their own undoing. And although erotic ties, like collective ones, also promise access to an enduring power, Warner takes the promise of both to be illusory. She therefore offers us the celibate collectivity, turned away from worldliness even as it must join with the world's labors, as the best picture, however odd, of revolutionary possibility. The celibate community figures the presence of collective life, of an integrated social totality, and at the same time it figures an absence of generative powers and securities that can eternize the powers either of individuals or of the community. In some way this *is* consonant with modern and Marxist revolutionism, for is it not in an attack on an all eternalizing stability in the order of things that modern revolution takes its rise?

The Corner That Held Them chooses for its drama an English era whose experience shows the necessity of speaking of all things, from Marxist theory to fantasy, in the light of death. The era is the more than forty years initiated by the arrival of the Black Death in England in 1349. Oby, the Benedictine priory that is the corner of the novel's title, is a fourteenth-century version of the limitary zone of unclassed women. It is far less a place of spiritual vocation than a matter-of-fact site of employment for unmarriageable daughters and sisters, who work as mediaries between the church's male-dominated order and the manorial peasantry. But the women's employment is also a shunting aside of them, into a condition in which they become unknown and unknowable. The bleak comedy of the novel has to do with the women's attempts to account for their lives economically and spiritually, both to themselves and to their male superiors. If almost every accounting reveals a loss (although the sisters have as good economists among them as any), it is just this failing that attracts Warner to the sisterhood. And the way the sisters suffer even more intensely than the men of their world the demographic shifts and class upheavals occasioned by the plague, which revolutionized the state of England more than the Peasants' Revolt, attracts Warner no less.

For the viral accident that is the Black Death collaborates with history and becomes history in *The Corner That Held Them*, by newly distinguishing men from women—freshly engendering their difference, as it were, because the plague intensifies the use by men of church and state as a defense against demise. One of the major male figures in the novel is Ralph Kello, a false priest who, during the chaos of the plague, stumbles upon the convent, insists that he has been deputized to serve the sisters, and takes up a life-long residence, cheating the nuns for the better part of thirty-odd years via the unhallowed sacraments they receive from his hands. Warner's narrative tolerates Ralph, but treats him as a prime instance of how the novel's men are closer to power and pleasure than the novel's women, because the men's possession of the world makes it easier for them to deny death. Ralph barely survives the plague, and in old age he loses his lay mistress to murder, but death does not seem to impress its finality upon him: when he himself dies, he is dreaming of immortality, thanks to yet another fraudulent act—his plagiarism of a contemporary epic poem he was to edit and copy so as to insure *another* man's immortal life.

From first to last the convent's story is about males attempting to surmount mortality, beginning with the convent's foundation as an act of reparation by a husband who has slain his wife's lover—and whose propitiatory act will immure females forever. Most significantly, there is Bishop Walter, the misogynist, whose deeply troubled death, with its relapse into paganism, shows his piety no less than his prudish populism to have been a desperate veneer over fear of his mortal vulnerability. The place in the novel of Henry Yellowlees, who becomes the convent's overseer when the bishop places the nuns in receivership, is also deter-mined by the narrative's desire to trace male fear of mortality. Henry finds a brief transcendence of death in the music of the *ars nova*, but he is then condemned to see the monk and the monk's leprous wards who have introduced him to the music slaughtered by peasants caught up in the revolt. The *ars nova* in England, the narrative suggests, is one of the responses to the plague, no less than is the freeing-up of the serfs from the feudal manors. Wherever the men in Warner's world turn, there is no corner that is free from the fear and the history of death. The women in Warner's world are more intimate than the men with this fact. Perhaps it is one more way of expressing this intimacy between women and knowledge of the mortality of male investments in the world that makes Warner suggest an insuperable distance between our corner of time's river, and the one we read about in the novel. Warner thought of the inspiration of the novel as Marxist, but would not Georg Lukács have found the tale guilty of what he would call an abstract particularizing of the past because it does not represent the fourteenth century as the "necessary prehistory" of the twentieth? I think Warner implicitly parries this question, with its paramount demand for continuity and for the confidence in forward progress dear to revolution-ary hope. To insist on the past as a conditioning mode of continuity with the present and the future is for us to be on the (perhaps decidedly male) defensive against the fact of death as a fact of history—against the disruptiveness of death to all the continuities that secure us, even when we are revolutionaries. We might number among those reassuring continuities the categories of intelligibility that structure our understanding (whether reactionary or radical) of the world—and upon which, as we have seen, the icon of revolutionary sisters throws a shadow.

Although most of *The Corner That Held Them* is about the noble fragility of the celibate collective, its final focus is on a pair of sisters who do not hold together. In the earlier novels I have considered, one of the pair remains fixed in the world's representational order, even though she is a rebel against that order (Madge Hopgood, for example), while the other sister implies a deeper, more radical distance from the world and from the modes of even a radical understanding of it; nevertheless, the sisters hold together. Like the bond of these sisters, Warner's narrative artistry holds on to the world-structuring Marxist-historicist mode of analysis even as it calls that mode into question. But the need for a sharper break with that mode seems always to threaten the balance signaled by the sororal icon in Warner. So we find *The Corner That Held Them* ends with a heart-stopping divorce between two of the convent's nuns, in a way that suggests a critical choice between honoring a revolutionary worldly engagement that ceaselessly enters and re-enters history—as if revolutionary historical engagement guaranteed the triumph of life—and a celibate disengagement from the world that is more intimate with mortality.

The sisters who break with each other are Dames Lilias and Sibilla. Lilias is in line to become the convent's infirmaress; her doctoring interest has much to do with a morbidity consequent on her being a child during the plague's outbreak. But Lilias' sisters jibe at her—too much of an interest in death won't do—in a way that isolates her and forces her to think that she had best become an anchoress. In imagining this character Warner actually submits to criticism her own fascination with mortality. But when Lilias, even in her morbidity, is weighed against Sibilla, the narrative tips the balance in the former's favor.

Sibilla has nursed the dying bishop and lyingly declares—out of a desire for self-promotion—that she has gained his deathbed approval for Lilias' anchorite scheme, of which she becomes the champion. But the advocacy becomes a cover-up for Sibilla's desire to find a way to escape the convent and join the world. The time for the success of Sibilla's double-dealing comes soon enough. During the Peasants' Revolt the nuns are accused, via earnest proto-Marxist typification, of being the representatives of the idle rich. We know that this typifying of them is not the truth; but the nuns give in to the analysis and are ruined financially. Lilias and Sibilla are sent to the city of Waxelby to beg alms, and at just the moment when the novelty of the city recalls Lilias from her hermetic ambitions, Sibilla concludes the process whereby Lilias will be immured in isolation. Having carried out this conscience-easing, phony devotion to her sister, Sibilla disguises herself as a secular pilgrim and sets out into the world, into revolutionary freedom from the corner and from the likes of Lilias forever.

But our sympathies remain with Lilias, even though she will be held to her restraints. Sibilla's apparently revolutionary impulse has her bishop-uncle's facti-tiousness inspired by the fear of death upon it; and she sets out into a belying of the women who have carried on together in spite of and even because of their unaccountability—even to Marxism's hope to empower the powerless. The novel's final sympathy is not with Sibilla's engagement with the world and its opportunistic individual freedom, but with ultimate disengagement. For Warner it appears that the isolated, chaste, odd Lilias is closer than Sibilla to an authentic and honest revolutionism. Better Lilias' withdrawal (even by such embittering means) than the alternative. The alternative—though enacted by a woman who desires freedom from conventual restraint—seems in spite of its world-centered care a trivializing, male, and hence fearful, mode of being.

Of course the likely political moral of the sisters' split is that the two modes of being and of analysis encoded in the sororal pair should not undergo a divorce. The cornered sister, Lilias, who exemplifies the mortality of even the visions of liberty—of the theoretical visions that are always beyond concrete embodiment—cannot be divorced from Sibilla, her more mobile and confidently aspiring partner in revolutionary speculation and the pursuit of power. The feminist criticism of Irigaray I have mentioned—which demands the submission of all interests to specific material and historical analysis of women's state—is in Warner's terms a call for a nefarious divorce, another split (however refined) between Lilias and Sibilla. In light of Warner, too, we must remember this call might be gendered, a vain *male* strategy (no matter how revolutionary in intention) of securing from demise the reliability of a by-now conventional radical habit of historical and sociological thought.

In this approach to Warner I have traced a feminism and a revolutionary politics responsive to death with the intensity of a dark mysticism. To feminists who might still wonder if such a responsiveness can enter into any liberating women's movement, Warner has left along with the novels I have discussed a fable with which further to answer their concern. At the end of the collection of stories called *The Cat's Cradle-Book* (1940) is a tale about Bluebeard's daughter, an unsung heroine (indeed!), who is no less curious than her doomed mother, but whose curiosity turns out to make her happy, not to curse her or others. Warner uses this figure to revolutionize the myths of Eve and Pandora, to picture a female curiosity that does not bring death into the world. But this story culminates a collection of tales, English equivalents of Kafka, that turn the coldest eyes upon life and probability; they treat human endeavor with the indifference of the gods—or the grave. By placing the tale of Bluebeard's daughter at the end of the collection, Warner's ordering of her book suggests that it is death that brings curiosity into the world and that gives woman a chance to reverse a father-engendered curse upon knowledge. The alliance with mortality is thus a revolution against patriarchy. Of course, even father Bluebeard here has contributed to the daughter's opportunity for happiness. Does this contribution echo the implication of male writers in Warner's favored picture of celibate sisters? Of course, the happiness, the lifting of the curse, is not available through the father's *generative* power or any celebration of it. In Warner and in her tradition only the path of celibate pairing, or of chaste community, of the self-possessed love between or among women that resists the erotic as well as the classificatory badge, can lead to a revolutionary feminist knowledge. The knowledge, with its resistance both to the indeterminacies of imagination and the determinacies of history, with its resistance to both the type and the instance, is a difficult one to bear and to apply. For the knowledge leaves out so much—the empowering heat of Eros, for one thing; and Warner's intercourse with Marx is so oddly a match and no match with him. Nevertheless, Warner's work, together with the long approach to it, provides us with reason to theorize that a feminist significance, correctness, and liberation need not and should not be disjoined either from an (as it were) chaste pairing with Marx or from a reiteration of the power of celibacy and of the fact of mortality.

17

(In)Visible Alliances:
Conflicting "Chronicles" of
Feminism

Robert Vorlicky

"Shifting Positions": An Off-Stage View

On 19 April 1988, the brutal beating and gang rape of a female jogger in New York's Central Park made headline news across the country and stayed at the top of the front page for weeks to come. It was one of those rare public tragedies that seemed to trigger within the public consciousness—nationally, not just locally— an uneasy admission of a truth Americans have always known but are most often willing to deny or diminish: the ferocity of the violence fostered in our culture against women.

A few days after the crime was reported in the press, a feminist friend and I struggled to talk about it after breakfast. The young woman was on our minds and in our hearts. "What is in men to make them do this?" she remarked. "In a woman-centered world this wouldn't have happened. The patriarchal structure sustains such oppression. It condones violence. Men, and boys, believe they have the right to violate anyone, anytime. It's against life. Men have nothing to offer me, as a woman." Echoing this general sentiment, Andrea Kannapell would write weeks later, "Everywhere we go, women are subject to this kind of violence. . . . I don't remember race or class. I remember that it's men."[1]

I, too, voiced outrage—at those men who abuse women, at a cultural ideology that condones oppression, at a violence that is random and inhuman. But I also couldn't help being struck by the familiar escalation of my friend's opinions. You see, we have had interactions like this before. Usually they end with some similar blanket rejection of "men." While not naive or insensitive to the differences in male and female experiences within our patriarchal culture, I nonetheless feel obliterated each time we reach this point in a conversation. Invisible. It's as though a formidable gap emerges between us, making it impossible for us to see, to speak, to hear one another as individuals. Such feelings, my women friends tell me, are frequent in their experiences. Women's practical response: men alone rule with their privilege to say and do as they like. Their theoretical explanation: women are objects, not subjects, in our capitalist patriarchal society. Men alone have the power to construct the visible. Yet, at that moment in conversation with my friend,

I truly felt as though I were unseen. It is a feeling that some other men, too, are finding increasingly more familiar.

To many it may be justified for me, as a male, to experience finally a position of invisibility. This notion, however, assumes that any position of invisibility is unfamiliar to me. In general, yes, my visibility is more likely to occur than for a female; my experiences of invisibility may be more the exception than the rule. But certainly not always. As an adult, I've learned what it's like to voice opposition within groups and be ignored, to be criticized if I did not want to follow the crowd, to resist group labeling in an effort to respect what I consider vital distinctions of my character and desires within my gender-inscribed body. While my life is not one characterized by its invisibilities, I am nonetheless hardly unfamiliar with that position. It's these exceptions (as few as they may be relative to women's experiences), when I (or other men) have felt invisible, that suggest a useful framework for exploring the too frequently overlooked area of male specificity.

Aside from men's biological bodies, we can no longer assume that the collective body of "men" is (if it ever was) a visible, cohesive identity. Historically this is certainly true of those males who have come of age with feminism, as well as those men who have come to feminism through other life experiences. For some time now, these men have remained an invisible minority to the culture at large. In making this observation, I am not immediately concerned with the issue of the suggested invisibility of (younger) male critics in feminist criticism, as debated by Joseph Boone and Toril Moi in *Gender and Theory* or as addressed by the present collection as a whole.[2] Rather, I am speaking of those men's lives—regardless of their profession, race, class, sexual preference, age, etc.—who embrace feminist ideology and goals of equality as *right* choices for their lives. In some cases, such men have also made these choices prior to any public or externalized appeal by the modern feminist movement. The politics is part of their being, one that has found expression through feminism. Yet, by actualizing (or making more visible) this personal choice, all these men, paradoxically, have become less visible within American society. It's as if the pervasive societal myths and assumptions about male identity and behavior are so firmly entrenched that they can withstand even demonstrated variation indicating the contrary. Therefore, the male feminists' choice of alternative action, of antipatriarchal positioning, is more often than not ignored, repressed, or outrightly denied by the culture at large, as well as even meeting opposition from some female feminists who may applaud the involvement of male feminists, but who oppose their involvement being activated in the name of (male) feminism.

The lives of these men are not often written about in the newspaper or in collections of essays, nor are they acknowledged as valid referents when constructing theoretical agendas. While invisible (or less visible), perhaps, on such fronts, they are nonetheless visible presences in life—men who are actively living the change. They can be seen in homes raising their children while their partners are at work; on the streets marching for Equal Rights and Pro-Choice movements; in conversations discoursing on their relationships to women and other men, mindful that the personal is political. Some of these men may also be theorizing about feminist ideology and its application, but not limiting themselves simply to intellectual involvement (which is not to be confused with some men's deliberate appropriation of feminism, most noticeably in academic contexts). Many support the feminist movement with their time, energy, and money.[3]

It is a reality, not just an idea, therefore, that heterosexual, bisexual, and homosexual male feminists are developing, as Toril Moi suggests, "an analysis of their own position, and a strategy for how their awareness of their difficult and contradictory position in relation to feminism can be made explicit in discourse and practice."[4] The present collection demonstrates, I hope, ways in which men are addressing these issues in their discourse. But during these increasingly polarized, reactionary times, it seems paramount that men and women who share feminist beliefs in practice—in our lives—be more openly supportive of one another. This is certainly not to suggest that such contexts—whether in discourse or practice—are beyond criticism. Quite the contrary. However, in validating one another's existence, we all contribute to undercutting polarization. We further close the gap that constantly threatens to keep us from communicating with one another—to keep us invisible within one another's visions.

So, as we sat in the diner, I couldn't help wondering who my friend thought I was at times like this. Why would I, a bodycoded male, sit here (or why would she, for that matter) if she truly felt that "men have nothing to offer"? If this were the case, who was her husband to her, and what must he represent? Who was her father to her? Her brother? Her male coworkers? The complexities of our gendered positions toward one another were evident. Certainly we all have made inflated, essentialist comments (regardless of the topic) during heights of rhetorical positioning and emotional responses. But while the tension in the air was inescapable and generally constructive, it bordered dangerously close to destructive ends. It's our teetering on this "edge," I believe, that is becoming all the more familiar to female and male feminists' interaction.

Once our dialogue resumed, I affirmed (to someone I have known on personal terms for twelve years), that I, too, was participating in this exchange. We were engaging one another, openly, as we had done countless times before. She and I could simply not ignore the reality that not all men are incapable of "offering" (in her words) her something "as a woman." Pluralities among men are a fact. It was time to stop dismissing some males as exceptions from the collective group of all men by simply saying, "Well, but you're/he's different" and then continuing to generalize as though that distinction had no relative, let alone long-range, value. What, after all, are we going to call this variation, and what are we going to do with it?

Faced with the complex issues raised by our conversation, my friend and I agreed to disagree and to see our contradictions as such. We were able to do so, however, only after affirming a mutual trust in one another; we acknowledged the visible positions to which feminism had brought us and those to which we had still to come. This trust among men and women, as individuals, activates a basic feminist premise of being aware of one's position, without which awareness the mobility for and toward change that is also the basis of a feminist politics will never occur. Unsettled as we may have been, my friend and I could recognize, finally, that we were experiencing what Elizabeth Weed calls "shifting positions": that which necessarily occurs when feminists "work against the erection of the same old phallocratic structures in the name of identity and the unifying subject."[5] But it is one thing to feel unsettled among feminists when you know it's part of a desired dynamic in the dialogic interaction; it is something quite different if it foreshadows a vacuum of no community, of no action, of no dialogue.

Nearly all of the men and women with whom I associate, both within and outside of the academy, are conscious, albeit with varying degrees, of feminism and the impact it has had on their daily lives. And yet, of late, I and a number of feminist friends have observed with real concern a rising tendency among many of these potential "allies" of feminism—as I'd choose to classify them—a tendency to reject any overt identification of themselves as "feminists." At issue here, I would suggest, is, once again, the need for "visible alliances" that emerged from my exchange with my angry friend, albeit now in a different guise. For the ironic fact is that most of the people I'm now talking about often quite vocally lend their public support to the feminist cause (through the Pro-Choice and equal wage movements, for instance) and equally often lead private lives that reflect a positive enactment of the basic premises of feminist ideology. Yet when it comes to naming themselves, many of these otherwise perceptive adults, men and women alike, are opting to call themselves *humanists*—not in the term's current academic usage to designate those generally conservative opponents of theory, but simply because they find it easier to grasp at the "human" in "humanism" as a more agreeable banner under which to claim allegiance to social change, the elimination of oppression, and equality for all people. From their perspective, these individuals perceive humanism as a more global, "human" (and therefore all-inclusive) ideology than the gender-specific focus presumed to be bounded within feminism. It's as though they believe that the latter word itself—*feminism*—has the power, if embodied, to render them invisible as "humans" (or paradoxically, to make them too visible).

Those "humanist" males who avoid being identified as feminists rarely do so, I think, because they presume that their gender-coded bodies have an impossible relationship to a female body-coded agenda. Nor do "humanist" females resist feminist labeling due to any assumption that they will be perceived necessarily as antimale. Rather, I believe, these individuals have a conflicted relationship to notions of power—a conflict that results in perpetuating both traditional notions of opposition between the sexes, as well as of the sexes as opposites. As such, "humanist" males often remain selective, for instance, about which of their powers they will part with. "Humanist" females, on the other hand, resist assuming powers completely unknown, as they often are hesitant to believe that any new power truly can be realized in a nonpatriarchal way. These would-be allies know that to take on the name of feminism is to demonstrate visibly their political selves. Out of a very accurate fear that feminism *is* political, they opt for humanism over feminism as a way, in effect, of remaining politically invisible.

In response to these observations, several crucial questions will continue in the 1990s to challenge all of us who are cognizant of feminism's impact on our daily lives, as well as its influence in shaping future generations. How would the self be constituted if we were to evolve from a phallocentric social identity and community to a nonphallocentric one? What would constitute our relationships to one another, as well as our manifestations of power? I believe that many men and women are now beginning to realize some of these possibilities from an experiential, and not simply theoretical, position. Many of these possibilities are coming to life because of feminism. Too few, however, are being claimed in the name of feminism. It is this latter experience that now needs to be written more deliberately, more visibly, into our work.

Upstaging Feminism: Wasserstein's *The Heidi Chronicles*

A week after the Central Park rape, I was at a Broadway theater blocks removed from the scene of this troubling act. Watching Wendy Wasserstein's acclaimed *The Heidi Chronicles*, I witnessed, in part, a dramatic interpretation of the complexities that surface between a female and the males in her life. There was neither rape nor violence of any kind on stage. Characters spoke wittily of their desires and fears; they depended upon words, not fists, in order to address their differences and to voice their needs. Wasserstein's female and male characters were white, privileged individuals, educated at the most prestigious institutions, and in professional positions of power and financial reward. The predominantly white audience generously acknowledged their identifications with the play, as rounds of laughter and applause filled the air throughout the evening.

Yet, as the play moved toward its final scenes, I couldn't help but wonder if men's and women's relationships had really come very far in the last twenty years . . . both off and on stage. Certainly, if focusing solely on the real tragedy in Central Park—and the countless rapes across America daily—one can conclude that our society has not matured past culturally conditioned rites of male sexual violence and female sexual abuse. Daily, it is a challenge for many to keep visible those men's lives that are distinct from the image of men created by these horrifying "off stage" manifestations of male behavior. But turning to a completely different type of "ritual"—the fictional on-stage world of theatrical performance and here specifically that in a commercial theater—I am again dismayed at which images of men's and women's lives are visible and which are not. Coming away from *The Heidi Chronicles*, I felt disturbingly distanced from a drama that created images, as well as raised issues, about which many of us care a great deal.

Nonetheless the press has been overwhelming in its praise of the New York productions of *The Heidi Chronicles*. By the spring of 1989, Wasserstein's work had become the most prized American play of the year, winning (among numerous awards) the Pulitzer Prize for Drama and Broadway's Tony Award for Best Play. Such distinctions virtually secure its future prominence in the canon. Despite these kudos, however, the play is not without its dissidents.[6] The nature of the controversy surrounding the play is complicated. On one level, it has to do with what *isn't* written into the text—specifically as a representation of a (would-be) feminist's life—as well as with the sociohistorical context in which the play is produced. For the purpose of illustrating this essay's immediate concerns, however, I suggest that there are two problematic aspects within the play proper of *The Heidi Chronicles* that contribute to this criticism: the play's unclear position on the relationship between humanism and feminism; and its presentation of men's incapacity to sustain a physically and psychologically satisfying intimate relationship with a (heterosexual) female feminist (accomplished through caricatures, as we will see, of polarized "classic" male types presented as the only males close to Heidi). The fact that Wasserstein has captured dramatically two such volatile issues that resonate within contemporary American culture is much to her credit. It has been a while since I've gone to a Broadway play that has stimulated as much opinionated discussion long after its performance. This is also no small feat for a play that many find immensely entertaining and humorous. This enthusiasm, however, does not diminish my concern for the play's apparent confirmation of an essentially white patriarchal ideology. Certainly, the mainstream audience and critics have eagerly embraced the play as such. In this regard, the play is a politically troubling phenomenon.

The Heidi Chronicles is the story of a woman who feels that feminism has let her down. Wasserstein's is the first major naturalistic play to be produced and to survive on Broadway that explicitly focuses on white Americans coming of age amidst the modern feminist movement. (This qualification distinguishes the Broadway production of Wasserstein's play from others with prominent feminist components, most notably the 1977 production of Ntozake Shange's choreopoem, *for colored girls who have considered suicide when the rainbow is enuf*, which focuses on women of color; and the 1986 presentations of Jane Wagner's multi-charactered one-actor *The Search for Signs of Intelligent Life in the Universe* starring Lily Tomlin.)[7] The fact that Wasserstein's play has been viewed as dramatizing the failure of the feminist movement has not gone unnoticed. The fact that the play is flourishing in the premier American theater showcase for mass audiences is also apparent. And these two facts are not unrelated.

Within thirteen scenes, Wasserstein chronicles pivotal moments during twenty-four years of Dr. Heidi Holland's life—from high school student in 1965 to art historian lecturer in 1989. In the course of time, Heidi comes to feel alienated from many of the goals of her generation, as well as from some of her closest friends who aspire to those goals. Arguably, that which is most painful for Heidi to face is her fear that perhaps she made the wrong choices in life, choices that were informed by her growing (feminist) consciousness. In confronting the core of her sadness, and subsequently revealing the heart of the play, Heidi confesses in "Women, Where Are We Going?", a 1986 luncheon address before her high school alumnae group: "I don't blame any of us. We're all concerned, intelligent, good women. It's just that I feel stranded. And I thought the whole point was that we wouldn't feel stranded. I thought the point was we were all in this together."[8]

For any number of reasons, many men and women have a vested interest in the failure of feminism as a movement and ideology. This is not news. These individuals choose to see feminism as a period piece with a limited agenda whose time has run out, only to leave its supporters "stranded." Its achievements and failures are now to be chronicled, measured, and shelved. From this perspective, feminism is not an evolving generational movement of change. This presumed failure of feminism is how many perceive Heidi's alumnae speech, as well as the overall meaning of *The Heidi Chronicles*. Within the context of the play's commercial production, mainstream audiences can assume that the play's popularity confirms that this message—the movement's failure—is one widely held among feminists today. After all, their "logic" may proceed, the play has all the elements popularly held as trademarks of a "feminist" play: the text is written by a woman; the story focuses on a woman whose life appears to be informed by (the unspeakable) feminism— Heidi's career is happily dedicated to reclaiming and teaching about "forgotten" women artists, which *is* the type of work feminists do; and yet this independent, resourceful single woman who is fast approaching forty holds on valiantly to the notion that her generation did not make "such big mistakes" (II, 3) despite her obvious unhappiness and alienation. Is it any wonder that many active feminists are challenging those who have called the play a feminist work? Meanwhile, nonfeminist critics and many in the mainstream audience eagerly see the play confirming their suspicions of the current state of feminism—that it has failed.

Although Wasserstein and her play are not responsible for chronicling a life that satisfies everyone's aesthetic or political expectations, there is a problem of what message is conveyed when conflicting signals arise surrounding the position of feminism in the play. This position is most prominently, and simultaneously ambiguously, dramatized within the politics of the heroine and, ultimately, her relationship to feminism (which includes her relationship to women) and to men.

It is precisely this confusion over perceptions of Heidi's politics—conveyed through Heidi's description of herself, Wasserstein's description of Heidi, and the popular audience's naming of Heidi—that should not be overlooked. The confusion illustrates the present situation, already noted, wherein many men and women find themselves caught between the conflicted claims of the implications of humanism and feminism. Consider first how Heidi identifies herself by way of addressing her work. At a consciousness raising group in 1970, Fran, a lesbian physicist, asks Heidi if she applies a "feminist interpretation" to her "interest in images of women from the Renaissance Madonna to the present." Heidi's reply: "Humanist." Soon after, another group member suggests that "maybe Heidi isn't at the same place we are":

Heidi: I *am* at the same place you are.
Fran: How are you at the same place we are?
Heidi: I think all people deserve the right to fulfill their potential.
Fran: Yeah, except for you.
Heidi: What?
Fran: Heidi, every woman in this room has been taught that the desires and dreams of her husband, her son, or her boss are much more important than her own. And the only way to turn that around, is for us, right here, to try to make what *we* want to be as vital to us as it would unquestionably be to any man. And then we can go out and really make a difference!
(I, 3)

Within this eclectic group of Ann Arbor women, Heidi's consciousness *is* raised, as she activates a main tenet of feminist ideology and community. For she follows Fran's suggestion that "nothing's going to change until we really start talking to each other" (I, 3). In a moment that acknowledges a crucial feminist premise that the personal is political, Heidi unself-consciously connects her private life and public work in ways that will clarify in the years ahead what it means to fulfill one's potential, "to make a better choice" (I, 3). Such choices, a close friend will later remind Heidi, also necessarily "change your life" (II, 5).

This feminist perspective, no matter how tentatively held by Heidi at any given moment throughout the remainder of the play, informs her personal and professional adult life. Whether marching in 1974 for equal representation of female artists in the Chicago Art Museum (I, 4), or being introduced on television in 1982 as a successful, published "essayist, curator, and feminist" (II, 2), or refusing in 1984 to participate in a sitcom project that would focus on women who "don't want to make the same mistakes" as Heidi's generation (II, 3), or placing female artists within art history during a 1989 college lecture (Prologues I, II), Heidi does so in the name of her individualism, in the spirit of feminism. But the latter is the name *she* refuses to speak—a name that she keeps inaudible/invisible. As critic Alisa Solomon observes, "In scene after scene, the dramatic action contradicts any gestures toward feminism Heidi feebly makes."[9] Yet, it is useful to identify the emerging if incoherent feminist components in the text not to vindicate the play necessarily, but rather to highlight the phenomenon that feminist-inspired discourse, and even actions, can occur despite very calculated and controlled efforts not to identify them as feminist.

Wasserstein tentatively provided some of the words lacking on Heidi's part during a 2 May 1989 interview at the New School for Social Research in New York City. As the guest speaker in Jay Fuchs's course, "From Page to Stage: The Playwright's

Point of View," Wasserstein opened her remarks by linking Heidi with the f-word by saying that her play is about a "feminist art historian who goes sad." Upon hearing this naming, several congenial but determined class participants, who had seen the recently designated Pulitzer Prize drama on Broadway, voiced opposing opinions, claiming that Heidi was "more than a feminist": she was a humanist whose story was "universal." When asked if she distinguished between these two terms, Wasserstein replied: "How can you be a humanist without being a feminist?" Perhaps. But precisely at moments like this, when terms are left embedded within arguable definitions, people are left without clarity, allowing them to retreat back to their previous assumptions. Consequently, any further attempts by others in the class to discuss Heidi's identification with the f-word, once humanism had entered the discourse, were dismissed. The proverbial gap was now widening off-stage, as it had been doing on the Broadway stage. Taking one step further the public's resistance to acknowledging any positive feminist impact on Heidi's development, critic Mimi Kramer identifies Heidi "not as an advocate of the women's movement but [as] one of its victims."[10]

On the other hand, accepting that Wasserstein and Heidi are consciously mining feminist territory, Solomon astutely challenges the quality of their engagement:

> And while Heidi's understanding of feminism is about as superficial as you can get (she refuses the f-word and insists on being called a "humanist") Wasserstein punishes her for it, as if it's feminism's fault that she didn't have both a career and a family. Of course, this fits in with play's general portrayal of the women's movement. [The scene] where Heidi visits a women's consciousness raising group is hilarious, but Wasserstein suggests that this touchy-feely fest, where women keep hugging one another and offering their support, is all feminism ever amounted to.[11]

Here again, it helps to recall Wasserstein's remark, "How can you be a humanist without being a feminist?" While this may be Wasserstein's personal belief based upon private definitions, many refuse to see (or outrightly refute) the connections as established on the *play's* terms. Even Heidi moves—in her own way and albeit slowly—from being a generalized humanist to an increasingly more conscious ally of feminism. While the consistency and scope of her politics may disappoint most feminists, like Solomon, they are nonetheless inspired by a germinating feminist awareness. How well she embodies that commitment is certainly debatable. On the one hand, Laurie Stone argues that "none of the choices Heidi makes connects up with feminism."[12] Although Heidi is unsatisfying as a feminist heroine, I suggest that feminism (in)directly informs several of her choices that we see dramatized during the last twenty years of her life. But, while making the links between an ahistorical humanism and the principles of feminism, and beginning to live accordingly, Heidi still *refuses to name feminism* as a developmental influence. This becomes a crucial omission given what the heroine does or doesn't say, what is or isn't written in the play, and how such omissions serve to reinforce the dominant ideology. Furthermore, it contributes to the confusion over the naming of the play if, as Stone claims, "The author purports to represent feminism from the inside, using the character of 'true believer' Heidi, a single working woman."[13]

Outside of Heidi's silence in the text, Wasserstein speaks of her own relationship to feminism in various contexts that reveal how her gradual opening to feminism, not unlike hesitant Heidi's, has evolved.[14] Like some allies of feminism, Wasserstein struggles with placing herself, as well as her work, within the feminist continuum. Her writing—from *Uncommon Women and Others* (1977) and *Isn't It Romantic* (1981) to *The Heidi Chronicles*—flirts with and invites such possible positionings. But her personal frame of reference continues to appear random; her resistance to becoming overly determined by a feminist label is apparent:

> Everytime I do a new play, I'm always asked if I am a feminist, and what are my thoughts on women. I'm waiting for someone to ask someone like Christopher Durang what are his thoughts on men. To me feminism is humanism.[15]

Certainly what one names oneself remains a personal choice. Such choices illustrate, nonetheless, the challenge before many female and male allies of feminism regarding the issue of one's private and public visibility via one's discourse. And for the artist, the choice to make his or her words political necessarily has an effect on one's artistic experience. But if, as Wasserstein's frequent producer Andre Bishop suggests, *The Heidi Chronicles* is the author's "most political" work to date, then both the heroine's and author's positions resist this basic premise out of which political theatre arises.[16] Or, from another perspective, the spirit of Heidi's life chronicle and to an extent Wasserstein's gradual political awareness illustrate the tendency among many of our current generation to claim that their achievements in the struggle for equality and quality in life, as well as in art, have been done in the name of an ahistorical humanism. In fact, they have often been *feminist* achievements—achievements that need to be named and claimed as such, and then positioned relative to their political coherency upon the evolving feminist continuum.

Part of Wasserstein's dramaturgy in *The Heidi Chronicles* is to present Heidi among women friends who fail her. This strategy—an understandably objectionable one to feminists—heightens not only Heidi's sense of being "stranded" by feminism, but draws all the attention to her male friends. As such, Wasserstein shifts the balance of power, which is held in check so long as Heidi is subject, to conventional male privilege that challenges female subjectivity. Furthermore, the two males whom the author presents as vying for Heidi's attention come to be seen as stereotypes in relation to the heroine. When in each other's company on stage, the men merely tolerate one another. The fact that both are close to Heidi initiates jealousy and suspicion, not civil bonding, between them. As Heidi describes them, they are "the cynic and the idealist. A real cross section" (II, 2). The former, Peter Patrone, is a homosexual who supports Heidi's feminist tendencies but desires no physical intimacy with her. When they first meet in 1965, Peter announces to her, "I want to know you all my life. If we can't marry, let's be great friends" (I, 1). Twenty-four years later, the two are still comrades.[17] The other man, Scoop Rosenbaum, is a heterosexual with whom Heidi shares a lingering love affair. Although still in love with "A+" Heidi, Scoop marries a more accommodating woman (a "secure 6" on his 10-point rating scale) while continuing to sleep around. Unlike Peter, Scoop is threatened by Heidi's independence and her desire to fulfill her potential. He is threatened by her feminism—and not her humanism, we can be assured. Yet Scoop gets a certain pleasure from anticipating that Heidi is destined to be part of "one generation of disappointed women. Interesting, exemplary, even sexy, but basically unhappy. The ones who open doors usually are" (I, 5).

Evident in the play's polarizing of male identity is Wasserstein's choice not to present a man who is a heterosexual or bisexual *ally* of feminism *and* befriends Heidi during twenty-four years of her life. If such a man (or men) ever existed in Heidi's chronicle, he is not visible on stage. In the face of her heroine's unspoken wish for more fulfilling intimacies with men (while not necessarily implying marriage), Wasserstein presents Heidi with no men who can meet her at the level on which she perceives herself to be existing. Rather, any such men in Heidi's (love) life remain offstage. They are reduced to an array of nameless males: an art dealer, an editor, a Londoner, a lawyer—about all of whom Heidi might as well conclude, "there's no one important" (II, 3). While it is certainly Wasserstein's prerogative to invent her own character's story, it is nonetheless poignant for her to omit any embodiment of or reference to a man with whom Heidi could have possibly had an "important" relationship. It is difficult to believe that such men would have been invisible, completely unavailable as allies of feminism *and* potential sexual intimates to a "serious good person" like Heidi Holland during her dramatic lifetime (I, 2).[18]

Within the paradigmatic triangle represented by Heidi, Scoop, and Peter's relationship, Wasserstein thus implies that a feminist (as she identified Heidi during the New School interview) cannot expect to exercise her political position *and* to engage in (let alone sustain) a physically intimate relationship with a man who respects, and possibly shares, that position. For the (heterosexual) female feminist in *The Heidi Chronicles*, politics and sex(ual love) are incompatible. The homosexual male accepts her as she is, but rejects her as a sexual intimate. The heterosexual male rejects her as she is, but accepts her as a sexual intimate. From the beginning, Heidi is set up to remain in limited situations with the only visible men in her story. These men can only disappoint her, in her deeper level of consciousness, through their inability to engage her fullest sense of her self. (Due to their visibility in Heidi's life, are we meant to see Peter and Scoop as representative "men"? Is Peter a sign that only homosexual men are capable of being active feminists? Is Scoop a sign of the heterosexual male as a whoring capitalist "master penis," despite his seemingly endearing efforts at repentance? Together, are both men signs that gay and straight men have nothing to say to one another?)

Rather, Wasserstein's play, taken on its own terms, risks this signal at the end: if a heterosexual woman hopes to maintain a "feminist" political position and to parent, she had best face the fact that she'll probably be doing it alone. The play's final scene suggests this reading when Heidi introduces to Scoop her newly adopted Panamanian infant, Judy. Heidi's choice to become a single parent takes the audience by surprise since she never discusses previously, in any revealing context, her wish to bear her own or to adopt a child, to parent, or to raise a family.[19] Instead, Heidi's action—which we may be tempted to read ironically but finally cannot—appears as a "natural" choice, following naturally (we are to presume) in her development to this point in the play. In utilizing a structure that moves from an established naturalistic mode to a wish-fulfilling conclusion, Wasserstein weakens her text. Parenting is presented too easily as a salvation for Heidi. Relevant information regarding this choice is omitted, which is particularly noticeable in light of the author's scrupulous attention to expository detail throughout the play. My hesitation is less with the fact that Heidi adopts a child, but rather with the invisibility of the process by which she comes to this decision. To ask the audience to accept that privileged Heidi just "got there" as a parent is playing right into the artistic expectations of (white) generations raised on fast food consumption. For some, however, such nurturance dished up without reference to what we are eating (or why) can not be easily swallowed. And because Wasserstein omits the process underlying Heidi's choice, failing to present any part of it dramatically, she sends an even more familiar (i.e., gender inscribed), conventional message to the audience: female=motherhood=fulfillment.

As if to confirm this cultural equation, the critic Mel Gussow praises Heidi's parenting choice by writing: "To our pleasure, the endearing character finally finds selfless fulfillment."[20] The unconscious irony in his word choice—"selfless fulfillment"—is obvious. "Selfless" Heidi borders on becoming self-less; her choice invites notions of female single parenting as an act of martyrdom possibly leading to the invisibility of her self.[21] While there are numerous plausible messages suggested by Heidi's choice (among them Heidi's ambivalence about motherhood, as well as her efforts to experience what she believes will bring her some happiness), my concern is that very complicated choices are often represented in commercial theater as being too easily realized. In *The Heidi Chronicles*, these choices involve other pressing topical issues besides parenting: the changing positions of women in American life, escalating alienation from peers and cultural values, the ambiguities inherent in creating and sustaining meaningful intimacies and friendships, and the urgency to do fulfilling work. In Wasserstein's handling of the parenting issue, in particular, the audience is finally not challenged to step away from the status quo, but rather left to wallow in it. This response is increasingly the case in recent American theater that has reached mass audiences. It is of particular concern where presented in a live context where quick resolutions, characteristic of television sitcom writings, are gradually becoming more acceptable within our dramaturgy. As Susan says in *The Heidi Chronicles*, "sitcom is big . . . women are big"—a combination that, at least in Wasserstein's dramaturgy, is almost realized.

Of course, socially provocative material by American authors is nearly invisible on today's Broadway stage. When the media suggest that such a play is on the Great White Way—and when a play wins every major award of the season, as is the case with *The Heidi Chronicles*—then our expectations are understandably peaked. But while a play's dramaturgy may indeed fall short of an individual's or a group's artistic and/or political expectations, the current mainstream audience attending Broadway theater also appears to be, on the whole, a less discerning audience than it once was. The commodification of commercial theater, causing the price of admission alone to be out of the range of many theater-goers, is an obvious sign of Broadway's bent toward a kind of homogeneity. It is a demanding challenge, therefore, to present socially relevant theater in a meaningful, truthful way before TV-conditioned audiences. When American playwrights find themselves in today's commercial theater, they are in a historically and politically critical position.

As George Bernard Shaw so aptly illustrated at the end of *Heartbreak House*, a writer cannot always assume that the public will grasp a play's universe, let alone its dramatic intentions. Anticipating that some in his audience might deny that the never-ending self-indulgence of his characters is occurring while a war rages in the distance, Shaw includes in *Heartbreak House* the sounds of artillery explosions off-stage just as the curtain is about to fall. The playwright does not hit us over the head with the play's social significance; but he also does not assume that all the vital connections have been made between the naturalistic stage world and the world at large—connections the writer *wants* established because his audiences have gotten dangerously far from knowing what it is to live purposefully and to survive with integrity. As a writer, therefore, he shows the way.

Without prescribing a specific dramaturgy to which writers like Wasserstein should adhere, I question the extent to which they are making the vital connections—so critical and fragile to dramatic realism—among the images conveyed in works, the relationship of those images to visible, experienced lives, and the interpretation of those images and relationships within commercial contexts. Our writers can more effectively "show the (alternative) ways" by making such connections, unsettling them, and offering still more organic ways to perceive and engage them. For our own good, as well as for future generations, those who are active feminists, as well as their allies—all who engage in feminist-principled work and living—must continually explore and represent those connections—connections that are first and foremost political.

Evolutionary Alliances, Revolutionary Stages

Feminism is a radical (re)visioning of the nature of power, its implementation, and its consequences. In the face of known patriarchal power relationships and their ensuing oppressions, it is often difficult to imagine feminist alternatives. The possibility of such alternatives being fully realized can sometimes seem even more remote for many of us. That is certainly one response I had to the male gang brutality that victimized the woman in Central Park. But also as I sat in the theater watching *The Heidi Chronicles*, I wondered how far we had *all* come in realizing, let alone imagining, these alternatives. There is formidable evidence both on- and off-stage suggesting the contrary (much of Western history as we know it). Yet, I couldn't deny the visible impact that feminism has already had, and will continue to have, on my life, as well as on the lives of countless other men and women. I was reminded of the importance of establishing contexts when speaking of feminism and of men's and women's relationships. But I also wondered how our alternative visions would alter if we continued to believe in the possibility of a world in which (more) men were feminists or self-proclaimed allies of feminism. Even more, I wondered how we would envision our future if we acknowledged that such men are already visible in our lives, while remaining relatively invisible in our theories and in our live art. At this point, an unsettling connection occurred to me: it has been as difficult in the wake of the Central Park rape for many to acknowledge that feminist men and their allies still exist as it has been for writers to create and audiences to expect diverse representations of such lives in contemporary works of art.

When faced with the possibility that radical change may not occur—whether in life or art—I often recall Adrienne Rich's words: "[I]f the imagination is to transcend and transform experience it has to question, to challenge, to conceive of alternatives, perhaps to the very life you are living at that moment."[22] Likewise, it is through the imagination that we can see our way to the (theoretical) possibilities within Stephen Heath's contention that "men's relation to feminism is an impossible one."[23] But if we stop there we have no where to go, since we run the risk of advocating that the relationship is only an imagined theoretical construct characterized by unresolvable contradictions. Rather, the ways in which male feminists and allies of feminism chose to live their lives is a pivotal determinant in the sequencing of changes within the feminist revolution. The quality of that engagement in many men's lives, imaginatively conceived and materially rendered, must never be underestimated—no matter how sparse its manifestations may now appear. It is an organic part of the whole that, while being imagined, is also now being realized. We are at a historic point when something other than, besides, current theory on men's relation to feminism—as well as current dramatic presentations of male characters on stage—must be equally considered and created.

Regarding this "something other," Alice Jardine remarks in *Men in Feminism:*

> for me, feminism can no longer be *only* about women or men as objects of study,
> but needs to be also about forming, encouraging, and protecting a certain shape
> of subjectivity that will be able to address the massive and urgent issues facing
> the entire planet. And so, for me, the issue of *alliance* between men and women

to these ends is clearly on the agenda. And yet there are still very few men in my opinion who have nurtured that subjectivity in themselves—even if they have theorized it ad nauseam.[24]

At this time, Jardine may very well be right that there is a gap between men who both theorize and subjectively experience feminism and those men who don't. But I would urge us also to acknowledge the impact of *active* alliances between men and women, alliances that include men who exist *outside* of those who theorize (as well as Jardine's "few" within). Again, I am referring to those men, not (necessarily) within the academy, whose daily lives reflect a sensitive alliance with feminism via their public and private relationships with women and other men—to men who are committed to living the change without being aware that others are theorizing about it. These alliances involving men who are active feminists exist, yet they all too readily go unacknowledged when essentialist opinions about men surface. It's as if the effort to differentiate and incorporate the reality of these alliances into our theories or to speak more candidly of their less common practices threatens to derail a more crucial essentializing agenda, an agenda that all too often serves only theoretical posturings that neglect to acknowledge that variations exist within *all* of our lives as we have come to experience them. Most importantly, such differences may just be vital links, still in the formative stages, to possible positionings of the male and female "alliance" within feminism. What, therefore, becomes of theory once men as feminists (or even as allies of feminism) are written into, not out of, critical discourse? As Boone rightly acknowledges, many male feminists (and I would clarify this body as men both within and outside of the academy) "are 'learning to speak as . . . body-coded male[s]' precisely in order to re-imagine man. Which is inevitably to change the shape of patriarchy and its discourses as well."[25]

But I would also suggest that while the theoretical discourse within feminism is changing, we have yet to write that discourse more fully from the perspective of Jardine's evolving alliance. It is absent not because men and women have failed to imagine, as Rich might encourage, new relationships to power, to change, to one another. It is absent not because we are still struggling to reconcile ourselves to a position between humanist and feminist ideologies. Rather, we have not yet been able to trust *all* that we know and live. Alliances exist. But many of us—male and female alike—need to speak and write more comprehensively about these visible active alliances. Upon doing so, we necessarily unsettle current theory and persistent cultural representations by positioning the materiality of such alliances more prominently within the evolving feminist movement.

We also know that some are now framing, just as more from our future generations will frame, feminist images that diverge from those represented in highly visible art like *The Heidi Chronicles*. These alternative images will come—as they have come for over thirty years—from playwrights across the country, from Off-Off-Broadway to San Francisco and Seattle, Minneapolis to Atlanta. Their images foreground and legitimize diversities among female subjects, including racial, ethnic, and class identities, as well as sexual preferences. Although many of these images now exist, they have yet to be seen with any frequency on the commercial stage. Faced with that dead end, feminists have often detoured and successfully established alternative routes for publicly presenting their creations. Soon, perhaps, one of the passages to evolve will involve more mainstream audiences.

And finally, as we turn back to consider what we know of our lives, we will find that we need to include men as part of the yet-to-be-seen images. As Wasserstein says, "What's missing is the 'We,' the making sure that not only can you pursue your potential, but that others can too. It's the thinking about others, as well as about 'me.' "[26] Ours is a world of otherness, a world of both women and men. It is perhaps the only essential, visible component we can neither question nor change. We are in this together.

Notes

Editors' Introduction

1. Adrienne Rich, "When We Dead Awaken: Writing as Re-Vision," in Adrienne Rich's Poetry, ed. Barbara Charlesworth Gelpi and Albert Gelpi (New York: Norton, 1975), pp. 90–91.

1. Of Me(n) and Feminism

This essay first appeared in a slightly longer version in Gender and Theory: Dialogues on Feminist Criticism, ed. Linda Kauffman (London and New York: Basil Blackwell, 1989). I am grateful for the comments given and interest shown in this essay when presented, in various stages of its composition, at Princeton University, Dartmouth College, the Graduate Center of the City University of New York, and the Feminist Doctoral Colloquium of the English Department at Harvard.

1. Stephen Heath, "Male Feminism," in Men in Feminism, ed. Alice Jardine and Paul Smith (London and New York: Methuen, 1987), p. 1. All further references to the essays in this collection appear in the text in parentheses.

2. Elaine Showalter, "Critical Cross-Dressing: Male Feminists and the Woman of the Year," Raritan (Fall 1983), reprinted in Men in Feminism, pp. 116–32. Page references are to the latter.

3. Despite theoretical problems I have with Jonathan Culler's attempt to talk about "reading as a woman" in On Deconstruction, my intuition is that he is a genuinely sympathetic ally of feminism, and I should not like my repetition of Showalter's criticisms to come to stand in my readers' minds for the person, a man who might be very different than the written traces embedded in a document composed nearly a decade ago. The same goes for all the critics I mention in the course of this essay, from Stephen Heath on: I am not judging, when I criticize, the individual person or critic, but rather his or her historical participation, at a given moment in time (a panel, a paper, a publication), in the articulation of a discourse on men and feminism that may extend beyond that critic's intention or awareness.

4. Among the men, two of the panelists, Paul Smith and Stephen Heath, were generally perceived as positioning themselves as outsiders wishing to be "in"/to feminism, while the third, Andrew Ross, avoided any direct commentary on his role as a male feminist by offering a specific case-analysis of sexual difference. In addition to Jardine, the women's panel included Judith Mayne, Elizabeth Weed, and Peggy Kamuf. All of their essays are reprinted in Men in Feminism. It should be added that Heath's essay, "Male Feminism," pp. 1–32, which circulated among all the panelists before the convention, is not the same as his final presentation paper ("Men in Feminism: Men and Feminist Theory," pp. 41–46), which, significantly, omits the opening argument about the "impossibility" of men entering

feminism and, in critiquing Smith and Derrida, attempts to refute the whole inclusion/exclusion proposition. But the fact was that everyone's earlier reading of Heath's original essay ensured that its discursive positionings were palpably *present* throughout the double session, both in rhetorical terms (as others quoted or cited the opinions expressed in it) and on an emotional level.

5. Not only did the format work to the men's detriment, it also channeled the *earned* authority of these women to criticize the men's arguments into a depressingly traditional "feminine" role: their authority suddenly capable of *appearing* merely that of the nagging mother scolding her wayward sons, their authority voicing itself only secondarily or reactively, in response to men's words—a point Jardine (54) and Weed (71) also make.

6. The papers were Laura Claridge's "Shelley's Poetics: The Female as Enabling Silence," Christina Zwarg's "Emerson as 'Mythologist' in *The Memoirs of Margaret Fuller Ossoli*," Margaret Higgonet's "Hardy's Tess—An Exchange of Voice," and Elizabeth Langland's "E. M. Forster's Right Rhetoric: The Omniscient Narrator as Female in *Howards End*." The two panelists whom Claridge and Langland selected out of those who responded to the call for papers, Zwarg and Higgonet, wrote extremely subtle and probing essays well worth inclusion on the panel; the irony is not in the quality of any of these presentations *individually* but in the way that *collectively* they delimited the topic announced in the session's title.

7. At this point in my original essay, I included an endnote in which I drew up a then hypothetical "table of contents" of gender-oriented work by male literary critics that might have formed a more "promising" volume. That list became the starting point, of course, of *Engendering Men*. In a response paired with my essay in Kauffman's volume, Toril Moi seizes upon this endnote to cinch her argument that my essay "is littered with comments antagonistic to older men or to men who are speaking when he is not." That is, by relegating this list to "a footnote which does nothing but list *twenty*(!) names of deserving 'invisible' men," I in effect silence their voices ("does nothing but") and ensure their continued "invisibility" (187). I trust the present collection goes some way in disproving Moi's theory. (True confessions: for a long time I fantasized publishing a response to Moi's response titled—to pun on my own title—"Of *Moi* and Feminism: The Terrifying Toril"— a response in which I would analyze the series of rather aggressive attacks that Moi has leveled against a number of American feminists, particularly those whose work disproves the American/ Continental opposition she constructs in *Sexual/Textual Politics*. But I'll leave well enough alone by containing my fantasy within these parentheses, in an aside relegated, appropriately enough, to a—merely—"silent" note.)

8. These included, in addition to a reprint of Showalter's *Raritan* essay, essays by Nancy Miller, Naomi Schor, Jane Gallop, Meaghan Morris, and Rosi Braidotti. I suspect that part of the problem I sense here has to do with the fact that some of these essays were either written or conceived before they were solicited for this collection—hence the degree to which they might not directly address the issue at hand.

9. Donoghue's review is reprinted in *Men in Feminism* after Miller's article "for the reader's convenience" (138); whether or not to include the piece was much deliberated by the editors, who ultimately decided Miller's analysis couldn't be understood without its referent. The "compromise" was to print the review in small type, in order to set it off from the other contributions.

10. I like the way in which Richard Ohmann's and Cary Nelson's titles ("In, With" and "Men, Feminism: The Materiality of Discourse," respectively) attempt to subvert what might be called the prepositional impasse of the collection's title; such plays with the pernicious *in* of "men in feminism," nonetheless, attest to the shaping influence the concept has exerted over the entire collection.

11. Ross makes this comment in a follow-up response to his original essay for the *Men in Feminism* volume (p. 86); all the original panelists were invited to contribute responses, one of its innovative features.

12. As I suggest in my prefatory note, my perception of the issue of "naming" or "labeling" has evolved considerably since I first wrote this essay. In many ways the introduction Michael Cadden and I have written to this volume begins at this point in order to move beyond it, explaining that the work we have included in *Engendering Men* is still in search of its "(im)proper name" and that its relationship to established feminist criticism thus necessarily—and perhaps fruitfully—remains in question.

2. Engendering F. O. M.

1. E. M. Forster, diary (25 October 1910), as quoted in introduction to *The Life to Come and Other Short Stories* (London: Edward Arnold, 1972), p. xv. This essay is a modified version of a lecture given at a conference, Lesbian/Gay Studies '87: Definitions and Explorations, at Yale University. I would like to thank Professor Ralph Hexter for his kind invitation to participate in such a lively event.

2. Quoted by F. O. Matthiessen in a letter to Russell Cheney (2 March 1925), *Rat and the Devil: Journal Letters of F. O. Matthiessen and Russell Cheney*, ed. Louis Hyde (Hamden: Archon Books, 1978), p. 101. Hereafter cited in the body of my essay as *Rat*.

3. W. K. Wimsatt, Jr., *The Verbal Icon* (Lexington: University of Kentucky Press, 1954), p. 100.

4. Jonathan Arac, *Critical Genealogies: Historical Situations for Postmodern Literary Studies* (New York: Columbia University Press, 1987), p. 175. A first version of Arac's chapter on Matthiessen appeared in *The American Renaissance Reconsidered: Selected Papers from the English Institute, 1982–83*, eds. Walter Benn Michaels and Donald E. Pease (Baltimore: Johns Hopkins University Press, 1985), pp. 90–112.

5. Arac, *Critical Genealogies*, p. 159.

6. Ibid., p. 175.

7. Ibid., p. 159.

8. Ibid.

9. May Sarton, *Faithful Are the Wounds* (New York: Norton, 1955). Hereafter cited in the body of my essay as *FW*.

10. Harry Levin, "The Private Life of F. O. Matthiessen," *The New York Review of Books*, (20 July 1978), p. 43.

11. William E. Cain, *F. O. Matthiessen and the Politics of Criticism* (Madison: University of Wisconsin Press, 1988), p. 47.

12. F. O. Matthiessen, *American Renaissance: Art and Expression in the Age of Emerson and Whitman* (Oxford: Oxford University Press, 1941), p. 535. Hereafter cited in the body of my text as *AR*.

13. On this subject, see especially Nina Baym, "Melodramas of Beset Manhood: How Theories of American Fiction Exclude Women Authors," in *The New Feminist Criticism: Essays on Women, Literature and Theory*, ed. Elaine Showalter (New York: Pantheon, 1985), pp. 63ff.

14. This formulation was suggested to me by Sandra Gilbert.

15. Joseph Summers and U. T. Miller Summers, "F. O. Matthiessen," *Dictionary of American Biography, Supplement Four: 1946–50*, eds. John A. Garraty and Edward T. James (New York: Scribner's, 1974), p. 560.

16. Eric Cheyfitz, "Matthiessen's *American Renaissance:* Circumscribing the Revolution," *American Quarterly* 41, 2 (June 1989):358.

17. Specifically, Woolf's speculations about "Shakespeare's sister" in *A Room of One's Own*.

18. E. M. Forster, "Terminal Note" to *Maurice* (New York: Norton, 1971), p. 249.

19. E. M. Forster, epigraph to *Howards End* (London: Edward Arnold, 1910, 1973), p. ii.

3. Redeeming the Phallus

This essay is a revised and expanded version of a lecture originally presented at a conference on Pedagogy and Politics sponsored in 1988 by the Center for Lesbian and Gay Studies at Yale. I would like to thank Wayne Koestenbaum for inviting me to participate on the panel discussing Gay/ Lesbian Literary Theory, and I would like to express my gratitude to Joseph Litvak for his generous comments and his always indispensable advice.

1. Llewelyn Powys, "The Thirteenth Way," *Dial* (July 1924); reprinted in *Wallace Stevens: The Critical Heritage*, ed. Charles Doyle (Boston: Routledge and Kegan Paul, 1985), p. 64.

2. Raymond Larsson, "The Beau as Poet," *Commonweal*, 6 April 1932; reprinted in *Wallace Stevens: The Critical Heritage*, p. 94.

3. *Letters of Wallace Stevens*, ed. Holly Stevens (New York: Knopf, 1977), p. 287.

4. William Empson, *Listener*, 26 March 1953; reprinted in *Wallace Stevens: The Critical Heritage*, p. 377.

5. Frank Lentricchia, "Frank Lentricchia," in Imre Salusinszky, *Criticism in Society* (New York: Methuen, 1987), p. 183.

6. In the final chapter of her pioneering study *Between Men*, Eve Kosofsky Sedgwick discusses the fate of publicly identifiable representatives of gayness in England and America in the aftermath of the Wilde trials. She notes that "the durable stereotype that came to prevail has been close to Symonds only as Symonds resembled Wilde: a connoisseur, an interpreter of aristocratic culture to the middle class, a socialist insofar as socialism would simply expand the venue of leisure, privilege, and high culture" (*Between Men* [New York: Columbia University Press, 1985], p. 217).

7. Offering a revision of Toril Moi's critique of feminist essentialism, Lentricchia asserts that "patriarchal oppression also consists of imposing certain social standards of masculinity on all biological men, in order precisely to make us believe that the chosen standards for masculinity are *natural*." Or, as he rephrases this a few sentences later: "the ancient social process called 'patriarchy' consists also in the oppression of patriarchs." ("Patriarchy Against Itself—The Young Manhood of Wallace Stevens," *Critical Inquiry* 13 [1987]:774. All future references to this essay will be given parenthetically in the text.)

8. Donald Pease, "Patriarchy, Lentricchia, and Male Feminization," *Critical Inquiry* 14 (1988):379.

9. Ibid.

10. This is immediately striking at the outset of Lentricchia's essay when, quoting from *The Hite Report on Male Sexuality*, he notes the anger of men's responses when asked "How would you feel if something about you were described as feminine or womanly?" (742). Surveying the comments (e.g., "Enraged. Insulted. Never mind what women are really like—I know what he's saying: he's saying I should be submissive to him"), Lentricchia concludes that "our relations with women are problematic, those with ourselves something worse" (743). What he leaves out of consideration completely is the historically specific overlaying of the question of sexuality and the question of gender in modern Western cultures. He ignores, that is, the way in which the issue of sexuality has been ideologically constructed upon a naturalized gender binarism that not only allows but, implicitly, requires that the image of a "womanly" or "feminine" man be interpreted within the field of associations that radiate from the culturally endorsed interpretation of male homosexuality.

11. Sedgwick, *Between Men*, pp. 88–89.

12. In *Love and Death in the American Novel* (New York, 1966), where he describes the tradition of male-male bonds, Fiedler comments tellingly on his own movement from the use of the word *homosexual* to the use of the word *homoerotic:* " 'Homoerotic' is a word of which I was never very fond, and which I like even less now. But I wanted it to be quite clear that I was not attributing sodomy to certain literary characters or their authors, and so I avoided when I could the even more disturbing word, 'homosexual' " (p. 349).

    Gilbert and Gubar, in their response to Lentricchia ("The Man on the Dump versus the United Dames of America; or, What Does Frank Lentricchia Want?" *Critical Inquiry* 14 [1988]:386–406), see him as reiterating claims made not only by Fiedler, but by Henry Nash Smith, Alfred Habegger, and Nina Baym (390) as well. It may be significant that Habegger's book, *Gender, Fantasy, and Realism in American Literature* (New York, 1982), is filled with offensively heterosexist assumptions about normal and healthy sexual development, and that Nina Baym's essay, "Melodramas of Beset Manhood: How Theories of American Fiction Exclude Women Authors" (in *The New Feminist Criticism*, ed. Elaine Showalter [New York: Pantheon, 1985]), articulates its often perceptive remarks about the fate of female authorship in American literary history side by side with expressions of unself-conscious homophobia in her description of male characters who disavow heterosexual relations in classic American fiction (e.g., "One should add that, for a homosexual male, the demands of society that link himself for life to a woman make for a particularly misogynist version of this aspect of the American myth, for the hero is propelled not by a rejected attraction but by true revulsion" [p. 73]).

13. Luce Irigaray, "Women on the Market," in *This Sex Which Is Not One*, trans. Catherine Porter with Carolyn Burke (Ithaca: Cornell University Press, 1985), p. 171.

14. Ibid., p. 172.

15. Henry Louis Gates, Jr., "Significant Others," *Contemporary Literature* 29 (1988):613.

16. Gilbert and Gubar make a similar point when they link the logic of Lentricchia's essay to the processes of cultural masculinization that it anatomizes. They describe Lentricchia, like Lentricchia's Stevens, as undertaking "virilization-as-defense" ("The Man on the Dump versus the United Dames of America," p. 406).

17. If academic life in general, and academic work in the humanities in particular, is "feminized" by the culture at large, within the humanities a microsociology prevails wherein "theory" generally is seen as having the effect of "masculinizing" a field—that is, of adding substance and weightiness to it, making it less "humanistic" and more like a (respectably masculine) science. Thus the prestige of feminist theory among some male academics is enhanced, ironically, by the extent to which its theoretical purchase assimilates it to a culturally coded masculinity. And, given the inevitable recapitulation of larger cultural patterns within the academic world, critical theory that focuses on issues of economics and materiality acquires an even greater force of "masculine" association.

18. Frank Lentricchia, "Andiamo!" *Critical Inquiry* 14 (1988):411.

19. Cited by Gilbert and Gubar, "The Man on the Dump versus the United Dames of America," p. 386.

20. "Andiamo!" p. 407.

21. Gilbert and Gubar, "The Man on the Dump versus the United Dames of America," p. 404. The "infamous photograph" is reprinted in Lentricchia's response. It is paired there, however, with another picture (subsequently used as the jacket photograph for *Ariel and the Police*) taken "later that same day" ("Andiamo!" p. 409) in which a kinder, gentler Lentricchia smiles engagingly from behind an array of candles, candlesticks, and wine bottles. If the earlier picture, in isolation, seemed to represent him, in Maureen Corrigan's words, as the "Dirty Harry of contemporary critical theory" (cited in Gilbert and Gubar, "The Man on the Dump," p. 404), the subsequent pictures

together could be seen to represent him as a sort of one-man Cagney and Lacey in their good cop/
bad cop mode.

22. "Andiamo!" p. 411.

23. "Andiamo!" p. 412.

24. "Life on a Battleship" (1939) was first published in *Parts of a World* (1942) but excluded, at Stevens'
request, from his *Collected Poems* (1954). The text from which I will be quoting appears in *Opus
Posthumous*, ed. Samuel French Morse (New York: Random House, 1957), pp. 77–81. All
subsequent references will be to this edition and the line numbers will be given in parentheses.

25. Harold Bloom, *Wallace Stevens: The Poems of Our Climate* (Ithaca: Cornell University Press, 1977),
p. 177.

26. Joseph Riddel, *The Clairvoyant Eye: The Poetry and Poetics of Wallace Stevens* (Baton Rouge:
Louisiana State University Press), p. 160.

27. On 5 November 1936, Stevens wrote a letter to Ronald Lane Latimer in which he declared, "I don't
believe in Communism; I do believe in up-to-date capitalism." Later in the same letter he goes on
to insist that "Whether or not all men are enemies, all egotisms are voluntarily antipathetic" (*Letters
of Wallace Stevens*, p. 292).

28. Sedgwick, *Between Men*, p. 14.

29. I have no quarrel with the usefulness of "homosociality" as a category through which to consider
the range of male-male relations. Sedgwick, in *Between Men*, does an exemplary job of articulating
the extent to which that category can be kept to disentangle the homosexual from the homophobic.
What I mean to suggest here, however, is that homosociality, as a signifier, can have the effect of
insulating the category of heterosexuality from ideological scrutiny. Not that homosociality is
necessarily located outside of the realm of the heterosexual, but *as a signifier* its prefix allows it
to be inscribed in the realm of that which is already identified with the homosexual—that is to say,
in the realm that Irigaray would read as the "hom(m)osexual." Yet what is at issue in my remarks
is precisely the extent to which the processes in question are characteristic of that which defines
itself as heterosexual. I should add that I do not intend, by this discussion, to privilege or reify the
opposition homosexual/heterosexual as in any way possessing a fixed transhistorical distinction.
This polarity, however, does have profound cultural power and can produce extraordinary experiential effects. For that reason, if for no other, it is imperative that the terms themselves not be
jettisoned or their utility in an identity politics slighted before the inequality of political and
discursive power that they label is redressed.

30. *Souvenirs and Prophecies: The Young Wallace Stevens*, ed. Holly Stevens (New York: Knopf, 1977),
p. 82.

31. To call this a "hom(m)o-sexuality" for which, as Irigaray puts it, "heterosexuality has been up to
now just an alibi" is to suggest that the category of heterosexuality has been unjustly impugned by
the mere lip-service patriarchy pays it and that "true" heterosexuality constitutes redemptive
territory in which a less oppressive relation between men and women may be found. What I am
trying to suggest, however, is that it is precisely the complicity of compulsory heterosexuality with
patriarchal structures of power that *produces* this repetitive scenario in which homosexuality is
discredited by being read as the "real meaning" of patriarchal organization while heterosexuality
is redeemed and positioned once again as an ideal that offers hope for a more progressive distribution
of power between the sexes.

32. "Andiamo!" p. 410.

33. Frank Lentricchia, "Anatomy of a Jar," *South Atlantic Quarterly* 86 (1987):390.

34. Lentricchia's gleeful imagining of the "TestaREEa" and its "big jars" would seem designed to ward
off the anxiety that finds expression in the tellingly worded paraphrase with which he dismisses

Sandra Gilbert's reading of Emily Dickinson: "Dickinson, therefore, not Whitman or Stevens, has real balls" (Ibid., p. 785).

4. "The Lady Was a Little Peruerse"

1. George Puttenham, *The Arte of English Poesie* (Kent, Ohio: Kent State University Press, 1970; facsimile reproduction of the 1906 reprint published by A. Constable and edited by Edward Arber), 153. Further references in the text, by page number.

2. See Patricia Parker's description of her book *Literary Fat Ladies: Rhetoric, Gender, Property* (London and New York: Methuen, 1987), 7: "The essays as a whole figure constructions of gender in relation both to the rhetorical tradition and to discourses of property. The concern with rhetoric throughout is in the conviction that only taking it seriously can make us better formalist readers of texts in a wide variety of periods; but that it is precisely such a concern with language and its ordering structures which might lead us to repose the question of moving beyond formalism, differently." See also 108ff.

3. See, among others, Barbara Johnson, *The Critical Difference* (Baltimore: Johns Hopkins University Press, 1980), for a polemical definition of gender as a tropological structure.

4. The influential exchange between Lacan and Derrida on "The Purloined Letter" records some consequences of the analogy between the indivisibility of the letter and that of the phallus. See the seminar on "The Purloined Letter," included in *Ecrits* (Paris: Seuil, 1966), and for Derrida's critique, which shows how Lacan is developing an *idealist* rather than a materialist concept of the letter (of the phallus), see his "Le facteur de la vérité," in *La Carte postale* (Paris: Flammarion, 1980), esp. 492–93 and 506ff.

5. See Fredric Jameson, *The Political Unconscious* (Ithaca: Cornell University Press, 1981), 45.

6. On the problematic status of the "beyond" of reading, see Wlad Godzich, "The Domestication of Derrida," in *The Yale Critics: Deconstruction in America* (Minneapolis: University of Minnesota Press, 1983), 20–40, and especially 31–32, where the displacement of the term *production* in Derrida in favor of *reading* in de Man is discussed.

7. On traditional definitions of rhetoric as *dicere ad persuadendum accomodate*—from Cicero's *De Oratore*—see among others Kenneth Burke, *A Rhetoric of Motives* (Berkeley and Los Angeles: University of California Press, 1950), 49ff; where a distinction is drawn between persuasion that includes "purely logical demonstration" and one that relies more heavily on *ingratiation* and *delight*.

8. See Luce Irigaray, *Speculum de l'autre femme* (Paris: Minuit, 1974), especially 288ff; on the instrumentality of male auto-affection. On the Timaeus' *chora*, see Julia Kristeva, *Revolution in Poetic Language*, Marguerite Waller, tr. (New York: Columbia University Press, 1984; French edition, 1974), 25ff.

9. See Kristeva, *Revolution in Poetic Language*, 25–26.

10. See Jean Paulhan, "La demoiselle aux miroirs" (1938), 183. In Jean Paulhan, *Oeuvres Complètes*, vol. 2: *Langage I (La marque des lettres)* (Paris: Gallimard, Cercle du Livre Précieux, 1945).

11. A reliance on experience draws Puttenham's Magistrate close to the poet. In a mode he shares with Sidney and that we encounter also in Vico and in Shelley, Puttenham in an earlier chapter suggests "How Poets were the first priests, the first prophets, the first Legislators and politicians in the world." The terms of the description are the familiar ones of *gravity, wisdom, age,* and *experience:* "And for all that [poets] were aged and graue men, and of much wisedome and experience in th'affaires of the world, they were the first lawmakers to the people, and the first polititiens, deuising all expedient meanes for th'establishment of Common wealth, to hold and containe the people in order and duety by force and vertue of good and wholesome lawes, made for the preseruation of the

publique peace and tranquillitie" (23). For the rationale of such defenses, see Margaret W. Ferguson, *Trials of Desire: Renaissance Defenses of Poetry* (New Haven: Yale University Press, 1983).

12. The Ciceronian subtext is much less elaborate. See *Tusculanarum Disputationum* I.xxxiv: "Death then withdraws us from evil, not from good, if truth is our object. Indeed this thought is discussed by Hegesias the Cyrenaic with such wealth of illustration that the story goes that he was stopped from lecturing on the subject by King Ptolemy, because a number of his listeners afterwards committed suicide. There is an epigram of Callimachus upon Cleombretus of Ambracia who, he says, without having met any misfortune, flung himself from the city wall into the sea after having read Plato's book. Now in the book of the Hegesias whom I have mentioned, *Apokarteron*, there appears a man who was passing away from life by starvation and is called back by friends, and in answer to their remonstrances, details the discomforts of human life. I could do the same, but I should not go so far as he does in thinking it no advantage at all for anyone to live." In *Cicero: Tusculan Disputations*, trans. J. E. King, tr. (Cambridge: Harvard University Press, 1945), 96–98.

13. The style that Hegesias is thought to have inaugurated, the so-called Asiatic style of rhetoric, was characterized by constant interruptions, aposiopeses, and parabases and contrasted with the Attic rhetoric later adopted by Cicero. See his *Epistularum ad Atticum*, XII.v–vi, in which he gives an example of interruption in the Asiatic mode: "As to Caelius, please see that there is nothing lacking in the gold. I know nothing about that. But anyhow there is loss enough in the exchange. If there is anything wrong with the gold on top of that—but what's the use of my talking? You will see it. There is a specimen of Hegesias' style, of which Varro approves." In *Cicero's Letters to Atticus, Book XII*, E. O. Winstedt, tr. (London: William Heinemann, 1925), 14–16.

14. The notion of similitude introduced at this point would thus appear to conform to Foucault's analysis of the epistemic convention of the Renaissance. See Michel Foucault, *Les Mots et les choses* (Paris: Gallimard, 1966).

15. It is no accident, in this reading, that the story's telling would tend to blur the lines that distinguish the court of law from a theater, in whose audience we would find Puttenham. Jonathan Crewe has argued ("The Hegemonic Theater of George Puttenham," *English Literary Renaissance* 16, 1986) that "Puttenham's account . . . implies a view of theater as a major hegemonic institution of the state; as one more important, in a sense, than the state's formal apparatus of legal, educational and bureaucratic institutions . . . public drama—and hence public theater—alone possesses the ability to institute hegemonic control in a situation otherwise insusceptible to 'enlightened' or 'lawful' rule, albeit rule in the manifest interest of a ruling *class*."

16. See, for instance, Daniel Javitch, *Poetry and Courtliness in Renaissance England* (Princeton: Princeton University Press, 1978), 58–67; and his "The Impure Motives of Elizabethan Poetry," in *The Power of Forms in the English Renaissance*, ed. Stephen Greenblatt (Norman, Ok.: Pilgrim Books, 1982). For a more specific treatment of rhetoric in the court and in particular for an elaboration of the social aspect of Puttenham's precepts, see Frank Whigham, *Ambition and Privilege: The Social Tropes of Elizabethan Courtesy Theory* (Berkeley: University of California Press, 1984), esp. ch. 2, "Rhetorical Semiotics at Court," 6.

17. See, for instance, Irigaray, *Speculum*, 285.

18. As it must, unless we define the decorum of reading *a priori* to exclude precisely the sort of reflection of the form in the content that constitutes "resemblance."

19. One could understand this double narrative, of collective suicides that cannot be predicated of the individual, proscribed by the act of the monarch and thus creating as it were the position of individuality, as a way of representing a particular historical formation arising in the transition from feudalism to an individuating notion of the subject (see, for instance, the work of Perry Anderson and Fredric Jameson, among many others). Hegesias thus becomes exemplary of a certain historical

necessity, and the fact that his story is told despite the magistrate's deciding against it becomes a way of representing the reemergence of historical categories in a formalist discourse. This apparent reemergence is structured in such a way as to bypass the discourse of the empirical subject, but it relies nonetheless on retaining the *form* of a subjective structure. This reliance on a fundamentally Idealist division creates certain complexities of formulation, in particular when the term it introduces to describe the mode of appearance and necessity of this form is *ideology*.

20. Puttenham: "Single words haue their sence and understanding altered and figured many wayes, to wit, by transport, abuse . . . first of *Transport*. There is a kinde of wresting of a single word from his owne right signification, to another not so naturall, but yet of some affinitie or conueniencie . . . therefore it is called by *metaphore*, or the figure of *transport*" (189). The Aristotelian use of transport—*epiphorein*—in defining metaphor is well known.

21. I follow Shoshana Felman, "Women and Madness: The Critical Phallacy," *Diacritics* 5, 4 (1975), in understanding this troubling of position to offer a critique of essentialist assumptions that structure any moment where one pretends to *speak for* or *as an example of* a class. See also Toril Moi, *Sexual/Textual Politics* (London and New York: Methuen, 1985), 138ff., for a discussion of such critiques, in particular as they concern the work of Irigaray.

5. Discipl(in)ing the Master, Mastering the Discipl(in)e

1. To make perhaps too fine a distinction, one might say that they promote themselves from disciples to apostles while doing so.

2. Examples include Rowland Mallet and Roderick Hudson, Olive Chancellor and Verena Tarrant, Ralph Touchett and Isabel Archer, Lambert Strether and Chad Newsome—and especially Strether and Little Bilham, the main scene between whom (in which Strether urges Little Bilham to "Live all you can!") James considered the kernel from which *The Ambassadors* grew.

3. Tzvetan Todorov, *The Poetics of Prose*, trans. Richard Howard (Ithaca: Cornell University Press, 1977) p. 143; "and in which he solves them," Todorov sanguinely continues.

4. Leon Edel, ed., *Henry James Letters* (Cambridge: Harvard University Press, 1984), vol. IV, p. 15. Hereinafter cited parenthetically in the text.

5. It is often noted that James seemed almost to have the capacity to predict his future relationships in his fiction. The "heroic young sculptor" (as James termed him) Hendrik Andersen, whom he met in 1899, bears a strong resemblance to Roderick Hudson, whom James invented in the early 1870s, just as Hugh Walpole, whom he met in 1909, does to Dr. Hugh, invented in 1893. Much has been written on James' homosexuality and the ways in which he manifested it in his writing. Two authors, Howard M. Feinstein, in *Becoming William James* (Ithaca: Cornell University Press, 1984, ch. 14, passim), and Richard Hall, in "An Obscure Hurt: The Sexuality of Henry James," *New Republic*, 180, 17:25–31, and 18:25–29, argue that Henry James' relations with his brother, William, were, if not actually incestuous, at least complicated by an incestuous desire on Henry's part that he partly worked through in his writing. Leon Edel has speculated frequently on James' homosexuality, most recently in his *Henry James: A Life* (New York: Harper & Row, 1985), pp. 82–83, 244–46, 497–98, 648–52, 722–25, and his introduction to volume four of *Henry James Letters* (Cambridge: Belknap, 1984), pp. xiii–xxxi. Eve Kosofsky Sedgwick, in "The Beast in the Closet: James and the Writing of Homosexual Panic," in Ruth Bernard Yeazell, ed., *Sex, Politics, and Science in the Nineteenth-Century Novel: Selected Papers from the English Institute*, 1983–84 (Baltimore: Johns Hopkins University Press, 1986), pp. 148–86), reads James' "The Beast in the Jungle" as a narrative of male homosexual panic, arguing that the central issue in the story is whether Marcher will ever recognize his potential for homosexual desire and suggesting a parallel with the author's life. While I would like to express in the strongest terms my gratitude to Sedgwick's inspiration and terminology, I want to distinguish my project here from hers in "The Beast in the Closet." Although

both of us offer readings of James' short stories to show how fictions situate relations between men along the continuum between homosexuality and homosociality, I limit my concerns solely to erotonomies of discipleship, while Sedgwick emphasizes the larger issue of male homosexual panic.

6. For a discussion of male homosexual panic see Sedgwick, "The Beast in the Closet."

7. Henry James, *The Art of Fiction*, in Henry James, *Literary Criticism: Essays on Literature, American Writers, English Writers*, selected and edited by Leon Edel (New York: Library of America, 1984), p. 43. Hereinafter abbreviated as *Essays* and cited parenthetically in the text.

8. René Girard, *Deceit, Desire, and the Novel: Self and Other in Literary Structure* (Baltimore: Johns Hopkins University Press, 1984), p. 2.

9. In "The Lesson of the Master," for example. One could argue that the description that follows of the triangular relations in James' literary tales resembles in some sense Sedgwick's description of the relations in Shakespeare's sonnets (*Between Men* [New York: Columbia University Press, 1985], Chapter 2). The trajectory of erotic energy emphasized in the sonnets, however, is one that flows *from* the poet to the young man and the dark lady. The trajectory emphasized in James' stories is significantly the reverse.

10. Todorov, *The Poetics of Prose*, p. 145.

11. James expresses a similarly vexed response to the publication of Hawthorne's private journals, letters, and "other personal memorials" in his review of the author's *French and Italian Notebooks* (*Essays*, p. 307).

12. Henry James, "The Real Right Thing," in Leon Edel, *The Complete Tales of Henry James* (Philadelphia: J. B. Lippincott, 1964), vol. 10, p. 471. Hereinafter cited parenthetically in the text as *Tales*.

13. *The Complete Notebooks of Henry James*, ed. Leon Edel and Lyall H. Powers (New York: Oxford University Press, 1987), p. 268.

14. Ibid., p. xiv. For another passage addressed to *mon bon* in which James' orgasmic language echoes his letters to Walpole and Fullerton, see ibid., p. 261.

15. In light of "The Real Right Thing," Leon Edel's act of naming the condensed version of his comprehensive biography of James' *A Life* takes on new resonance. He all but invites us to compare the relation between himself and James with that between Withermore and Doyne, thereby forcing the inference that his lifelong project would unequivocally be considered by James to constitute chronic torture.

16. For those unfamiliar with Benjamin's terminology, a hasty explanation of it may be helpful. An aesthetic artifact, according to Benjamin, has "cult value" and/or "exhibition value." It has cult value to the extent that its existence and role in a specific rite or practice are more important than its capacity to be exhibited before a wide public. Detailed carvings high on a cathedral, for example, have great cult value, because, although they cannot readily be perceived, their representations are known as significant to, and indeed partake in, the religious rituals associated with the cathedral. Painting on canvas, by contrast, have great exhibition value and, often, little cult value; because their primary function is to be appreciated "aesthetically," they can be transported and displayed almost anywhere. Benjamin uses the terms *information* and *wisdom* to detail modes of communication. He distinguishes between storytelling and simply transmitting information by arguing that "wisdom" is conveyed in the former practice but absent from the latter. Storytelling, related originally to the giving of counsel, refuses to separate from the storyteller, the benefit of whose deep experience, in the end, the story means to convey. See Walter Benjamin, "The Storyteller," "The Work of Art in the Age of Mechanical Reproduction," and "On Some Motifs in Baudelaire," in *Illuminations*, trans. Harry Zohn (New York: Schocken Books, 1969), especially pp. 86–89, 159, and 222–26.

17. The fear of feminization is also expressed in the thematization of ludicrous androgyny, as represented not only by Guy Walsingham and Dora Forbes—a peculiar doubling of the character of the

androgynous author whose textual body and physical body are gendered differently—but also by the edificial princess.

18. Girard, *Deceit, Desire, and the Novel*, p. 7.

19. In "The Figure in the Carpet" the narrator's friend, George Corvick, evidently insists that marriage be the price Gwendolyn Erme must pay to learn the secret "figure" in the author Vereker's literary works. "The Aspern Papers" analyzes an interestingly similar case where the roles are reversed: the gay male narrator, unable to face the marriage to Tina that the culture's positive presumption of heterosexual attraction leads her to propose in return for sharing Aspern's letters with him, ultimately relinquishes his effort to attain them.

6. Cowboys, Cadillacs, and Cosmonauts

An earlier version of this article appeared in *East-West Film Journal* (Fall 1989).

1. Carey McWilliams describes this appropriation at length in *North From Mexico* (Philadelphia: J. B. Lippincott, 1948).

2. The "denigration" of the genre reached its delightfully campy zenith in Warhol's *Lonesome Cowboys* (1968), where the fun-loving posse, agonizing over hair-styling and ballet moves, wrestles throughout the film with the maxim "We're not out here to raise cain, we're here to raise families."

3. Ralph Brauer and Donna Brauer, *The Horse, the Gun, and the Piece of Property: Changing Images of the TV Western* (Bowling Green: Bowling Green University Popular Press, 1975). Like the TV Western, the dime novel from 1875–1895 and the Hollywood Western from 1937–1957 had both moved through a whole succession of historical inflections of the genre.

4. Rita Parks, *The Western Hero in Film and Television: Mass Media Mythology* (Ann Arbor: UMI Research Press, 1983), p. 163.

5. The suppression of these two histories has not gone completely uncontested in Hollywood—in the case of genocide, by the so-called Cinema Rouge of the 1960s (*A Man Called Horse, Soldier Blue, Little Big Man*) and, in the case of the cattlemen's associations, by neopopulist films from *The Man Who Shot Liberty Valance* to *Heaven's Gate*.

6. The pioneer family was undoubtedly a favored populist model for the countercultural family bent on some degree of agrarian self-sufficiency. But the more politically resonant version of an extended kinship community was provided in the figure of the Native American tribe, more properly egalitarian and thus stripped of the Hollywood Western's historically inaccurate fondness for the absolute sovereignty of the patriarchal"chief." The counterculture's nostalgic "reinvention of the Indian" in the 1960s did not, however, arise solely out of a surplus of white guilt generated by a historical reexamination of the Old West. In most instances the new primitivistic attention to the Native American was articulated within the critical evaluation of the United States' advanced technological intervention in the non-Western world, especially in Southeast Asia. Thus arose a double identification with East and with the prewhite West; the hippie earth mother could carry a papoose and sport "Oriental" cheesecloth without any sense of cultural contradiction. Ironically, this dual identificatory practice reproduced the vestigial association of the Native American with the Orient, perpetuated ever since Columbus' grand navigational/cartographic blunder. It is no surprise, then, that the films of the Cinema Rouge would each come to be interpreted as allegories of the intervention in Vietnam, or that President Johnson would compare the defense of Vietnam to the defense of the Alamo.

7. Marshall McLuhan, "Television in a New Light," in *The Meaning of Commercial Television*, ed. Stanley T. Donner (Austin: University of Texas Press, 1967), pp. 87–89.

8. Andrew Ross, *No Respect: Intellectuals and Popular Culture* (New York: Routledge, 1989), p. 132.

9. Jane Tompkins, *Sensational Designs: The Cultural Work of American Fiction 1790–1860* (New York: Oxford University Press, 1985).

10. For a fuller description of the ideology of conservative familialism, see Michélle Barrett and Mary McIntosh, *The Anti-Social Family* (London: Verso, 1982).

11. The inverted image of this conceit can be found in John Carpenter's *They Live!* (1988), an allegory of aliens as the ruling class, especially the Republican elite, who have taken over the world and are altering the atmosphere through pollution and acid rain in order to make it more comfortable for them to breathe; Earth is their third world to colonize and exploit.

12. Robin Wood, *Hollywood from Vietnam to Reagan* (New York: Columbia University Press, 1986), pp. 162–88.

13. Vivian Sobchak, "Child/Alien/Father: Patriarchal Crisis and Generic Exchange," *Camera Obscura* 15 (1986):7–36.

14. *The Man Who Shot Liberty Valance*, for example, where the youthful memories of Valance the elder statesman are allowed to flesh out the film's famous parable about the mythical West: "When the legend becomes fact, print the legend."

15. Dale Carter, *The Final Frontier: The Rise and Fall of the American Rocket State* (London: Verso, 1988).

16. Ibid., p. 257.

17. The famous film of the *Challenger* disaster ironically reproduced the kind of special-effects spectacle (like the destruction of the Death Star) that had thrilled *Star Wars* audiences, just as the Zapruder footage of the Kennedy assassination in Texas had recalled a furtive ambush scene in a Western.

18. Carter, *The Final Frontier*, p. 258.

19. A similar gender-coded conflict is played out in *Barbarella* (1968), the Pop fantasy film that features a different kind of space heroine for the 1960s and an earlier discourse around reproductive technologies like the birth control pill, whose recent advent is represented in the film as indicative of a passionless, technocratic future that must be prevented in the name of old-fashioned (male-dominant) pleasure.

7. "Meat Out of the Eater"

In some of the seventeenth-century passages, I have silently modernized or regularized punctuation for ease of reading.

1. See, for example, Edmund S. Morgan, *The Puritan Family* (New York: Harper & Row, 1944), and Edmund Leites, *The Puritan Conscience and Modern Sexuality* (New Haven: Yale University Press, 1986).

2. Edmund S. Morgan, "The Puritan's Marriage with God," *South Atlantic Quarterly* 48, 1 (1949):107–12; Philip J. Greven, *The Protestant Temperament: Patterns of Child-Rearing, Religious Experience, and the Self in Early America* (New York: New American Library, 1977), pp. 124–40.

3. *The Diary of Michael Wigglesworth, 1653–1657*, ed. Edmund S. Morgan (New York: Harper & Row, 1965), p. 13. Page numbers of quotations taken from this work will be placed in the body of the text.

4. *The Poems of Edward Taylor*, ed. Donald E. Stanford (New Haven: Yale University Press, 1960), p. 230. Quotations from the *Preparatory Meditations* will be identified in the body of the text by the series number and the meditation number. Stanford glosses "spermodote" as "giver of seeds" (p. 541).

5. Perry Miller, *The New England Mind: The Seventeenth Century* (Cambridge: Harvard University Press, 1939), pp. 3–34.

6. Andrew Delbanco, *The Puritan Ordeal* (Cambridge: Harvard University Press, 1989), p. 152.

7. Morgan suggests in "The Puritan's Marriage With God" that the erotic metaphor allowed Puritans to "sublimate" their heterosexual desires. Greven, in *The Protestant Temperament*, claims that "evangelical" Puritan males "feminized" themselves in order to become "brides of Christ" and that this tendency may have encouraged homosexuality; he also suggests that their anxiety over this feminization was expressed as misogyny and hatred of effeminacy.

8. *The Works of Anne Bradstreet*, ed. Jeannine Hensley (Cambridge: Harvard University Press, 1967), p. 282. Page numbers of quotations from this work will be placed in the body of the text.

9. Jonathan Ned Katz, *Gay/Lesbian Almanac* (New York: Harper & Row, 1983), p. 95.

10. Michael Wigglesworth, *Meat Out of the Eater* (Boston: F. Allen, 1717), p. 52. Passages from this poem can be found in Perry Miller and Thomas H. Johnson, eds., *The Puritans*, volume II, (New York: Harper & Row, 1938), pp. 617–30. Wigglesworth's description of these "satanical injections" vividly depicts his state of sexual panic:

> Blasphemous hellish thoughts
> Into his mind are cast
> Concerning God; which make him quake
> And stand like one aghast.
> Imaginations black
> And fancies filthy foul
> Are darted in with violence,
> Which stab him to the soul.

11. Richard Crowder, *No Featherbed to Heaven: A Biography of Michael Wigglesworth, 1631–1705* (East Lansing: Michigan State University Press, 1962), p. 90.

12. The origin of the terms *positive* and *privative* in reference to sin is unclear; they are at least as old as Emerson, who uses them in his "Divinity School Address." The best discussion of the terms is in Delbanco, *The Puritan Ordeal*, pp. 22–27.

13. Katz, *Gay/Lesbian Almanac*, pp. 95–96.

14. Ibid., p. 46.

15. Michael Wigglesworth, "The Day of Doom," in Miller and Johnson, eds., *The Puritans*, pp. 587–606. It might be worth noting that Wigglesworth spent the proceeds from his best-selling poem on a year in Bermuda with a "companion" named John Younglove. See Crowder, *No Featherbed*, p. 124.

16. Michael Wigglesworth, "God's Controversy with New England," in Alan Heimert and Andrew Delbanco, eds., *The Puritans in America* (Cambridge: Harvard University Press, 1985), pp. 231–36.

17. Michel Foucault, *The Care of the Self*, trans. Robert Hurley (New York: Random House, 1986), pp. 115–16. Wigglesworth certainly consulted some medical texts to find out about his "disease"; he complains in the diary that reading about "afflux" makes it worse.

18. Wigglesworth, "God's Controversy," pp. 234–35.

19. Alan Bray, *Homosexuality in Renaissance England* (London: Gay Men's Press, 1982), p. 26.

20. Wigglesworth, *Meat Out of the Eater*, pp. 27–28. The poem's title is derived from Samson's riddle in the Book of Judges.

21. Wigglesworth, *Meat Out of the Eater*, pp. 29–30.

22. Wigglesworth, *Meat Out of the Eater*, p. 153.

23. Michael Wigglesworth, "The Prayse of Eloquence," in Miller and Johnson, eds., *The Puritans*, pp. 674–75.

24. This letter is reprinted in Donald E. Stanford's introduction to *The Poems of Edward Taylor*, p. xlii.

25. Heimert and Delbanco, eds., *The Puritans in America*, p. 297.

26. Leo Bersani, "Is the Rectum a Grave?" in *October* 43 (1987):222.

27. John Winthrop characterizes the antinomian heresy this way in *A Short Story* in David D. Hall, ed., *The Antinomian Controversy, 1636–1638* (Middletown, Conn.: Wesleyan University Press, 1968), p. 205.

28. Walt Whitman, "Song of Myself," in *Complete Poetry and Collected Prose*, ed. Justin Kaplan (New York: Literary Classics of the United States, 1982), p. 29.

29. Emily Dickinson, *Final Harvest*, ed. Thomas H. Johnson (Boston: Little, Brown & Company, 1961), p. 5.

8. Hester Prynne, *C'est Moi*

An earlier version of this essay was delivered as a public lecture at the University of Calgary. I want to express my appreciation to my hosts there, particularly Eric Savoy and Helen Buss. Eric Savoy has also been a discriminating and generous reader.

1. Letter to Ticknor, 19 January 1855, in *Letters of Hawthorne to William D. Ticknor* (Newark: Carteret Book Club, 1910), 1:75

2. See Hawthorne's description of himself as a young man as "a scribbler by profession" in a letter dated 12 April 1838, as well as his youthful description of British writers as "the scribbling sons of John Bull" in a letter of 13 March 1821. Both letters are in *The Centenary Edition of the Works of Nathaniel Hawthorne*, ed. William Charvat et al. (Columbus: Ohio State University Press, 1962), 15:270 and 15:139, respectively. All further quotations from Hawthorne's works are from this edition and are indicated in the text by volume number and page number.

3. For instance, Nina Baym's very important work on Hawthorne has by and large dealt with the question of Hawthorne's representation of women without raising larger issues across gender. Recently, there have been a few exceptions, notably Leland S. Person, Jr.'s *Aesthetic Headaches: Women and a Masculine Poetics in Poe, Melville, and Hawthorne* (Athens: University of Georgia Press, 1988). His explorations of Hawthorne's "feminized masculine poetics" (p. 174) are intriguing, and he more than anyone has shown Hawthorne's attempt to subvert a traditional masculine poetics. His study seems to me nonetheless too optimistic in its evaluation of this subversion, largely because of his relative neglect of the anxieties it produces, particularly with regard to gender identity and heterosexual certainty.

4. Hélène Cixous, "The Laugh of the Medusa," trans. Keith Cohen and Paula Cohen, first published in *Signs* (Summer 1976) and reprinted in *New French Feminisms*, ed. Elaine Marks and Isabelle de Courtivron (New York: Schocken, 1981), p. 247.

5. *The Letters of Margaret Fuller*, ed. Robert N. Hudspeth (Ithaca: Cornell University Press, 1983–1987), 1:198.

6. John Irwin, *American Hieroglyphics* (New Haven: Yale University Press, 1980), p. 276.

7. There may be another complex relationship between Hawthorne and Hester here. Both names begin with *H*, of course, and the transformation of an *H* into an "*A* requires only a "steeple-crown." Perhaps more significantly, both names involve a missing, or supplementary, letter. Hester recovers

her biblical origins if her *H* is shifted to Esther, while Hawthorne marks off his distance from his origins by adding a *W*. The *W*, we might say, is *his* scarlet letter, one that seeks to unwrite the legend of past evil, even while reminding us of it.

8. John P. McWilliams, Jr., *Hawthorne, Melville, and the American Character: A Looking-Glass Business* (Cambridge: Cambridge University Press, 1984), p. 68.

9. On needlework and narrative, see Elaine Showalter, "Piecing and Writing," in *The Poetics of Gender*, ed. Nancy K. Miller (New York: Columbia University Press, 1986), pp. 222–47. She terms the quilt a "hieroglyphic or diary" (p. 241).

10. Nina Baym is right, I think, to link the Indian woman in Hawthorne to a suppressed matriarchy, although she does not pursue the point, especially in *The Marble Faun*, where the idea of matriarchy is crucial as the Etruscan counterpoint to papal Rome. See Baym, *The Shape of Hawthorne's Career* (Ithaca: Cornell University Press, 1976), p. 120.

11. See, for example, Joanne Feit Diehl, "Re-Reading *The Letter:* Hawthorne, the Fetish, and the (Family) Romance," *New Literary History* 19 (Spring 1988):655–73. Diehl's emphasis on Hawthorne's desire for the mother seems to me somewhat overstated, especially since it entails neglect of the male relationships in his fiction. It was, after all, Hawthorne's *father* who died when he was young. (The figure of the sea-captain father is almost certainly present in the sea captain of *The Scarlet Letter*, who would take Hester and Dimmesdale away, but who will inevitably bring Chillingsworth along as well. What ship could take Dimmesdale and Chillingsworth away? Only, one might answer, one captained by Melville.)

12. In Peggy Kamuf's very acute commentary, Hester's embroidery is "a speculation . . . on the position of the symbol of the guilty subject, the subject of nonidentity, the 'woman' presented in *Appliquée*" ("Sexual Politics and Critical Judgment," in *After Strange Texts: The Role of Theory in the Study of Literature*, ed. Gregory S. Jay and David L. Miller [n.p.: University of Alabama Press, n.d.], p. 83).

13. Sentimentality, as Michael Davitt Bell shows in *The Development of American Romance: The Sacrifice of Relation* (Chicago: University of Chicago Press, 1980), is "a medium of psychological repression and social control" (p. 191).

14. For more on the demonized and empowered nineteenth-century woman, see Nina Auerbach, *Woman and the Demon* (Cambridge: Harvard University Press, 1982).

15. This apparent difference is largely erased in the scene of Zenobia's drowning, when her body is penetrated by the grappling hook. Both Zenobia and Priscilla in the end bear the traces of their sexuality on their (maimed) bodies. Zenobia's flower recalls Hester's *A*, for both are ways of proclaiming sexuality as sign and story. Dimmesdale, like Priscilla, keeps his bloody scars concealed, even as he renews them regularly. There is an interesting discussion of sewing and the body, with particular application to *The Mill on the Floss*, in Helena Michie, *The Flesh Made Word: Female Figures and Women's Bodies* (New York: Oxford University Press, 1987), p. 42.

16. Hawthorne regularly uses horticultural figures for sexuality, most strikingly in "Rappaccini's Daughter." While his usage is fairly conventional, it was sufficiently pronounced to be picked up by Melville in his "Monody" for Hawthorne ("the cloistral vine / That hid the shyest grape"). I believe the association is linked to Hawthorne's troubled relationship to his uncle Robert Manning, a noted horticulturist; in this regard see James R. Mellow, *Nathaniel Hawthorne in His Times* (Boston: Houghton Mifflin, 1980), p. 15.

17. One might also note how the world of women remains the object of the male gaze even as it finally eludes male comprehension. When Coverdale continues to watch Zenobia and Priscilla through the window of the house in the city, Zenobia finally lets down the curtain, a barrier explicitly compared to "the drop-curtain of a theatre" (3:159). The scene anticipates by a number of years the famous episode in Proust's *A la recherche du temps perdu* where Marcel watches through a window the

lesbian relationship of Mlle. Vinteuil and her friend, until they close the shutters, an act proclaiming their love-making as a realm closed off to the male gaze.

18. The genital nature of the threat in this story was obscured in its revision in 1837, the same occasion that led Hawthorne to delete from another story the account of a meeting with a group of carnivalesque actors of uncertain sexuality—the first version of this obsessive scene. See Mellow, *Hawthorne in His Times*, pp. 77–78. For a text of the passage deleted from "The Gentle Boy," see the *Centenary Edition*, 9:617, a note to 9:92.

19. Hawthorne's awareness of historical shifts in the construction of gender is clear from his contrast early in *The Scarlet Letter* of sixteenth-century women of the time when "the man-like Elizabeth had been the not altogether unsuitable representative of the sex" and "their fair descendants" of his own day who have "a fainter bloom" (1:50).

20. Michel Foucault, *La volonté de savoir (Histoire de la sexualité*, vol. 1) (Paris: Gallimard, 1976), pp. 66–67. Foucault's wonderful phrase for this is "la consolidation des sexualités périphériques" (p. 67).

9. The Love-Master

I want to thank Shirley Samuels, Andrew Ross, Joseph Boone and Michael Cadden for responding to earlier drafts of this paper—a paper which is not, by the way, about "the question of male feminist criticism."

1. Ernest Thompson Seton, *Boy Scouts of America: A Handbook of Woodcraft, Scouting, and Life-Craft* (New York: Doubleday, Page, 1910), pp. xi, xii, 1–4, 34–38; Seton, "History of the Boy Scouts," p. 10, as cited by Michael Rosenthal, *The Character Factory: Baden-Powell and the Origins of the Boy Scout Movement* (New York: Pantheon, 1986), p. 65. On the relations and rivalries between the Woodcraft and scouting movements and between Seton and Baden-Powell, see, in addition to Rosenthal, David I. Macleod, *Building Character in the American Boy: The Boy Scouts, YMCA, and Their Forerunners, 1870–1920* (Madison: University of Wisconsin Press, 1983). Macleod, more generally, provides a lucid and informed account of the making of middle-class Americans at the turn of the century.

2. Theodore Roosevelt, "The Strenuous Life," in *The Works of Theodore Roosevelt*, Memorial Edition (New York: Scribner's, 1924–1926), vol. 15, pp. 267, 271.

3. Frederick Jackson Turner, *The Frontier in American History* (New York: H. Holt, 1920), pp. 1, 4. See also Roderick Nash, *Wilderness and the American Mind* (New Haven: Yale University Press, 1973), pp. 141–60.

4. Ronald T. Takaki, *Iron Cages: Race and Culture in Nineteenth-Century America* (New York: Alfred A. Knopf, 1979), pp. 253–79.

5. BSA, *Handbook for Scout Masters* (New York: National Council Boy Scouts of America, 1914), p. 102.

6. As Ernst Haeckel observed in his widely influential *The Riddle of the Universe* (New York: Harper, 1900): "We can only arrive at a correct knowledge of the structure and life of the social body, the state, through a scientific knowledge of the structure and life of the individuals who compose it, and the cells of which they are in turn composed" (p. 8). See also S. J. Gould, *Ontogeny and Phylogeny* (Cambridge: Harvard University Press, 1978); and Leo W. Buss, *The Evolution of Individuality* (Princeton: Princeton University Press, 1987).

7. Seton correspondence, as cited by Macleod, *Building Character in the American Boy*, p. 101; G. Stanley Hall, *Adolescence: Its Psychology and Its Relations to Physiology, Anthropology, Sociology, Sex, Crime, Religion, and Education* (New York: D. Appleton, 1904), vol. 2, p. 648.

8. To anticipate: The notion of *wilding* governs at least the media accounts of the recent brutal attack in New York City on a woman by a "pack" of youths in that nature preserve at the heart of the city, Central Park, which was designed by Frederick Law Olmsted as a remedy for the "over-civilized" and degenerate urban dweller. The account invokes the naturalist idiom of a violent primitivism and regeneration: a regeneration that takes place in the reproduction of "the natural" represented by the park or "nature museum" and a primitivism, at once antinatural and antifemale, that is here racialized, not merely in the races of the attackers and victim, but also in the racial idea of the "gang period" itself. Across from the park stands the Museum of Natural History and Roosevelt Memorial, with their visual reproductions of Nature—nature as *nature morte*.

9. These case studies include: "The Naturalist Machine," in *Sex, Politics, and Science in the Nineteenth-Century Novel: Selected Papers from the English Institute, 1983–84,* ed. Ruth Bernard Yeazell (Baltimore: Johns Hopkins University Press, 1986), pp. 116–47; "Physical Capital," in *New Essays on The American,* ed. Martha Banta (Cambridge: Cambridge University Press, 1987), pp. 131–67; "Statistical Persons," *Diacritics* 17, 3 (Fall 1987):82–98. Versions of these pieces and of the present paper form parts of my *Bodies and Machines,* forthcoming from Routledge.

10. In addition to the sources already cited, see, for instance: H. W. Gibson, *Boyology; or Boy Analysis* (New York: Association, 1918); Thorton W. Burgess, "Making Men of Them," *Good Housekeeping* 59 (July 1914); William Byron Forbush, *The Boy Problem,* 6th ed. (Boston, 1907).

11. Jean Baudrillard, *For a Critique of the Political Economy of the Sign,* trans. Charles Levin (St. Louis: Telos Press, 1981), p. 85.

12. Seton, *BSA Handbook,* pp. 3–4.

13. *Congressional Record,* 47th Congress, 2d Sess., 14 (1 March 1883), p. 3488.

14. Baden-Powell, *Headquarters Gazette* 5 (November 1911), p. 2, as cited by Rosenthal, *The Character Factory,* p. 6.

15. See Macleod, *Building Character,* pp. xi, 28, 104–6. As the social historian Samuel Haber has shown, in his *Efficiency and Uplift: Scientific Management in the Progressive Era, 1890–1920* (Chicago and London: University of Chicago Press, 1964), "The literature of system leaned heavily upon analogies to the human body, the machine, and the military. The body and the machine usually illustrated the need for close integration within the factory while military organization exemplified hierarchy and discipline" (p. 19). The scouting organization efficiently coordinates the body and the machine, in its physical cultures, in its quasimilitary troops of boys, and in its hierarchical organization.

16. Galton, "Eugenics: Its Definition, Scope and Aim," *Nature* 70 (1904), 82; Pearson, *Darwinism, Medical Progress, and Eugenics* (London: Dulan, 1912), p. 27; Arthur Conan Doyle, preface to *The Construction and Reconstruction of the Human Body* (London: John Bale and Davidson, 1907), p. x. On Sandow and the physical cultures movement generally, see Harvey Green, *Fit for America: Health, Fitness, Sport, and American Society* (New York: Pantheon, 1986).

17. Seton, *The Birch-Bark Roll of the Woodcraft Indians* (New York: Doubleday, Page, 1906), p. 4. "Honors by standards"—or, more familiarly, the merit badge system—forms part of the more general merit system of standardized individualism I outline here.

18. This treatment of rival styles of individualism is indebted to Foucault's accounts of the "government of individualization" and the making of individuals and individuality as an effect of disciplinary technologies and systematic management. See, for instance, "The Subject and Power," *Critical Inquiry* 8 (Summer 1982) and *Discipline and Punish: The Birth of the Prison* (New York: Pantheon, 1977), esp. pp. 135–69. The following discussion extends and redirects the account of individualization, discipline, and desire in the American culture of managerialism set out in my *Henry James and the Art of Power* (Ithaca: Cornell University Press, 1984), pp. 96–145.

19. James R. Beniger, *The Control Revolution: Technological and Economic Origins of the Information Society* (Cambridge: Harvard University Press, 1986), pp. 49, 185; Alfred D. Chandler, Jr., *The Visible Hand: The Managerial Revolution in American Business* (Cambridge: Harvard University Press, 1977), pp. 27, 1; Daniel Boorstin, *The Americans: The Democratic Experience* (New York: Random House, 1973), part 5. On "mechanical prime movers" and machine culture generally, see Thorstein Veblen's *The Place of Science in Modern Civilization and Other Essays* (New York: B. W. Huebsch, 1919).

20. For Veblen, the uneven transition from the invisible hand of the market to the visible one of managerialism is in fact seen as a tension between honors and standards—or, in Veblen's terms, between "exploit" and "industry." The distinction between exploit and industry is, for Veblen, a distinction between the rival tendencies of market culture and machine culture. If the first remains attached to the body and its desires—to an "interpretation of human nature in terms of the market" (that is, in terms of "the sensations of consumption"), the second transcends body and desire both (*Place of Science*, pp. 141, 231–51).

Exploit, for Veblen, includes but is not limited to the "archaic survivals" of the predatory impulse evident in the militarism and "the boys' brigades and other quasi-military organizations," in the cult of the wild, and big game trophy-hunting that proliferated in the 1890s. These survivals are, in Veblen's view, not *alternatives* to market culture but rather *instances* of market culture itself. And these instances include not merely the "buccaneer" capitalism of corporate raids and head-hunting, the predatory "pecuniary exploits" of market culture and its "captains," but also the forms of competitive or possessive individualism and the rituals of competitive, or conspicuous, consumption. (Corporate head-hunting might form a subject of its own: in order to join Roosevelt's Boone and Crockett Club, it was necessary to have collected at least three trophy heads; Roosevelt himself had eight.) (See Veblen, *The Theory of the Leisure Class: An Economic Study of Institutions* [1899] [New York: New American Library, 1953], pp. 27–29, 170–74).

Exploit remains, on all counts, bound up with the "radiant body": with the reassertions of physical prowess and with the understanding of the economy in "sensuous terms." The logic of exploit, which is also the logic of market culture, thus remains tied to "animistic and anthropomorphic explanations": to the understanding of the economy in terms of the "disintegrating animism" of an "unseen hand." "Industry"—what Veblen calls "the metaphysics of the machine technology"—involves, precisely, a transcendence of the natural body and such anthropomorphic and animistic explanations. The logic of industry calls for, in short, a transcendence of the "ordre physique." The logic of industry demands the replacement of the radiant body by the "disciplinary effects" of the "machine process" and by an *im*personal "body of matter-of-fact knowledge." (*Theory of the Leisure Class*, pp. 81–82, 28–31; *Place of Science*, pp. 1–31, 55, 82–113).

The *commuting* between these rival logics—between the logic of market culture and possessive individualism, on the one side, and the logic of machine culture and disciplinary individualism, on the other—such a commuting might be taken to define the double logic of desire and discipline in the culture of consumption. (For an extended account of that double logic, see my "Advertising America," *Henry James and the Art of Power*, pp. 96–145.) But it may be noted that a good deal of recent work on turn-of-the-century American culture continues precisely the "interpretation of human nature in market terms"—the equations of economics and desire within the logic of possessive individualism and an abstractly, and anachronistically, conceived notion of "the market." It is not merely that the generalization or inflation of C. B. Macpherson's "political theory of possessive individualism" to explain later nineteenth-century social conditions makes for contradictions and historical inaccuracies. The "new historicist" account of the market is not historical but methodological or theoretical. That account *posits* a tautological relation between individual desires and social demands—the logic of sheer culturalism. (On some of the problems such a logic entails, see my "The Aesthetics of Consumption," in *Bodies and Machines*, forthcoming, which also treats more specifically than I have here the matter of the working body.) Finally, the persistence of the understanding of the visible hand of the managerial economy in terms of the animistic and invisible one of the market economy is, of course, one of the regenerative rituals of consumerism: consumption as a paying homage to the radiant body, albeit in mass-produced and standardized form. Consuming as the call of the wild. And if recent cultural criticism tends to ratify such an understanding, this is certainly not the only way in which recent criticism replays the panic about agency and self-possession that it takes as its subject.

21. Veblen, *The Theory of the Leisure Class*, pp. 26–29.

22. Henry Ford, *My Life and Work* (Garden City, N.J.: Doubleday Page, 1923), pp. 108–9.

23. James Howard Bridge, *The Inside History of the Carnegie Steel Company: A Romance of Millions* (New York: Aldine, 1903), p. 85.

24. Harry Braverman, *Labor and Monopoly Capital: The Degradation of Work in the Twentieth Century* (New York: Monthly Review Press, 1974), p. 125. See also: Howard P. Segal, *Technological Utopianism in American Culture* (Chicago: University of Chicago Press, 1985), pp. 19–32, 98–99.

25. Niklas Luhmann, "Modes of Communication and Society" (1984), as cited by Beniger, *The Control Revolution*, p. 38. See also Luhmann's "The Individuality of the Individual: Historical Meanings and Contemporary Problems," in *Reconstructing Individualism: Autonomy, Individuality, and the Self in Western Thought*, ed. Thomas C. Heller et al. (Stanford: Stanford University Press, 1986), pp. 313–25.

26. Beniger, *The Control Revolution*, p. 10. On Loeb and biomechanics, see Philip Pauly, *Controlling Life: Jacques Loeb and the Engineering Ideal in Biology* (New York: Oxford University Press, 1987).

27. "The Crown Princes of Business," *Fortune*, XLVII (October 1953), as cited by David F. Noble, *America by Design: Science, Technology, and the Rise of Corporate Capitalism* (New York: Oxford University Press, 1977), p. 321.

28. Muybridge's model is mentioned in Miles Orvell, *The Real Thing: Imitation and Authenticity in American Culture, 1880–1940* (Chapel Hill: University of North Carolina Press, 1989), p. 311.

29. Gilles Deleuze, *Masochism: Coldness and Cruelty* (New York: Zone Books, 1989), pp. 20, 69, 76.

30. References to *The Red Badge of Courage* are to the Norton Critical Edition, ed. Sculley Bradley et al. (New York: Norton, 1976) and are included in parentheses in the text.

31. Klaus Theweleit, *Male Fantasies*, vol. 1, trans. Stephen Conway (Minneapolis: University of Minnesota Press, 1987), p. 233.

32. Freud, *New Introductory Lectures, The Standard Edition of the Complete Psychological Works of Sigmund Freud*, trans. James Strachey, vol. 22, p. 80.

33. Beniger, *The Control Revolution*, p. 321; Boorstin, *The Americans*, p. 549.

34. Jack London, *White Fang*, in the Library of America edition of *Jack London: Novels and Stories* (New York, 1982), pp. 92, 161. References to *White Fang (WF)* and *The Sea-Wolf (SW)* are to this edition. References to *John Barleycorn (JB)* are to the Library of America edition of *Jack London: Novels and Social Writings* (New York, 1982). References to *The Call of the Wild (CW)* are to the casebook edition, ed. Earl J. Wilcox (Chicago: Nelson Hall, 1980). All references are included parenthetically in the text.

35. It would be possible to trace the links between the coldness and cruelty of this logic and what will reappear as the "white terror" of the fascist state. That is, it would be possible to explore, in "the pitiless, spectral syllogisms of the white logic" seen "from his calm-mad height" (*JB*, 940), the terroristic racial and sexual violence "naturalized" (in the sense I have tried to indicate) in London's stories of the great white male North. On the "White Terror," see Klaus Theweleit, *Male Fantasies*, vol. 2, trans. Erica Carter and Chris Turner (Minneapolis: University of Minnesota Press, 1989). American imperialism, at the turn of the century, is bound up with the syllogisms of such a white logic. Hence the set of analogies that structure Richard Harding Davis' observation that "the Central American citizen is no more fit for a republican form of government than he is for an arctic

expedition." See *Three Gringos in Venezuela and Central America* (New York: Harper & Brothers, 1896), p. 146.

36. Baden-Powell, *Young Knights of the Empire: Their Code and Further Scout Yarns* (London: C. Arthur Pearson, 1916), p. 163.

37. See also *The Call of the Wild:* "His muscles became hard as iron . . . He could eat anything, no matter how loathesome or indigestible, and, once eaten, the juices of his stomach extracted the last particle of nutriment . . . building it into the toughest and stoutest of tissues" (25).

38. See also *White Fang:* "Another advantage he possessed was that of correctly judging time and distance. Not that he did this consciously, however. He did not calculate such things. It was all automatic. His eyes saw correctly, and the nerves carried the vision correctly to his brain. The parts of him were better adjusted than those of the average dog. They worked together more smoothly and steadily . . . When his eyes conveyed to his brain the moving image of an action, his brain, without conscious effort, knew the space that limited that action and the time required for its completion" (203). London's consummate version of the call of the wild as the call to systematic management also invokes the later nineteenth century updating of the Cartesian notion of the animal machine. See William Coleman, *Biology in the Nineteenth Century: Problems of Form, Function, and Transformation* (Cambridge: Cambridge University Press, 1977), pp. 120–30.

39. On the discipline of desire in the naturalist workplace, with particular reference to the erotic violence of segregation and transgression (walls and openings) in Zola's fiction, see my *Henry James and the Art of Power*, pp. 181–83.

40. On what I am here calling the compulsory perversity of "modern sexuality," see Jean Laplanche, *Life and Death in Psychoanalysis*, trans. Jeffrey Mehlman (Baltimore: Johns Hopkins University Press, 1976); and Susan Stewart, "The Marquis de Meese," *Critical Inquiry* 15 (Autumn 1988):162–92.

41. Oliver Wendell Holmes, "The Stereoscope and the Stereograph," *Atlantic Monthly* 3 (June 1859), repr. in *Photography: Essays and Images*, ed. Beaumont Newhall (New York, 1980), p. 60. In his "The New Story-Tellers and the Doom of Realism" (1984), William Thayer also makes explicit the association of realism and skin games—with what he calls "epidermism." See *Realism and Romanticism in Fiction: An Approach to the Novel* (Chicago: Scott, Foresman, 1962), p. 158.

42. I am here indebted to Donna Haraway's extraordinary essay, "Teddy Bear Patriarchy: Taxidermy in the garden of Eden, New York City, 1908–36," repr. in *Primate Visions: Gender, Race, and Nature in the World of Modern Science* (New York: Routledge, 1989), pp. 26–58.

43. Ernest Hemingway, *The Sun Also Rises* (New York: Charles Scribner's Sons, 1926), p. 72.

44. Antonin Artaud, *Van Gogh, the Man Suicided by Society*, trans. Mary Beach and Lawrence Ferlinghetti, in *Artaud Anthology* (San Francisco: City Lights Books, 1965), p. 158.

10. Are We (Not) What We Are Becoming?

1. While reading a working draft of this essay, a lesbian friend and colleague inscribed the following criticism in the margins of my text:

> Isn't it primarily gay male issues which have been receiving high priority in these periodicals? Lesbian concerns have received a more or less fair hearing in the feminist journals (*Signs, Feminist Issues, Feminist Studies* . . .) for over a decade now, but I'm not aware of the journals you cite paying too much attention to lesbian scholarship.

For me the implications of this comment work two ways. On the one hand, the privilege accorded to men within academics is not necessarily mitigated when men begin to consider gender as a salient category of analysis; indeed, quite often the opposite obtains, as the recent debates around "Men in Feminism" underscore (see Alice Jardine and Paul Smith, eds., *Men in Feminism* [New

York: Methuen, 1987]). On the other hand, the acceptance of feminism as both a methodology and an institutional formation has created the space for producing a legitimate "lesbian" discourse, while gay academic men heretofore have had few equivalent opportunities. Thus, although it is easy for me to slip into the mistake of metonymically eliding "lesbian" into "gay," the specific histories and power relations that organize the emergence of these "identities" into the academy insure that they are not and cannot be symmetrical categories.

2. My essay appeared as "Writing Gone Wilde: Homoerotic Desire in the Closet of Representation," *PMLA* 102, no. 5 (October 1987): 802–13. *PMLA* is the acronym for the *Publication of the Modern Language Association*; it designates the official journal of the Modern Language Association, a professional organization composed of those in higher education who teach, write, research, and publish in the fields of literature, language, and linguistics. As an institutional entity the MLA plays a major role in organizing both the epistemological and professional domains of American literary studies. Largely operating in the absence of other institutionally based organizing bodies such as unions or guilds (the major exception perhaps being the more broadly based American Association of University Professors), this disciplinary association not only effectively constitutes the range of disciplinary subspecialties (so that an essay appearing under its imprimatur is granted de facto legitimacy) but also concretely coordinates and oversees the process of job hiring for the majority of four-year colleges and universities.

3. Adrienne Rich, "Invisibility in Academe," *Bread, Blood, and Poetry* (New York: Norton, 1986), p. 199.

4. Jacques Lacan, "The Mirror Stage as Formative of the Function of the I," *Ecrits*, trans. Alan Sheridan (New York: Norton, 1977), pp. 1–17.

5. Teresa de Lauretis, "Issues, Terms, and Contexts," in *Feminist Studies/Critical Studies*, ed. Teresa de Lauretis (Bloomington: Indiana University Press, 1986), p. 9.

6. The phrase "technologies of gender" was introduced by Teresa de Lauretis in *The Technologies of Gender* (Bloomington: Indiana University Press, 1987).

7. Michel Foucault, "Friendship as Lifestyle," *Le Gai Pied* 25 (1981). For a more detailed consideration of Foucault's writings on gay politics see my "Foucauldian Necrologies: 'Gay' 'Politics'? Politically Gay?" *Textual Practice* 2 (Winter 1988):87–102.

11. Wilde's Hard Labor and the Birth of Gay Reading

1. See the several volumes of Michel Foucault's *History of Sexuality*, particularly *Volume I: An Introduction*, trans. Robert Hurley (New York: Random House, 1980). See also John D'Emilio, *Sexual Politics, Sexual Communities: The Making of a Homosexual Minority in the United States, 1940–1970* (Chicago: University of Chicago Press, 1983), and Jeffrey Weeks, *Sexuality and Its Discontents: Meanings, Myths, and Modern Sexualities* (London: Routledge & Kegan Paul, 1985).

2. Roland Barthes, *S/Z: An Essay*, trans. Richard Miller (New York: Farrar, Straus and Giroux, 1988).

3. D. A. Miller, *The Novel and the Police* (Berkeley: University of California Press, 1988).

4. See Ed Cohen, "Writing Gone Wilde: Homoerotic Desire in the Closet of Representation," *PMLA* 102, 5 (October 1987):801–13; Jonathan Dollimore, "Different Desires: Subjectivity and Transgression in Wilde and Gide," *Genders* 2 (July 1988):24–41; Regenia Gagnier, *Idylls of the Marketplace: Oscar Wilde and the Victorian Public* (Stanford: Stanford University Press, 1986). I have had the privilege of reading important unpublished work on Wilde and on gay theory by Christopher Craft, Bruce Hainley, Patrick Horrigan, Michael Lucey, and Eve Kosofsky Sedgwick; I am grateful, as well, to the students in my 1988 undergraduate seminar at Yale on gay and lesbian literature.

5. See Walter Benjamin, "The Work of Art in the Age of Mechanical Reproduction," in *Illuminations* (New York: Schocken Books, 1969), pp. 217–52.

6. E. M. Forster, *Maurice* (New York: W. W. Norton, 1987), 156.

7. This reader resembles Proust's Albertine. Wilde, like Marcel, turned fear of infidelity into a prose-engendering germ.

8. Oscar Wilde, "De Profundis," in *De Profundis and Other Writings*, ed. Hesketh Pearson (Harmondsworth: Penguin, 1986), 97. Further references appear in my text.

9. See Richard Ellmann, *Oscar Wilde* (New York: Knopf, 1988), 508–9.

10. Quoted in Robert Ross, "Preface," in Oscar Wilde, *De Profundis* (London: Methuen, 1905), vii.

11. Susan Gubar, " 'The Blank Page' and the Issues of Female Creativity," in Elizabeth Abel, ed., *Writing and Sexual Difference* (Chicago: University of Chicago Press, 1982), 73-94.

12. Oscar Wilde, "The Decay of Lying," in Wilde, *De Profundis*, 74.

13. Oscar Wilde's petition, written in Reading Gaol, to the Secretary of State for the Home Department; quoted in H. Montgomery Hyde, *Oscar Wilde: The Aftermath* (London: Methuen, 1963), 71.

14. Typing—defined as the ability to make a fatal impression on a lover or on the next generation—resembles the poetics of infection that dominates homophobic constructions of AIDS: sexual magnetism as a contagion.

15. *The Chicago Manual of Style*, 13th ed. (Chicago: University of Chicago Press, 1982), 587.

16. Robert Ross, "Preface," ix.

17. Quoted in Hyde, *Oscar Wilde*, 173.

18. Ibid., 89.

19. Quoted in ibid., 90.

20. Quoted in ibid., 90.

21. Vyvyan Holland, "Introduction," in Wilde, *De Profundis and Other Writings*, 91.

22. Abraham Horodisch, *Oscar Wilde's "Ballad of Reading Gaol": A Bibliographic Study* (New York: Aldus, 1954), 84, 59.

23. "The Story of Oscar Wilde," Advertising brochure for the Patrons' Edition De Luxe of Oscar Wilde (New York: Doubleday, Page).

24. Karl Beckson, ed., *Oscar Wilde: The Critical Heritage* (London: Routledge & Kegan Paul, 1970), 243.

25. Ibid., 247.

26. Ibid., 222.

27. Hester Travers Smith, *Oscar Wilde From Purgatory* (New York: Henry Holt, no date), 97.

28. *Oscar Wilde: The Critical Heritage*, 322.

29. See Horodisch, *Oscar Wilde's "Ballad of Reading Gaol"*, 14.

30. "The Ballad of Reading Gaol," in Wilde, *De Profundis and Other Writings*, 239. Page numbers will appear in my text.

31. Ellmann, *Oscar Wilde*, 503–4.

32. The *red* room, in which Charlotte Brontë's Jane Eyre is locked for hitting John *Reed* over the head when he forbade her to *read* one of his books is another exemplary conflation of redness and reading.

33. See John Addington Symonds, *In the Key of Blue and Other Prose Essays* (London: Elkin Mathews, 1893).

12. Homo-Narcissism; or, Heterosexuality

1. The question of what is "modern" can here get a bit tricky. At this point, I mean only the broadest extension of the term: heterosexuality as a cultural system does not date from prehistory, nor is it universally the same. Later on, however, I shall be speaking of links between the sex/gender system of heterosexuality and "modern society." The task then will be to describe the relation of that sex/gender system not simply to a recent period of history, but to the set of social forms and normative principles that are programmatically linked together as "modernity." Included under this heading are the imperatives of universal law and morality, rationalized social life, autonomous disciplines of art, and objective science. And although this development in social organization has sources in the Renaissance, its full and classic expression comes with the height of the Enlightenment and its liberal aftermath. The key descriptions of this term and its history are by Jürgen Habermas; although his defense of modernity is highly controversial, his exposition of its meaning remains unmatched. See, for a brief version, "Modernity—An Incomplete Project," in Hal Foster, ed., *The Anti-Aesthetic* (Seattle: The Bay Press, 1983), 3–15. The much more developed version is in Jürgen Habermas, *The Philosophical Discourse of Modernity*, trans. Frederick Lawrence (Cambridge: MIT Press, 1987), esp. chapters 1 and 2. For the debate about the ongoing value of modernity and Habermas' use of the notion, see the essays in Richard Bernstein, ed., *Habermas and Modernity* (Cambridge: MIT Press, 1985).

2. Simone de Beauvoir, *The Second Sex*, trans. H. M. Parshley (1952; rpt. New York: Vintage, 1974), 44.

3. The best recent example of this tradition is Jessica Benjamin's *The Bonds of Love: Psychoanalysis, Feminism, and the Problem of Domination* (New York: Pantheon, 1988).

4. De Beauvoir, *The Second Sex*, 79.

5. Juliet Mitchell, *Psychoanalysis and Feminism* (New York: Random House, 1974), 34 (summarizing Freud).

6. This appears in a voluminous literature on sexuality in other cultures. For a general survey of the problem of "homo" and "hetero" sexualities, along with the projection of these categories onto cultures that order sexuality differently, see David Greenberg, *The Construction of Homosexuality* (Chicago: University of Chicago Press, 1988).

7. De Beauvoir, *The Second Sex*, 55 (italics in original). In *Psychoanalysis and Feminism*, Juliet Mitchell offers a critical but, in my reading, not entirely fair account of de Beauvoir's rejection of Freud. See pp. 305–18.

8. Sigmund Freud, "On Narcissism," in James Strachey, ed., *The Standard Edition of the Complete Psychological Works of Sigmund Freud*, 24 vols. (London: Hogarth, 1953–1974), 14:88.

9. "As always where the libido is concerned, man has here again shown himself incapable of giving up a satisfaction he had once enjoyed. He is not willing to forgo the narcissistic perfection of his childhood; and when, as he grows up, he is disturbed by the admonitions of others and by the awakening of his own critical judgement, so that he can no longer retain that perfection, he seeks to recover it in the new form of an ego ideal" ("On Narcissism," 94).

10. Several commentators have noted the evaluative instability of the term, usefully surveyed by Arnold Cooper, "Narcissism," in an excellent collection edited by Andrew Morrison: *Essential Papers on Narcissism* (New York: New York University Press, 1986), 112–43.

11. In *The Ego and the Id*, trans. Joan Riviere (New York: Norton, 1962), by which time Freud has begun to treat the ego ideals as the superego, he writes that "the super-ego manifests itself essentially as a sense of guilt (or rather, as criticism—for the sense of guilt is the perception in the ego answering to this criticism)" (43). This narrowing of the dissonance of the ego ideals is, in my view, too simple and indicates a symbolic valence that has since eroded. For describing the dissonance between ego and its ideals in modernity, "criticism" is probably more accurate.

12. Kaja Silverman, "Masochism and Male Subjectivity," *Camera Obscura* 17 (1988):41.

13. Jacqueline Rose, *Sexuality in the Field of Vision* (London: Verso, 1986), 170 (emphasis added).

14. For a much fuller version of this argument, see John Brenkman, *Culture and Domination* (Ithaca: Cornell University Press, 1987), especially chapter 5, "The Social Constitution of Subjectivity." Explicating the *fort-da* game, Brenkman writes: "It is essential not to collapse the distinctive moments of the dialectic of desire and interaction; the child's mirror play is already marked with the liberating negativity of speech" (165).

15. There are a number of general surveys on this subject. None, as far as I know, is really satisfactory. The most recent is Kenneth Lewes, *The Psychoanalytic Theory of Male Homosexuality* (New York: Simon and Schuster, 1988).

16. Freud to Sandor Ferenczi, 6 October 1910, quoted in Ernest Jones, *The Life and Work of Sigmund Freud*, 3 vols. (New York: Basic Books, 1953), 2:83. On the erotics of Freud's collaborative friendships, see Wayne Koestenbaum, *Double Talk: The Erotics of Male Literary Collaboration* (New York: Routledge, 1989), 17–42.

17. Freud, *The Ego and the Id*, 21.

18. Ibid., 23–24.

19. Sigmund Freud, *Group Psychology and the Analysis of the Ego*, trans. James Strachey (New York: Norton, 1959), 37.

20. See Silverman, "Masochism and Male Subjectivity," 39ff., for a discussion of the implications of this scenario.

21. Mikkel Borch-Jacobsen, *The Freudian Subject*, trans. Catherine Porter (Stanford: Stanford University Press, 1988), 93. The passage continues: "To recognize that I resemble the other, that I resemble myself in him even in my own desire, would be tantamount to admitting the inadmissible: that I am not myself and that my most proper being is over there, in that double who enrages me."

22. Jacques Lacan, *Seminaire* 1 (Paris: Seuil, 1975), 162. Translation modified from the English version: *The Seminar of Jacques Lacan: Book I*, trans. John Forrester (New York: Norton, 1988), 141.

23. Lacan, *Seminar*, 1:142.

24. Ibid., 1:221.

25. There is an excellent article by Wilfried Ver Eecke on this subject: "Hegel as Lacan's Source for Necessity in Psychoanalytic Theory," in Joseph Smith and William Kerrigan, eds., *Interpreting Lacan* (New Haven: Yale University Press, 1983), 113–38.

26. De Beauvoir, *Second Sex*, 464–65.

27. Christopher Lasch, Introduction to Janine Chasseguet-Smirgel, *The Ego Ideal*, trans. Paul Barrows (New York: Norton, 1984), xiii–xiv.

28. Jacques Lacan, "Aggressivity in Psychoanalysis," *Écrits*, trans. Alan Sheridan (New York: Norton, 1977), 27.

29. Jacques Lacan, "On a Question Preliminary to Any Possible Treatment of Psychosis," *Écrits*, 194.

30. Lacan, *Seminar*, 1:141.

31. In this way the discourse on narcissism and homosexuality bears an important resemblance to the psychoanalytic discourse on femininity. See Shoshana Felman, "Rereading Femininity," *Yale French Studies* 62 (1981):19–44.

32. Michel Foucault, *The History of Sexuality, Vol. 1: An Introduction* (New York: Pantheon, 1978). I have no interest in minimizing the value of work that has followed in the same general direction, especially in its value as a critique of the liberal-essentialist discourse of sexuality. For versions that specifically treat the question of homosexuality, see especially Jeffrey Weeks, *Sexuality and Its Discontents: Meanings, Myths, and Modern Sexualities* (London: Routledge, Kegan, Paul, 1985); or the work of Eve Sedgwick, most recently exemplified in "Across Gender, Across Sexuality: Willa Cather and Others," *South Atlantic Quarterly* 88 (Winter 1989):53–72; or David M. Halperin, *One Hundred Years of Homosexuality and Other Essays on Greek Love* (New York: Routledge, 1990).

33. Christopher Lasch, *The Culture of Narcissism* (New York: Norton, 1979).

34. See especially Jürgen Habermas, "Moral Development and Ego Identity," in *Communication and the Evolution of Society*, trans. Thomas McCarthy (Boston: Beacon Press, 1979), 69–94. Habermas argues, for instance, that the subject of modernity "takes into account that traditionally settled forms of life can prove to be mere conventions, to be irrational. Thus he has to retract his ego behind the line of all particular roles and norms and stabilize it only through the abstract ability to present himself credibly in any situation as someone who can satisfy the requirements of consistency even in the face of incompatible role expectations and in the passage through a sequence of contradictory periods of life. Role identity is replaced by ego identity; actors meet as individuals across, so to speak, the objective contexts of their lives" (85–86).

35. Freud, "On Narcissism," 75.

36. See, for instance, Lacan, "Aggressivity,", 27.

37. Charles Brockden Brown, *Arthur Mervyn* (1799–1800), ed. Sydney Krause et al. (Kent, Ohio: Kent State University Press, 1980), p. 434.

13. Rebel Without a Closet

I wish to thank Chris Reed for unending support and editorial rescue.

1. Eve Kosofsky Sedgwick, *Between Men: English Literature and Male Homosocial Desire* (New York: Columbia University Press, 1985), pp. 3–4, 21, 25.

2. Robert K. Martin, *Hero, Captain, and Stranger: Male Friendship, Social Critique, and Literary Form in the Sea Novels of Herman Melville* (Chapel Hill: University of North Carolina Press, 1986), p. 5.

3. Michel Foucault, *Discipline and Punish: The Birth of the Prison*, trans. Alan Sheridan (New York: Pantheon, 1977). See also Foucault, *The History of Sexuality*, trans. Robert Harley (New York: Vintage, 1980).

4. D. A. Miller, *The Novel and the Police* (Berkeley: University of California Press, 1988), pp. viii, viii–ix, ix.

5. Stewart Stern, the screenwriter of *Rebel Without a Cause*, notes that the photo of Alan Ladd was one of many props deployed to mark Plato as "the one who would have been tagged as the faggot character." Quoted in Vito Russo, *The Celluloid Closet: Homosexuality in the Movies* (New York: Harper & Row, 1981), p. 110.

6. For a fuller discussion of Frank Stark's power to name, see Marguerite Waller, "Poetic Influence in Hollywood: *Rebel Without a Cause* and *Star Wars*," *Diacritics* 30 (1980):57–66.

7. For another discussion of the patriarchal economic and emotional control at stake in *Consenting Adult*, see John R. Leo, "The Familialism of 'Man' in American Television Melodrama," *South Atlantic Quarterly* 88 (1989):31–51. I agree with Leo that "the crisis to be resolved" in *Consenting Adult* "is the nuclear nest's repugnance and intransigence before an unrelentingly unrepentantly gay son whose aberration in the post-Stonewall context is officially no longer a sickness" (p. 38). But I don't agree with Leo's conclusion that Jeff is "reincorporated, as the rebel body returned, back into the bourgeois family and its attendant obligations of fealty, kinship, and property" (p. 43). As my discussion makes clear, I see the conclusion of the film as significantly more subversive than does Leo.

8. Sigmund Freud, *Character and Culture*, trans. Philip Rieff (New York: Collier, 1963), pp. 265, 264.

9. Ibid., p. 266.

10. Ovid, *Metamorphoses*, trans. Rolfe Humphries (Bloomington: Indiana University Press, 1955), p. 239.

11. At the conclusion of *Nightmare on Elm Street 2*, Freddy is momentarily resurrected (on the bus taking Jesse and Lisa to school, Freddy's razored glove shoots out from the seat cushion). On one hand, this gesture simply informs viewers to keep an eye out for future *Nightmare* sequels. However, Freddy's final appearance deconstructs the film's depiction of the tranquil suburban domesticity purchased with Freddy's destruction. More subtly, Freddy's return signals his function as the representative of a taboo desire. Freud notes that a taboo can never fully be repressed because renunciation is crucial in the ritual of taboo; Freddy must be resuscitated so he can again be vanquished. But Freud also argues that taboos persist because societies' attitudes towards the taboo are ambivalent; people desire what they also fear (taboo is, according to Freud, the objectified fear of a deep desire). The connection between desire and prohibition, as Freddy's final appearance shows, lies at the heart of *Nightmare on Elm Street 2*, in which the desires of "normal" and of "perverse" persons (the police and Schneider, Mr. Walsh and Freddy) are almost indistinguishable. That the taboo represented by Freddy is related to homosexuality is suggested by the music that accompanies the closing credits: Bing Crosby crooning, "Have You Ever Seen A Dream Walking?" This final campy gesture revives a homosexual code that the film itself, nominally, seeks to repress. See Sigmund Freud, *Totem and Taboo*, trans. James Strachey (New York: Norton, 1950).

12. See Carol J. Clover, "Her Body, Himself: Gender in the Slasher Film," *Representations* 20 (1987):211.

13. Simon Watney, "The Spectacle of AIDS," *October* 43 (1977):71–86. See also Watney, *Policing Desire: Pornography, AIDS and the Media* (London: Methuen, 1987).

14. Caged Birds: Race and Gender in the Sonnet

1. Anna Julia Cooper, *A Voice From the South*, ed. Mary Helen Washington (New York: Oxford, 1988), 31.

2. Washington, ed., *A Voice From the South*, xlii.

3. W. E. B. Du Bois, "The Damnation of Women," *Writings*, ed. Nathan Huggins (New York: Library of America, 1986), 959.

4. Ibid., 968.

5. Mary Helen Washington, ed., *Invented Lives: Narratives of Black Women, 1860–1960* (New York: Anchor-Doubleday, 1987), xxvii.

6. Ann Rosalind Jones, "Assimilation with a Difference: Renaissance Women Poets and Literary Influence," *Yale French Studies* 62 (1981):135.

7. Sandra Bermann, *The Sonnet Over Time: A Study in the Sonnets of Petrarch, Shakespeare, and Baudelaire* (Chapel Hill: University of North Carolina Press, 1988), 23.

8. Jones, "Assimilation with a Difference," 136.

9. James M. Mueller, "On Genesis in Genre: Milton's Politicizing of the Sonnet in 'Captain or Colonel,' " in *Renaissance Genres: Essays on Theory, History, and Interpretation*, ed. Barbara Lewalski (Cambridge: Harvard University Press, 1986), 215.

10. See Joan R. Sherman, ed., *Collected Black Women's Poetry: Vol. III* (New York: Oxford University Press, 1988).

11. Ibid., 78.

12. Ibid., 83.

13. Paul Laurence Dunbar, *The Complete Poems of Paul Laurence Dunbar* (New York: Dodd, Mead, 1980), 208.

14. Wayne F. Cooper, *The Passion of Claude McKay, Selected Poetry and Prose, 1912–1948* (New York: Schocken Books, 1973), 116.

15. Claude McKay, *Harlem Shadows: The Poems of Claude McKay* (New York: Harcourt, Brace, 1922), 53.

16. Cooper, *Claude McKay: Rebel Sojourner in the Harlem Renaissance* (Baton Rouge: Louisiana State University Press, 1987), 65.

17. Ibid., 100–1.

18. Gwendolyn Brooks, *Selected Poems* (New York: Harper & Row, 1963), 22.

19. Ibid., 54.

15. Homelessness at Home: Placing Emily Dickinson in (Women's) History

I wish to thank Susan Stanford Friedman and Lynn Keller for their close attention to earlier versions of this essay. I am also grateful to Jane Marcus for her suggestions and assistance.

1. Emily Dickinson,*The Letters of Emily Dickinson*, eds. Thomas Johnson and Theodora Ward (Cambridge: Belknap Press of the Harvard University Press, 1958), vol. 1, 211–12.

2. F.O. Matthiessen's "The Private Poet: Emily Dickinson," in *The Recognition of Emily Dickinson: Selected Criticism Since 1890*, eds. Caesar R. Blake and Carlton F. Wells (Ann Arbor: University of Michigan Press, 1965), 224–35, marks the beginning of this debate in the modern criticism. For two representative feminist positions on this question, see Suzanne Juhasz, *The Undiscovered Continent: Emily Dickinson and the Space of the Mind* (Bloomington: Indiana University Press, 1983), 1–3; and Sharon Leder with Andrea Abbott, *The Language of Exclusion: The Poetry of Emily Dickinson and Christina Rossetti* (New York: Greenwood Press, 1987), 2.

3. For a discussion of Dickinson's "emotional and erotic ties" to both women and men, see Adelaide Morris, " 'The Love of Thee—A Prism Be': Men and Women in the Love Poetry of Emily Dickinson," in *Feminist Critics Read Emily Dickinson*, ed. Suzanne Juhasz (Bloomington: Indiana University Press, 1983), 98–113.

4. In "Zero Degree Deviancy: The Lesbian Novel in English," in *Writing and Sexual Difference*, ed. Elizabeth Abel (Chicago: University of Chicago Press, 1982), Catharine Stimpson points to the lesbian kiss as a literary device that encodes both transgression and permissibility, possibility and impossibility, because it both reveals and conceals sexual activity (246–47).

5. Nancy Walker, " 'Wider Than the Sky': Public Presence and Private Self in Dickinson, James, and Woolf," in *The Private Self: Theory and Practice of Women's Autobiographical Writings*, ed. Shari

Benstock (Chapel Hill: University of North Carolina Press, 1988), describes how Dickinson's letters seem intended to function as both private and public discourse (274–75; 281).

6. Julia Kristeva, "Women's Time," trans. Alice Jardine and Harry Blake, in *Feminist Theory: A Critique of Ideology*, eds. Nannerl O. Keohane, Michelle Z. Rosaldo, and Barbara C. Gelpi (Chicago: University of Chicago Press, 1982), 33.

7. I am here suggesting that what Sandra Harding calls "the instability of the analytical categories of feminist theory" can be understood in terms of Jacques Derrida's account of deconstruction as a "double gesture" that both retains and displaces oppositional categories like gender. See Harding, "The Instability of the Analytical Categories of Feminist Theory," in *Feminist Theory in Practice and Process*, eds. Micheline R. Malson, Jean F. O'Barr, Sarah Westphal-Wihl, and Mary Wyer (Chicago: University of Chicago Press, 1989), 15–34; and Derrida, *Margins of Philosophy*, trans. Alan Bass (Chicago: University of Chicago Press, 1982), 329.

8. Gayatri Spivak, "The New Historicism: Political Commitment and the Postmodern Critic," in *The New Historicism*, ed. H. Aram Veeser (New York: Routledge, 1989), 283. For another formulation of this problem, see Spivak, *In Other Worlds: Essays in Cultural Politics* (New York: Methuen, 1987), 205.

9. In other words, Dickinson poses to me the same question that she posed to the only male literary critic with whom she had contact during her life, Thomas Wentworth Higginson. After visiting Dickinson in Amherst, Higginson wrote his wife that Dickinson asked him, "Could you tell me what home is?" (Higginson's letters on this occasion are appendèd to Dickinson's initial letter of invitation to Higginson, dated 16 August 1870; *Letters*, vol. 2, 475). The real question here, I would argue, is whether the male critic will responsibly use his power to place the woman writer and thereby possibly displace her from her own self-representations.

10. Harding, "Instability," 17.

11. Sheila Rowbotham describes the double gesture I am trying to define here in terms of the necessity to resist two types of "patronage," both "the assumption that everyone must naturally want to be what you are or what you hope to be" and "the assumption that other human beings are a different order of creature from yourself and therefore would never share your aspirations" (*Women, Resistance and Revolution: A History of Women and Revolution in the Modern World* [New York: Vintage, 1974], 244).

12. However, see Leder and Abbott, *Language of Exclusion*, 133–47, on Dickinson's use of "the vocabulary of the marketplace" as evidence of her self-consciousness about her exclusion from that social space (133).

13. Mary P. Ryan, *Womanhood in America: From Colonial Times to the Present*, 3rd ed. (New York: Franklin Watts, 1983), 113–19; 115, 165.

14. Nancy F. Cott, *The Bonds of Womanhood: "Woman's Sphere" in New England, 1780–1835* (New Haven: Yale University Press, 1977), is the classic work on this transition.

15. Nina Baym, *Woman's Fiction: A Guide to Novels by and about Women in America, 1820–1870* (Ithaca: Cornell University Press, 1978), 28, 48. The best study of this project of widening "woman's sphere" is Martha Vicinus, *Independent Women: Work and Community for Single Women, 1850–1920* (Chicago: University of Chicago Press, 1985). Though Vicinus discusses English women exclusively, she also makes the general point that the uncritical acceptance of a domestic femininity led many women reformers to conceptualize the widening of the female sphere in terms of colonization, an imposition of middle-class values on workers and the unemployed (39–40, 219–21).

16. Mary Kelley, *Private Woman, Public Stage: Literary Domesticity in Nineteenth-Century America* (New York: Oxford University Press, 1984), 222.

17. Suzanne Juhasz, *Undiscovered Continent*, 24, defines the typical treatment of spatial imagery in Dickinson's poetry when she argues that both home and homeland are best understood as versions

of "mental space," as Dickinson attempts to create psychological and literary room for the expression of a nonconformist feminine sensibility. Such readings seem to me to neglect the possibilities for materialist analysis that are opened by a more literal reading of Dickinson's representation of the domestic.

18. Jean McClure Mudge, *Emily Dickinson and the Image of Home* (Amherst: University of Massachusetts Press, 1975), 11–12, lists these definitions, which also include the "dwelling house," the "seat" or "place of constant residence," and the "grave, death; or a future state." Mudge draws on the 1844 edition of Webster's dictionary, a copy of which the Dickinson family owned.

19. Kelley, *Private Woman, Public Stage*, 111.

20. Gayatri Chakravorty Spivak, "Displacement and the Discourse of Woman," in *Displacement: Derrida and After*, ed. Mark Krupnick (Bloomington: Indiana University Press, 1983), 186.

21. Elizabeth Fox-Genovese and Eugene Genovese, *Fruits of Merchant Capital: Slavery and Bourgeois Property in the Rise and Expansion of Capitalism* (New York: Oxford University Press, 1983), 318.

22. Dolores Hayden, *The Grand Domestic Revolution: A History of Feminist Designs for American Homes, Neighborhoods, and Cities* (Cambridge: MIT Press, 1982), offers a historical account of feminist attempts to articulate alternative domestic economies. My essay reads Dickinson in the context of what Hayden calls a "material feminist" tradition (3).

23. Emily Dickinson, *The Poems of Emily Dickinson*, 3 vols., ed. Thomas Johnson (Cambridge: Belknap Press of Harvard University Press, 1955). Individual poems will be identified in the body of this essay according to the numbering system Johnson uses in this edition.

24. Sharon Cameron, *Lyric Time: Dickinson and the Limits of Genre* (Baltimore: Johns Hopkins University Press, 1979), 112–21.

25. Sandra M. Gilbert and Susan Gubar, *The Madwoman in the Attic: The Woman Writer and the Nineteenth-Century Literary Imagination* (New Haven: Yale University Press, 1979), 631–32, read this poem as a confrontation with those forces of decay and mortality that cannot be excluded even from the supposedly secure interior of the home and particularly as an attempt to come to grips with the social stigma of spinsterhood.

26. Jacques Derrida, *Of Grammatology*, trans. Gayatri Chakravorty Spivak (Baltimore: Johns Hopkins University Press, 1976), 60–62, 69–70.

27. Cameron, *Lyric Time*, 115.

28. Sheila Rowbotham, Lynn Segal, and Hilary Wainwright, *Beyond the Fragments: Feminism and the Making of Socialism* (Boston: Alyson, 1981), 146.

29. Gilbert and Gubar, *Madwoman*, 82, 64.

16. Celibate Sisters-in-Revolution

1. Virginia Woolf, *Three Guineas* (New York: Harcourt, Brace, Jovanovich, 1966), 82.

2. Jane Marcus, *Virginia Woolf and the Languages of Patriarchy* (Bloomington and Indianapolis: Indiana University Press, 1987), 117, 132, 128, 135.

3. Catherine Gallagher, *The Industrial Reformation of English Fiction* (Chicago and London: University of Chicago Press, 198), 240.

4. Indeed, because adverse criticism of Irigaray has been so often repeated, with little variety and thoughtfulness of attack on the part of the adversaries, I have begun to think that the adversaries rather than their brilliant object are on the misguided side of the conflict.

5. Toril Moi, *Sexual/Textual Politics: Feminist Literary Theory* (London and New York: Methuen, 1985), 147. See also the remark "*Speculum* cannot really address the question of historical specificity" (148).

6. For an expression of discontent more recent than Moi's, see Dorothy Leland, "Lacanian Psychoanalysis and French Feminism: Toward an Adequate Political Psychology," *Hypatia* 3 (Winter 1989):83–90. Leland asserts that "the issue of empirical warrants does not enter into [Irigaray's] analysis at all" (87).

7. John Goode, *George Gissing: Ideology and Fiction* (London: Vision Press, 1978), 80. All other references to this edition appear in the text.

8. George Gissing, *The Odd Women* (New York: New American Library, 1985), 153. All other references to this edition appear in the text.

9. George Gissing, *The Unclassed* (Brighton, Sussex: Harvester Press, 1976), Preface to the New Edition.

10. Drawing upon Mary Barfoot's lecture on women, Goode writes, "The odd woman, alone or in the more violent isolation of sexual relations, measures the 'nature' of woman at the point where it is no longer sustained by the artifices of incorporation. . . . Speaking to us from the silence left by the voice of power, [the odd woman] is the object of question—what are we to do with those we cannot fit in?" (161).

11. Mark Rutherford, *Clara Hopgood* (London: Hogarth Press, 1985), 176–77.

12. Arnold Bennett, *The Old Wives' Tale* (New York: The Modern Library, n.d.), 599. All other references to this edition appear in the text.

13. This both hidden and open political engagement is exemplified by Gerald Scales no less than by Sam, Constance, and Sophia. Gerald's last significant action in the novel, precipitating the break with Sophia, is his "inexplicable" ambition to witness a public execution. But this is inexplicable more to him and Sophia than to the reader. For Bennett contrives the narrative so as to parallel Gerald's ambition with Sam's political agitation on Dan's behalf. Gerald's desire to witness a guillotining strikes him as only a desire to share in what is typically French ("In France it's quite the proper thing to go to [guillotinings]"), but since he pursues this desire against Sophia's wishes, he is unconsciously enacting a revolutionary disruption—of marital domesticity and so of the bourgeois typicality he seems to be imitating.

14. I echo Goode's language above, quoted in note 10.

15. Sylvia Townsend Warner, *Four in Hand: A Quartet of Novels* (New York: Norton, 1986), 119. All other references to this edition appear in the text.

16. Sylvia Townsend Warner, *Summer Will Show* (New York: Viking, 1936), 278. All other references to this edition appear in the text.

17. (In)Visible Alliances

1. Andrea Kannapell, "The Pro-Rape Culture," *Village Voice*, 9 May 1989, p. 39.

2. See Joseph Boone's essay in this volume and Toril Moi, "Men Against Patriarchy," in *Gender and Theory: Dialogues on Feminist Criticism*, ed. Linda Kauffman (New York: Basil Blackwell, 1989), pp. 187–88.

3. See Alisa Solomon, "Top Girls, Bottom Line," *Village Voice*, 27 June 1989, p. 58. Writing of a financial crisis at "Judith's Room," a New York women's bookstore, when it was turned down for a guarantee loan by the Small Business Administration because of selling "specialized" publications, Solomon singles out one man whose efforts are exemplary: "After recovering from this absurdity,

[Sally] Owen and [Carol] Levin [the bookstore owners] sent hundreds of women fundraising letters; in less than six months, they had collected $50,000 in loans which they have promised to pay back within five years. But some lenders, like Mark Glucksman, a 33-year-old neurobiologist who pores over Mary Daly in his spare time, don't even remember the exact terms of their loans, since, as he puts it, 'it's not an investment, but a cause.' Outraged to read . . . that the SBA had stiffed Levin and Owen, Glucksman phoned them to offer a $10,000 loan. Levin thought at first that it was a crank call. 'Why would a man be doing this?' she wondered. But it turns out that Judith's Room is getting a modest but loyal following of male customers."

4. Moi, *Gender and Theory*, p. 184.

5. Elizabeth Weed, "A Man's Place," in *Men and Feminism*, eds. Alice Jardine and Paul Smith (New York: Methuen, 1987), p. 75.

6. *The Heidi Chronicles* also received the 1989 Best Play distinction from the Drama Desk, the New York Drama Critics' Circle, and the Outer Critics' Circle, as well as the Dramatists Guild's Hull Warriner Award and the Susan Smith Blackburn Prize (awarded to "a woman who deserves recognition for having written a work of outstanding quality for English-speaking theatre"). On the other hand, critics who registered varying degrees of dissatisfaction upon the play's New York productions (at Off-Broadway's Playwrights Horizons or on Broadway) include Clive Barnes (*New York Post*, 12 December 1988); Alisa Solomon (*Village Voice*, 20 December 1988); John Simon (*New York*, 2 February 1989); William Henry III (*Time*, 20 March 1989); and Laurie Stone (*Village Voice*, 13 June 1989).

7. Two recent Broadway productions featuring white female characters in naturalistic settings may be seen as qualified exceptions to the historical position in which I place *The Heidi Chronicles*: Marsha Norman's 1986 Pulitzer Prize–winning drama, *'night Mother* (1986) and Tina Howe's *Coastal Disturbances* (1987). Although the principles of feminism are not explicitly present within the discourse of either play, Norman's text, in particular, has become the focus of debate as feminist drama critics consider the issue of (traditional) realist narrative (viewed as an inscription of patriarchal ideology) and feminist playwriting practice. See, for example, Jeanie Forte, "Realism, Narrative, and the Feminist Playwright—A Problem of Reception," *Modern Drama* 32, 1 (March 1989):115–27. Forte concludes that although "['*night Mother*] may not be feminist or political in terms of its writing strategies, or in its naive conception of the self/subjectivity" (122), the play "may be *perceived* as a feminist text, in that it challenges on some material level the reality of male power" (123). Forte's conditions for activating a "feminist theory of reception" to evaluate Norman's realistic narrative drama might usefully be extended to reevaluating the impact of *The Heidi Chronicles* as a feminist text. See also Jill Dolan's discussion of *'night Mother* in *The Feminist Spectator as Critic* (Ann Arbor: UMI Research Press, 1988), pp. 27–34. Among the most notable Off-Broadway realistic plays, some of which included characters of color, whose feminist component may or may not be disputed, are Kathleen Tolan's *A Weekend Near Madison* (1983), Tina Howe's *Painting Churches* (1983), Jane Chambers' *Last Summer at Bluefish Cove* (1982), Marsha Norman's *Getting Out* (1980), Wendy Wasserstein's *Uncommon Women and Others* (1977), Marie Irene Fornes' *Fefu and Her Friends* (1977), and Alice Childress' *Wedding Band* (1973). Off-Broadway nonrealistic feminist works have proliferated since the 1960s, and they include the plays or performance pieces of Rochelle Owens, Megan Terry, Rosalyn Drexler, Adrienne Kennedy, Honor Moore, Alice Childress, Eve Merriam, Paula Wagner, Ursule Molinaro, Corinne Jacker, Joanna Russ, Julie Bovasso, Gretchen Cryer, Nancy Ford, Susan Griffin, Tina Howe, Irene Fornes, Karen Malpede, Judith Malina, Ntozake Shange, Myrna Lamb, Mary Gallagher, Muriel Miguel, Lynne Alvarez, Migdalia Cruz, Milcha Sanchez-Scott, Rachel Rosenthal, Karen Finley, Ann Magnuson, Linda Mussmann, Deborah Margolin, Linda Montano, Holly Hughes, Lisa Jones, Kaylynn Sullivan, Joyce Scott, Reno, Kathy Najimy, Mo Gaffney, and Sandra Bernhard. See Forte, who argues convincingly for the appeal of the nonrealistic, rather than realistic, form for many women playwrights. Forte contends that classic realism, unlike nonrealism, "perpetuates narrative closure and Oedipal constructions of identity" (122) which inhibit the construction of female subjectivity.

8. "The Heidi Chronicles," unpublished manuscript. All quotations from the play will be followed by the act and scene in which they appear. Wasserstein's play opened on Broadway at the Plymouth Theatre on 9 March 1989.

9. Alisa Solomon, "feminism-something," *Village Voice*, 20 December 1988, pp. 121–22.

10. Mimi Kramer, "Portrait of a Lady," *New Yorker*, 26 December 1988, p. 81

11. Solomon, "feminism-something," p. 122.

12. Laurie Stone, "The Women's Movement Carried Off My Baby in a Flying Saucer," *Village Voice*, 13 June 1989, p. 36.

13. Ibid.

14. See Wasserstein quoted in "Women Playwrights: Themes and Variations": "[W]hen I did *Uncommon Women and Others* [1977] someone said to me, you know, are you a feminist; do you see yourself as a woman playwright? And I said, no, I'm a writer. . . . But then, in the past three years [1986–1989], I began to have a change of heart. . . . I am a woman playwright and I want to write stories about women. I feel a need to see these stories on stage, both as an artist and as, in a way, a political action."

15. Quoted in Diane Stefani, "Women Pump New Life into Old-Boy Broadway," *New York Post*, 4 November 1986, p. 27.

16. Quoted in Christa Santangelo, "Wendy Wasserstein Writes Plays that Touch Audiences on a Personal Level," *West Side Spirit*, 6 March 1988, p. 13.

17. It should be noted that Wasserstein contributes to relatively new territory for an American commercial playwright in the frankness with which she handles the sexual tension between a single heterosexual woman and a single homosexual male. In the depiction of the Heidi-Peter relationship, Wasserstein presents adults who are to be "family" for one another (II, 5) and not sexual intimates. Upon hearing that Peter is gay (I, 4), Heidi strikes her friend on the arm, saying, "And that's for liking to sleep with men more than women . . . and that's for not being desperately and hopelessly in love with me." Peter's declaration of his sexuality, however, does not automatically erase all traces of unspoken desire between the couple. In Joan Allen's subtly modulated performance as Broadway's original Heidi, for example, the impact of what might have been but never will be between Peter and Heidi is not very far from Heidi's surface—especially when she meets or must speak about Peter's lovers (I, 4; II, 5). In the smallest gestures the actress acknowledges her character's sadness: a bowed head, a slight turning away, a depletion of facial expression. For Heidi, such movement is unobtrusively poignant; generally, it has been either unnoticed or misrepresented by the critics (see Kramer, "Portrait of a Lady").

18. When an entirely recast Broadway production of *The Heidi Chronicles* opened on 5 September 1989, Wasserstein had rewritten the play's controversial last scene. Christine Lahti, the actress who succeeded Joan Allen in the role of Heidi, spoke of these changes: "Part of the way to clarify [the scene] is to show that Heidi has a relatively successful relationship with a man at the end—she doesn't adopt a baby just to fill a void" (quoted by Phillip Lopate in "Christine Lahti Tries to Fashion a Spunky 'Heidi,' " *New York Times*, 3 September 1989, sec. H, p. 8). To date, it is unknown which version of the scene will be published, let alone if Wasserstein's changes were a response to commercial pressure or aesthetic revision. Nonetheless, Heidi now says to Scoop in the staged production of Act II, Scene 6: "I'm seeing an editor I seem to like. . . . He's moving in next door. . . . We're investigating separate but equal." The significance of this insertion is ambiguous since now both the baby's adoption and Heidi's admission of having a (invisible) male lover in her life appear as conveniently coincidental events in Heidi's chronicle, rather than as convincing choices. Wasserstein's revision still keeps invisible the *process* by which Heidi comes to realize her relationship to parenting as well as to a "separate but equal" relationship with a man.

19. The only time Heidi initiates a comment on parenting is in 1984, when she says to Susan: "I'm planning to start my family at sixty. I hear there's a hormone in Brazil" (II, 3). The only other reference to parenting occurs in 1980. Replying to Denise's question regarding whether she "want[s] to have a family," Heidi answers, "Yes, I hope so" (II, 1).

20. Mel Gussow, "A Modern Day Heffalump in Search of Herself," *New York Times*, 12 December 1988, sec. C, p. 13.

21. As directed by Daniel Sullivan on Broadway, the visual framing of the final scene—its iconographic images with their metaphoric associations—is arresting in its almost religious "leap of faith" affirmation of Heidi's single parenting position: in the foreground, white-robed Heidi sits in a rocker amidst streaming sunlight in a stark, white, empty loft space; behind her, Scoop drapes himself along the mantel top in a cruciform position. Breaking this pose, Scoop (the "dying" child/lover) comes to the foreground and sits at the base of Heidi's (the virginal mother's/lover's) feet. Unlike Mary of the Pieta who cradles the body of her immaculately conceived dying son, Heidi chooses not to embrace the needy Scoop. Instead, she gathers up in her arms her adopted child, the embodiment of Heidi's delayed gratification. Judy, after all, will be nurtured to be "a heroine for the twenty-first century," a hope that suggests to Heidi that "things will be a little better" during her daughter's lifetime than they were during her own (II, 6).

22. Adrienne Rich, "When We Dead Awaken: Writing as Re-Vision," in *On Lies, Secrets, and Silence* (New York: Norton, 1979), p. 43.

23. Stephen Heath, "Male Feminism," in *Men and Feminism*, p. 1.

24. Alice Jardine, "A Conversation," in *Men and Feminism*, p. 263.

25. Boone, p. 24.

26. Quoted in Mervyn Rothstein, "After the Revolution, What?" *New York Times*, 11 December 1988.

Selected Bibliography

The following is a list of essay collections that in part address the kinds of issues surrounding the "question of male feminist criticism" that we have attempted to highlight in the present volume:

Butters, Ronald R., John M. Clum, and Michael Moon, eds. *Displacing Homophobia: Gay Male Perspectives in Literature and Culture*. Durham and London: Duke University Press, 1989.

Claridge, Laura and Elizabeth Langland, eds. *Out of Bounds: Male Writing and Gender (ed) Criticism*. forthcoming University of Massachusetts Press.

Jardine, Alice and Paul Smith, eds. *Men in Feminism*. London and New York: Methuen, 1987.

Kauffman, Linda, ed. *Feminism and Institutions: Dialogues on Feminist Theory*. London and New York: Basil Blackwell, 1989.

————, ed. *Gender and Theory: Dialogues on Feminist Criticism*. London and New York: Basil Blackwell, 1989.

Kaufman, Michael, ed. *Beyond Patriarchy: Essays by Men on Pleasure, Power, and Change*. Toronto and New York: Oxford University Press, 1987.

Showalter, Elaine, ed. *Speaking of Gender*. New York and London: Routledge, 1989.

The following is a highly selective list of individual examples of what might be called "engendered male criticism" written by men (we also recommend to the reader the books and articles written by our contributors):

Aers, David. *Community, Gender, and Individual Identity: English Writing 1360–1430*. London and New York: Routledge. 1988.

Awkward, Michael. *Inspiriting Influences: Tradition, Revision, and Afro-American Women's Novels*. New York: Columbia University Press, 1988.

Bergman, David. "Changing our Fathers: Gender and Identity in Whitman, Ashbery, and Richard Howard," *American Literary History* 1, no. 2 (1989): 383–403.

Bernheimer, Charles. "Huysmans: Writing Against (Female) Nature" in *The Female Body in Western Culture*. Ed. Susan Rubin Suleiman. Cambridge and London: Harvard University Press, 1985. 373–386.

Bersani, Leo. "Is the Rectum a Grave?" *October* 43 (1987): 197–222.

Bray, Alan. *Homosexuality in Renaissance England*. London: Gay Men's Press, 1982.

Brod, Harry. *The Making of Masculinities: The New Men's Studies*. Boston: Allen and Unwin, 1987.

Cheyfitz, Eric. *The Trans-Parent: Sexual Politics in the Language of Emerson*. Baltimore: The Johns Hopkins University Press, 1981.

Craft, Christopher. " 'Descend and Touch and Enter': Tennyson's Strange Manner of Address," *Genders* 1 (1988): 83–101.

Crompton, Louis. *Byron and Greek Love: Homophobia in 19th-Century England*. Berkeley and Los Angeles: University of California Press, 1985.

Dellamora, Richard. *Masculine Desire: The Sexual Politics of Victorian Aestheticism*. Chapel Hill: University of North Carolina Press, 1990.

Dijkstra, Bram. *Idols of Perversity: Fantasies of Feminine Evil in Fin-de-Siècle Culture*. New York: Oxford University Press, 1988.

Dixon, Melvin. *Ride Out the Wilderness: Geography and Identity in Afro-American Literature*. Urbana: University of Illinois Press, 1987.

Dollimore, Jonathan. "Different Desires: Subjectivity and Transgression in Wilde and Gide," *Genders* 2 (1988): 24–41.

Duyfhuizen, Bernard. "Deconstruction and Feminist Literary Theory," *Tulsa Studies in Women's Literature* 3 (1984): 159–69.

Erickson, Peter. *Patriarchal Structures in Shakespeare's Plays*. Berkeley: University of California Press, 1985.

Gates, Henry Louis, Jr. "Significant Others," *Contemporary Literature* 29 (Winter 1988): 606–623.

Gilman, Sander. *Difference and Pathology: Stereotypes of Sexuality, Race, and Madness*. Ithaca and London: Cornell University Press, 1985.

Habegger, Alfred. *Gender, Fantasy, and Realism in American Literature*. New York: Columbia University Press, 1982.

Halperin, David M. *One Hundred Years of Homosexuality and Other Essays on Greek Love*. New York and London: Routledge, 1990.

Heath, Stephen. "Difference," *Screen* 19 (Autumn 1978): 51–112.

Kimbrough, Robert. "Macbeth: The Prisoner of Gender," *Shakespeare Studies* 16 (1983): 175–90.

Leverenz, David. *Manhood and the American Renaissance*. Ithaca and London: Cornell University Press, 1989.

Litvak, Joseph. "Charlotte Brontë and the Scene of Instruction: Authority and Subversion in *Villette*," *Ninteenth Century Literature* 42 (Winter 1988): 467–489.

Miller, D. A. Chapters 5 and 6, *The Novel and the Police*. Berkeley: University of California Press, 1988.

Moon, Michael. " 'The Gentle Boy from the Dangerous Classes': Pederasty, Domesticity, and Capitalism in Horatio Alger," *Representations* 19 (1987): 87–110.

Parker, Andrew. "Holding the *Fort!* Instituting Genders, Engendering Insitutions." *Genders* 1 (1988): 75–82.

Person, Leland, Jr. *Aesthetic Headaches: Women and Masculine Poetics in Poe, Melville, and Hawthorne*. Athens: University of Georgia Press, 1988.

Pleck, Joseph. *The Myth of Masculinity*. Cambridge: MIT Press, 1981.

Schwenger, Peter. *Phallic Critiques: Masculinities and Twentieth-Century Literature*. London and Boston: Routledge and Kegan Paul, 1984.

Snow, Edward. "Sexual Anxiety and the Male Order of Things in *Othello*," *English Literary Renaissance* 10 (1980): 384–412.

Stallybrass, Peter. "Reading the Body: *The Revenger's Tragedy* and the Jacobean Theater of Consumption," *Renaissance Drama* 18 (1987): 121–48.

Stoltenberg, John. *Refusing to be a Man: Essays on Sex and Justice*. Portland, Oregon: Breitenbush Books, 1989; rpt. New York: Meridian, 1990.

Theweleit, Klaus. *Male Fantasies, Volume One: Women, Floods, Bodies, History*. Trans. Stephen Conway, in collaboration with Erica Carter and Chris Turner. Minneapolis: University of Minnesota Press, 1987.

———. *Male Fantasies. Volume Two: Male Bodies: Psychoanalyzing the White Terror*. Trans. Erica Carter and Chris Turner in collaboration with Stephen Conway. Minneapolis: University of Minnesota Press, 1989.

Van Leer, David. "The Beast of the Closet: Homosociality and the Pathology of Manhood," *Critical Inquiry* 15 (1989): 587–605; see also Eve Kosofsky Sedgwick's response and Van Leer's reply: 745–763.

Watney, Simon. *Policing Desire: Pornography, AIDS, and the Media*. Minneapolis: University of Minnesota Press, 1987.

Weeks, Jeffrey. *Sexuality and Its Discontents: Meanings, Myths, and Modern Sexualities*. London: Routledge and Kegan Paul, 1985.

Winkler, John J. *The Constraints of Desire: The Anthropology of Sex and Gender in Ancient Greece*. New York and London: Routledge, 1990.

Wittreich, Joseph. *Feminist Milton*. Ithaca: Cornell University Press, 1987.

Woods, Gregory. *Articulate Flesh: Male Homo-Eroticism and Modern Poetry*. New Haven: Yale University Press, 1987.

Yingling, Thomas E. *Hart Crane and the Homosexual Text: New Thresholds, New Anatomies*. Chicago: University of Chicago Press, 1990.

Index

Contributors

Marcellus Blount, Assistant Professor of English at Columbia University, is currently completing a book, *In a Broken Tongue: Rediscovering Afro-American Poetry*.

Joseph A. Boone, Associate Professor of English at the University of Southern California, is the author of *Tradition Counter Tradition: Love and the Form of Fiction* (1987) and is working on a companion volume, *Sexuality, Narrative, and Modernity* (forthcoming, Chicago).

Former Dramaturg at the Yale Repertory Theatre, *Michael Cadden* is Assistant Professor of English at Princeton University. His book on contemporary theatre, *The Body Politic/The Body Theatrical*, is forthcoming from Routledge.

The author of *Plot, Story, and the Novel* (1979), *Robert L. Caserio* is at work on *The Novel in England since Conrad and Woolf: Theory and History*. He is Associate Professor of English at the University of Utah.

Visiting Assistant Professor in English at Colorado College, *Christopher Castiglia* is completing his dissertation as a graduate student at Columbia University on narratives of women captives from Mary Rowlandson to Patty Hearst.

Ed Cohen is Assistant Professor of English at Rutgers University. He is completing a book entitled *Talk on the Wilde Side: Towards a Genealogy of the Discourse of Male Sexuality* (forthcoming, Routledge), and is the recipient of the 1987 Crompton-Noll prize of the MLA.

A graduate student at Harvard University, where he is writing a dissertation on "apostolary" narrative, *Michael A. Cooper* is Lecturer at Wellesley College.

Lee Edelman, Associate Professor of English at Tufts University, is the author of *Transmemberment of Song: Hart Crane's Anatomies of Rhetoric and Desire* (1987) and is writing *Homographesis: Essays in Lesbian and Gay Literary Theory*, forthcoming from Routledge. "Redeeming the Phallus" is the winner of the 1989 Crompton-Noll prize.

Thomas Foster has recently completed a dissertation entitled "Homelessness at Home: Oppositional Practices and Modern Women's Writing," at the University of Wisconsin-Madison. He is Assistant Professor of English at Illinois State University.

Until recently *Walter Hughes* was, like his hero Michael Wigglesworth, a tutor at Harvard University, where he wrote a dissertation on models of social and erotic love from the Puritans to Whitman; he is now Assistant Professor of English at Princeton University.

Wayne Koestenbaum, Assistant Professor of English at Yale, is the author of *Double Talk:*

The Erotics of Male Literary Collaboration (1989) and is currently writing a book on opera and homosexuality entitled *The Queen's Throat*. He was co-winner of the 1989 "Discovery"/ *The Nation* poetry contest.

Robert K. Martin is the author of *The Homosexual Tradition in American Poetry* (1979) and *Hero, Captain, and Stranger: Male Friendship, Social Critique, and Literary Form in the Sea Novels of Herman Melville* (1986). He is Professor of English at Concordia University in Montreal.

Jacques Lezra, Assistant Professor of Spanish and Comparative Literature at Yale, is co-translator of Paul de Man's *Blindness and Insight* into Spanish and has published articles on Shakespeare, Cabrera Infante, and Don Juan Manuel.

Andrew Ross teaches at Princeton University, where he is an Assistant Professor of English. He is the author of *No Respect: Intellectuals and Popular Culture* (1989) and *The Failure of Modernism* (1986) and has edited *Universal Abandon?: The Politics of Postmodernism* (1989).

The author of *Henry James and the Art of Power* (1984), *Mark Seltzer* is Associate Professor of English at Cornell University; "The Love-Master" is included in his book *Bodies and Machines* (forthcoming, Routledge).

Robert Vorlicky, Associate Professor of English and Theatre and Chair of the Division of Humanities at Marymount Manhattan College in New York City, is currently completing *America's Power Plays*, and analysis of male cast plays in American drama.

Michael Warner, Associate Professor of English at Rutgers University, is the author of *The Letters of the Republic* (forthcoming, Harvard). He has also co-edited, with Gerald Graff, *The Origins of Literary Studies in America* (1988).

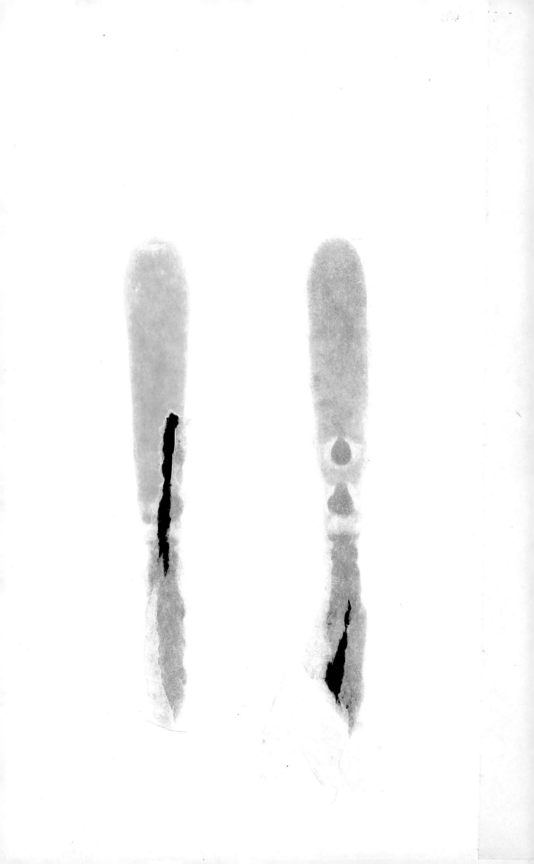